AGAINST THE
MEGAMACHINE

Illustration by Freddie Baer

AGAINST THE MEGAMACHINE:

ESSAYS ON EMPIRE & ITS ENEMIES

David Watson

Against the Megamachine: Essays on Empire & Its Enemies
by David Watson

ISBN 1-5027-063-5

Autonomedia
P.O. Box 568 Williamsburgh Station
Brooklyn, NY 11211-0568
Phone & Fax: 1-718-963-2603

Fifth Estate
4632 Second Avenue
Detroit, MI 48201

Printed in the United States of America

Book layout and design donated by Freddie Baer; cover collage based on
a painting by Peter Breughel, "Tower of Babel," (Rotterdam, Museum
Boymans-Van Beuningen).

Also by David Watson:

How Deep Is Deep Ecology?
Beyond Bookchin: Preface for a Future Social Ecology

For Marilynn Rashid —
contigo pan y cebollas

"I myself am an anarchist, but of another type. . . ."

— *M.K. Gandhi*

TABLE OF CONTENTS

Author's Note & Acknowledgments _____ vi

Introduction by Richard Drinnon _____ 1

I. Catching Fish in Chaotic Waters _____ 5
    Catching Fish in Chaotic Waters:
    An Essay on Empire & Mass Society _____ 7

II. We All Live in Bhopal _____ 25
    1. Notes on the Disappearance of History _____ 27
    2. Earth Day? We Want a Festival of the Oppressed! _____ 34
    3. We All Live in Bhopal _____ 42
    4. Stopping the Industrial Hydra _____ 48
    5. Biosphere 2 and the Future of the Earth _____ 71
    6. Six Theses on Nuclear Power _____ 75

III. Against the Megamachine _____ 83
    1. The Fall of Communism & the Triumph of Capital _____ 85
    2. Against the Megamachine _____ 117
    3. The Snowmobile Revolution _____ 146
    4. The Language of Domestication
      & the Domestication of Language _____ 152
    5. Anarchy & the Sacred _____ 159
    6. The Failure of Civilization & the Failure of Noam Chomsky ___ 175
    7. A Humble Call to Subvert the Human Empire _____ 179

IV. Civilization in Bulk _____ 185
    1. Civilization Is Like a Jetliner _____ 187
    2. Civilization in Bulk: Empire & Ecological Destruction _____ 189
    3. Insurgent Mexico: Redefining Revolution
      & Progress for the 21st Century _____ 202

4. Deep Ecology & Environmental Philosophy:
   On the Ethics of Crisis & the Crisis in Ethics _____ 224
5. Homage to Fredy Perlman _____ 244
6. The Unabomber & the Future of Industrial Society _____ 252

V. These are Not Our Troops _____ 269
   1. 1492–1992: The End of the 500-Year Reich _____ 271
   2. Looking Back on the Vietnam War _____ 278
   3. War in the Persian Gulf: Imperial Death Trip to Nowhere __ 300
   4. These Are Not Our Troops; This Is Not Our Country_____ 305
   5. Watching the Dogs Salivate: Notes on the 1992 Elections __ 318
   6. On the Road to Nowhere: The New Nomadism _____ 327

AUTHOR'S NOTE & ACKNOWLEDGMENTS

Illustration by David Watson

Illustration by Johann Humyn Being

AUTHOR'S NOTE & ACKNOWLEDGMENTS

Nearly all the essays in this book were first published in the *Fifth Estate*, which, as the archivists at the University of Michigan Library Labadie Collection have informed us, is now the longest enduring English-language anarchist newspaper in North America. Written at different times under different conditions, their format is irregular; I saw no benefit in trying after the fact to make them consistent. Some have been dramatically changed; for example, the title piece, "Against the Megamachine," is a compilation and reworking of several articles written during the early 1980s, with some material added, and much rhetoric excised. All the essays have been revised to some degree; those significantly altered show both the earlier and later date.

The *Fifth Estate* is a collective effort. Everything here was read and discussed by several people, in different combinations, before being published in the paper. Thanks most of all to Peter Werbe, Marilyn Werbe, Marilynn Rashid, Kathleen Rashid, Lorraine Perlman, Rob Blurton, Ralph Franklin, Bill Boyer, Harry Schnur, Alan Franklin, Fran Shor, and Federico Arcos for their comments and suggestions over the years. Three essays were originally written for *The New Internationalist*: "Notes on the Disappearance of History," "On the Road to Nowhere: The New Nomadism," and "A Humble Call to Subvert the Human Empire." I thank NI editors Richard Swift and Wayne Ellwood for their encouragement and suggestions, and for permission to reprint those essays here. Fredy Perlman and Bob Brubaker read and influenced my work before their untimely deaths. I still feel the loss of their intellectual camaraderie and miss their friendship.

Steve Welzer, Kathleen Rashid, Marilynn Rashid, Lorraine Perlman, Daniel Grobani and Peter Werbe all helped to edit and proofread this text. I'm also grateful to Richard Drinnon, whose own work both confirmed and helped to shape the essays in this book, for writing his generous introduction.

Thanks to Johann Humyn Being for his collages, Ralph Franklin for technical assistance, and Jim Fleming for bringing this to fruition at Autonomedia. Finally, the indefatigable Freddie Baer has once more worked mightily to present my work, providing art and designing the book. This is our fourth book collaboration.

The graphics heading each essay are from a nineteenth century Catalan *aleluya* or broadsheet, "Lo mon al revés" (the world upside down). This motif, with its deep roots in art and folklore, is a powerful idea of reversal in which animals hunt the hunter, fish catch the fisherman, death is killed by a mortal, donkeys ride on the backs of people, and so on. Its subversive ambivalence may suggest either an alienated world or the festival of the oppressed that overturns alienation—an image appropriate to a text attempting to understand modern mass society.

Any selection from work penned over a decade and a half requires not only inclusion but exclusion. This anthology in fact had to be limited to core themes in my writing, leaving aside other topics I've treated and key texts from other *Fifth Estate* contributors—material we intend to publish in a *Fifth Estate Reader*. I should also add that though these essays were greatly improved by editing and rewriting, they still reflect only a stage in an unfinished journey, a process of political, philosophical, and ethical inquiry I continue, however haphazardly, to confront. Thus, they may not prove true in every detail, and there may be conceptual errors in them; certainly, they seem to me only "resemblances of what is true," as Xenophanes of Colophon described his own practice of questioning some two and a half millennia ago.

As reality evolves, many of our best ideas about it turn out to be only fragmentary moments in life's larger intelligence. Consequently, I believe these essays to be more useful for the questions they raise than for any specific response they recommend. We find ourselves in a profoundly restless age—interesting times (a curse according to the ancient Chinese) when every logic and tradition has proven somehow incomplete and inadequate, even an impediment to the promise of what it means to be human. It is left to those of us living at the turn of this millennium to prevent the hubris-caused apocalypse foreshadowed in our stories and myths by reassessing the whole of human experience and finding an appropriate place in it.

In a sense this means abandoning much of what we have learned while rediscovering much of what we have forgotten—allowing ourselves to be guided as much by our uncertainties as by what we think we know. Not all these essays were written in such a spirit—I only started learning to think and to write by writing them. But in that spirit I have gathered them into a single book; if they help others to question, to feel, and to express themselves in their own way, then I will be profoundly gratified.

—D.W.

INTRODUCTION

Illustration by Freddie Baer

Illustration by Johann Humyn Being

INTRODUCTION

by Richard Drinnon

Thirty years ago this fall the flower-power contingent of the antiwar movement requested permission to levitate the Pentagon and the General Services Administration (GSA) graciously allowed they might raise the building to a maximum of ten feet. Very recently a humorless reviewer pointed to this incident as a graphic illustration of the raging silliness that has kept so many from getting a "fix" on the sixties. But could it be that to earn that fix you need at least a GSA level of irony and just a flicker of vision?

David Watson attended his first national protest against the war that October at the Pentagon at the age of fifteen. The previous fall he had attended his first antiwar teach-in and, as he reports in the introduction to "Looking Back on the Vietnam War," thereupon determined "not to be an oppressor or to tolerate oppressors." Over the years he did what he could to stop the war, demonstrating, leafleting, burning his draft card, agitating on street corners, and, yes, waving a "VC" flag at the gates of a tank factory. Today he can see that his admiration for the Vietnamese people blinded him to the authoritarianism of their leaders but he offers no apology for waving the NLF flag in the face of the U.S. empire, and only regrets not having done more to undermine it. That first teach-in continues in these essays and shows how consistently he has tried to do more, from 1967 to the present, a thirty-year hitch in the resistance with no end in sight.

Watson's youthful flag-waving certainties, later sloughed off like so much baby fat, came out of a style that had long since run down. By the sixties the traditional left had become a patchwork of brittle slogans, with anti-Stalinists locked in seemingly endless battle with Stalinists, shadow boxers united only by their mutual fear of radical change. In the name of Progress, Science, and Reason, both sides celebrated industrialism and embraced technology that was destroying the last possibilities of individuality and community. When at last a "new" left rebelled against this programmatic accommodation, one vivid strand of that rebellion was Luddite. And it was in this counter-tradition that Watson put down roots and grew into the sensitivity and caring patience evident in these essays and in his just published treatise on social ecology, *Beyond Bookchin: Preface for a Future Social Ecology* (1996).

In "Homage to Fredy Perlman," Watson records that "our community in Detroit, being far greater than the sum of the individuals who make it up, was much diminished by his untimely passing [in 1985]." A onetime student of C. Wright Mills and a gifted thinker in his own right, Fredy Perlman had earned that esteem by stripping off his Marxist presuppositions and taking the lead in the search for libertarian alternatives. Perlman participated in the Paris May Days of 1968 and on his return to the United States explored the implications of this explosion of possibilities for the rest of his life, mainly through the Black & Red publishing project and the Detroit Print Co-op, the journal *Fifth Estate*, and through "stories, essays, plays, music," as Watson notes, "and by his participation in many anticratic and communitarian projects." Perlman's study of native peoples and their cultures had led to his discovery that "the state of nature is a community of freedoms." As for the Pentagon also called Leviathan, it is not a prospective horror: "It is our world," Perlman wrote in *Against His-story, Against Leviathan!* (1983), a book Watson has drawn on for his own title and much more.

The essayist is also a close student of the work of Lewis Mumford and indebted to that of Jacques Ellul, Marshall Sahlins, Stanley Diamond, Vandana Shiva, Ivan Illich, Carolyn Merchant, Gary Snyder, and many others — he seems to have read everybody. Shaped by such diverse influences and written over more than a decade for different occasions, and in some instances in response to specific catastrophes, his pieces have their ups and downs and are repetitious now and again. Moreover, this is not a monograph but a collection and, as we all know, essays are wont to wander down paths of their own. But here they do have an underlying unity laid down by the coherence of Watson's outlook and by the unwavering intensity of his search for some way out of the labyrinth — I think of these essays as so many steel files smuggled into our iron cage.

Anarchism may offer a way out but not, Watson believes, through its classical nineteenth-century formulations. He easily demonstrates that Bakunin shared in distressingly full measure Marx's glorification of progress and so did Kropotkin in his less reflective moments. But there were "contradictory currents," as Watson also recognizes, some of which presciently anticipated his own critique of domination. Said by Emma Goldman to be "the greatest woman Anarchist of America," Voltairine de Cleyre, for instance, rejected the centralization she saw turning people into robots and in 1900 wanted to make things new and preindustrial again so one might "watch things grow and blossom, and feel again the joy of life and the sweet kinship with all living things — learn the forgotten lore of the savage who knew all the colors of the leaves, and the shapes of them, and the way they turn to the sun...." There in embryo was Watson's goal of an anarchism shorn of progressivism and reunited with the forgotten lore that was "anarchist" eons before the term was coined.

Here and now, I venture, Watson's breathtakingly ambitious project is no less than to have us look at the world with our eyes wide open. In William Blake's famous words:

If the doors of perception were cleansed every thing would
appear to man as it is, infinite.
For man has closed himself up, till he sees all things thro'
narrow chinks of his cavern.

Unclosed and open-eyed we can see that Blake's insight reaches back to the ecstatic wisdom called shamanism— in *Primitive Man as Philosopher* (1957) Paul Radin said that his subject lived "in a blaze of reality." And at that level of awareness we will begin to find our way out of the cavern.

Or so the vision promises. Irving Howe, the old left defender of original sin and Civilization, would have surely seen it as yet another expression of sixties barbarism, however belated, and included it in his indictment of "neo-primitivism," that state of nongrace destined never to win a national election. Correct in his identification, if not in his fiery dismissals, the departed critic's certain disapproval would merely underscore my argument that these essays bring one of the millennial aspirations of the sixties straight down to the present moment. In so doing they provocatively question anew the left's efforts — extending over a span of two centuries — to integrate itself into the established political system of the industrialized West. And they challenge it in the name of a critical neo-primitivism that would restore the abandoned radical vision.

So in the light of all this, what is our final fix on Pentagon levitation in the sixties? The late and revered Allen Ginsberg — he has just died as I conclude this introduction — persuasively argued some years ago that the demonstration has to be understood as "a poetic metaphor" that had in fact been "a triumph of the human imagination over heavy metal materialism": the authority of the Pentagon had been demystified and "in that sense we did levitate it."

In the selfsame sense David Watson's *Against the Megamachine* raises the Pentagon for us and that is a timely exploit in these grim last days.

April 1997

I.
CATCHING FISH IN
CHAOTIC WATERS

Illustration by Freddie Baer

Illustration by Johann Humyn Being

CATCHING FISH
IN CHAOTIC WATERS:
AN ESSAY ON EMPIRE
AND MASS SOCIETY

In his book *Shadow Work* (1981), Ivan Illich describes three kinds of issues: "Some are considered legitimate. Others are not to be raised in polite society. A third kind seems to make no sense at all. If you raise these, you risk being thought a fiend or impossibly vain."[1] (See page 22 for endnotes.) The *Fifth Estate*, in which most of these essays were published, has tried to engage contemporary conditions in a creative way that has often brought the kind of response Illich describes — even from and sometimes especially from those who claim to be the revolutionary enemies of those conditions.

But contemporary conditions demand a different order of creative thinking. It's more than a question of socialism or barbarism, as Rosa Luxemburg stated it three quarters of a century ago. We've been enmeshed in a deepening barbarism since before her time, a barbarism of which much of the experience of socialism turned out to be just another variety. I am talking rather of a plague of much greater dimensions, worthy of poetic, tragic or mythic terms, like the plagues of the classic Greek drama.

Like Oedipus, we still face the riddle of the sphinx: who are you? what are you? Yet what it means to be human is now in flux, is being contested, in fact, by rival parties. And the old political terms, never entirely useful, don't work. "I'd rather be a cyborg than a goddess," we're told by an ostensibly radical feminist critic.[2] But there is the ominous sense that we will not even get to choose. Other possibilities are equally grim — including the total physical extinction of our species, and much of the present configuration of complex life along with us. The green world in which we evolved is being shredded by our instruments, our way of life, our very rationality. Yet here, too, we haven't determined the outcomes; they are largely occurring behind our backs.

Neither our technique nor our problem-solving rationality yield adequate responses to this catastrophe. It is a crisis rooted in character and culture, and hard to reach. This became clearer than we would have liked to believe during the 1991 war in the Persian Gulf. It would be difficult to find a more dramatic example of societal denial, compulsion and voluntary servitude, when a nation of ostensible environmentalists was rapidly herded into cheering from its living rooms as the empire devastated an entire country, in large part to defend claims to one of the key substances destroying the biosphere.

That demonstrated what some of us had been arguing — that environmentalism was a mile wide and an inch deep, and Earth Day a version of bread and circuses. It showed that even our own well-honed paranoia underestimated the power of the totalitarian state, but it said just as much about mass society and its communications system and techniques, and even more importantly, about the quality of subjectivity and consciousness they imply. That the war hysteria was almost forgotten a year later, like some tv mini-series, was no less disturbing.

Mass society lurches along from war to war, technological disaster to disaster, while a slow-acting catastrophe continues silently and incrementally, in natural cycles, in human society, in the psyche. True, the Captain Ahabs at the control panels administer it, usually making horrendous decisions rather than humane ones, but they only direct it to a degree. The man or the occasional woman at the controls is just another drudge, a creature of the lever. And in ways both great and small, the levers are tending not to function as designed or anticipated.

That tells us something crucial about the tragedy that is history, a tragedy of hubris and unforeseen consequences. Prometheus steals fire, but leaves his dull-witted brother Epimetheus to invent the nuclear reactor. History is filled with prometheans — Sargon, Caesar, Columbus, Ford, Lenin, Einstein; it's their story. Francis Bacon, perhaps the exemplary promethean, urged the disciples of his new scientific method in the seventeenth century "to unite forces against the nature of things," bind "the harlot" nature "into service," "storm and occupy her castles and strongholds … and thus extend the bounds of human empire." The human empire is Epimetheus, filled with hubris, domesticating chaos, splitting the atom and the gene, all to a utopian, messianic fanfare. We're now living half inside the leaky, malfunctioning satellite fabricated by both his rationality and his irrationality, and we go day to day wondering when it will disintegrate altogether.

We are typically and frequently asked how we might practically get from here to there with the modern-primitive synthesis explored in the *Fifth Estate*. We all wonder how to bring about change; we'd like to find a fulcrum. But there isn't any, and "what to do" can fall into an instrumentality reminiscent of Lenin, whose methodology didn't help him predict the upheavals of 1917, and who, by the time he was done, described his sense of being at the control of a vehicle which did not obey his commands. Furthermore, we are standing at a vague moment not only along the continuum of modern capitalism, but at a crisis akin to the decline of ancient empires. If you have any humility at all, you don't look around in the midst of the fall of Sumer and propose a program. We have to talk tentatively about how an unprecedented, megatechnic empire and its corresponding constellation of cultures might become a qualitatively different kind of society; how a grid might become an organic weave of diverse, egalitarian, communal societies; and how an atomized, mass human being might become a whole person embedded in a community.

No generation has ever faced such prospects. Even many of the former wards of collapsing empires probably had memories of tribal community and convivial skills to sustain themselves. In fact, the greatest revolutions in history were carried out by people with direct connections to archaic communal societies. We, in contrast, face the greatest crisis of detribalization and social decomposition since the birth of the state. Trying to make sense of mass society, to respond practically, is as the Chinese say, like catching fish in chaotic waters.[3] And in some way *we* are the fish. It goes without saying that we are oppressed by the institutions of industrial capitalism. But we also find that people have been conditioned to be cogs, both functional and dysfunctional (and more and more they are dysfunctional, like all instruments of an instrumental world). We may have nothing to lose but our chains, but they are our own pathological behavior patterns, and conform to an enormous social and material terrain, a terrain we tend to reproduce even as we oppose it.

The language of the empire reproduces it. Thus to consider practical technique alone would be to repeat the same arrogant folly we are trying to subvert. And the irrational will still be there, one way or another, to exact its revenge. For, contrary to the declarations of faith of one well-known rationalist defender of order, history is *not* "precisely what is *rational* in human development," but also what is non-rational, what is hidden or unknown.[4] Order and disorder, the rational and the non-rational, are organic unities not only in myth and tragedy but in life and history. After centuries of culture and character change in an economic, instrumental civilization, our notions of these polarities are deceptive. Method, practical politics, theory only tell a part of the story; we have to find a way to respond with the whole of being. Without the extra-rational and intuition, reason is incomplete, gaunt.

Here I wish to speak for something simpler and more subtle than programs: a mindfulness about where we find ourselves, our context (certainly a green sensibility), and a respect not only for what we know but also for what we do not know and especially for what we *cannot* know. This demands some humility, and epimetheans don't care for humility. For some reason they still can't distinguish humility toward what taoists call the "sacred vessel" of the world, and humility toward one's boss. But when the Lakota medicine man Black Elk, sounding exactly like the old taoists, said, "We should even be as water which is lower than all things, yet stronger than the rocks," he wasn't counseling servility.[5] He was telling us something valuable about strength not as force but as endurance, about radiating power rather than possessing or controlling it, about listening to nature instead of fantasizing about mastering it — all evocative of the kind of character change necessary to sustain us, even if the state succeeds in mowing down yet another generation of us. Without certain insights into who and what we are, we could never become the seeds of a new society; even our victory would turn into defeat. Those are some of the subtle intuitions that a modern-primitive synthesis suggests. It is also a topic that brings us well into that third realm of discourse with which I began this discussion.

In classic tragedy, as in primal societies, the sacred and profane commingle. They do for us, too, even if we don't admit it. We should be cautiously open to the spiritual and non-rational, and skeptical of the more invisible magical thinking — what we might call "magical rationalism" — pervading secular thought and experience in modern society. Science and technology are for most people a new religion, and their orthodoxies are believed with the same fervor. Questioning their monopoly on reason is considered heresy, when not altogether ignored.

What science claims to know is based on a vast body of unexamined assumptions about the nature of language and the language of nature. Even on its own terms, it's worth asking, if all scientific paradigms tend to wear out with time, why shouldn't science as a whole do the same? A future metaphysics, as Mexican poet Octavio Paz once suggested, might begin as a critique of science, asking "the same questions as in classical philosophy," starting not at the traditional moment "*before* all science but *after* the sciences."[6] And by classical philosophy we should understand not only western philosophical traditions, obviously, but the Chinese, Indian, aboriginal Australian, Native American, and others.

It follows that the "merciless criticism of all things," that now decayed modernist project which claims to be the science of sciences, must also be scrutinized, as we recognize the compulsions and superstitions of a rationalist, instrumental civilization that it celebrates — among others, the fantastic idea uttered by Marx that the "practical construction of an objective world, the manipulation of inorganic nature, is the confirmation of man as a species being." Such instrumental rationality, as Jacques Ellul has written, seeks "to transform everything into means," to abolish mystery. But in the process of disenchanting the world it has itself become the repository of the sacred, celebrated through world's fairs, space launches, televised spectacles, and the promise of a bioengineered cornucopia. Thus even those marginalized and ruined by technology, Ellul argues, cannot find a compensating force to resist. Their "bad conscience," as he calls it, is what Lewis Mumford called the myth of the machine: the belief that megatechnic civilization is not only irresistible but ultimately beneficial, a view generally shared by the rulers and those who contest their rule.[7]

The green sensibility, on the other hand, with its attentiveness to the whole of life, suggests to us that this "objective" world is so because it is alienated. The world is not objective — that is a Cartesian fantasy wedded to the imperial designs of rationalist science. Rather, in a subtle way that it is our responsibility to engage, and not in the inane, literalistic sense that rationalists enjoy refuting, the world is alive, inspirited. This recognition that the world is alive, now being discussed and debated seriously by scientists, is a metaphor already very familiar to primal and classical societies, is in fact one of their key intuitions.

Many such intuitions are now being "discovered" by science the way the Europeans discovered America. For example, that everything is interconnected was demonstrated with a vengeance when pesticide residues, blowing off fields in Mexico, ended up in a small lake on Lake Superior's Isle Royale. But some people didn't need lab tests to understand it. The rediscovery of such traditions and counter-traditions must be that intelligence, the spirit of the land, slowly working its way into us, as the Lakota philosopher Luther Standing Bear predicted it would. Some social ecologists warn that these ideas, coming from intuitive modes of thought, are unreliable, even dangerous.[8] But since when have rationalism or revolutionary reason been any more reliable? How many people were exterminated in the name of dialectical materialism? One-dimensional irrationality and rationality have both turned our century into a charnel house.

Some people believe that if the voice can't be picked up by a recording device, or sent by fax, I suppose, it isn't there. They don't recognize their own epoch's magical thinking. The green idea, on the other hand, open to the wholeness of human experience during our million or so years here on this star, suggests that our adventure is not to be found in the manipulation of "inorganic nature," but in that ineffable, numinous relationship with an intelligent, animate world that only a renewed mythopoetics can approach. "The White people never cared for the land or deer or bear," says an old holy Wintu woman. "The White people plow up the ground, pull down the trees, kill everything. The tree says, 'Don't. I am sore. Don't hurt me.' But they chop it down and cut it up. The spirit of the land hates them … Everywhere the White man has touched it, it is sore."[9]

The testimony of native peoples and the idea of union with nature may strike some as sentimental nostalgia; there is a fearful reaction when not only the land claims of native peoples are affirmed (as all good progressives agree they should be), but their *vision*. That is understandable. We have been shaped by the scientific revolution with its single vision, as Blake called it, and then by multiple waves of permanent industrial revolution that have commodified and mechanized every sphere of life. In contrast to so-called "pre-scientific" peoples' intimate relation to being, mass technics has allowed (or rather, forced) us to live in our heads, shutting out the phenomenal world by constructing an artificial one. As Norman O. Brown points out, "Capitalism has made us so stupid and one-sided that objects exist for us only if we can possess them or if they have utility." Brown's provocative work condemns the dehumanized nature of modern rationalist subjectivity, which makes the land sore with its calculus of efficiency, compulsion to dominate nature through work, and mania for money and quantification. In contrast to these compulsions, he argues, a nonmorbid science would be erotic. "Its aim would not be mastery over but union with nature."[10]

Such talk may not seem very practical, and some are impatient to get to nuts and bolts. Learn patience; we are going to need it. What appears practical and possible defines the parameters of the ruling ideology. In fact, capitalism now presents itself as life's only option — either we continue technological development (we can argue about who administers it or reaps the profit) or we'll face collapse and all the horsemen of the apocalypse. Question technicization, mass communications, electrification, medicalization, organization, and you are looked at like the malicious child who lets the barbarians in through the back gate (all those forces capitalism worked so hard to suppress, witches perched on the compound wall), or you're treated like a lunatic (or dilettante) speaking a language hardly anyone even faintly comprehends.

In any case, capitalism no longer needs to justify itself with claims to be good or eternal, it appears eternal because it's the only game in town.

As for the critics, and the people in the path of the bulldozer who find it more and more untenable, *los perros ladran y la caravana pasa* ("the dogs bark and the caravan passes"). Nuts and bolts rule; the machine trudges on. So the Ukrainian state, in desperate need of energy (meaning capital, growth, production, technology, jobs, commodities, and then all the same in an increasing upward spiral), has decided to continue operating the nuclear station at Chernobyl. Talk about a character crisis! Don't the scientists' and bankers' children also get leukemia?

A synthesis of primitive, archaic and modern, given the whole range of a million years or so of human experience, would judge the decision of the Ukrainian politicians differently from the way world bank technocrats do. Since the decision affects life for tens of thousands of years, going well beyond the proverbial seventh generation that native peoples have said must determine their actions, it makes sense to seek a similarly deep social perspective. In natural terms, we humans are but one leaf on the enormous world tree of four and a half billion years of Gaian evolution, a marvelous and unique leaf to be sure. In human terms, the last ten thousand years of human society represent one percent of our time on earth. The other ninety-nine percent was lived in small, stateless, propertyless, egalitarian, visionary societies like the Wintu. Only perhaps two hundredths of a percent has been lived in the experiment of urban industrialism. Civilization could arguably be described as an aberration. A deep critique, "after the sciences," would gain from looking at the industrial world, as the Haudenosaunee or Iroquois recommend in their famous *Basic Call to Consciousness*, "through Pleistocene eyes."[11]

Such a perspective not only encourages a tough-minded humility, it gives us some insight into the origins of the plague we are discussing. I discuss elsewhere the rupture that transforms a harmonious human community, with its myriad reciprocities, into a work pyramid, the ancient slave state, in a process described by Fredy Perlman, Lewis Mumford and others.[12] A discussion of primal society and the different notions of origins would be a discussion easily as long as this overview. Instead, I want to focus briefly on what emerged to discern its parallels with today.

It was one of Mumford's great contributions to recognize this new reorientation and reorganization of society into a big machine, or megamachine, as the first machine. The general characteristics of such megamachines are fairly constant: the circle becomes a pyramid. Mutualities become hierarchies, otherhood is suppressed — in woman, in nature, and eventually in the conquered peoples along a widening frontier. Elites and the drudgery of the oppressed are institutionalized. Monoculture emerges to feed the empire's army — labor gangs organized for production and armed gangs for destruction — both using, as Mumford noted, roughly the same methods and principles. Civilization always demands empire, to seize colonies for cheap labor and materials to build its temples and military juggernauts. Every civilization has its empire, and every empire its frontier, with its wretched colonies and denuded sacrifice zones.

A second great mutation was the rise of the capitalist world system — the first global megamachine or system of interlocking megamachines; the scientific and the industrial revolutions occurring in production and later in culture and consumption have managed to internalize the empire, wire it into subjectivity, in a way no previous form could. Capitalism, first financed by the mutation resulting in the vast discovery and plunder of Africa and the Americas in particular, has become itself a system of permanent revolution, constantly finding new commons to enclose and new colonies to vampirize. For the first time in history, the instrumental and economic transformation of the world has become the central cultural motive.

This process of conquest, looting, regimentation of labor and leisure, and growing dependency on an energy/capital/production grid continues today, not only in the hinterlands of India, Mexico and the Amazon, where remnants of vernacular cultures persist, but in the soil, seeds, oceans, sky and gene pool. The empire of man over things has been firmly established. We marvel at its miracles and disasters, take for granted its transubstantiation of the life web into resources, of real plenitude into pseudo-wealth. As if watching a televised war, we cannot avert our gaze from the spectacles that its official loudspeakers and apologists, in a duckspeak both sophisticated and simple, call Progress. But of course, in a fundamental sense, we are still in ancient Mesopotamia, even more deeply mired in it. And nature, for us, is mostly dead. In its place a machine is telling us, "Stay tuned."

In old mythic terms, we have been taught to revere not life but a two-headed Beast: the promise of mastery over mechanical slaves and the bribe of a world awash in artifacts. Both idols require our skeptical attention. Yet a critical skepticism of megatechnics and industrial pseudo-plenitude is exactly what elicits the most resistance, bringing accusations of indifference to the suffering of the poor, irresponsible technophobia, or utter incoherence. This is the myth of the machine in operation, where the denial is strongest, and the fetters most difficult to break. Again, each area deserves a full treatment that is not possible here. We can only review them briefly.

The empire is a brutal, mechanized pyramid that cannot exist without colonies and sacrifice zones: once established, quantitative value flows from one direction to another. Thus at one end of the spectrum we find an idyllic, manicured park, and at the other the slag heap which paid for it. At one end society chokes on its waste and excess, while at the other, starvation is permanent, institutionalized. The "winners" in the imperial war-of-all-against-all now find themselves in the industrial enclaves, where they can shop at air-conditioned malls or snow-ski on indoor, ambient-controlled ski-slopes, as one can now do in Japan. The losers are in places like Bhopal, Serra Pelada or the slums of Detroit. Except for the high rise bastions of the rich (which are also turning out to be toxic with synthetics, electromagnetic radiation, antibiotics and stress), the world is being reduced to a junk pile, a slum, a cesspool, a barren mountain of debris picked over by hungry ghosts.

In the high rises those who long ago would have had little but been much, to use Fredy Perlman's incisive formulation, now have much but are little.[13] With global industrialization and the modernization of poverty, the others who continue to have little are tending also to *be* less and less. In the train stations of India, I've been told, where poor people actually live, there are public monitors broadcasting American television programs. Some of the world's poorest people are vicariously witnessing the transubstantiation of spirit into money, and they are now craving that impossible living death in the tower, when in fact only the village can save them. Indigenous zapatista revolutionaries demand, along with respect for their culture and their autonomy, the televisions that will eventually implode both.

Various reformers and noble souls, be they leftist revolutionaries with political programs or U.N. technocrats with satchels full of blueprints, are determined to deliver the "much" to the have-nots. If you suggest that bringing an industrial existence to the poor is neither ecologically feasible nor culturally desirable you are usually accused of privileged elitism. Yet not only is this viewpoint connected to age-old insights of both primal societies and classical philosophy, it is coming to be taken seriously by radical critique in the so-called underdeveloped world and in indigenous communities. "My people are tired of development," one activist told a development conference in the mid–1980s, "they just want to live." "More commodities and more cash mean less life," Indian ecofeminist Vandana Shiva has written. Or as Illich has noted, the organization of the economy toward a "better" life is undermining the possibility of a good life.[14] People in rich nations and poor are beginning to realize that we must all get off the treadmill, that what we need is not a higher standard of living but a deeper one.

This is fertile anti-imperial discourse, not a rigid position, as both the defenders and the reformers of empire usually maintain. But the critique of empire has other crucial applications. It doesn't just focus on peons working the banana plantation to feed the global supermarket, the image of empire to which we are accustomed; industrialism is structurally and ecologically an empire in other ways. You cannot have petrochemicals without colonies and sacrifice zones — waste pits, oil spills, refinery row, ruined areas and lives. You can't have mass dependence on a global chemical-industrial grid without unanticipated incidents and accidents. You can't have the empire of man over things and mastery over a complex of mechanical slaves without feedback and without becoming, like Dr. Frankenstein, the creature of your monsters.

The common attitude toward technology is a weird amalgam of optimism, resignation and denial. While explicitly acknowledging the profound changes in culture and social institutions, in the rare instances when it ponders the shifting social contract mass technics have imposed, the ruling ideology concludes that we must adapt. The gigantic technological structures, the reorganized forms of life and new reorientation in thought, and the very modification of the experience of reality itself, are all considered necessary "trade-offs" for the industrial bribe. Contained in the idea that we cannot get the genie back into the bottle, that there is "no going back," is a dim recognition that technology can indeed undermine human autonomy.

Yet strangely, technology is usually thought to be neutral, or the product of social relations, never a determinant that itself imposes conditions. This is true even among radical greens and others critical of technology, expressed for example in Brian Tokar's remark in *The Green Alternative*, "Technologies are only as good as the society that creates them; the more powerful the technology, the more it can amplify the qualities of the society it was designed to serve."[15] Missing from this view is the recognition that technology — actually an interlocking system of apparatus, rational techniques and organization — doesn't merely follow design but changes the world in a systemic, *ecological* way.[16]

Neither tools nor technology are neutral. They are inevitably powerful constituents of our symbolic world. Technology imposes not only form but content wherever it comes into use. Industrialism is the grand example, shattering the medieval world with its dynamism and synergy, its tendency to irreversibility and pervasiveness. (Here it is important to emphasize that modern industrialism and capitalism emerged in tandem as a unitary phenomenon. Industrialization and capital accumulation have always occurred synergistically, both in the period of the early rise of capitalism, and later in the various state formations of industrial capitalism during the nineteenth and twentieth centuries.) But even one supposedly isolated technological addition can easily come to reshape society, creating qualitatively different conditions, a famous example being how the introduction of snowmobiles rapidly exploded Sami (Lapp) society in the 1960s. In a matter of a few years, the snowmobile undermined ancient modes of life of the reindeer-herding people, altering the behavior of the reindeer, further opening the society to the world market, and creating new dependencies and a class society where there had previously been none. Proving again that everything is interconnected.[17]

The process is not entirely deterministic, but clearly, technology is more than the sum of its parts. The automobile, for example, is more than a tool; it is a component in a total system of production, energy, distribution, roadways, techniques, laws and other attendant processes that extend throughout the culture and reshape it behind our backs. Thinking in terms of our individual, enlightened use of the single component — be it a car, computer or television — misses the whole picture. We forget that a socialization process is taking place in individuals and their society, that the totality of means, apparatus and organization is having its effect.

"Seen as a way of ordering human activity," writes Langdon Winner in *Autonomous Technology*, "the total order of networks is anything but neutral or tool-like. In its centrality to the daily activity and consciousness of … the function-serving human component, the technical order is more properly thought of as a *way of life*." "Machinery is aggressive," commented Emerson. "The weaver becomes the web." By this he meant that gradually the means come to undermine and reshape the ends, and the world is qualitatively altered. And what is worse, the system, once fully in operation, no longer responds to human guidance. The dream of mastery gives way to desperate attempts to manage the feedback. "The means," writes Winner, "accomplish results that were neither anticipated nor chosen and accomplish them just as surely as they had been deliberate goals." He quotes Nietzsche on the utilitarians, who knew the next step or two, but no more: "They have no conception of the grand economy, which cannot do without evil."[18]

Today's utilitarians are the crackpot realists (to borrow C.Wright Mills' rich term) in the research labs, military command centers, board rooms and universities planning out each new stage of a new-improved world, free of war, hunger and disease — or so they promise. Meanwhile they have created an exterminist system with its daily litany of death — Bhopal, Prince William Sound, Minamata, Chernobyl, Love Canal, the burning Amazon, the Gulf War. And let us not forget the invisible, undramatic, slow-acting catastrophe — the "climate death" now discussed by climatologists, the depleted ozone, the pervasive contamination of the food chain, a ton of toxic waste a year per person in the U.S. — not the products, like the styrofoam cup or the microwave oven, which are also toxic, but the production waste. A ton a year: happy birthday.[19]

But it's not just corporate criminals who are to blame (though we have plenty of them, too). It's also Nietzsche's grand economy. Incidents, accidents and systemic disasters are inevitable. No amount of citizen control, double-hulled tankers or fail-safe back-up systems will prevent them. To think otherwise is to fall into what has been called the engineering fallacy, a form of denial. As Charles Perrow writes in *Natural Accidents: Living With High-Risk Technology*, "Systems that transform explosive or toxic raw materials or that exist in hostile environments [and this could almost serve as a basic definition of industrialism itself], appear to require designs that entail a great many interactions which are not visible and in expected production sequence. Since nothing is perfect — neither designs, equipment, operating procedure, materials and supplies, nor the environment — there will be failures ... These accidents then are caused initially by component failures, but become accidents rather than incidents because of the nature of the system itself; they are system accidents, and are inevitable, or 'normal' for these systems." This passage should bring to mind not only single dramatic disasters like Bhopal, but the systemic catastrophe that industrialism is for the entire web of life. [20]

CFCs are an example of a combination of the grand economy and capitalist greed. The refusal to stop using chlorine-based compounds is certainly a kind of denial based on greed. But CFCs were originally a result of fragmented, "problem-solving" science, produced to replace toxic compounds with an environmentally more benign alternative, not simply to generate profits. No one could have known all the far-reaching effects they would have.[21] This is true of pesticides, biomedical technologies, synthetic chemicals, mass communications, and electromagnetic grids— all seen as beneficial developments, tools that need proper and responsible management. We don't yet know their total impact, since even with toxic chemicals and the ozone depletion we are only seeing the results of activities of decades ago. We notice what we think are the aberrations in the system, even protest them, without realizing that industrialism itself is one vast Bhopal.

Television is another example, in the realm of meaning. Television has changed language and culture, is even changing the shape of the human brain. Computers and nintendo have added to the equation. Selective viewing — or not viewing at all, for that matter — is to some degree only a private response to a pervasive environment. The 1991 Persian Gulf War reminds us that the effects of the technology are systemic. Memory has come to resemble what the machine records, and sensual reality is eroding into a labyrinth of mediatized images. People can focus less than they once could. Discourse is being reduced to simple signals. The culture is increasingly fast-paced, frenetic, technicized, numb. Silence and the art of sitting still are all but extinct. The human subject is becoming what Mills called "the spectator of everything and the human witness of nothing." "The sight of immediate reality," said the prescient Walter Benjamin, "has become an orchid in the land of technology."[22]

Nevertheless, because of greed, ignorance and universal character malaise, the command remains the same: "full steam ahead," either to create post-modern paradise or to ameliorate the disasters already upon us. When, to give a small personal example, I ask the teachers with whom I work how we decided that elementary school children needed computer literacy rather than gardening, I am either told to "get with it," or given a blank, somewhat puzzled look. The technology is "here to stay"; we have to learn to use it or be left behind. Yet we are not certain what it is doing to us or what it will do to our children. This passivity among people whom I respect in other regards brings to mind Mumford's comment that even when dangers or malfunctions are suggested, people can "see no way of overcoming them except by further extension of automation and cybernation … It is the system that, once set up, gives orders." This "self-inflicted impotence [is] the other side of 'total control.'"[23]

The tree says, "Stop. I am sore." But the technician doesn't listen. The life web says, "Stop. I am suffering." But the empire plants more surveyor stakes, isolates the genetic Holy Grail, hooks its children to a keyboard, demands more studies. And the life web suffers, as the immune systems of plants, animals and people, undermined by this pervasive Bhopal, succumb to viral and bacterial predators they once could resist. In many places mother's milk — it is difficult to find a more powerful representation of the sources of life — is so contaminated with dioxins and other chemicals that it is thought to be dangerous to the nursing child. The sources of life become the sources of death — the ultimate feedback.

So, what to do? I'm glad I'm no political organization with a need to invent a nuts-and-bolts plan for everything from what to do with toxic waste to the health care system to a green party program. We're all droplets of water in the stream described by Black Elk, carving away at the rock of history. There is plenty to do. If transformation is a question of culture and character, and doesn't depend on a single method, or on our ability to manipulate the dialectic, then on a certain level we can, in fact we must, relax. (A key taoist principle, by the way.) That will help us to endure. In some contexts that simply means showing concern and affection for life around us, proof we exist not because we know, as the decaying world view has it, but because we care. In our daily life, respect for both what we know and for what we cannot know might mean learning patience, or the attentiveness with which we drink our tea. An ecological society knows how to drink its tea properly, and mindfully.

It may sound strange to hear me describe the apocalypse called modernity, then counsel something sounding like "everything I know I learned in kindergarten." I'm in no way nullifying analysis, critique, social action. I'm proposing to harmonize them to the fullness of life. As for proposing global strategies, let's be careful not to fall into instrumentalism in our desire to be practical. In the final sections of *The Myth of the Machine*, Mumford writes, "To describe even in the barest outline the multitude of changes necessary to turn the power complex into an organic complex, and a money economy into a life economy, lies beyond the capacities of any individual mind. . . ."[24] He thought the reemergence at a new level of the organic vision and its corresponding lifeways would take at least as long as it did for the modern megamachine to replace medieval society.

Mumford believed the necessary planet-wide reorientation of culture would first appear in evidence of inner change, and in a wide variety of gestures of refusal, non-conformity and creative, alternative forms of practice. Like a diverse constellation of radical greens, native traditionals, ecofeminists, anarchists, libertarian socialists and many others drawing from an enormous wealth of traditions and counter-traditions, he understood that below the surface of the empire, ancient forms of human sociation and alternative forms of reason continue to work organically, even if under harsh conditions and in distorted ways: mutual aid, solidarity, community, love, friendship, affection, celebration, self-reflection, the struggle for personal autonomy, the arts as a school of wisdom, and the manifold, archetypal forms of the nurturance of life. Thus much of the transformation is already going on around us, within us. People in wide-ranging projects are already answering the question, "what to do." I wouldn't presume to tell them. Mistakes will surely be made, but the important point is to *keep* doing what we think enhances community, solidarity, the nurturance of life — to endure. There are many areas where this can occur. They tend to coalesce as we begin to make the connections.

I do think creative response points to a basic frame of mind and practice beyond the tepid proposal to democratize industrialism; we have to find ways to challenge its basic assumptions. A radical vision for today demands a luddite politics starting from a technological skepticism toward the entire structure and content of technological society. It demands a focus on the process of empire, not only the innumerable hydra heads that are its symptoms. Such a practice would ask the fundamental philosophical questions I mentioned earlier — question number one being how to prevent the mystique of a mechanized paradise from destroying the possibility for a deeper form of life.

Global industrialism is a dead end, in social and in evolutionary terms. We can choose to abandon it voluntarily, through a new reorientation in our values and our practice, or it will occur in a different way, suggested by what we have seen happen to people in places like the former Yugoslavia or Iraq during the Gulf War. Such a new orientation would seek to turn society into a school of inquiry for deconstructing industrial and technological dependencies. I am thinking here of a kind of great moratorium on development and scientific-technological expansion that would renew the vernacular domain of doing for self by exploring how to create subsistence and culture at home in one's community.

Restoration and renewal would be key values — of wilderness, the land, community, and the self, all presently contaminated and eroded by the external and internal structures of the megamachine. This suggests a kind of salvage operation, from the rich compost of former cultures and from the industrial junkyard we are gradually going to have to clean up. Realistically, it will also mean a prosthetic technics, as Theodore Roszak once suggested, but consciously in a direction far different than either "going back" — which we have never proposed and which could never occur anyway — or going forward into technotopia.[25] It means a third way that will come from asking the kinds of questions and raising the kinds of issues that make no sense either to business-as-usual or to palliative reform. Isn't the green idea potentially the exemplar of a "third way"?

Finally we must remember to approach this with the entirety of being. What does that mean? To see the world as ourselves. Writing of the Chipko movement in northern India, which has hugged trees to keep loggers from cutting them, Vandana Shiva tells how at one point village women suffered brutal beatings by hired thugs from the logging companies, but still held their ground. Shiva asked a woman how she could keep going, keep smiling. The woman replied, "Can you see all this grass growing? We come to cut this grass and every year it grows back. And the power in that grass is the power in me. Do you see those trees growing? They're two hundred years old. Every year we lop those trees to feed our cattle and to keep our children alive, so that the children have milk, and still the trees keep growing and still keep nurturing us, and that *shakti* [energy, the life principle] is in me."[26]

To see the world as yourself means to practice in the same manner, no matter what your expectations of winning or losing. It's the kind of organic reason that compels us to plant a tree, even on the last day of the world — how human community will endure this long wandering through civilization and empire, mass society and catastrophe. If you think these ideas seem impractical, remote from what many people see as their immediate concerns, you are right. But in relation to mass society, even a more pragmatic, green reform appears impossible. We need to be realistic by demanding the impossible. If we don't, who will? To paraphrase Eugene Debs, we are better off fighting for what we want and not getting it than fighting for what we don't want and getting it.

"On the terms imposed by technocratic society," Mumford writes, "there is no hope ... except by 'going with' its plans for accelerated technological progress, even though [our] very organs will be cannibalized in order to prolong the megamachine's meaningless existence." Here we are reminded of the current fascination with cyborgism that I mentioned earlier. "But for those of us who have thrown off the myth of the machine," says Mumford, "the next move is ours: for the gates of the technocratic prison will open automatically, despite their rusty hinges, as soon as we choose to walk out."[27]

There are no easy answers to the question of how can we open those rusty gates once and for all and walk free. That isn't the adventure any of us would have chosen, but it's the one we all face. It is an adventure, nevertheless. Let's be worthy of it.

(1994)

Endnotes

1. Ivan Illich, *Shadow Work* (Boston and London: Marion Boyars, 1981), p. 29.
2. Donna Haraway, "A Manifesto for Cyborgs: Science, Technology and Socialist Feminism in the 1980's," *Socialist Review* 80 (1985), pp. 65–107.
3. The "catching fish" idea comes from N. J. Giradot, *Myth and Meaning in Early Taoism* (1983; Berkeley and London: University of California Press, 1988), p. xiii.
4. Murray Bookchin, "History, Civilization and Progress: Outline for a Criticism of Modern Relativism" (*Green Perspectives* 29, March 1994), pp. 4-5, emphasis in original. For a critique of Bookchin's work, see my *Beyond Bookchin: Preface for a Future Social Ecology* (Detroit and New York: Black & Red/Autonomedia, 1996).
5. Black Elk quoted in Joseph Epes Brown, *The Spiritual Legacy of the American Indian* (1982; New York: Crossroad, 1985), p. 43.
6. Octavio Paz, *Alternating Current* (New York: The Viking Press, 1973), p. 116, emphasis in original. See also Morris Berman's inspired *The Reenchantment of the World* (Ithaca: Cornell University Press, 1981), which takes Paz's idea as its starting point.
7. The "merciless criticism" is the marxist revolutionary project, the idea of "species being" from Marx's *Economic and Philosophic Manuscripts*. Jacques Ellul's remarks are from *The Technological Society* (1964), pp. 141-6.
8. I mean in particular Murray Bookchin and his associate Janet Biehl, in a number of recent books and articles, especially Bookchin, *Remaking Society: Pathways to a Green Future* (Boston: South End Press, 1990), and Biehl, *Rethinking Ecofeminist Politics* (Boston: South End, 1991).
9. Quoted in T.C. McLuhan, *Touch the Earth: A Self-Portrait of Indian Existence* (New York: Simon & Schuster, 1971), p. 15.
10. Norman O. Brown, *Life Against Death: The Psychoanalytic Meaning of History* (1959; Middletown: Wesleyan University Press, 1977), pp. 238, 236.

11. *Basic Call to Consciousness,* edited by *Akwesasne Notes* (1978; Mohawk Nation, via Rooseveltown NY, 1982), p. 69.

12. See "Civilization in Bulk," in part IV of this book.

13. Fredy Perlman, *The Reproduction of Daily Life* (Detroit: Black & Red, 1972), p. 24.

14. Vandana Shiva, *Staying Alive: Women, Ecology and Development* (London: Zed Press, 1989), pp. 13, 7; Ivan Illich, *Tools for Conviviality* (New York and London: Harper & Row, 1973).

15. Brian Tokar, *The Green Alternative: Creating an Ecological Future* (second edition, San Pedro: R. & E. Miles, 1992), p. 83. This same idea of a neutral technology is common in the works of Bookchin as well. See, for example, his comment that technology only *"magnifies* more fundamental economic factors" (in *Remaking Society*, page 93, emphasis in original), and in *Social Anarchism or Lifestyle Anarchism: An Unbridgeable Chasm* (San Franscisco and Edinburgh: AK Press, 1995), that capitalist relations "blatantly determine *how* technology will be used. . . ." (pp. 28-9, emphasis in original).

16. This discussion is informed by Langdon Winner's indispensable *Autonomous Technology: Technics-out-of-Control as a Theme In Political Thought* (Cambridge and London: MIT Press,1977). See also Neil Postman's *Technopoly: The Surrender of Culture to Technology* (New York: Knopf, 1992) for the use of the idea of "ecological" change.

17. See "The Snowmobile Revolution," in part III of this book.

18. Winner, *Autonomous Technology*, pp. 201; Emerson's *Works and Days* cited p. 195, Nietzsche's *The Will to Power* cited p. 96.

19. C. Wright Mills, *The Causes of World War Three* (New York: Simon & Schuster, 1958). For discussion of climate death, see Tim Thompson, "Where Have All the Clouds Gone?," *Earth Island Journal*, Spring 1992.

20. The "engineering fallacy" idea comes from Michael Edelstein, *Contaminated Communities: The Social and Psychological Impacts of Residential Toxic Exposure* (Boulder and London: Westview Press, 1988). Perrow quoted in Tara Jones, *Corporate Killing: Bhopals Will Happen* (London: Free Association Books, 1988), p. 243. This theme is discussed in "Stopping the Industrial Hydra," in part II of this book.

21. CFCs were of course used by corporations to clean components and for other industrial tasks *after* the problem with aerosols was discovered. But they and many other such products, nevertheless, came from problem-solving science, not simply from irresponsible greed.

22. Mills, ibid., p. 78; Walter Benjamin, *Illuminations* (New York: Schocken Books, 1969), p. 233.

23. Lewis Mumford, *The Pentagon of Power: The Myth of the Machine Volume Two* (New York and London: Harcourt, Brace Jovanovich, 1970), p. 184.

24. Mumford, ibid., p. 433.

25. Theodore Roszak, *Where the Wasteland Ends: Politics and Transcendence in Postindustrial Society* (1972; Garden City: Doubleday/Anchor, 1973), pp. 379-408.

26. Quoted in a review by Frederique Apffel-Marglin of Vandana Shiva's *Staying Alive*, in *Capitalism, Nature, Socialism* (Summer 1989, Volume 1, Number 2).

27. Mumford, ibid., pp. 435.

II.
WE ALL LIVE
IN BHOPAL

Illustration by Freddie Baer

Illustration by Johann Humyn Being

NOTES ON THE DISAPPEARANCE OF HISTORY

" ... so that when there is no more
story that will be our
story when there is no
forest that will be our forest"
— W.S. Merwin, "One Story"

I've spent most of my life in the inner city of Detroit, a place both like and unlike many others in the industrialized world. I still live in the neighborhood where I did my growing up, attended school, met and married my wife. Despite the urban desolation, I'm tied to the place; even after long sojourns abroad, I always return to the same few square blocks.

Our house looks out on land that was gradually cleared of buildings after the 1967 black rebellion and the city's economic decline in the 1970s. During the 1960s it had been a thriving community of poor whites and blacks, students, longhairs and young radicals. I found the local anti-war committee, a friendly poor peoples' diner, communes, poor churches, and a sense of community there.

Like so many of the decade's dreams, the neighborhood was demolished. At the far west end, on the other side of the expressway, was left a fascinating miniature wilderness of great, old trees, wildflowers mixed with perennials where once were gardens, and rich bird habitat. Eventually this green place was also flattened and a typically ugly housing development constructed in its place. (Named, nightmarishly, "Freedom Place," a huge sign at the entrance lists a dozen or more prohibitions, each with the word "NO" twice the size of the rest of the lettering.)

Recently the builders returned to the section directly across from us. In a few days it was fenced, and all the trees were smashed. Expensive apartments, almost completed, are being leased at rents well beyond the means of most locals. Our view of a park and the sunset is blocked. Someone is getting upscale, sterile housing, and someone else is getting rich, but our lives seem to be incrementally poorer.

Such things happen all the time, happen everywhere. One might wonder what they have to do with history and its abuses. I think that in a small, perhaps obscure way, our experience is like the one many people have had walking down a familiar street and realizing some landmark is missing, but not quite remembering what. It is somehow emblematic of the disappearance of memory occurring relentlessly around the globe. The process may seem anonymous because it is inertial, or because nearly everyone assumes it to be perfectly natural. But history, big and small, is not just disappearing; it is *being disappeared* just as surely as human beings are disappeared by dictatorships.

Of course, history has always been an ambiguous affair — a (consciously and unconsciously) constructed official story employed by powerful men to legitimate and sacralize their rule ever since the armed Mesopotamian god-kings conquered the wilderness to build their sacred city-states. Since then, history has been a long series of cataclysms. In the 1930s, Walter Benjamin described the "angel of history" being thrown backwards by a storm out of Paradise. At the angel's feet lies "one single catastrophe which keeps piling wreckage upon wreckage." While he would like to "make whole what has been smashed," the storm "irresistibly propels him into the future to which his back is turned, while the pile of debris before him grows skyward. The storm is what we call progress."

Despite its many disasters, there have always been counter-stories to imperial myth, and history has remained contested ground. Individual memory is a knot in the web of collective memory, and this shared history is an immense, diverse psychic commons sustaining our sense of human community, a reservoir where glimpses of freedom, and the remembrance of atrocities and triumphs are all preserved. We need this common historical space to replenish our inner capacity to remain human in the same way that forests and wild places are needed to nourish and renew the lands that sustain human communities. But just as the world's forests are being destroyed, so too is memory's commons.

Empires have always worked to undermine authentic memory — for example, the book burnings by the the Ch'in emperors, a method still employed in our time. (This strategy was updated in 1970s China by the Maoist regime, when photographs of a lineup of party leaders were retouched to turn purged bureaucrats into shrubs.) Monumentalism is another age-old form of control. One grotesque recent case was the construction by the Balaguer government in the Dominican Republic of an enormous lighthouse, far from the sea, to honor Columbus and his "discovery" — a project which levelled poor *barrios* of Santo Domingo and now causes frequent electricity shortages throughout the city.

Despite their destructiveness, such methods have limited results, to which the patent shabbiness of the Columbus story and the toppling monuments of the Soviet bloc dramatically testify. There are now greater threats to memory, greater weapons in power's arsenal. The modern transformations in consciousness brought about during the last century by mass communications and consumer society seem to be changing the *form* memory takes. And history's form shapes content as surely as it takes particular words or kinds of words to make a certain kind of statement. This change evokes the legend of the Chinese emperor who decreed for himself the exclusive use of the pronoun "I." The modern media have now donned such imperial robes, speaking while everyone else listens. One can no longer even make a revolution without making sure to seize the television stations (as was apparently the case in Romania), since instead of directly *making* history, people watch the screen to see what is happening. The contemporary erosion of people's capacity to think for themselves, and the monopolization of meaning by the media, seem to be succeeding at what the legendary emperor might only have imagined.

A new society emerged in Western Europe and North America during the last century as the organic structures of life began to unravel. In the United States, where this development seems most pernicious, the colonization and control of culture was an explicit strategy for labor discipline and goods distribution. As historian Stuart Ewen writes in *Captains of Consciousness: Advertising and the Roots of Consumer Culture*, by the early twentieth century, business leaders, coming out of a period of mass labor unrest, recognized the need to manage not only production but consumption. A new kind of citizen had to be shaped to respond appropriately to the plethora of industrial products offered by the emergent corporate market system. Scientific time management studies in the factory were mirrored by expanding techniques of human management. One businessman wrote in the 1920s that education must teach "the masses not what to think but how to think, and thus ... how to behave like human beings in the machine age."

By the 1950s, industrial expansion and economic growth had become a universal secular religion, and consumerism an unquestioned cultural norm. Of course, the rapid obsolescence of commodities and a throwaway society was also a conscious, explicit strategy of managerial elites. One prominent marketing consultant, for example, urged "forced consumption," arguing, "We need things consumed, burned up, worn out, replaced, and discarded at an ever increasing rate." Now that the ethos of consumerism (if not necessarily its material benefits) is quickly spreading to the countries of the post-colonial world and the former Soviet empire, the question culture critic Vance Packard asked about North American culture in the 1950s is increasingly relevant. "What is the impact on the human spirit," he wrote, "of all these pressures to consume?"

The impact of television — which has become the key vehicle for consumer culture worldwide — has more than confirmed Packard's fears. Television flattens, disconnects and renders experience and history incoherent. Its seemingly meaningful pastiche of images works best to sell commodities — fabricated objects devoid of any authentic history. But more importantly, it also affirms the whole universe of commodity consumption as the only life worth living. Wherever the set is turned on, local culture implodes.

Though sold as a tool that could preserve memory, television utterly fragments and colonizes it. What remains is a cult of the perpetual present, in continual, giddying motion. The jumbled, packaged events of recent and remote history come to share the relative weightlessness of soap operas and dish detergent, and perspective evaporates. Power no longer needs to shout; as Mark Crispin Miller once remarked, Big Brother isn't watching you so much as Big Brother is you, watching. Henry Ford's cynical quip that history is bunk comes true as people grow up more and more on television, rather than hearing about events through convivial conversation. Historical memory is now becoming what was televised, while that commons of the mind, domesticated and simulated by the media, is receding.

A striking case in point is the way people (especially North Americans) were manipulated into supporting the 1991 Persian Gulf War. Someone who has already seen tens of thousands of people "killed" on tv has a difficult time understanding the human suffering caused by the technological special effects that tv is good at presenting. Yet even the war hysteria, which one journalist described as a "nightly electronic Nuremberg Rally," faded with time, as the images crystallized into scraps of last year's mini-series. When Iraq was later attacked and several civilians killed on a couple of different occasions, many passive patriots who had been glued to their sets during the height of the war were now barely aware of it. It was all, as is often said, "history" — which is to say, in the common parlance, *it no longer existed.* Their indifference today is as disturbing as their spasm of enthusiasm was before.

The "information society" and the culture of its mass media-driven market system are doing something to human meaning far more serious than organized government propaganda or censorship ever could. Now that the peoples of the former colonies (as well as women and other formerly invisible groups) are beginning to rediscover the stories that official history formerly suppressed, modern technique is poised to shape everyone's story, to make them all a fragment in one long photomontage. But, to paraphrase Packard, how will so many different peoples tell their unique histories when tv itself has become the dominant mode of communication and recall? How will memory express diverse modes of being when work, buying and selling are the core of what is rapidly becoming a global monoculture? Will those cultures that aren't as compatible with the television sensibility, and even memory of them, just disappear altogether, like the trees that once stood across from my window?

The disappearance of languages and cultures is as terrifying a prospect as the current mass extinction of species. At current rates, some ninety percent of the world's languages will be dead or moribund in the next century. And without language, there can be no memory. Ironically, the greatest threat is to those scattered cultures whose memory *precedes* official history — primal and indigenous peoples, some with traditions reaching back to the Pleistocene.

The native Hawaiians, for example, have seen their culture wither under the onslaught of progress. Today many Hawaiians speak only the language of their American conquerors, and remembrance has eroded as the places to which words and sensibilities were bound now come under the bulldozer's blade. Enormous resorts, shopping malls and golf courses (as well as military bombing ranges) have devoured burial grounds, old fishing villages and sacred sites.

I will give just one devastating example. On the island of Hawai'i, where the active volcano Kilauea constantly creates new land, is some of the richest lowland tropical rainforest left in the island chain (only about ten percent survives). Even according to the conqueror's laws, the forest, called Wao Kele O Puna, was to be held in perpetuity for Hawaiians to practice subsistence activities and to gather ceremonial and medicinal plants, many of which grow only there and nowhere else.

To some, the volcano is simply a resource from which geothermal energy could be tapped by harnessing volcanic steam. Though risky, it could provide energy to fuel the already obscene growth ravaging the islands. There are few meaningful memories of the place in the minds of the developers that would recommend restraint; so, in the late 1980s the state government of Hawai'i traded the 27,000-acre forest to corporate geothermal developers for some lava-covered lands where earlier drilling sites had been destroyed by the volcano.

The Hawaiians, however, have an entirely different way of seeing things; their concept of *aloha aina* is far more subtle, complex and fleshy than the simple translation we might give it of "love for the land." To a Hawaiian, the terms connote not two separate elements, love on the part of a subject for an object called land (something real estate agents deal in), but rather interconnectedness and kinship, reciprocity and subjectivity, impassioned desire and an attentiveness rooted to the spirit and the specifics of place. Thus, the volcano is a living being, the goddess Pele. She created and continues to create the islands, and her family is not only the diverse life forms that slowly turn burnt land into verdant forest, but the Hawaiian people themselves.

The Hawaiians and their allies have many good reasons to fight geothermal development — its risks, its cost, its violation of native land rights, its inevitable destruction of pristine forest. (One University of Hawai'i biologist called it a place where one could see "where life comes from.") But the project is above all an assault on the heart of their culture and religion, and thus on a tangible reminder of what it means to be Hawaiian. As Pualani Kanehele, a respected teacher of the sacred Hawaiian dance, the *hula kahiko*, argued, to cap Pele's steam would be "putting a cap on the Hawaiian culture ... and Hawai'i will be dead. [Then] this may as well be new California. Because we'll all be *haoles* [foreigners, strangers] with the same goals as the *haoles*: make money."

Meaning, like ecology, is context: everything is connected to everything else. As strands are pulled from the skein of memory, what it means to be a person within a human community shifts toward some troubling unknown. The experience of the Hawaiians, who have seen their ancestors' bones turned up by machines where someone else's paradise will be fabricated, lends special resonance to Benjamin's warning that even the dead are not safe when power triumphs.

If, as Czech novelist Milan Kundera has written, "the struggle ... against power is the struggle against forgetting," the need to remember must also inevitably confront power. We may come to need truth commissions to recover shared memory, like those organized to uncover and preserve the lost stories of disappeared persons in Latin America. Taking responsibility for our past might help us uncover the complex weave of histories that now connect us all in our shared suffering and grandeur.

As I write this I imagine the new tenants across the street plugging into the free cable television they've been promised, staring at the instantaneous news on their dizzying array of channels, and seeing "history" in the moment it is conjured. I hear the heavy equipment beeping as the machinery backs up over the past, shifts into forward, and growls into the future.

(1993)

Postscript, 1994: After I wrote this essay, Pele's eruptions probably did more to stop geothermal development than anything else. A Supreme Court decision allowing native Hawaiians access to Wao Kele O Puna has also brought the battle to a standstill and partial victory. Many questions remain open and much destruction has already occurred. As I said, the Wao Kele O Puna struggle is only one example of the multiple wars against the Hawaiian land and people. To support native Hawaiian struggles contact/donate to the Pele Defense Fund, P.O. Box 404, Volcano HI 96785.

EARTH DAY?
WE WANT A FESTIVAL
OF THE OPPRESSED!

Earth Day or Capital's Spectacle?

If there was ever a need for an "Earth Day," "Earth Week," or "Earth Year" "to get people thinking creatively about the problems we now confront, and looking for new ways to tackle them," in the words of Earth Day 1970 organizer (and Earth Day 1990™ CEO) Denis Hayes, now is certainly the time.

Twenty years after the original Earth Day demonstrations in April 1970, the ecological crisis is far more grave, with major organs of the living ecosphere apparently taking a rapid slide downhill. Now everyone is climbing on the bandwagon — not only the suckers but the confidence men, the victims as well as the executioners, the contaminated communities and the powerful institutions that profit from their contamination. Hands across America, everybody, let's save the Earth; and if we can do it by satellite hookup with corporate sponsorship, well, all the better.

Everyone wants a piece of Hayes's "outpouring of public concern," concern being one of those low-overhead factors of continuing production that make such good corporate publicity. Big Oil wants a piece of the action, and the politicians, and the Utilities — even the Pentagon must be scheming up an announcement for an "Earth-friendly" war. Every company and promoter with something to sell is giving an Earth Day spin to the sales pitch. The environment is "in." Yet somehow the contamination and plunder are accelerating even as the noise about saving the planet becomes loudest.

Whose Day? Whose Earth? Do the military-industrial-financial ghouls at Death's control panel think that by donating a few trees to be planted on wasted soils they can postpone the inevitable breakdown of their crumbling megamachine? One is reminded of the Puritan sabbath, when the land grabbers, Indian-killers and witch burners contemplated the pieties of their savior in whose name they perpetrated their slaughters. Once April 22 passes, the show will end, and that holocaust of holocausts, the normal state of affairs and its corresponding affairs of state will resume, full steam ahead.

No kidding: there is a profound biocrisis occurring. It isn't radicals who are sounding the alarm about this crisis, but mainstream scientists. Industrialism has now caused some five holes in the ozone layer in the Earth's upper atmosphere and is heating up the planet in unprecedented ways, the results of which can only be guessed.

Then there is destruction of habitat for the Earth's species, in fact of entire planetary organs. The rainforests are being lost at the rate of some hundred acres a minute, and will disappear by early in the next century. Not only the rainforests, which contain perhaps half of the world's species of plants and animals, are threatened: an acre of trees is levelled every eight seconds in North America, and biologists believe twenty percent of plants in northern temperate zones will be gone by the next century. In the oceans, the same massacre is going on, as they are simultaneously poisoned and denuded of their living organisms.

Forest death from acid and toxic rain, diminishing topsoil, nuclear waste, wandering garbage barges, global urbanization — the list goes on and on. Everywhere, uncountable species and ecosystems — including most of those that make the world recognizable to us, and many more that we will never encounter before they vanish forever — are going down capital's drain.

I say capital's drain, for isn't it investment, capital expansion, economic growth, and the drive for profit that are torching the forests and raking the seas? Listen to the words of Lowell Moholt, director of investor relations for Weyerhaeuser, the ten billion dollar logging company that is the biggest private possessor of forests (in Deathspeak: timberland) in the world, presently felling some of the last remnants of North American old-growth forests in the Pacific Northwest: "We are rational people ... We have to run our company to the best of our ability for shareholders ... You can't ignore that a lot of our products are just commodities." This is the rationality that is dragging the entire world to its doom, led along by powerful institutions administered by the experts of "practical next steps," practitioners of what C. Wright Mills, in a prescient book written in 1958 about the nuclear war establishment, *The Causes of World War Three*, called "crackpot realism."

"In this society," Mills wrote, "between catastrophic event and everyday interests there is a vast moral gulf ... The atrocities of our time are done by men as 'functions' of a social machinery — men possessed by an abstracted view that hides from them the human beings [and, we would add, those *other* beings] who are their victims and, as well, their own humanity. They are inhuman acts because they are impersonal. They are not sadistic but merely businesslike; they are not aggressive but merely efficient; they are not emotional at all but technically clean-cut."

Such "moral insensibility," Mills writes, was dramatized by the Nazis, but it has also been demonstrated in wars like Korea and Vietnam, in the planning agencies for World War Three (yes, and believe it or not, they are also planning World War Four), and in the corporate headquarters where blueprints for cutting down the Tree of Life are continuously revised, updated, and embellished by well-fed, well-paid functionaries.

Thus it should come as no surprise that every year, more than a ton of hazardous waste is produced for every man, woman and child in the United States. These are the *production* wastes, mind you, not the toxic products themselves, like the automobiles and electronic and plastic gizmos, the pesticides and chemical compounds that appear in the marketplace. And technicians work every day to find "new disposal methods" — constructing ziggurats of garbage and high tech incinerators — while publicists get paid to assure toxic victims that all is well with the world and that we are achieving "better living through chemistry."

The economy — that is, the accumulation of capital — is the bottom line. The year that *Time* dubbed the Earth "planet of the year," profits for basic extractive/exploitive industries increased across the board, with metals up 110 percent, petroleum refining up 63 percent, forest products up 45 percent, chemicals up 35 percent, electronics up 19 percent, pharmaceuticals up 17 percent, and motor vehicles up 12 percent. It's no accident that the Earth (and our communities along with it) is being reduced to a cesspool — the entire world is being mined and the work machine of the Empire is riding the crest of the contamination from which it profits.

1970–1990: Whose Earth?

If Earth Day 1970 was one of many manifestations in the 1960s of the desire to become a "friction against the Machine," it also suffered from domesticated qualities that blunted its potential radicality from its inception. In fact, Earth Day had the full support of the establishment and the press. In Washington, D.C., maverick journalist I.F. Stone noted that half of Nixon's cabinet was on the speakers' platform.

"Looking out at that tumultuous sea of sweet faces," he wrote, "I felt that just as the Caesars once used bread and circuses so ours were at last learning to use rock-and-roll, idealism and non-inflammatory social issues to turn the youth off from more urgent concerns which might really threaten the power structure. And I said so in my speech." Stone underestimated the seriousness of the ecological crisis but he had a point. "Here was the country slipping into a wider war in Southeast Asia," he observed, "but we were talking as if we had nothing to worry about but our drains."

In fact, that spring brought the invasion and massive bombing of Cambodia in a war which at the time inspired conservation biologists to coin the term *ecocide*. In some places (for example Flint, Michigan where anti-war radicals waving Viet Cong flags chased Michigan Governor William Milliken away during an Earth Day speech), connections were made; but generally they were missed. At the University of Michigan, for example, students listened to representatives of the Dow Chemical Company, which in addition to being a major contaminator of Michigan land and waters, manufactured napalm (jellied gasoline) and chemical defoliants to be used in Vietnam, a war against the entire natural and human ecology. (Describing the massive destruction of Vietnam's forests by Agent Orange and other deadly chemicals to starve out and expose the resistance, one military officer remarked, "The trees were the enemy.")

Capitalists such as Henry Ford II and Laurance Rockefeller were prominent and widely published Earth Day promoters, with Hank the Deuce promising to install "the cleanest coke ovens in the world" in his auto factories. (Rockefeller's name appears among the Earth Day 1990™ International Board of Sponsors, along with that of Vietnam era war criminal Robert McNamara.)

The ecological imbalances caused by industrial capitalism are now approaching dangerous and unprecedented thresholds; mass starvation is a permanent fixture of the world global economy, while in the industrialized world elites are achieving unparalleled and obscene consumption levels. If the last twenty years have demonstrated anything, it is the failure of environmentalism to halt the process of planet-wide destruction. Yet the Earth Day revival is predicated on the same failed strategy and the same reformism.

Most significant is the liberal assumption or at least the implication that ecological devastation is an aberration, a well-intentioned error (just as Vietnam was seen as a mistake in the 1960s) rather than the direct result of programmatic policies (even if ultimately suicidal) on the part of elites to expand exploitation, extraction and imperial power. Or it is seen as a feedback of the "good life" brought by modern industrialism, which can be corrected by a mix of technofix fine-tuning and personal piety. The official Earth Day 1990™ "Green Pledge" urges its adherent "to adopt a lifestyle as if every day were Earth Day," and "to buy and use those products least harmful to the environment and ... to the maximum extent possible do business with corporations that promote global environmental responsibility." Of course, what corporation doesn't promote environmental responsibility? That's what public relations departments are for. Nowhere is the comparatively recent social system of buying and using products, of corporate power, ever questioned, even though the ecological crisis is one of *geological* dimensions. Nor is the possibility ever mentioned that the very structures and content of industrialized society are inherently anti-ecological. Instead, Earth Day recruits are reduced to eco-production, eco-work, eco-investing and eco-shopping in a world that functions essentially in the same manner as the present one.

Schizophrenia about commodity production (a more technical term for what has been called the "throwaway society") runs through the Earth Day literature. Even Henry Ford could write, in a *Look* magazine essay in 1970, "Modern industrial society is based on the assumption that it is both possible and desirable to go on forever providing more and more goods for more and more people. Today, that assumption is being seriously challenged. More goods do not necessarily mean more happiness. More goods may eventually mean more junk, and the junk in the air, in the water and on the land could make the earth unfit for human habitation before we reach the 21st century." Yet Hank's entire existence was geared to the economic necessity of manufacturing more cars for more people. The capitalist enterprise must either expand its empire, its markets, its exploitation of "resources" (read: nature and humanity reduced to commodities) or it will die. Earth Day 1990™ — however sincere it may be — takes for granted the working and the buying that keep capital reproducing itself at the expense of the planetary web of life, and recommends that capital expand into the production of "Earth-friendly" commodities. It fails to see what might become the revolutionary insight of a radical ecological perspective that challenges the production system itself. High energy/commodity consumption is fundamentally destructive not only to the natural world, but to human personhood, autonomy and community as well.

Industrialism promises a "higher" standard of living by undermining the possibilities of a deeper kind of life, one characterized by such values as autonomy, community, direct control by individuals and communities over tools and forms of subsistence, access to clean air and water, silence, green areas and even wilderness. As Ivan Illich observes in *Tools for Conviviality*, "The individual's autonomy is intolerably reduced by a society that defines the maximum satisfaction of the maximum number as the consumption of material goods ... The organization of the entire economy toward the 'better' life has become the major enemy of the *good* life." Industrialism is a cultural and political dead-end.

Thus, correspondingly, the political illusions of mass technology's republic are also affirmed by the Earth Day pledge, with the signer agreeing "to vote and support those candidates who demonstrate an abiding concern for the environment" (once more, concern!), and "to support the passage of local, state and federal laws and international treaties that protect the environment." This pledge constitutes a massive, societal denial. What candidates are not so enmeshed in the business-as-usual of politics as to have all their alleged "concern" over present conditions completely undermined? And where have laws and regulations ultimately done much more than to provide flimsy *assurances* of protection in the face of actual capital expansion? A strategy of negotiated regulation with the contaminators and the exploiters can only result in tragedy, farce or both.

Toward a festival of the oppressed

Industrialism is also an evolutionary dead-end. We are against a wall and cannot wait twenty more years for the lessons of another Earth Day. An entirely new kind of politics, a far more profound response, is needed, something Rudolf Bahro, in *Building the Green Movement*, has called "an anti-investment and a deconcentration strategy, an emergency brake against any further 'progress' in the fateful direction which the accumulation of capital, driven by the world market, is taking."

Such a response would have to move rapidly beyond environmentalism, beyond even radical environmentalism (to the degree that the latter has only employed "radical" tactics to further environmental reforms). It would need to create a social movement that clearly recognizes the myriad connections between global capital, nation-state empires, industrial growth, the disabling impact of mass technics on human culture, and the social and ecological chaos which result — a social movement which begins by elaborating a profound critique of the global urban-industrial megamachine and which bases its practices on this outlook. Neither a reform environmentalism that leaves the capitalist economy in place, nor an eco-leftism that leaves industrial civilization intact by placing it under the direction of some spurious form of socialist commonwealth can be enough; we must challenge not only the motor forces of urban-industrial expansion presently fraying the very tissue of life, but their technological and cultural content as well. *Ecological conversion demands technological inversion.* Human autonomy and a renewal of authentic planetary energies can only be expressed by starting with the prime task at hand: the critical and practical deconstruction of the power grid and its corresponding industrial work pyramid. Any "democratically managed" megamachine would simply allow capital to reorganize without the former owners.

The two currents that brought about the first Earth Day are in motion once more. On the one hand, there is a growing, genuine desire to turn things back, to stop the runaway colossus from dragging all of human society and several hundred million years of evolutionary development hurtling into the abyss for which it is surely headed. A radicalization among young people is occurring on many levels, and to an extent not seen during the last decade; young people seem to be linking the large questions of militarism, social oppression, ecological destruction, megatechnics, and alienation into a vibrant radical response. They are responding to the idea of Earth Day out of the desperate sense that time is running out, and they are correct. Many of the activists among the organizers of Earth Day are impelled by the same desperation.

But the same powers of manipulation continue to function: the chemical manufacturers will plant some trees, and even the "forest products" magnates, as they generally do, will plant some trees. President George Bush called for the planting of a billion trees — but none of the rulers or their allies mention the possibility of refraining from *cutting* a billion trees (in particular say, the last few remnants of old growth forests, but also anywhere where woods are coming under the developers' blades). These forces, these institutions, are concealing their grisly, daily business with a multi-media extravaganza, a spectacle that converts a natural love of what is alive into a pointless civic ritual.

What would an authentic Earth Day look like? Wouldn't it look like a general strike, a moratorium on production, a reduction of mechanical movement, and with it of the industrial noise that drowns out the wind; when all of the former cogs of the megamachine take a long look at the world, perhaps for the first time, and begin the process of becoming living subjects once more? Wouldn't they engage one another in a face-to-face discourse for the first time taking stock of hands and feet and head and heart as the real material bases for a new society? Wouldn't they simply ignore the television stations, rather than attempting to capture them to broadcast the pronouncements of the latest revolutionary-industrial junta? Wouldn't they begin to retrace their steps, back away from the edge of the precipice, turning things off and beginning to rely on their communities and their own human powers to meet their few trifling needs so as to get on with the real adventure of living, of singing, of dreaming? And that first night — wouldn't the sky be dark and beauteous and studded with stars for the first time in memory? Wouldn't a different language, spangled with eternity, find its way into daily discourse as the conditioning of industrialism and manufactured values began to be shed?

Couldn't it be, rather than one more supervised saturnalia for the inmates, a festival of the oppressed capable of bursting its limits and calling a new culture into being? (And who might be the oppressed? Surely not only human victims, but all the branches of life's tree. The very stones groan under this civilization's weight.)

Let us be clear to those who propose only negotiated half-measures and "practical politics" for fear that anything more will be too radical, too "utopian." Collaboration with the wide array of the forces of extermination now facing us will bring only extermination, whether it be in a general conflagration or in small graduated doses. Surely a new defiant outlook starting with what is impossible for this world can lead us to those measures necessary to realize our desires.

(April 1990)

WE ALL LIVE IN BHOPAL

The cinders of the funeral pyres at Bhopal are still warm, and the mass graves still fresh, but the media prostitutes of the corporations have already begun their homilies in defense of industrialism and its uncounted horrors. Some 3,000 people were slaughtered in the wake of the deadly gas cloud, and 20,000 will remain permanently disabled. The poison gas left a 25 square mile swath of dead and dying, people and animals, as it drifted southeast away from the Union Carbide factory. "We thought it was a plague," said one victim. It was: a chemical plague, an industrial plague,

Ashes, ashes, all fall down!

A terrible, unfortunate, "accident," we are reassured by the propaganda apparatus for Progress, for History, for "Our Modern Way of Life." A price, of course, has to be paid since the risks are necessary to ensure a higher Standard of Living, a Better Way of Life.

The Wall Street Journal, tribune of the bourgeoisie, editorialized, "It is worthwhile to remember that the Union Carbide insecticide plant and the people surrounding it were where they were for compelling reasons. India's agriculture has been thriving, bringing a better life to millions of rural people, and partly because of the use of modern agricultural technology that includes applications of insect killers." The indisputable fact of life, according to this sermon, is that India, like everyone else, "needs technology. Calcutta-style scenes of human deprivation can be replaced as fast as the country imports the benefits of the West's industrial revolution and market economics." So, despite whatever dangers are involved, "the benefits outweigh the costs." (December 13, 1984)

The *Journal* was certainly right in one regard — the reasons for the plant and the people's presence there are certainly compelling; capitalist market relations and technological invasion are as compelling as a hurricane to the small communities from which those people were uprooted. It conveniently failed to note, however, that countries like India do not import the benefits of industrial capitalism; those benefits are exported in the form of loan repayments to fill the coffers of the bankers and corporate vampires who read *The Wall Street Journal* for the latest news of their investments. The Indians only take the risks and pay the costs; in fact, for the immiserated masses of people living in the shantytowns of the Third World, there are not risks, so much as certain hunger and disease, and the certainty of death squad revenge for criticizing the state of things as they are.

Industrialization a nightmare

In fact, the Calcutta-style misery is the result of Third World industrialization and the so-called industrial "Green Revolution" in agriculture. The Green Revolution, which was to revolutionize agriculture in the "backward" countries and produce greater crop yields, has only been a miracle for the banks, corporations and military dictatorships which defend them. The influx of fertilizers, technology, insecticides and bureaucratic administration exploded millennia-old rural economies based on subsistence farming, creating a class of wealthier farmers dependent upon western technologies to produce cash crops such as coffee, cotton and wheat for export, while the vast majority of farming communities were destroyed by capitalist market competition and sent like refugees into the growing cities. These victims, paralleling the destroyed peasantry of Europe's Industrial Revolution several hundred years before, joined either the permanent underclass of unemployed and underemployed slum-dwellers eking out a survival on the tenuous margins of civilization, or became proletarian fodder in the Bhopals, Sao Paulos and Djakartas of an industrializing world — an industrialization process, like all industrialization in history, paid for by the pillage of nature and human beings in the countryside.

Food production goes up in some cases, of course, because the measure is only quantitative; some foods disappear while others are produced year round, even for export. *But subsistence is destroyed.* Not only does the rural landscape begin to suffer the consequences of constant crop production and use of chemicals, but the masses of people — laborers on the land and in the teeming hovels growing around the industrial plants — go hungrier in a vicious cycle of exploitation, while the wheat goes abroad to buy absurd commodities and weapons.

The industrialization of the Third World is a story familiar to anyone who takes even a glance at what is occurring. The colonial countries are nothing but a dumping ground and pool of cheap labor for capitalist corporations. Obsolete technology is shipped there along with the production of chemicals, medicines and other products banned in the developed world. Labor is cheap, there are few if any safety standards, and costs are cut. But the formula of cost-benefit still stands: the costs are simply borne by others, by the victims of Union Carbide, Dow, and Standard Oil.

Chemicals found to be dangerous and banned in the U.S. and Europe are produced instead overseas — DDT is a well-known example of an enormous number of such products, as is the unregistered pesticide Leptophos exported by the Velsicol Corporation to Egypt which killed and injured many Egyptian farmers in the mid–1970s. Other products are simply dumped on Third World markets, like the mercury-tainted wheat imported from the U.S. which led to the deaths of as many as 5,000 Iraqis in 1972. Another example was the wanton contamination of Nicaragua's Lake Managua by a chlorine and caustic soda factory owned by Pennwalt Corporation and other investors, which caused a major outbreak of mercury poisoning in a primary source of fish for the people living in Managua.

Union Carbide's plant at Bhopal did not even meet U.S. safety standards according to its own safety inspector, but a U.N. expert on international corporate behavior told the *New York Times*, "A whole list of factors is not in place to insure adequate industrial safety" throughout the Third World. "Carbide is not very different from any other chemical company in this regard." According to the *Times*, "In a Union Carbide battery plant in Jakarta, Indonesia, more than half the workers had kidney damage from mercury exposure. In an asbestos cement factory owned by the Manville Corporation 200 miles west of Bhopal, workers in 1981 were routinely covered with asbestos dust, a practice that would never be tolerated here." (December 9, 1984)

Some 22,500 people are killed every year by exposure to insecticides, a much higher percentage of them in the Third World than use of such chemicals would suggest. Many experts decried the lack of an "industrial culture" in the "underdeveloped" countries as a major cause of accidents and contamination. But where an "industrial culture" thrives, is the situation really much better?

Industrial culture and industrial plague

In the advanced industrial nations an "industrial culture" (and little other) exists. Have such disasters been avoided as the claims of these experts would lead us to believe?

Another event of such mammoth proportions as those of Bhopal would suggest otherwise — in that case, industrial pollution killed some 4,000 people in a large population center. That was London, in 1952, when several days of "normal" pollution accumulated in stagnant air to kill and permanently injure thousands of Britons.

Then there are the disasters closer to home or to memory, for example, the Love Canal (still leaking into the Great Lakes water system), or the massive dioxin contaminations at Seveso, Italy and Times Beach, Missouri, where thousands of residents had to be permanently evacuated. And there is the Berlin and Farro dump at Swartz Creek, Michigan, where C-56 (a pesticide by-product of Love Canal fame), hydrochloric acid and cyanide from Flint auto plants have accumulated. "They think we're not scientists and not even educated," said one enraged resident, "but anyone who's been in high school knows that cyanide and hydrochloric acid is what they mixed to kill the people in the concentration camps."

A powerful image: industrial civilization as one vast, stinking extermination camp. We all live in Bhopal, some closer to the gas chambers and to the mass graves, but all of us close enough to be victims. And Union Carbide is obviously not a fluke — poisons are vented into air and water, dumped in rivers, ponds and streams, fed to animals going to market, sprayed on lawns and roadways, sprayed on food crops, every day, everywhere. The result may not be as dramatic as Bhopal (which then almost comes to serve as a diversion, a deterrence machine to take our minds off the pervasive reality which Bhopal truly represents), but it is as deadly. When ABC News asked University of Chicago professor of public health and author of *The Politics of Cancer*, Jason Epstein, if he thought a Bhopal-style disaster could occur in the U.S., he replied: "I think what we're seeing in America is far more slow — not such large accidental occurrences, but a slow, gradual leakage with the result that you have excess cancers or reproductive abnormalities."

In fact, birth defects have doubled in the last 25 years. And cancer is on the rise. In an interview with *The Guardian*, Hunter College professor David Kotelchuck described the "Cancer Atlas" maps published in 1975 by the Department of Health, Education and Welfare. "Show me a red spot on these maps and I'll show you an industrial center of the U.S.," he said. "There aren't any place names on the maps but you can easily pick out concentrations of industry. See, it's not Pennsylvania that's red it's just Philadelphia, Erie and Pittsburgh. Look at West Virginia here, there's only two red spots, the Kanawha Valley, where there are nine chemical plants including Union Carbide's, and this industrialized stretch of the Ohio River. It's the same story wherever you look."

There are 50,000 toxic waste dumps in the United States. The EPA admits that ninety percent of the 90 billion pounds of toxic waste produced annually by U.S. industry (70 percent of it by chemical companies) is disposed of "improperly" (although one wonders what they would consider "proper" disposal). These deadly products of industrial civilization — arsenic, mercury, dioxin, cyanide, and many others are simply dumped, legally and illegally, wherever convenient to industry. Some 66,000 different compounds are used in industry. Nearly a billion tons of pesticides and herbicides comprising 225 different chemicals were produced in the U.S. in 1984, and an additional 79 million pounds were imported. Some two percent of chemical compounds have been tested for side effects. There are 15,000 chemical plants in the United States, daily manufacturing mass death.

All of the dumped chemicals are leaching into our water. Some three to four thousand wells, depending on which government agency you ask, are contaminated or closed in the U.S. In Michigan alone, 24 municipal water systems have been contaminated, and a thousand sites have suffered major contamination. According to the *Detroit Free Press*, "The final toll could be as many as 10,000 sites" in Michigan's "water wonderland" alone (April 15, 1984)

And the coverups continue here as in the Third World. One example is dioxin; during the proceedings around the Agent Orange investigations, it came out that Dow Chemical had lied all along about the chemical's effects. Despite research findings that dioxin is "exceptionally toxic" with "a tremendous potential for producing chloracne and systemic injury," Dow's top toxicologist, V. K. Rowe, wrote in 1965, "We are not in any way attempting to hide our problems under a heap of sand. But we certainly do not want to have any situations arise which will cause the regulatory agencies to become restrictive."

Now Vietnam suffers an epidemic of cancers and health problems caused by the massive use of Agent Orange there during the genocidal war waged by the U.S. The sufferings of the U.S. veterans are only a drop in the bucket. And dioxin is appearing everywhere in our environment as well, even in the form of recently discovered "dioxin rain."

Going to the Village

When the Indian authorities and Union Carbide began to process the remaining gases in the Bhopal plant, thousands of residents fled, despite the reassurances of the authorities. The *New York Times* quoted one old man, "They are not believing the scientists or the state government or anybody. They only want to save their lives."

The same reporter wrote that one man had gone to the train station with his goats, "hoping that he could take them with him — anywhere, as long as it was away from Bhopal." (December 14, 1984) The old man quoted above told the reporter, "All the public has gone to the village." The reporter explained that "going to the village" is what Indians do when trouble comes.

A wise and age-old strategy for survival by which little communities always renewed themselves when bronze, iron and golden empires with clay feet fell to their ruin. But subsistence has been and is everywhere being destroyed, and with it, culture. What are we to do when there is no village to go to? When we all live in Bhopal, and Bhopal is everywhere? The comments of two women, one a refugee from Times Beach, Missouri, and another from Bhopal, come to mind. The first woman said of her former home, "This was a nice place once. Now we have to bury it." The other woman said, "Life cannot come back. Can the government pay for the lives? Can you bring those people back?"

The corporate vampires are guilty of greed, plunder, murder, slavery, extermination and devastation. And we should avoid any pang of sentimentalism when the time comes for them to pay for their crimes against humanity and the natural world. But we will have to go beyond them, to ourselves: subsistence, and with it culture, has been destroyed. We have to find our way back to the village, out of industrial civilization, out of this exterminist system.

The Union Carbides, the Warren Andersons, the ever "optimistic experts" and the lying propagandists all must go, but with them must go the pesticides, the herbicides, the chemical factories and the chemical way of life which is nothing but death.

Because this is Bhopal, and it is all we've got. This "once nice place" can't be simply buried for us to move on to another pristine beginning. The empire is collapsing. We must find our way back to the village, or as the North American natives said, "back to the blanket," and we must do this not by trying to save an industrial civilization which is doomed, but in that renewal of life which must take place in its ruin. By throwing off this Modern Way of Life, we won't be "giving things up" or sacrificing, but throwing off a terrible burden. Let us do so soon before we are crushed by it.

(1985)

STOPPING THE INDUSTRIAL HYDRA

Remember the Exxon Valdez? The ship was the source of the worst oil spill to date in U.S. history, spilling eleven million gallons of oil in Alaska's Prince William Sound, where it ran aground in March 1989. By the time it had limped into San Diego Harbor in July, it also left at least one other oil slick some eighteen miles long off the California coast.

The spill at Prince William Sound was the grand prize in a season of spills. In December 1988, 230,000 gallons of oil were spilled, fouling 300 miles of coast in the Canadian-U.S. Pacific Northwest.[1] (See page 70 for endnotes.) In January 1989, an Argentine ship broke apart, spilling 250,000 gallons of oil off Antarctica's Palmer Peninsula near penguin, seal and seabird colonies. In the four months prior to the Valdez disaster, Alaska suffered several spills, including a 52,000 gallon spill at a Kenai refinery, a city pipeline rupture that spilled jet fuel into a creek in Anchorage, and a ship grounding in Dutch Harbor that closed down fish plants temporarily and killed more than 500 birds.

In January alone, the environmental organization Greenpeace recorded six ship, barge and boat wrecks in Alaskan waters "that released or threatened to release large quantities of oil." One accident dumped two million gallons of diesel fuel into the ocean.[2] Then, in February, Exxon leaked 117,000 gallons of oil in Hawai'i. Again, in April, another 10,000 gallons of oil from a mystery spill fouled beaches on the Hawaiian islands of Moloka'i and Lana'i. Later in the spring, over 300,000 gallons were spilled in the Delaware River, another 420,000 gallons were spilled in Rhode Island's

Narragansett Bay, and the collision of a tanker and a barge in Texas's Houston Channel dumped 252,000 gallons of oil.

Still remember the Valdez? In a petrochemical civilization, oil and chemical spills go with the territory. Nevertheless, life — or rather, organized death — goes on as usual. The refineries, mines and factories continue to operate, and the traffic continues to roar relentlessly. Oil spills have now, with only sporadic exceptions, dropped out of the mass media, replaced by "crime" and drugs — "America's number 1 problem." As the apparatus turns, its media machine churns. The oil spill in Prince William Sound has become yesterday's newspapers, entering the exterminist Hall of Fame to join, along with other disasters, such jewels as the Santa Barbara off-shore oil rig spill in 1968, the sinking of the Amoco Cadiz off of Brittany in 1978, and the Ixtoc oil well spill off Mexico's Caribbean coast in 1979, as well as Bhopal, Love Canal, the Rhine River, Three Mile Island and Chernobyl, and on and on — a toponymy of extinction.

As the hustlers say, pick a card, any card. Survival, increasingly diminished and constrained, goes on, leaving an array of victims in its wake to pick up what little they can salvage. Everyone else adjusts to the increasing velocity of Progress, putting the wrenching and infuriating media images of dying animals behind them. They still have to get to work, to play, and to Grandma's house, which is invariably on the other side of Hell six dozen freeway interchanges away. A few pious calls to drive less are heard, but in the absence of a mass strike *today* against the Machine, everyone keeps driving. The tyranny of mechanized daily life remains intact, and, in fact, is extended by the disasters it unleashes.

Autopsy of a petrochemical disaster

Nevertheless, in magnitude and in terms of the rich ecosystem in which it occurred, the Valdez spill was exceptional. It occurred in an area containing one of the richest concentrations of animals in North America; 219 separate species of birds alone have been recorded in the Sound. Situated at an important point in the Pacific migratory route of northern latitude breeders, the spill happened just in time to greet millions of birds on their way back north.

From late April to mid-May, the nearby Copper River delta is the world's largest resting area for shore birds, many on their way to nest in the Canadian Arctic. Flocks of as many as a hundred thousand birds stop two or three days to feed, foraging in shallows and at the water's edge, where much of the oil accumulates. Nearly entire populations of certain species pass through the area — twenty million western sandpipers and dunlins alone. It is also rich with hundreds of thousands of black turnstones, tens of thousands of lesser golden plovers, redknots and whimbrels, and thousands of oystercatchers, ruddy turnstones, puffins, tundra swans, Canada geese, snow geese, gulls, cormorants, fifteen species of ducks, peregrine falcons and other birds. Some five thousand bald eagles — the largest concentration in the world — are found in the area. As of September 1989, some 146 eagles were found dead; as many as seventy percent of mothering eagles abandoned their nests, leaving behind oil-soaked eggs and dead chicks.

The world's largest concentration of northern sea otters, some ten to twelve thousand, were also found in the Sound. Probably half died from the spill, but many more are at risk. The effects on seals, walruses and whales are not clear, though they have not been affected as dramatically as the otters. While many animals have been killed by asphyxiation and freezing (one drop is enough to destroy protective coverings on birds and otters and kill them), not much is known about the toxicity of seawater contaminated by oil. Sitka black-tailed deer, feeding on the kelp along the beach, and bears feeding on carrion left by the spill, have died. Deadly chemicals found in oil such as xylene, benzene and toluene not only damage the intestines of large animals and kill them, but threaten the entire food chain by killing and disrupting the zoo-plankton on which it depends. Herring, salmon and shellfish will be adversely affected as well. All in all, some 400,000 animals may have been affected. About 33,000 birds and 980 otters were found dead by official counts, but biologists consider such a number to be only ten to thirty percent of animals poisoned by the spill.

The long-term consequences on the marine ecology are, as is to be expected, also disastrous. Little has been known until fairly recently, but a study by the Smithsonian Tropical Research Institute in Panama, describing the biological consequences of a major oil spill in the Caribbean Sea off of Panama in 1986, found "dramatic effects" both more severe and longer lasting than previously thought. Judging from laboratory tests, scientists once had considered coral relatively immune from oil residues, but this has not turned out to be true. Organisms affected are more susceptible to epidemic disease and are likely to grow and reproduce more slowly than unaffected colonies.

Reports on the aftermath of the Amoco Cadiz spill off France's Brittany coast in 1978 also show that oil remains a serious problem for marine life long after a spill. In this case, the massive elimination of bottom dwellers such as urchins, razor clams and tiny crustaceans called amphipods brought about the decline and disappearance of fish species that feed on them. According to a *New York Times* report, "On exposed mudflats that are continually covered and uncovered by the tides, almost all animal life was wiped out." (April 2, 1989)

Figures vary on the extent of the area contaminated by the Exxon Valdez, but it was, at a bare minimum, 3,000 square miles, including at least 1,000 to perhaps 1,600 miles of shoreline. The long-term effects are particularly hard to determine, given the cold waters and rough seas characteristic of the area. Recovery rates, if such a term can even be used meaningfully, vary widely as well. ("Recovery" can only signify a relative biological stability at a diminished level for a given ecosystem, since none can ever return to the pre-spill state with its full panoply of species diversity.) Furthermore, scientists judge "recovery" to be the ocean's ability to disperse and wash away oil, a view implying that dilution of contaminants in the larger ecosystem is recovery. But the oil always goes somewhere, and with it, a steady, generalized contamination of the whole living planet. While the consequences of the overall contamination can never be precisely measured by scientists, the silent pall over inlets and coves around the Sound, once teeming and noisy with wildlife, should serve as an indication.[3]

The failure of technology

Even "cleanup" represents one of those cruel language jokes that mask a grisly reality. Not only do many containment and cleaning techniques prove ineffective, they are often worse on the environment than the oil itself. Chemical dispersants, which are considered to be only ten to thirty percent effective under ideal conditions, are themselves highly toxic. High-pressure water treatment on beaches is very destructive to beach organisms, and the fertilizer used to clean beaches is also toxic. Traffic from workers doing cleanup weakens bottom sediment and destroys habitat. Rescue efforts only save a minute fraction, perhaps ten percent, of animals found, and many tend to return to the same area to be fouled once again. Birds cleaned and returned to the environment rarely, if ever, reproduce, and so are, in ecological terms, already dead.

One great irony is the utter uselessness of the complex technological apparatus that has been developed to respond to oil spills. As Eugene Schwartz has written in *Overskill: The Decline of Technology in Modern Civilization* (1971), technological ingenuity came to nothing in the Santa Barbara spill; the only relatively effective response ended up being the low tech strategy of spreading straw as an absorbent and collecting it with rakes and pitchforks.

The immense failure of mass technics is vividly illustrated by Schwartz's description of two oil spills that took place during another season of spills — February 1970, when in a period of sixteen days four major oil spills occurred in North America: a 3.8 million gallon oil spill in Chedabucto Bay, Nova Scotia; an oil platform fire in the Gulf of Mexico near New Orleans, fed by crude oil and gas escaping from wells drilled into the seabed; a spill in Tampa Bay from a grounded ship that eventually covered a hundred square miles of ocean before washing ashore and killing thousands of birds; and the spilling of 84,000 gallons of gas and diesel fuel when a barge collided with a jetty in California's Humboldt Bay. Such accidents are "powerful reminders" of the helplessness of human ingenuity in disasters, Schwartz writes. "The Gulf of Mexico accident unfolded like a Greek tragedy ...:

> After the fire had been extinguished with the help of dynamite on March 10, oil began to pour from the wells and to form a heavy oil slick. On the same day, the National Wildlife Refuge on Breton Island was menaced when an oil collecting boom broke. The cleanup was reported to be "going well" as the boom of heavy mesh fence covered with vinyl was repaired — only to break again. On March 11 the vinyl and plywood dams collapsed in heavy seas and over 1,500 barrels of crude oil began to move toward the oyster beds. The skimmer boats could not operate because of wind and high seas. On March 12 the incident was officially termed a "disaster" as oil slicks covering fifty square miles of the Gulf neared the oyster beds. If necessary, it was planned to set off fireworks to startle a quarter-million geese to begin an earlier migration northward. On March 13 officials considered setting the oil on fire. An oil slick moved into the marshes of a wildlife refuge the next day while officials scanned wind notices to determine the course of the oil slicks. A well head used to cap a spouting well blew off on March 15, and the escaping oil added to the fifty square mile slick.

> Faced with a growing oil slick, the oil well's owners smothered the spouting wells with tons of mud and dynamite. They poured dispersant chemicals on the slicks though the effects of these chemicals on the marine life threatened by the oil had not been established. ...

> The Chedabucto Bay spill transformed the bay into a cold-water laboratory — with primitive measures taking precedence over scientific ones. Efforts were made to burn the spilled oil, but low sea temperatures frustrated ignition efforts with benzine, magnesium, and flame-throwers. Old tires filled with napalm burned doughnut-shaped holes in the congealed oil and sank to the bottom. Chemical dispersants were halted by the government as being harmful to marine life. As at Santa Barbara, sawdust and peat moss were used to soak up the oil on the beaches, and bulldozers scraped up the contamination.

While some of capital's advanced technology may have improved slightly since the 1970s, no equipment is capable of responding to spills in heavy seas. Oil starts sliding under booms in currents of only seven tenths of a knot, and goes over the top in wind and waves. Even large skimmers can only pick up small amounts and can only be used in calm seas. When gale force winds came up in Prince William Sound, the booms just blew away. And in the December 1988 spill along the northwest Pacific coast, high seas thwarted any response. Said a Canadian official, "It was simply a matter of waiting for the oil to hit the beach and clean it up manually." (*Toronto Globe and Mail,* April 1, 1989)

Ultimately, efforts were to prove so ineffectual that the term "cleanup" was replaced with that of "treatment" and "stabilization" of shorelines. After Exxon workers had cleaned up only a half mile of beach, and an Exxon spokesman claimed that the beach had been left "cleaner than we've found it," the *Times* reported that "some of the painstaking cleanup is only spreading the oil around, moving from the high-tide mark down to the water's edge." A state official in charge of an inquiry into the spill remarked, "The cleanup is just not working. It's like trying to get the toothpaste back into the tube." By September, when Exxon announced that it was going to end the effort, the Alaska Department of Environmental Conservation reported that more than 300 miles of "treated" shoreline were still coated with oily muck as much as three feet deep.[4]

The earth is a company town

For the institutions that administer and benefit from the petrochemical megamachine, the spill was a "terrible disaster," too, if only a temporary one. The spill indicated, contrary to corporate reassurances of infallibility, that not everything went exactly according to plan, and that can make the natives restless.

Exxon and the oil company pipeline consortium Alyeska, along with the usual government and corporate allies, immediately followed the strategy always employed in the wake of a toxic accident — managing appearances with the appearance of management. Thus the reassurances and declarations of concern came rolling off production lines along with slick photos of Exxon workers holding cleaned up, healthy looking otters and ducks.

The model for capitalist crisis management of such disasters remains the toxic chemical gas leak at a Union Carbide factory in Bhopal, India, in 1984. As Tara Jones has written in *Corporate Killing: Bhopals Will Happen* (Free Association Books, 1988), "The crisis Bhopal created was one which required both immediate and long-term management. In the management of this crisis, the victims' needs were totally neglected: the predominant priorities were the economic interests of [Union Carbide] and the Indian state. In the ensuing macabre dance of death, the dead and walking wounded were left by the wayside, while the main protagonists acted to minimize damage to their own interests." For the continuance of industrial capitalism, the accident at Bhopal was not an ecological or even a technological crisis (accidents being inevitable) but rather a public relations crisis, and thus, potentially, a social crisis if people began to take the lessons of the gas leak seriously. Hence, the entire chemical industry worked "to reassure the general public that Bhopal was a rare, chance occurrence that would not be repeated," rather than a dramatic example of a continual process of toxic contamination.

As soon as the news hit about the oil spill in Prince William Sound, Exxon followed Union Carbide's strategy of cleaning up ... the propaganda environment. By hiring nearly every boat in Valdez and Cordova harbors, and with the stipulation that no media would be allowed on them without permission from the company, Exxon prevented most environmental groups and critical journalists from even getting to Bligh Reef to survey the damages. The crew of a fishing boat nicknamed "the Hearse," which brought garbage bags filled with dead animals into Valdez harbor every few days, was told not to bring in animals that had been dead more than two weeks to avoid stirring up reporters.

Exxon's body counts varied wildly from all others. "The numbers just don't match," one disgusted worker told George Michaels of *The Animals' Agenda*. "The [Exxon] press release says that 500 otters have been brought in dead in the past six weeks. I've counted 600 myself in the past week."

Exxon continued to release regular notices that the spill had been contained and cleaned up even as it continued to grow in size and severity, and produced a video entitled "Progress in Alaska," which extolled the corporation's environmental commitment and the success of its response to Valdez, as well as the benefits the industry has brought to a state which receives 85 percent of its revenues from oil. Full-page ads in newspapers across the country were bought by Exxon to defend its role in the affair, and Exxon maintained tight control of emergency response efforts, much in the way, say, that a mass murderer might be hired to head up the forensics study of the massacre.

The propaganda blitz was intense because the stakes were high. Suddenly, offshore drilling and exploration of sensitive wilderness areas (policies contested even before the spill) were getting the spotlight along with information about oil company practices — leaks of far greater concern to capital than a few million gallons of oil. Speaking before the National Ocean Industries Association, an organization of companies linked to off-shore oil extraction, Interior Secretary Manuel Lujan warned his corporate cronies, "If the image of an uncareful and uncaring industry prevails among the

U.S. public, then we can kiss goodbye to domestic oil and gas development in the Arctic National Wild life Refuge, offshore and in the public lands." For Lujan, the Valdez spill might hinder oil exploitation much in the same way that the accident at Three Mile Island stalled the construction of nuclear power projects. And he did not hesitate to call further exploration and extraction, including in wilderness areas, a matter of "national security," even though the coveted Arctic National Wildlife Refuge is estimated to have only enough oil for a mere six months supply for U.S. cars and trucks. To the industrialists, the oil must keep flowing at all costs, and one terrifying question — when will society begin to do without oil — is not even allowed. It is a matter of state security: industrial capitalism cannot exist without oil.

Meanwhile, the image of a "caring" corporation is disseminated for the gullible. One Exxon publicist called a boycott of the company "unjust," adding that the spill "was an accident — a bad one. But accidents can happen to anyone." This was the accident, of course, that such publicists had formerly claimed would never happen.

Economic boom = ecologic bust

Ever since the construction of the Prudhoe Bay oil field on the Arctic Ocean (said to be the largest contiguous industrial complex in the world), the oil industry provided every assurance of safety to those uneasy with oil development in Alaska's pristine waters and wilderness. Flush with petrochemical plunder, the State of Alaska and the corporations that had staked it out rode a giddy wave of technological hubris and gold-rush corruption. Alaska became a Boom state, providing one quarter of all U.S. domestic oil. In exchange for Prudhoe Bay, the state doubled its budget on public services, repealed personal income taxes, and created a trust fund out of which it pays an annual dividend to all Alaska residents.

Some Alaskans resisted oil development in the beginning, but Big Oil swept all opposition aside, both by using the law to further its own interests and by circumventing it whenever necessary. In the 1970s, fishing communities and environmentalists fought the Alyeska pipeline all the way to the Supreme Court and won, but Congress simply declared the project exempt from environmental laws. State laws were also overrun and modified to accommodate the nine-company consortium seeking to build the pipeline across 800 miles of Alaska wilderness to the port at Valdez.

Oil development came accompanied by promises of the "best technology," safety reviews, and an upgrading of facilities as volumes rose. Not even these dubious promises materialized. Instead of cleaning up toxic pits left in drilling, it is cheaper for oil companies to pay penalties for abandoning them, and even the inadequate environmental protection laws are routinely ignored. As John Greely notes in *The Nation*, Port Valdez was already considered one of North America's most "chronically polluted marine environments" by scientific agencies. Small spills — some 400 before the Valdez spill — were an ongoing problem.

Big Oil built itself not just a few company towns but a company state. The wave of new immigrants brought by an expanding economy continued to erode opposition to development and the corporations. Housing, schools, roads, power projects — the whole infrastructure of the modern capital-energy-commodity-intensive society — were constructed with oil revenues. And when society-wide corruption and collusion didn't work, Alyeska used a mix of cover-up, publicity campaigns and legal maneuvers to continue operations unimpeded, for example going into court in May, after the spill, to block more stringent pollution controls at Valdez. Greely quotes a toxicologist, "If Alyeska is an example of how these oil companies operate in an environmentally sound manner, what are the companies doing in more remote wilderness areas with even less supervision?"

A good question. If the idea of a "third world" suggests a plundered colony where brute force, super-exploitation, and a veil of secrecy prevail, then Prudhoe Bay is a kind of third world colony. The complex, encompassing a 900-square-mile wasteland of prefab buildings, drilling pads, pipelines, roads and airstrips, matches any nightmare in the industrialized world. Burning fuels blacken the Arctic sky, causing air pollution that rivals the city of Chicago. According to the March-April 1988 *Greenpeace Magazine*, "Some 64 million gallons of waste water containing varying amounts of hydrocarbons, chemical additives, lead and arsenic have been released directly into the environment. Regulators report up to 600 oil spills a year, and five hazardous waste sites at Prudhoe are already candidates for clean-up under Federal Superfund law. In addition, the oil companies have been cited for numerous violations of federal and state environmental laws," which does not reveal how bad things are, since many violations obviously go unreported. Road and building construction has thawed the tundra permafrost and caused flooding; this has spread toxic chemicals, and affected an area much greater than the actual development itself.

Hundreds of waste pits overflow during the late spring thaw, killing off small fresh water animals low on the food chain, but also causing dramatic poisoning incidents. Last year, for example, a polar bear was found dead, stained pink from drinking industrial poisons not even normally found together. Other wildlife has been affected. The oil companies are quick to point out that the caribou population is up, but that is largely due to the mass extermination of wolves during 1977-78 by hunting guides when road construction created more access to remote areas. In reality, many questions remain about the caribou and how they will be affected over the long run.

In a letter to the *New York Times*, two people who had been weathered in at Deadhorse (at the heart of the Prudhoe complex) on their way to the wildlife refuge to the east, describe seeing "thousands of vehicles in use and abandoned, ranging from pickup trucks to massive mobile drilling equipment, stacks of discarded oil drums, small ponds with greasy slicks and general debris." Dozens of abandoned structures stand in and around the development at Deadhorse, with no indication that any is to be re-used or removed as oil exploitation (which has already reached its peak) starts to wind down. "Merely to remove the accumulated vehicles, buildings and drilling equipment," they continue, "not to mention detoxifying the polluted tundra and dismantling the roads, airstrips and pipelines, would take years and hundreds of million of dollars. Who will pay?" (April 4, 1989)

Another good question. When one considers what the actual energy expense of building and operating such a vast and remote complex might be, even before an attempt at any kind of "stabilization" of the environment, the realization sinks in that this development is representative of the entirety of industrialism: a massive pyramid scheme that will collapse somewhere down the line when all the major players have already retired from the game. Of course when the last of these hustlers cash in their chips, there won't be any place left to retire to.

The greenhouse effect: capital's business climate

It should go without saying that Exxon and its allies don't try their best to protect the environment or human health. Capitalist institutions produce to accumulate power and wealth, not for any social good. Predictably, in order to cut costs, Exxon steadily dismantled what emergency safeguards it had throughout the 1980s, pointing to environmental studies showing a major spill as so unlikely that preparation was unnecessary. So when the inevitable came crashing down, the response was complete impotence and negligence.

Yet to focus on disasters as aberrations resulting from corporate greed is to mystify the real operational character of an entire social and technological system. The unmitigated disaster of daily, undramatic activities in places like Prudhoe Bay and Bhopal — even before they enter the vocabulary of doom — is irrefutable proof that Valdez was no accident but the norm. Modern industrialism cannot exist without its Prudhoe Bays. Capital must always have a super-exploited colony, a "sacrifice area" of some kind — the sky, a human community, a watershed, the soil, the gene pool, and so on — to expand and extend its lifeless tentacles.

The real spillage goes on every day, every minute, when capitalism and mass technics appear to be "working" more or less according to The Plan. The Exxon Valdez contained some 1.2 million barrels of oil; at any given time 750 million barrels are floating on the world's waters. In 1979, the amount of oil lost worldwide on land and sea through spillage, fire, and sinkings reached a peak of 328 million gallons; since then it has dropped to between 24 and 55 million a year, except for 1983, when tanker accidents and oil blowouts in the Iran-Iraq War brought the total up to 242 million gallons.[5]

Most of the oil in the oceans comes not from accidents but municipal and industrial run-off, the cleaning of ship bilges and other routine activity. Industry analysts say that major oil spills have declined, but that "smaller" spills continue to take place all the time, a phenomenon paralleled in the chemical industry by focusing on major leaks to conceal the reality of a slow-moving, low-level, daily Bhopal. And no matter how carefully industry tries to prevent accidents, they are going to occur; the larger and more complicated the system, the more certain the breakdown. As the head of the Cambridge-based Center for Short-Lived Phenomena (!), which keeps tracks of oil spills, commented after the Valdez spill, because such an event "takes place so infrequently, and the resources are never available in a single location to deal effectively with it" (meaning because booms can't be stationed every hundred yards along the route, etc.), major spills are inevitable. In any case, mass society is a continual oil spill, just as it is a constant chemical leak. As petrochemicals are necessary to industrialism whatever the form of management, spills are also integral to petrochemicals.

And what chemicals and oil spills are to a society addicted to industrialism, industrialism is to the living fabric of the planet. This observation was raised by writer Bill McKibben in an essay published in the *New York Times* on April 7, 1989. McKibben asked, what would have been the result had the Exxon Valdez gotten through without a hitch? If ten million gallons had gotten through to be consumed, they would have released about 60 million pounds of carbon dioxide into the atmosphere. Carbon dioxide is the major component gas causing the greenhouse effect, in which gases emitted in enormous quantities by industrial civilization will trap heat in the atmosphere and raise global temperatures, disrupting and profoundly transforming the planet's ecology — capitalism's 21st century Global Business Climate, so to speak.

McKibben writes that in the next century, "There will be twice as much carbon dioxide in the atmosphere as there was before the Industrial Revolution." The effects are unclear to scientists, but nearly all agree that the burning of fossil fuels combined with the release of chemicals that destroy the planet's ozone layer in the upper atmosphere, the generation of heat from all sources, deforestation and other factors will bring about massive species extinctions, climate and weather changes, flooding and other havoc.

The average car reproduces its own body weight in carbons each year. This is "another oil slick," McKibben notes, being released every day. And while technological modifications to make "clean-burning" cars may reduce pollutants such as carbon monoxide and hydrocarbons as much as 96 percent, such cars will emit as much carbon dioxide as a Model T. Electric cars will pose a similar problem if their energy comes from fossil fuel sources. The production of automobiles, and the production of anti-pollution technology itself, are not even taken into account by this analysis, but the inherent failure of technological rationality can be seen. The rate of climate change over the next hundred years may dwarf by thirty times the rate of global warming that followed the last Ice Age. Reducing what comes out of tail pipes won't even put a slight dent in that problem.

"The greenhouse effect," McKibben observes, "is not the result of something going wrong. It doesn't stem from drunken sailors, inadequate emergency planning or a reef in the wrong place. It's harder to deal with than that because it's just a result of normal life." Leaving aside the question of whether or not the phrase "normal life" appropriately describes industrial capitalism, if McKibben's recommendation that "less energy" be used is to confront the looming greenhouse crisis meaningfully, such a reduction in industrial activity will have to be far more dramatic than almost any sectors of society have been willing to ponder so far. It would signal a deconstruction process more profound than any revolutionary transformation of society ever seen previously. Whether or not this prospect is possible is an open question. Whether or not it is necessary is a question that must include the recognition that present environmental effects are the results of activities which occurred several decades ago. And since modern science cannot understand thresholds, there is no telling how much time is left, only a certainty that it is running out.

Disaster fuels the machine

Warnings of the inevitable crash of urban-industrialism's house of cards now appear often in the leading capitalist newspapers. The ruling classes cannot help but suspect that their system is drawing the world toward a cataclysm. Yet they cannot respond, and grimly go about their business like distracted Ahabs trying to maintain control of their foundering ship. The entropy inherent in their system overwhelms them as they grapple for a helm that does not exist. In this respect they resemble any ruling class nearing the end of its historic journey.

French president Mitterand seemed to sense as much when he remarked at summit discussions on the environment in 1989 that there was "no political authority capable of making decisions on a global scale." The authority of the modern state cannot find a solution, of course, because it has come to encompass every aspect of the problem itself. Only a planetary revolutionary transformation from the ground up — a revolution now fragmentarily glimpsed in aspects of the radical fringe of the ecology movement, in the indigenous-primitive revival, in anti-authoritarian movements, and the new social movements against mass technics, toxics, and development could bring the death train to a halt before it disintegrates and finally explodes under its own inertia.

That revolution remains beyond our reach. Our revolutionary desire must squarely face the fact that disaster itself tends to fuel the system that generates it, which means that we must abandon the pathetic hope that perhaps this latest horror will be the signal that turns the tide (as Chernobyl was supposed to be, and Bhopal). In *Where the Wasteland Ends* (1972), Theodore Roszak points to "the great paradox of the technological mystique: its remarkable ability to grow strong by virtue of chronic failure. While the treachery of our technology may provide many occasions for disenchantment, the sum total of failures has the effect of increasing dependence on technical expertise."

That economic and technological spheres are one is confirmed by the way capital rushes into the vacuum momentarily caused by its own crisis, renewing operations and finding new ways to expand and reinforce its global work machine. Thus even the oil spill became good for business once crisis management was functioning, as Exxon took tax breaks, raised prices, and took charge of the "cleanup." Valdez and other towns boomed again as thousands of people and hundreds of vessels and aircraft were hired. (Boomtowns quickly folded to shambles when the company closed its operations, but by then investment had already moved on.) San Diego, where the ship was moved for repairs, also enjoyed its 25 million dollar mini-boom. Other beneficiaries included companies developing new cleanup techniques, scientific organizations doing studies on the after-effects, the media and public relations.

And extraction continues, with exploration now underway in Alaska's Bristol Bay and Chukchi Sea, and drilling platforms operating just off the coast of the ostensibly "protected" Arctic National Wildlife Refuge.[6] After the repair, the Valdez will even be given a new name, according to an Exxon executive, so that the ship can "start a new career." The natural world reels, but the business of business marches on.

Because they are isolated, localized events, or because they are generalized, global ones, the calamities of industrialism erode the common conditions of life without necessarily posing any alternatives. Local communities affected by disasters are forced into rearguard, defensive struggles while having to survive under severely deteriorated conditions. Other communities, not directly affected, go on with "normal life," holding out the faint hope that the oil, toxic cloud, contaminated water, etc., won't drift in their direction.

The growing awareness of widening catastrophic conditions is insufficient to bring about a response as long as the structures of daily urban-industrial-commodity life are not materially challenged. When they separately confront the various manifestations of the crisis, communities are left on the terrain of emergency response, demands for technological and regulatory reform, and, ultimately, "treatment" of an increasingly denuded world. That is to say, we remain on the terrain of a system that thrives on disaster, grasping at measures that may at best only achieve the same diminished stability in the social sphere that they do ecologically in places like Prince William Sound.

Roszak observes, "If modern society originally embraced industrialism with hope and pride, we seem to have little alternative at this advanced stage but to cling on with desperation." Of course, this is to cling to a sinking ship, but cling we do. Mass society has taken its predictable revenge on those forced to inhabit it, eroding the inner strength and visionary impulses of human beings as ruinously as it has degraded and simplified the natural world. Disaster being a permanent condition of life, so quickly is one horror followed by the next, we have been disciplined to focus on the mediatized version of this season's industrial plague while all around us the hundred hydra heads flourish.

The image of the hydra occurred to me while driving my car to an event organized to show opposition to one of the hydra's local manifestations — the world's largest trash incinerator, which burns about a mile from where I live. Hearing the news of Prince William Sound, I saw the whole series of misfortunes originating in Prudhoe Bay (or rather, in some board room), and running through Prince William Sound down to me filling my gas tank in Detroit.

While I was gassing up to get to some modest attempt to oppose a piece of the monster, it had knocked off a whole section of the planet. Every day, in fact, it is the same concatenation of misery and desolation that does not in any meaningful way, ultimately, serve the long-term interests of even those who administer it. It's exterminism in action: the hydra. In the myth, Heracles was at least able to cut off a head before two appeared in its place; we don't even have that small satisfaction before a hundred more appear.

Limits of environmentalism and leftism

The profound break necessary to contest this horror and create a liberatory, ecological society in its place clearly reveals the limitations of two currents of fragmented opposition to it, environmentalism and leftism.

Environmentalism emerged as an ethical reassessment of humanity's relation to and a protest against the wanton exploitation and destruction of the natural world. As a social movement it has sought to set aside and protect nature preserves, while trying to institutionalize, within modern capitalism and through the state, various safeguards and an ethic of responsibility toward the land.

Despite its appeal to a non-anthropocentric ethical perspective and its often vigorous and courageous battles to defend nature, environmentalism has lacked an acute critique of key social forces that propel ecological destruction: capitalism, empire and the state. Even where it has elaborated a partial critique of industrialism and mass society, it has generally failed to recognize the close connection between urban industrialism and capital. Rather, it has attempted to reform the existing system by rationalizing and humanizing it.

This perspective is illustrated by a comment made by David Brower, an indefatigable environmental crusader who inspired many of the radical environmental activists today. Speaking to author John McPhee, Brower remarked, "Roughly ninety percent of the earth has felt man's hand already, sometimes brutally, sometimes gently. Now let's say, 'That's the limit.' We should go back over the ninety and not touch the remaining ten percent. We should go back, and do better, with ingenuity. Recycle things. Loop the system." (*Encounters with the Archdruid*, 1971) Even if Brower's figures are true (and even if the ten percent could remain unaffected by the activities in the other ninety), his statement provides little in the way of a critique of the world of the ninety percent and says nothing about the forces and institutions that determine "normal life" there.

As for those institutions, they have in many cases recognized the benefits of conservation and have preserved areas and natural objects, but they have always chosen to exploit such preserves when it was decided that the "benefits" outweighed the "costs." (One cannot help but be reminded of the remark of an oil company executive, in the manner of a vampire, "The day you see gas lines in the Lower 48 [the Alaskan wildlife refuge] will open to us.")

The environmental movement has been, from the beginning, one of retrenchment, temporary stalemate, defeat and retreat. As Brower comments, "All a conservation group can do is defer something. There's no such thing as a permanent victory. After we win a battle, the wilderness is still there, and still vulnerable. When a conservation group loses a battle, the wilderness is dead."

The same holds true for communities defending themselves from corporations seeking to site landfills and toxic production facilities. In his painful and often extremely enlightening study of such communities,

Contaminated Communities: The Social and Psychological Impacts of Residential Toxic Exposure (1988), Michael R. Edelstein describes a successful fight in Richton, Mississippi to stop a nuclear waste repository. "Even with the project now abandoned," he writes, "there remains a feeling of 'perpetual jeopardy' in Richton resulting from the likelihood that so visible a site will attract some other hazardous waste proposal."

Lacking a perspective that challenges the capitalist order, environmentalists have seen their rhetoric captured and employed by the contaminating corporations and the state. The bureaucrats administering hazardous waste and garbage incinerators can be found parroting the environmental slogan "reduce, re-use, recycle," and conservation is touted as a patriotic duty. All such rhetoric on the part of the contaminators amounts to an enormous scam, since capitalism — at least in its present configuration, which could not be abolished without a civil war — is based on extractive-exploitive industries such as mining and metals, petrochemicals, forest products, etc. No matter how assiduously the average person recycles household waste, these industries will continue to operate, and there is a direct correlation between the economic well-being of these industries and destruction of the environment. Economic growth demands ecologic bust. If capitalist concerns do not grow, they will lapse and die. The privileged functionaries of such institutions have already clearly expressed their preference that everything else die first.

As for municipal recycling, that pet panacea of liberal environmentalism, not only is capitalism capable of rationalizing its production through such piecemeal reform, it will soon do so in North America once the waste management industry has created technical and economic infrastructures to make it profitable. (Until that time, recycling will, for the most part, fail, which is what is already happening in many municipalities that now find themselves sitting on tons of recyclable materials that can find no market.) In places such as Japan and Western Europe, where materials recycling can sometimes reach more than half of the municipal waste stream, widespread contamination continues. Factories, energy facilities, airports, mines and the rest remain. As it becomes profitable and necessary, recycling will certainly be institutionalized within the system, but it will not significantly alter the suicidal trajectory of a civilization based on urban-industrial-energy development and the production and circulation of commodities.[7]

Despite numerous insights into commodities and the market economy, the left historically has always embraced the industrial, energy-intensive system originally generated by private capitalism as a "progressive" force that would lay the basis for a free and abundant society. According to this schema, humanity has always lacked the technological basis for freedom that industrial capitalism, for all its negative aspects, would create. Once that basis was laid, a revolution would usher in communism (or a "post-scarcity" society, in one formulation) using many of the wonders of technology that were capitalism's "progressive" legacy. Presently, capitalism has allegedly outlived its progressive role and now functions as a brake on genuine development. Hence it is the role of the left to rationalize, modernize, and ultimately humanize the industrial environment through socialization, collectivization, and participatory management of mass technics. In fact, in societies where the bourgeois class was incapable of creating the basic structures of capitalism — urban-industrial-energy development, mass production of consumer goods, mass communications, state centralization, etc. — the left, through national revolution and state-managed economies, fulfilled the historic mission of the bourgeoisie.

In the leftist model (shared by leninist and social democratic marxists, as well as by anarcho-syndicalists and even some social ecologists), the real progressive promise of industrialization and mechanization is being thwarted by private capitalism and state socialism. But under the collective management of the workers, the industrial apparatus and the entire society can be administered safely and democratically. According to this view, present dangers and disasters do not flow from contradictions inherent in mass technics (a view considered to reflect the mistake of "technological determinism"), but rather from capitalist greed or bourgeois mismanagement — not from the "forces of production" (to use the marxist terminology) but from the separate "relations of production."

A mechanized pyramid

The left, blinded by a focus on what are seen as purely economic relations, challenges only the forms and not the material, cultural and subjective content of modern industrialism. It fails to examine the view — one it shares with bourgeois liberalism — that human freedom is based necessarily on a material plenitude of goods and services. Parroting their prophet, marxists argue that the "appropriation" by the workers of the "instruments of production" represents "the development of a totality of capacities in the individuals themselves." Conquest of the "realm of necessity" (read: conquest of nature) will usher in the "realm of freedom." In this view, the material development of industrial society (the "productive forces") will make possible the abolition of the division of labor; "the domination of circumstances and chance over individuals" will be replaced "by the domination of individuals over chance and necessity." (Marx and Engels, *The German Ideology*) Mastery of nature by means of workers councils and scientific management will put an end to oil spills. Thus, if mass technics confront the workers as an alien power, it is because the apparatus is controlled by the capitalist ruling class, not because such technics are themselves uncontrollable.

This ideology, usually accompanied by fantasies of global computer networks and the complete automation of all onerous tasks (machines making machines making machines to stripmine the coal and drill the oil and manufacture the plastics, etc.), cannot understand either the necessity for strict and vast compartmentalization of tasks and expertise, or the resulting social opacity and stratification and the impossibility of making coherent decisions in such a context. Unforeseen consequences, be they local or global, social or ecological, are discounted along with the inevitable errors, miscalculations and disasters. Technological decisions implying massive intervention into nature are treated as mere logic problem or technical puzzles which workers can solve through their computer networks.

Such a view, rooted in the nineteenth century technological and scientific optimism that the workers' movement shared with the bourgeoisie, does not recognize the matrix of forces that has now come to characterize modern civilization — the convergence of commodity relations, mass communications, urbanization and mass technics, along with the rise of interlocking, rival nuclear-cybernetic states into a global megamachine. Technology is not an isolated project, or even an accumulation of technical knowledge, that is determined by a somehow separate and more fundamental sphere of "social relations." Mass technics have become, in the words of Langdon Winner, "structures whose conditions of operation demand the restructuring of their environments" (*Autonomous Technology*, 1977), and thus of the very social relations that brought them about.

Mass technics — a product of earlier forms and archaic hierarchies — have now outgrown the conditions that engendered them, taking on an autonomous life (though overlapping with and never completely nullifying these earlier forms). They furnish, or have become, a kind of total environment and social system, both in their general and in their individual, subjective aspects. For the most part the left never grasped Marx's acute insight that as human beings express their lives, so they themselves are. When the "means of production" are in actuality interlocking elements of a dangerously complex, interdependent global system, made up not only of technological apparatus and human operatives as working parts in that apparatus, but of forms of culture and communication and even the landscape itself, it makes no sense to speak of "relations of production" as a separate sphere.

In such a mechanized pyramid, in which instrumental relations and social relations become one and the same, accidents are endemic. No risk analysis can predict or avoid them all, or their consequences, which will become increasingly great and far-reaching. Workers councils will be no more able to avert accidents than the regulatory reforms proposed by liberal environmentalists and the social-democratic left, unless their central task is to begin immediately to dismantle the machine altogether.

The left also fails to recognize what is in a sense a deeper problem for those desiring revolutionary change, that of the cultural context and content of mass society — the addiction to capitalist-defined "comforts" and a vision of material plenitude that are so destructive ecologically. The result is an incapacity to confront not just the ruling class, but the grid itself — on the land, in society, in the character of each person — of mass technics, mass mobility, mass pseudo-communications, mass energy-use, mass consumption of mass-produced goods.

As Jacques Ellul writes in *The Technological System* (1980), "It is the technological coherence that now makes up the social coherence. . . . Technology is in itself not only a means, but a universe of means — in the original sense of *Universum*: both exclusive and total." This universe degrades and colonizes the social and natural worlds, making their dwindling vestiges ever more perilously dependent on the technological environment that has supplanted them. The ecological implications are evident. As Ellul argues, "Technology can become an environment only if the old environment stops being one. But that implies destructuring it as an environment and exploiting it to such an extreme that nothing is left of it."

We are obviously reaching that point, as capital begins to pose its ultimate technology — bioengineering and the illusion of total biological control — as the only solution to the ecological crisis it has created. Thus, the important insights that come from a class analysis are incomplete. It won't be enough to get rid of the rulers who have turned the earth into a company town; a way of life must end and an entirely new, post-industrial culture must also emerge.

Revolution against the megamachine

A new kind of thinking presently haunts the despair and bad faith that now rule the world. It recognizes that a whole order must be abolished, that we must retrace our steps, that the machine must stop once and for all, if we are to avoid going over an abyss. Yet this vision for the most part remains hidden; the necessary shift in thinking and the practical strategies that it suggests have not generally occurred even in many of those human communities most adversely affected by growing social and ecological degradation.

Michael Edelstein's discussion of the impact of contamination on communities takes up this problem. Edelstein studied several communities reeling from the consequences of contamination or in the process of trying to stop industrial projects that are proposed. He describes how these experiences can dramatically radicalize people, create the basis for communities of resistance (if only temporarily), and ultimately, inspire people to begin to "challenge core assumptions of the overall society." Any doubts about the far-reaching radical, even revolutionary, potential of the anti-toxics and anti-development movements will be dispelled by this book.

Nevertheless, as Edelstein points out, it is the failure to recognize and confront the context and social content of mass contamination that finally leaves these communities powerless to halt it. Society as a whole engages in "denial and rationalization" in thinking that a single accident or problem can be resolved in isolation from the total fabric, in thinking that the mass urban-industrial society can continue to operate without contamination and ecological destruction. "We no longer deny the existence of pollution," he writes; "instead we adopt the engineering fallacy — that pollution simply needs to be 'cleaned up.' Landfills or other technological systems can be designed to securely contain hazards; pollution is merely a technological problem waiting to be solved. This is societal denial!"

Without an authentically alternative perspective, Edelstein argues, even the victims of direct contamination "are left to deal with toxic exposure in ways that force them to continue participating in the system that caused the pollution. Toxic activists seek 'cleanup' and other engineering solutions," pressing for health testing and compensation for victims. While Edelstein does not discount the necessity for such defensive strategies, he maintains that they nevertheless "serve to institutionalize and legitimate as a problem what might otherwise be viewed as a fundamental crisis and, thus, a challenge to our modern, industrial way of life."

As for people not directly affected, even if they sympathize with toxics victims and express a strong desire (in polls) to defend the environment, they do not recognize their own personal participation in the machine or what will be required to make changes. "Their lives are so compartmentalized that they live a lifestyle that supports the pollution habit, without even seeing the contradiction." The life-or-death biological crisis facing the earth becomes just one more abstract issue rather than a life-or-death crisis for the individual and community that demands immediate and radical response. As with the weather, natural and inevitable, everyone talks about the crisis, but no one does anything about it. The masses, a product of the mass society they have produced, continue in their domesticated lives, suiciding themselves, future generations, and the land.

Even more militant responses are limited by the uncanny ability of the system to overcome and grow from its crises. After the Exxon spill, for example, thousands of credit cards were returned and gas stations felt the impact of a consumer boycott. The petrochemical industry, of course, continued operating. For a brief moment, Exxon served as the media "bad guy" and contributed a small share of its business to other oil companies, while managing to be consoled by its other sources of profit — plastics, paints, textiles, detergents, and services to the pulp and paper industry. Boycotts, demonstrations and other forms of militant response focus on some of the real culprits who benefit from ecocide, yet fall short of an adequate challenge to the system as a whole. On the other hand, to call for a boycott of all oil and gas as a strategy is the same as calling for an immediate mass strike against industrialism. It is provocative, but few are listening; even those who are listening are also trapped in the machinery, burning gas to stay alive.

Our house is on fire

Such a commentary should not be interpreted as a call to abandon practical struggles in local communities and workplaces or around specific problems. For many, these battles are desperate measures, and when the house is on fire, one tends to save whatever is in reach. It would be a grave error to give up such struggles on the basis of a more abstract image of a larger totality, for it is in such experiences where many people learn to fight and where the possibility of a larger perspective begins to present itself. We are also talking about people's communities and their deepest loyalties, in any case.

But now that industrial capitalism is fast burning down the entire ecosphere, the problem has become more than ever how to link local and partial struggles to a larger vision that can assert itself as a movement and a cultural transformation carried out by millions of people. We must begin to talk openly and defiantly of the mass strike and revolutionary uprising that it will take to stop the megamachine from grinding up the planet. We must begin to consider what it will mean to put ourselves out of work, to halt production and destroy the economy, creating a free society based on social and ecological cooperation in place of the work pyramid.

Those who might tremble at the idea of disemploying the working class and dismantling mass technics and the economy of industrial dependence should know that this prospect was raised by revolutionaries a century ago. Kropotkin, for example, took up the question of the fate of thousands of workers involved in producing luxury and export commodities during a revolutionary period, when there would suddenly be no use and no market for them. To tell the laborers to become the masters of such factories "would be a cruel mockery," Kropotkin wrote. Instead, facing the inevitable breakdown of the system, workers must learn to provide themselves with the basic necessities of life, food and shelter. Such facilities would simply be abandoned.[8] When petrochemical workers and the rest of us working at meaningless jobs to prop up urban-industrialism confront our daily activities, won't our choices be the same?

The idea of a revolution against urban industrialism may seem far-fetched today. But in the future this idea may prove to have come so late as to be insufficient and not radical enough, given the conditions in which we find ourselves. While the question of violence remains an open one, no image of revolutionary uprisings of the past will serve us well in articulating the idea. Yet they may indicate to us what they proved to revolutionaries of the past, that a population that at one moment appears defeated and quiescent can rapidly transform itself and create sweeping changes. As Rudolf Bahro wrote in *Socialism and Survival* (1982), "The decision can suddenly take hold of millions — tomorrow or the day after — and expand the horizon of political possibility overnight."[9]

Such a process would not be motivated by a vision of negation only, but rather should affirm the idea of restoration of human community and the integrity of the land organism, affirm a natural world and a social world renewed unto themselves and reconciled to one another. The critical luddite sensibility that underlies it would make society as a whole a kind of philosophical school, through which deconstructing or unbuilding the megamachine — on the land and in our social relations — would become a form of inquiry, its foremost spiritual, critical and practical project. By exploring this vision, we can perhaps begin to break out of our conditioning and domestication to create an entirely new life combining the deep wisdom of primal animism with the humility that the harsh lessons of history and modernity have brought.

Last spring, a fisherman told a journalist that when he was done working on the Exxon fiasco, he would load his boat and take his family away. When asked where, he replied, "Someplace where the water's still clean." One can only wish him luck. But like the birds that once more headed south through Prince William Sound only to face poisoning again, we've all run out of places to hide. If the anti-industrial perspective now seems too radical, too visionary, too impractical, future generations, if there are any, will wonder why it took so much time and anguish to recognize it and to make it a practical reality. It remains as yet only a weak approximation of the road that lies ahead of us if we are to save some remnant of ourselves and this planet from the catastrophe whose engines were set in motion long ago. Let us begin to throw off our chains and win back the world while there is still something left of it to win.

(1989)

Endnotes

1. For an excellent essay on the Pacific Northwest spill, see Mikal Jakubal's "With Enough Toothbrushes," *Live Wild or Die*, Number 1.

2. See "What's Behind the Spills," *Greenpeace Magazine,* June 1989, and "The Spills and Spoils of Big Oil," by John Greely, *The Nation,* May 29, 1989.

3. For a chilling eyewitness account of the spill's effects, see "The Dead Zone: Disaster in Alaska," by George Michaels, in the September 1989 issue of *The Animals' Agenda.*

4. The *New York Times,* April 23 and September 10, 1989; "Exxon Reneges on Cleanup," *The Guardian,* August 30, 1989. In one report, Jill C. Kunka asks, "What about the waste from the cleanup? Waste disposal may be the climax of Exxon's cleanup nightmare. According to the *Anchorage Daily News,* one ton of spilled crude turns into ten tons of toxic garbage — bags of oily gravel, mountains of synthetic absorbent booms and pads, discarded coveralls and the assorted refuse of 10,000 cleanup workers ... Service barges are collecting about 250 tons of waste per day. Much of this will be burned; the rest will be sent to hazardous-waste landfills, probably in Oregon." A friend from Detroit also reported after a trip last summer to Alaska that several temporary incinerators were working around the clock in Valdez harbor. As Kunka writes, "With almost any environmental cleanup ... the problem just gets moved around." "Report from Alaska," *Detroit Metro Times,* Sept. 27-Oct. 3, 1989.

5. The 1991 Persian Gulf War spilled many more millions of gallons into the Persian Gulf and even caused black, oily rain contaminated by burning oil fields to fall in western Iran.

6. In his 1987 book *The Toxic Cloud,* Michael Brown reports that one exploratory drillship alone "can produce as much smog as twenty-five thousand cars each travelling eighteen thousand miles."

7. The capitalist state has previously implemented recycling as public policy in times of war to gather materials at home in order to blow them to smithereens overseas.

8. See "Revolution and Famine," in *Act for Yourselves* (London: Freedom Press, 1988). Presumably, many anarcho-syndicalist defenders of industrialism will object, furnishing quotes from Kropotkin in which the anarchist prince reveals the optimism toward technology so common in his time. There will always be those who insist on overlooking what is most visionary and far-seeing in writers like Kropotkin while clinging to what has not withstood the test of historical experience. The myth of progress has become the real "dead weight of the past" weighing like a nightmare on the imagination of the present.

9. Bahro's apparent political and intellectual deterioration is extremely regrettable, if not unheard of in any radical movement. His early work is nevertheless valuable — see my "Swamp Fever, Primitivism and the 'Ideological Vortex': Farewell to All That" (Fall 1997 *Fifth Estate*) for more discussion of this.

BIOSPHERE 2 AND THE FUTURE OF THE EARTH

 In late September 1993, after two years of being shut away in a 315-acre terrarium called Biosphere 2, eight "biospherians" — four men and four women — emerged to breathe the (comparatively) natural air of the Arizona desert. The experiment was advertised as an attempt to simulate the earth's ecosystems on a small scale with the idea of long-term outer space travel and interplanetary colonization in mind. Located, significantly, near the town of Oracle, it was hailed by its protagonists as "one of the magic moments in history," and "a new science of life as a total system."

While the New Age hyperbole surrounding the project made most professional scientists shudder, it was not because of the sinister, totalitarian implications of designing a "new science of life as a total system" — a notion as old as the scientific revolution that continues to have great appeal for scientific elites — but because it was closer to a theme park than what is generally considered rigorous experimental science.

At one point, for example, the "self-contained" technocratic idyll began to break down, and project administrators had to pump in 600,000 cubic feet of additional fresh air, introduce a carbon dioxide scrubber, extra food (biospherians were supposed to grow their own) and other emergency supplies. Nothing to worry about, since this was only the "inaugural voyage" of what was supposed to be a hundred-year project. After all, they hadn't actually gone out into space, where by now, under similar conditions, they would be little more than high tech mummies.

The fastidious scientists critical of Biosphere's hype and lack of precision forget that such hype elicits the very hazy zeal that has fueled science's power as a vast social movement since the early modern epoch. And if they shuddered, it might also be in part because their own grand experiment — modern scientific technics and industrialism — is faring so poorly. In its pathetic ambition to prepare for Martian colonies and the like, this "magic moment in history" reflected the not-so-fanciful dread haunting the modern mind that industrialism is indeed rendering "Biosphere 1" — the earth — uninhabitable.

Reproducing in miniature climates such as a rainforest, a savannah, a marsh, a desert, and an ocean with tides, as well as a tiny farm on which the biospherians were supposed to raise their food, could be rightly considered a monstrous act of hubris, if it weren't so patently silly. Who could be simultaneously so innocent and presumptuous to consider a six-block patch of tropical garden a rainforest, a formidably complex organism that science has barely fathomed? But Biosphere 2 is, perhaps more interestingly, an exceedingly baroque exercise in imperial denial, sharing with the original baroque (another period of imperial decline and ideological tension) a fascination with the miniature, the simulated and the mechanical — a kind of highly elaborated strategy of pseudo-utopian escape in the midst of generalized disaster.

That the biospherians considered their greenhouse space capsule "a key to the future of the planet" reflects the impoverished imagination of decaying industrial civilization and its popular scientific culture. (Even the scientists who criticize Biosphere share its sensibility, if not its methodology.) In an indirect, metaphorically cunning sense, its desire to escape the flaming ship points to the catastrophe now unfolding and the grim horizon ahead. As George Wald wrote in *CoEvolution Quarterly* back in the mid–1970s, "[T]he very idea of space colonies carries to a logical — and horrifying — conclusion processes of dehumanization and depersonalization that have already gone too far on the Earth. In a way, we've gotten ready for Space Platforms by a systematic degradation of human ways of life on the Earth."

According to David Ehrenfeld, the so-called space age and the "spaceship earth" idea that accompanies it are foolish delusions. In his book *The Arrogance of Humanism* (in which Wald's essay is cited), he argues that pointing out superficial similarities between a spaceship and the planet fails to recognize that the "'life-support systems' of earth are vast, complex, poorly understood, very old, self-regulating, and entirely successful." The very idea of a life-support system is in fact more an engineering concept than an ecological one.

"On earth, the life and the 'life-support systems' are not separable," Ehrenfeld writes, "they are part of the same whole," whereas in a space station the system would be a machine, which would inevitably, periodically, fail, since "all machines fail. When the failure is minor and of short duration, the space colony will survive, and when it is serious and long-lasting the inhabitants of the colony will die — unless, of course, they can go home to earth."

But the biospherians seemed to share no such circumspection about technology's claims, despite having lived through a lifetime of nuclear melt-downs, oil spills, exploding space ships and urban blackouts. When they "re-entered" Biosphere 1, one of them told journalists that their work had provided "an operating manual for the world," and another ardently enthused that it demonstrated a lifeway "closer to the idea of natural paradise such as the earth should be and could be."

Lewis Mumford had an apt analogy for this artificial paradise and its air of devotion in his comparative critique of ancient and modern megamachines, *The Pentagon of Power*. A space capsule with its astronaut, he wrote, "corresponds exactly to the innermost chamber of the great pyramids, where the mummified body of the Pharaoh, surrounded by miniaturized equipment necessary for magical travel to Heaven, was placed." Thus, the biospherians really were practicing to become mummies.

To the degree that the living planet is reduced to a contaminated industrial wasteland, the dream of colonizing space and escaping into heavenly spheres will gain increasing appeal. It's noteworthy that the entire project was bankrolled by a Texas oil billionaire, whose source of income has far more to do with the terrifying future of the planet than his sideline hobby. Also of emblematic significance was the constant hunger experienced by the eight space travellers — a poignant reflection in miniature of the mass starvation that has become a permanent feature and direct consequence of the capitalist world economy currently dominating the real biosphere. But most striking perhaps was their acknowledgement that their greatest accomplishment was simply getting along with one another — not unremarkable in a world increasingly shredded by war and xenophobic bloodletting.

In the September 27, 1993 *New York Times*, where I read of these cosmic exploits, there was another small news item next to the Biosphere story about an accident at a plating company in California in which one worker died and seventeen were injured by exposure to toxic wastes. The stories make perfect sense together — an absurd fantasy of deluded futurists sharing the ruling optimistic mythos of a cruel and destructive age, next to a small, sordid example of the reality underlying it.

Space exploration has already made a junkyard of the space around earth, with some five thousand discarded objects now in orbit (including several nuclear reactors that will inevitably fall back into the atmosphere to the planet's surface). Space exploration itself is a horribly toxic industry connected intimately and inseparably to the global war machine. Such is the reality of the space paradise touted by modern confidence men and hustlers, just as the industrial accident in California is but a glimpse into the truth of the technological paradise that modern industrialism promises.

Human destiny and our relationship to the rest of the cosmos will be decided once and for all (and in the not-too-distant future, one might add), here on earth, not wandering in space. We have to learn — relearn, one should say — to live on what already was earthly paradise when we started out.

This is it. Not only are there no lifeboats; the idea that such artificial paradises might be a tolerable alternative to the planet itself is an indication of how far we've already wandered, and how far we have to go to find our way home.

(1993)

Postscript, 1996: According to the November 19, 1996 *New York Times*, the $200 million project, now under new management from Columbia University, is being retooled into an "atmospheric nightmare," a "controlled habitat for exploring how the earth's ecology would respond to global warming." They just don't get it, do they?

SIX THESES ON NUCLEAR POWER

I. The nuclear power complex is inherently totalitarian.

The apparent controversy over nuclear power is not really a matter for debate, but rather reflects the underlying question of social power. Its history makes this clear. First developed as a weapon of war under the veil of military secrecy, and then in coordinated efforts with enormous corporate interests, it was never publicly debated before the whole society was heavily committed to it. At its inception, public opposition would have brought charges of treason, and nuclear technology and materials are still considered a matter of strict state security.

Instead of genuine public discussion, concerns about this dangerous technology have been marginalized by the monologue of advertising and enforced patriotism. To the nuclear power conspirators, talk is a smoke screen. It's not a matter of technics or simple procedural decisions, "cost-benefit" analyses, or "risk-assessment" to be conferred on by well-mannered experts and citizens. Life is one thing; sophistry, meaningless jargon and mystification in the service of naked domination are another. Over the last two decades, the extravagant claims of technological utopia and unlimited abundance have eroded. The dream of nuclear power has come to look more like a nightmare of terrifying accidents, dazzling cost overruns and the unending problem of nuclear waste. Yet public discussion remains little more than a tactical diversion as far as those who administer the nuclear industry are concerned, a manner of periodically changing the Emperor's clothes to hypnotize the populace. They have no intention of giving up, whatever the costs.

The fact is that nuclear power is necessarily totalitarian. From the beginning, nuclear technocrats experimented on whole populations, like the mad doctors of Buchenwald. Countless innocent people were treated as secret experimental subjects; entire towns and cities like Los Angeles were purposefully dosed with fallout; native peoples were driven from their land so it could be obliterated in tests; and soldiers were marched into radioactive sites to test exposure results. These are only the experiments we know about and occurred not only in the dictatorships of the Eastern Bloc, but in the "democratic" West.

Nuclearism cannot exist except in a society based on class or caste division — whereby one group commands authority for itself, increasing its wealth and power at the expense of the rest. Nuclearism can only operate under some form of authoritarian rule using commissions and cops to enforce and regulate its power. Thus, "discussing" the merits or problems of nukes with utility companies and government bureaucrats is like debating the meaning of life with a murderer who has a knife to your throat.

The nuclear power question also exponentially complicates the question of social power. Even the dream of abolishing nuclearism contains the potential for authoritarianism and centralized control: the technology has created technological and social problems that simply may have no adequate solution. Not only the problem of dismantling nukes, but the more far-reaching dilemma of containing the already present nuclear and industrial wastes (and the wastes which are being produced today, as this is being written, and tomorrow, as it is being read) makes the need to halt it all as soon as possible ever greater.

2. Nuclear power is fundamentally a matter of psychology.

Nuclear power is at the center of a configuration of questions facing humanity today which can be posed in the words *life against death*. To "favor" nuclear power means desiring your own techno-bureaucratically administered annihilation. To fear and oppose nuclear power, whether out of scientific ("rational") or intuitive ("irrational") reasons, is to some degree to resist inertia, to glimpse life beyond the shroud of business-as-usual in a civilization listing toward self-destruction. Nuclearism is therefore more than a technology (a word that renders it deceptively innocuous). It is, rather, the materialization of the death-wish itself.

Nuclearism is the centerpiece of a system that, as its most far-seeing and thoughtful scientific minds now recognize, is undermining complex life on earth. Even the champions of this system can see many of its consequences — the Chernobyl disaster, for example — yet they continue. This suicidal compulsion compels us to consider nuclear power in terms of pathology: fascination with self-destruction and a reckless disregard for life, a diminishing capacity in the integrity and autonomy of individuals, and the psychology of addiction and denial. What else explains the continuing romance in some sectors with a technology capable of bringing about unspeakable disaster, and the general indifference and psychic numbing in others?

Even if more Chernobyl-like disasters were a remote possibility (they are in fact inevitable, given the aging apparatus and the corruption and incompetence of the social forces managing it), the risk of perhaps millions of illnesses and deaths, and the need to evacuate whole regions permanently would seem sufficient reason to abandon nuclearism. We are told "we" must have the energy — but for what? Are people really willing to trade their children's future in order to run an industrial empire producing things they not only don't need but in many cases would be better off without? Could we lead fulfilling lives and use dramatically less energy? Is it necessary to sacrifice the genetic integrity of future generations to keep shopping malls lit at night and televisions on? Why, given the horrors of Chernobyl, is no one except a radical fringe asking, *energy for what?*

This is mass denial. A mass circulation science magazine intones, "The prospect of nuclear war is fading. But nuclear weapons, radioactive waste, and poorly designed reactors are here to stay." But with more fissionable material and nuclear technology around than ever, more nation states trying to get their hands on it, and an epidemic of plutonium smuggling from the former Soviet Union, why would anyone think nuclear war is less likely? The author of this typical article breezily reports on the calamities of Soviet nuclearism, but concludes, "Marxist technology was the culprit."

How reassuring! Yet what exactly is "Marxist technology"? There once were marxists, like those Chinese pilots who claimed they could fly through storms by applying the wisdom of Mao Tse-tung Thought, who believed that a marxist science and technology were something more than a wish-fulfillment. But all that has been discredited. Every single nuclear military facility in the United States has been heavily contaminated; was that "Marxist technology"? Will we learn tragically after the fact that some containment structure designs in American reactors suffered the errors of marxism? Was the Union Carbide gas leak at Bhopal, India, from which people continue to die, marxist? The space shuttle disaster? Love Canal? Blaming the empire's enemy ideology is a pathetic form of denial.

3. Technolatry is a form of denial.

Technolatry assures people that backup systems will work, alloys will not corrode or wear out prematurely, landfills will never leak, and technicians will make the correct decisions, pushing the right buttons in the right sequences, with the buttons functioning as intended, and the computers responding appropriately. All this, of course, is massive, utterly irrational denial — a denial weirdly coexisting with a pervasive, society-wide suspicion that nothing in this society works, that all systems are failing and no expertise is very trustworthy or machinery reliable, that everything has been produced by the lowest bidder, a lowest bidder cutting corners to cut costs. And yet this vast, complex, and dangerous technology, we are assured by its operatives and paid publicists, will work just fine. In any event, we have no choice, they tell us; we simply cannot do without it.

Of course, only the most venal and desperate community would willingly site a nuclear plant or waste repository nearby. People recognize that no technical system is fail-safe, be it for nuclear production or storage (there being no such thing as "disposal"). In complex industrial systems, accidents are inevitable. Most landfills of any kind are already leaking, and all must eventually leak, since nature allows no container to remain intact forever. Geological and chemical phenomena are more complicated than was once thought, and recent research has increased scientists' sense of uncertainty. Though there are some 400 nuclear reactors operating in the world, there is not one long-term waste storage program in place.

Yet the nuclear empire continues its march to oblivion. As of late 1993, some 50,000 people had died of illnesses resulting from the April 1986 nuclear explosion and fire at Chernobyl. People involved in the emergency response are dying in droves and the populations of Belarus and Ukraine are suffering pandemics of cancer, birth defects and other diseases. Nevertheless, in need of "energy independence," Ukraine has decided to keep the remaining reactors running and to lift a moratorium on new plants. In the United States, the mentality is the same. Bureaucrats at Detroit Edison and other associated institutions have undoubtedly seen ample illustrations in the media of Chernobyl's grim results, without wavering in their commitment to the exterminist system they manage. Why?

It was Wilhelm Reich who argued in his studies on the mass psychology of fascism that a large portion of the German people desired fascism even though it was not in their interest. I thought of mass psychology recently while at the Edison offices in downtown Detroit. A small group of us were crowded around a reception desk where one anti-nuclear activist was attempting to deliver a dead fish to a public relations clone at the utility headquarters. The office workers and executives coming in and out of the sterile concrete, glass and steel lobby barely noticed us. Those who did seemed to enjoy a passing smirk as they went to lunch before getting back to their desks and the routine of creating more Chernobyls, more genetic monsters, more thyroid cancers, more leukemia.

In the short term (until next payday, at least), people who blandly walked by are making money (and for most, not much money) unraveling life's fragile web. In the longer term, however, they'll see the same cancers, immune disorders and other illnesses in their own families as the rest of us, and face the same dismal radioactive cloud when the geiger counters spin out of control and the pointers hit jackpot. Denial maintains their addiction to the industrial bribe (the cars, boats and VCRs they cannot do without) and to power and prestige (their position in the necktie hierarchy). Denial and psychic numbing keep a suicidal system on automatic. And it isn't just at Edison; to one degree or another, we're all involved.

4. Nuclearism undermines human autonomy.

Of course, the defense of nuclear power routinely presents itself as a defense of the rights of individuals — the right of the power companies to turn a profit, the right of individuals to obtain the "good life" through unlimited access to energy. But industrial capitalism, based as it is on the looting of nature and humanity for capital accumulation and power, can only take place where human autonomy itself has been looted. This process began with violent coercion during the rise of industrial capitalism and is now culminating in rule by hypnotic suggestion.

The industrial system could not survive without the passive cooperation of human beings who trust and obey their leaders, have faith in the abstruse newspeak of experts, and accept at face value every step of technological progress unleashed upon them by government and corporate bureaucracies as quite naturally an enrichment of their impoverished lives. They seem barely capable of living autonomously, making decisions, or critically examining their lives and society. Having abdicated responsibility for themselves, they simply recite the litanies of their leaders and bosses.

At its inception capitalism proclaimed the primacy of the individual only to bring about, in its maturity, the suppression and disappearance of authentic individuality. Today the inmates sense what they have lost but cannot name. Anxiety is pervasive, along with rage. In its attempt to expand its artifactual, depersonalized world while ameliorating the subsequent collapse of selfhood, capital mines and degrades the earth to produce a world of consumable objects, programmed entertainments and prefabricated "communities."

The domesticated creatures who continue to repeat capital's rationalizations in the wake of dramatic accidents and the continuous reports of failed-technology events that might have broken through their conditioning the way a flood in the laboratory destroyed the conditioning of Pavlov's dogs, according to one story — are reminiscent of the people who craved fascism. (Many now also crave fascism.) They are painful reminders that time really is running out. Without social and personal change as dramatic as the events that now demand it, life as it will soon come to be lived (if at all) may no longer be worth fighting for.

5. "No nukes" is not enough: industrial capitalism is the enemy.

According to the official view, the suits and skirts at Edison were, of course, normal and rational — we were fringe wackos. Just as nuclearism complicates power relations, it turns reason inside out. Unlike Captain Ahab in Melville's Moby Dick, nuclear power cannot claim that either its means or ends are sane — both are mad. Nevertheless, it poses as the pinnacle of reason, as the normal, natural state of affairs. Its warped, crackpot realism serves to legitimate what is in reality only one component of a runaway industrial juggernaut bent on bringing about the compulsive and suicidal "conquest of nature" which is the core spiritual value of capitalism.

The conquest of nature, of course, has its revenge in the unintended consequences it produces; nature is not so easily conquered. The industrial system is causing an increasingly precarious, global destruction of diversity — cultural, biological and agricultural. It functions by undermining the natural world; obliterating peoples, places and species; recklessly poisoning the ecosphere with deadly pollutants; blindly degrading natural cycles; and accelerating and growing for the sake of growth itself. Operating under the guise of normalcy, it pulverizes wilderness, wreaks havoc on delicate ecological harmonies, fills the sacred earthy silence with the white noise of industrial civilization, and shreds human communities. Having already obliterated much of human memory, it works to obliterate the future by imposing increasingly rigid, brittle and dangerous technical and institutional systems on society and nature that are guaranteed to bring about unforeseen, catastrophic results.

A focus on nukes alone is therefore not enough; resistance against nuclear power must become a starting point in the critique of the system in its entirety. This means finding ways to resist capitalism's reduction of the living world to production and commodities, to stop the plunder of seas, soils, forests and the gene pool, to reverse the reduction of culture to mass media noise — to take none of modern civilization's propaganda for granted. It means turning the terrain of capital into a terrain of resistance, restoring and reinhabiting the earth in a manner consonant with the natural world and the possibilities of genuine human community and solidarity.

Those who might argue that we can maintain a "user friendly" urban industrial civilization without nuclear power don't realize that the growth economy of mass production itself (fueled by any power whatsoever) devours the world to shit out toxic waste and toaster ovens. The addiction to profit, power and an ever-expanding megalopolis will continue to undermine life, with or without nuclear power.

The Persian Gulf War was one powerful example of capitalism's addiction to energy having relatively little to do with nuclear power. As an anti-war demonstrator's placard put it, "Oil is capitalism's crack." An anti-nuclear movement that does not begin to confront the industrial capitalist system as a whole — not just nukes but oil, production and markets, militarism, cybernetics, the media, genetic engineering — will confront only one of its hydra heads, leaving the root intact. Such an approach is not only bound to fail, it could strengthen the forces that we most need to destroy if life is to prevail.

6. Industrialism is an empire — life is the colony.

The nuclear power system grew out of war and cannot be separated from the accumulation of nuclear weapons by nation states and the unavoidable drift toward more war. Thus any resistance to nuclearism must of necessity confront not only nuclear arms but the military machine. To fail to see that the demand for nuclear disarmament logically leads to war against the imperial state itself is to defy reason. Again, one begins with a single, isolated aspect of the problem and ends with the totality of interconnections. Opposition to nuclearism must eventually become linked to the demand to abolish the armies, states and rival empires which control it.

The nuclear power system is not only a key component of military-industrial empires like the United States, France, Britain, Israel, etc., it fits the structural model of all empires, starting from the earliest slave states of the ancient middle east. Every empire demands a work hierarchy, military machine, sacrifice colonies and the wanton destruction of nature and human communities, and all have been pyramid schemes that exploited and wasted some areas and communities to enhance and enrich elites elsewhere. In the end, they all brought about massive destruction before collapsing under their own weight.

The nuclear power complex is no different, bringing to mind historian Gordon V. Childe's remark that the first imperial civilizations of Mesopotamia "probably did directly destroy more wealth than they indirectly created." Similarly, if one were to calculate the amount of energy the nuclear industry has produced against that expended in mining, processing, maintaining, and eventually mothballing nuclear materials and reactors, it would obviously represent a net loss in energy — an imperial shell game. The artifactual "wealth" that global urban industrialism creates is likewise a deficit to real social and natural plenitude.

To capital, a forest is worthless until it is shattered into lumber, just as people growing their own food and meeting their own needs are an economic loss. To life, on the other hand, the vast, toxic necropolis we are constructing represents an irreplaceable loss, an imponderable violence. If confronting nuclear power during its early days signified an act of treason against the state, today it means no less an act of treason, this time against the entire empire system — most specifically the religion of growth now bringing about the demise of complex life forms on earth.

The nuclear problem appears insurmountable; to challenge the industrial system may seem utterly out of reach. But we must begin to face this challenge; otherwise we surrender to a fatal inertia. If nothing else, let this sense of urgency sustain us.

(1979/1994)

III.
AGAINST THE MEGAMACHINE

Illustration by Johann Humyn Being

Illustration by Freddie Baer

THE FALL OF COMMUNISM & THE TRIUMPH OF CAPITAL

I.

"Governments come and go, but business stays." — Anatoly Skopenko, president of the Ukrainian Renaissance Bank, to a global investment scout for the Asia Bank in New York, New York Times, *August 31, 1991*

"The U.S. and the U.S.S.R., I understood, were the two portions of the Empire as divided by the Emperor Diocletian for purely administrative purposes; at heart it was a single entity, with a single value system." — Philip K. Dick, Radio Free Albemuth

When the Wall came down in Berlin, the people immediately went shopping. In this apparently mundane act of acquiring what has a price, they entered, in a manner whose symbolism was as material as its materiality was symbolic, that world which is called "free." They were now free to go in search of products unobtainable in the society calling itself marxist, ironically recalling Marx himself (wise enough once upon a time to deny being a marxist), who wrote, quoting himself in the first line of the first chapter of the first volume of *Capital*: "The wealth of those societies in which the capitalist mode of production prevails, presents itself as 'an immense accumulation of commodities'...."

Now this immense accumulation presented itself as the key to their desires. It wasn't only dictatorship, secret police and thought control they had overthrown, but everything that had kept them from everything beyond the Wall. Even the Wall itself succumbed to market forces, was chipped away and sold as souvenirs of a moment rapidly fading into the vacuum vortex of mediatized history.

Simply put, capitalism had triumphed. Prices, of course, rose. "With the better packaging and the greater variety of the new goods from the West there are also higher costs," reported the *Toronto Globe and Mail.* (July 3, 1990) Only with time will the feckless shoppers discover what the real costs actually are. They are exchanging a dictatorship of paupers for intensified pauperization under the dictatorship of money. Their socialism failed, and now they are being re-educated to the first lessons of capital, foremost being that Money Talks, Bullshit Walks. And unfortunately for them, they are at the bullshit end of the spectrum. What was always potent in Marx — his critique of the commodity, the market, and alienation — now weighs like a nightmare on the brain and backs of the living not because it represents the dead weight of the past but because it reveals the dead weight of the present.

"The exchangeability of all products, activities, and relations with a third, objective entity which can be re-exchanged for everything without distinction — that is, the development of exchange values (and of money relations) is identical with universal venality, corruption," wrote Marx in his notebooks (*Grundrisse*). "Universal prostitution appears as a necessary phase in the development of the social character of personal talents, capacities, abilities, activities. More politely expressed: the universal relation of utility and use. . . ." The former inmates of the East Bloc lost their chains, but the world they won was that universal prostitution described by their official prophet — a world we inmates of the West Bloc know too well. "We're going to McDonaldize them," commented a McDonald's executive to the *New York Times* (January 28, 1990) in a summary of the company's "cultural conquest" of the Soviet Union and its opening of a restaurant in Moscow. Capitalism triumphed. The "Free World" triumphed. The former East Bloc is now free — free to be McDonaldized.

In the same passage of the *Grundrisse*, Marx observed that in societies with "underdeveloped" systems of exchange (feudalism, traditional or vernacular societies, and one might now tentatively add bureaucratic collectivist societies of the East), individuals enter into relations with one another "imprisoned" within certain rigidly defined roles (and here he revealed his own imprisonment within the bourgeois ideology of progress to the degree that he saw all such relations as rigidly defined, despite the validity of the contrast he was trying to elaborate). The roles to which Marx referred might include lord and vassal, or those specifically defined by clan relations, but perhaps could also suggest those of party bureaucrat and worker in the bureaucratic party states of the East.

Under developed capitalism, however, "the ties of personal dependence, of distinctions of blood, education, etc., are in fact exploded, ripped up ... and individuals seem independent (this is an independence which is at bottom merely an illusion, and it is more correctly called indifference), free to collide with one another and to engage in exchange within this freedom; but they appear thus only for someone who abstracts from the conditions of existence within which these individuals enter into contact. . . ." Put again more simply in the ABCs of capitalism, there is no such thing as a free lunch; the freedom promised by capital also has its hidden costs. The "free relations" are themselves determined by a more complex kind of dictatorship than the state-collectivist dictatorships could ever muster.

"A particular individual may by chance get on top of these relations," continues Marx — and one is reminded of the myriad former functionaries of the communist bureaucracy now becoming budding capitalists — "but the mass of those under their rule cannot, since their mere existence expresses subordination, the necessary subordination of the mass of individuals." In other words, McDonaldization demands low-paid shit workers if there are to be high-paid investors. Everybody can't be rich. Capitalism needs a colony, and someone has to be that colony.

Thus, when researcher David Lempert asked a Soviet economist what kind of economic rights and protection against exploitation there would be for people lacking capital after the transition to a "free market" he was told, "They will have the right to work. They will work for people who have capital." In Leningrad (now St. Petersburg), a "Free Economic Zone" was created to make the city, in the words of one elected city-council member, "just like Mexico." A law student "put it to me even more bluntly," Lempert goes on. "We're not interested in the ideas of democracy," the student told him. "We need to eat. Help us with our English so we can work for joint ventures." ("Soviet Sellout," *Mother Jones*, September/October 1991)

The market economy even has its Stakhanovite heroes. (Stakhanov was the legendary self-sacrificing worker of socialist production.) Drowsy from working long late-night hours at a kiosk used as an all-night convenience store in view of the Kremlin, an entrepreneur displays high-priced vodka, chewing gum, used clothes, and other desired items. (The kiosks cannot close at night or they would be looted, and are "protected" from small "mafias" by bigger ones. One can almost hear the Godfather whisper, "It's only business. . . .") The kiosk owner dreams of a large walk-in store (his very own Seven Eleven?) and tells a Westerner, "We must grow by stages, with setbacks and progress until maybe, in 15 or 20 years, we reach your knees," thus revealing that not only the entrepreneurial spirit, but the envy and sense of inferiority bred by colonialism, are making headway in the former powerful empire. (*New York Times*, January 24, 1992)

"It's inevitable," whispered a newspaper editor to Lempert. "We're going to be a colony." And an old Siberian exclaimed, "Sell the forests. Sell the minerals ... Let the West take what they want. Let them come in and give us what we need to start over." Of course, the West has every intention of giving them what they need ... to be just like Mexico.

2.

"The theater, like the plague ... releases conflicts, disengages power, liberates possibilities, and if these possibilities and these powers are dark, it is the fault not of the plague nor of the theater, but of life." — Antonin Artaud, The Theater and Its Double

An empire in disarray, the monuments lurching in history's whirlwind and falling. The statues of notorious executioners being sledgehammered by a giddy crowd. Unarmed people facing down tanks, and the tanks withdrawing. Perhaps the empire is actually falling; for now there is only the whirlwind, dangerous, intoxicating.

And the miraculous comes so close
to the ruined, dirty houses —
something not known to anyone at all,
but wild in our breast for centuries.

(Anna Akhmatova, 1921)

The people triumphed over the dictators in the streets of the East Bloc cities, if only for a time. Their great refusal crippled the gulag state momentarily, even if it did not break its back.

How and why events unfolded in the way they did will remain a speculative question. A combination of elements seems to have brought about what no single one could. There was a rebellion from below, a "counter-revolution" from the outside, a palace coup from above, and a generalized economic crisis. All of the aspects are woven together; none is entirely distinct from the others. All make the situation more a multiplicity of unique, incommensurable situations — geographically, culturally, and politically — which may explain why no single force or sector in East Bloc societies can yet respond coherently to the changes. The popular revolution that coincided with national bankruptcy had been simmering for decades, in fact, for generations. Contrary to the fantasies of right-wing academics (some of them former leftists) in the West, even soviet totalitarianism could not achieve the nightmare of a total, irresistible monolith. (The "authoritarian-totalitarian" contrast so fashionable among reactionary U.S. academic and diplomatic circles under reaganism was thus thoroughly discredited without any comment from its purveyors.)

As historian Geoffrey Hosking points out, the ancient forms of mutual aid of the traditional community (the *mir*) and the cooperatives formed by peasants who moved to the cities (the *arteli*), were the deep roots of the new forms of association in the latest upheavals, showing the "extraordinary capacity to improvise humane and functioning grassroots institutions in extremely adverse circumstances." He argues that local labor groups, intellectuals, and marginals who created the counter-cultural opposition have their roots in the 19th century; "the traditions of the peasantry and the intelligentsia ... underlie such habits of community as have survived at all into the modern Soviet Union." (See *The Awakening of the Soviet Union*, 1991; reviewed by Peter Reddaway in "The End of the Empire," *The New York Review of Books*, November 7, 1991.)

Even the infrastructure and economic problems were at least in part a consequence of work resistance and work refusal, rather than simply of the failure of "socialism" or bureaucracy. (Within the military-industrial and space industry complexes, where such refusal would have brought about much harsher reprisals and repression, the machine functioned quite efficiently. The inefficiency of the civilian sector became a low grade kind of sabotage or class war and a part of the unspoken social contract, an inevitable feedback.)

In the society as a whole, the population slowly and inexorably applied the brakes; when this was combined with a certain lack of will on the part of the ruling elites, power tended to erode. Even repression probably ceased to work as effectively. This itself could be attributed to an aspect of caste or class struggle as well, probably aggravated by the war in Afghanistan and the concomitant growth in counter-culture movements against the war and for nuclear disarmament, ecological justice, free expression, democracy, and cultural autonomy (including nationalist independence movements). Many Westerners commented on the resemblance of 1980s movements in the U.S.S.R. to 1960s movements in the U.S. The breakdown of authority was partly, at least, both a consequence and a cause of the Soviet Union's "Afghanistan Syndrome."

Consequently, there emerged a kind of cautious refusal at one end of the power spectrum and a tenuous lack of will at the other that tended to reinforce one another. No one could have known where it was leading, though the vast majority of people being persuaded by the dissidents (people, say, who might simply want to know what really happened to Uncle Vanya after he was disappeared by the "workers state") carried out their own personal and collective acts of refusals with few clear goals, and even less with the idea of establishing Western-style corporate capitalism. They were more inclined to some kind of "socialism with a human face." Their gesture was not a "yes" to any programmatic change, but rather a broad "no" to what power and universal servility had done to life. (See D.M. Borts, "They Just Said 'No,'" in the Winter 1990-91 *Fifth Estate*.) They were tired of the cops and the bosses, sick of lies. Once granted a moment of indecision from the rulers, they were never going back.

This, more than an abiding loyalty to the Napoleonic Yeltsin, explains much of the crowd (as small as it was) in front of the Russian parliament building in August 1991. The coup plotters were as interested in going ahead with privatization as Yeltsin and his gang — but with their own power structure and privileges intact. They wanted to preserve the established ensemble of the military-industrial-police apparatus and were certain that the impending All Union Treaty spelled their doom, as well as signaling further imperial fragmentation. But it was too late; the refusal had already spread even to their own ranks. People were not following orders. Those who stood in front of the tanks included die-hard Yeltsin loyalists, but most must have been choosing to land a blow against the old guard and for fragmentation.

Many others ignored both Yeltsin and the coup organizers. For the most part, workers did not strike, and only a few blocks from the confrontation, people were going about their daily routine. (Some families took turns standing in food lines and at the barricades.) In some sense, too, this must have reflected an unwillingness to be drawn into the schemes of politicians. Hatred and contempt for politicians of all stripes is the attitude most shared by the population.

Of course there was also significant support for the coup — a reaction, certainly from "law and order" traditionalists, among them probably the Russian nationalists who wave placards with Stalin's picture at demonstrations, but also from those who are seeing their living conditions being shredded as former communist bureaucrats and others enrich themselves at the rest of society's expense. And because all the agents of repression, in power and out, hate a "power vacuum" more than anything else, they are actively recruiting, each faction for its own millennium. This includes everyone from reorganized Communist Party groups and other leftist parties, to nationalist parties and religious groups, fascists, criminal mafias, even the Hare Krishnas. One looks almost in vain for evidence of those forces which played such a large role in the humanization of the society and the social changes that followed — the peace and ecological groups, for example — but not only are they blocked out of the Western press for all the usual reasons, the whirlwind seems to have kept them mostly at the margins. (See David Porter, "The Anarchist Spectre in Eastern Europe," in the Winter 1990-91 *Fifth Estate*.)

Nevertheless, the changes reflected just as much a palace coup among the elites; seeing the increased difficulty in proceeding in the old way, a faction of the stalinist bureaucracy chose to ride the crest of change rather than to resist it. For them, it was preferable to face the unknown of transition to an economy more integrated into global capital with them still in command than to share the fate of some of their cronies in Poland, East Germany, and Romania. What has followed has been an environment of generalized piracy, with the little mafias only reflections of the big ones, and the sale of ostensibly public property to joint ventures and the creation of new business concerns with communist bureaucrats at the helm and the cash register.

"Democracy" is the code word, signaling the freedom to McDonaldize. "Democracy" is the high card they play in a high stakes game to keep their power and privilege. Like Yeltsin, with the right-wing Western think-tank technocrats who advise him, they mouth the rhetoric of "free market democracy" effectively enough to pass as stolid Rotarian Republicans (with about the same amount of genuine concern and respect for individual rights and social well-being). In one well-known estimation, only a rapid, 500-day transition to capitalism, as gentle as Stalin's collectivization of the peasants — a bitter "shock treatment," as it has been called in the press — will work to bring the former empire into line with the rest of the world. That is, with the Third World, and the world of the brutalized inner cities of the U.S. Yeltsin and others, down to the entrepreneur in the kiosk, call for sacrifice on the part of the people to bring about this Latin-Americanization. Some will get rich; some will get cholera. That, after all, is what made America great.

The conflict between Yeltsin and Gorbachev, or between them and the hapless military conspirators of August 1991, was not between totalitarian socialism and democracy. The coup and counter-coup were mostly a struggle between elite factions. As historian James Petras commented, "The real conflict was and is between a dying patronage machine controlled by party bureaucrats and a rising class of professionals intent on turning the state into a vehicle for privatizing national resources, promoting privileges and incentives for private business owners, especially foreign ones — particularly by selling off vast amounts of energy resources."

For the great majority, this will mean "decades of sacrifice for the market" — not much of a prospect. "The problem with the marketeers," Petras continues, "is that there are no risk-taking capitalists who make long-term investments capable of reorganizing the economy and replacing the disintegrating bureaucratic apparatus. And foreign investors will not make large-scale, long-term investments under a ruling elite that lacks decisive control over the society, except in a few strategic sectors. The result is likely to be economic cannibalism, with each firm manager grabbing a piece of the action — leaving the economy in chaos." ("Decades of Sacrifice for Free Market?" *The Guardian*, September 11, 1991)

The nationalist politicians in the various republics are no better. In Uzbekistan, for example, the Communist Party apparatus, firmly entrenched, announced plans to follow the "Chinese model" for "economic reform." Georgia is now in a lull in what appears to be a civil war after electing a nationalist-fascist to power and then overthrowing him. Baltic, Ukrainian, Russian and other nationalists are threatening one another in various regions where different nationalities have long mixed and coexisted in relative peace. Anti-semitism and Great Russian chauvinism and fascism are on the rise. According to the Helsinki Watch, the society is increasingly militarized, "a dozen areas of the country are now under states of emergency" and more than a thousand people have been killed in sectarian violence. The spectre of Yugoslavia — a "Yugoslavia with nukes," as U.S. Secretary of State Baker declared ominously — hovers over the entire society.

As social chaos and resistance threaten the smooth transition to colony status, many would welcome a military coup — particularly the Russian nationalists and some of the managerial bureaucrats who want privatization with the iron fist that the August junta promised. But no elite faction, East or West, entertains the idea of a return to the days prior to the unravelling of the stalinist state, notwithstanding the fantasies of the unfortunates who wave placards with photos of Stalin and Lenin. The reconstructed stalinists need the West to get their noses barely above the quicksand, and for its own sake the West needs to get them on their feet, if only on the level of Mexico or Brazil (where social chaos is dealt with as decisively as possible). Just as some stability was essential during the Cold War, when the rival blocs played out their exterminist standoff, rockets at the ready, stability is of the utmost importance now, when events in the former East Bloc could threaten not only the relative social peace but the very existence of the West Bloc.

One of the things that has kept such a coup from occurring is the possibility that it could be drawn into the post-imperial whirlwind. Would the army split along national lines, or its mostly Russian officer corps bog down (a mega-Afghanistan?) in an attempt to quell unrest and nationalist aspirations in the republics? Already the republics are wrangling over who controls what section of the military, which led one admiral to warn, "This is a mine that will slowly explode." Civil war? A Yugoslavia with nukes? During negotiations, the commander of strategic forces in Ukraine, Major General Vladimir Bashkirov, reminded stalinist-turned-nationalist Ukrainian president Leonid Kravchuck with a smirk, "In my division I have more buttons than the President, so you better be careful of me." (*New York Times*, January 10, 1992)

"The theater like the plague is a crisis which is resolved by death or cure," wrote Antonin Artaud. In the post-imperial theater of cruelty, as in the imperial one, no cure appears to be forthcoming.

3.

"Whilst in ordinary life every shopkeeper is very well able to distinguish between what somebody professes to be and what he really is, our historians have not yet won even this trivial insight. They take every epoch at its word and believe that everything it says and imagines about itself is true." — Marx and Engels, The German Ideology

Things are rarely what they seem. An epoch inherits a language that in turn becomes a mystique, a falsification. Thus the early Christians, turning their backs on the crumbling Roman colossus, used the anti-imperial message of their prophet to found new imperial cities of god.

So too in the age of the world-historic struggle between capitalism and communism. Appearances masked reality; the revolution against capitalism only gave it new expression. The communists were not communists and the free world never free. The political typology served the interests of hierarchs and hirelings in both camps. The stalinist artistocrat's actual role as functionary in a new statified, hybrid form of capital was concealed behind a revolutionary rubric that garnered enormous sacrifices of a quasi-religious character, both from within the regime and from supporters outside. For their part, the old ruling classes of the West had a godless external enemy to scapegoat wherever imperial pillage and military adventures were questioned. It was an elegant if gruesome system, and it survived for most of the century.

Their essential convergence does not mean that the interests of the two blocs weren't diametrically opposed. There was an ongoing effort by the West (punctuated by alliance and economic exchange) to undermine and overthrow its rivals in the self-proclaimed socialist world. This is partly because all empires struggle ruthlessly for dominance. But the private capitalist powers had even greater reasons to oppose the formal property relations of the state capitalist regimes. The West longed to reopen those same countries to inter-imperial exploitation and to eliminate the revolutionary mystique that inspired colonial nationalists to impede private capital's smooth accumulation of value at bargain rates.

But the ultimate collapse of the soviet regime was partly the result of the 75-year war against a state which, despite its failed promise to usher in a toilers' paradise, did physically liquidate the traditional hierarchies, sending the same shiver of dread through the rulers of the West that news of the French guillotine had caused among English and Russian wealthy classes at the end of the eighteenth century. The oppressors, like millions of the world's oppressed, took the communists at their word. In fact, any challenge to established power was automatically labeled communist and dealt with by the same iron fist.

The Cold War intensified and "rationalized" what was already essentially a war of aggression by the West against any stripe of rebel threatening to carry out the kinds of nationalizations of Western-controlled resources that the Bolsheviks had in the 1920s, as well as against the only regimes willing to ally with such nationalist upstarts. This permanent, institutionalized campaign turned the Western restorationist project into a veritable culture. Paranoia, brutality, conformism, and regimentation assured obedience to the empire and social peace at home, while the greatest arms race in history (linked to continuous military bloodbaths in the so-called peripheries) was generated to ensure domination of the post-world-war neocolonies, to maintain the military-industrial basis of the economy, and to force a both socially and economically costly defense posture on the state capitalist adversary. This arms race played a decisive role in finally doing in the stalinist regime.

President Reagan was once asked if the U.S. strategy of "spending Russia into a depression" might backfire on the already troubled U.S. economy. He replied, "Yes, but they will bust first." (M. Kaku, "No Milk and Honey in the Soviet Future," *The Guardian*, September 11, 1991) That is essentially what occurred; the U.S. economy also started down the tube in the process, just a few steps behind its adversary. From 1949 to 1989, the total military budget of the U.S. in 1982 dollars was $8.2 trillion — as one commentator noted, "more money than it would cost to replace all of the human-made machines and structures in the entire country." (Morris Gleicher, "America in Decline," *Detroit Metro Times*, July 24-30, 1991) Not that American capital could eliminate its military budget without unravelling the whole economic system itself; as someone once remarked, the U.S. doesn't have a war machine, it *is* a war machine.

Yet despite the differences between the two rival blocs, the Soviet Union was ultimately only a poorer version of private capital, indeed, the only kind of capitalist development generally available to poorer nations lagging behind in the race for industrial growth. And because it was a poorer version, a kind of weak link in a way perhaps that tsarist Russia was in 1917, and because the new social-economic configuration could neither retreat to its former colonial position nor rise to become a competitive empire, it fell victim to the fabulously expensive arms race and to a deepening international recession that tended to make all weak national capitals teeter on the edge of bankruptcy. When its Eastern European client states began to fall under the sway of the vampires at the International Monetary Fund and the World Bank, the writing was on the wall.

Economic stagnation and a weak ruble, low productivity and social unrest flowing from the stalemate in Afghanistan, ecological degradation and other grievances all combined to bring about the changes that would consign the U.S.S.R. to the "dustbin of history." But it was, to be precise, neither a revolution nor a counter-revolution. Only a minuscule amount of property has so far been privatized to individuals, and more or less the same caste remains in power, with an infusion (usually a healthy development for any power structure) of critics and reformers from outside. Had the U.S.S.R. been a client rather than a rival of the U.S. — say, a Saddam Hussein or a Marcos or a junta-run state like the Salvadoran — major loans would have been expedited and the CIA sent in to crush the troublemakers. That didn't happen, of course, and the rest is television.

And so the Fall of Communism/Triumph of Capitalism is the official imperial history as conceived, produced, and directed by the victors. And the victors are not the common people of the two blocs whose living conditions decline as international capital reorganizes around a still more exploitative "social contract," but rather the class and caste hierarchs who administer and who benefit from international capital accumulation, East and West. The narrow definition of capitalism that served the managers of both blocs must be rejected for a broader one if this epoch is ever to be understood.

Ideology East and West has reasons to deny it, but the truth is that to focus on juridical property relations and the terms by which hierarchically organized societies name themselves is to commit a grave, formalistic error. Modern state socialism was only a manifestation of the capitalism it claimed to supersede. Capitalism and socialism must be understood in an anthropological and historical sense that sees through the veils of ideological mystification. By doing so, we understand not only the difference between the blocs but their fundamental identity. What was capitalist about Soviet socialism?

Cornelius Castoriadis argued in 1977 that the social regime in the Soviet Union would better be described as "total bureaucratic capitalism" in contrast with private "fragmented bureaucratic capitalism" in the West (though "total" does not imply that there is no opposition or antagonism within the regime). It was (and remains) "an asymmetrical and antagonistically divided society — or, in traditional terms, a 'class society' ... subject to the domination of a particular social group, the bureaucracy."

This domination, Castoriadis continues, was "concretized in an economic exploitation, political oppression, and mental enslavement of the population" for the bureaucracy's benefit. Exploitation — the extraction of value from nature and human labor for reinvestment in the enterprise and for the enrichment of the ruling group, flows from antagonistic relations of production "based on [a] division between managers and operatives" separate from formal or legal property relations. Whether the factory manager holds the deed to the place or runs it on behalf of an abstraction called the State (in reality a country club to which he and his cronies belong) is irrelevant. The result is the same for him and for those who work under him.

"[S]ubject to a 'wage' relation as any other working class," the operatives "have control of neither the means nor the product of their labor, nor of their own activity as workers. They 'sell' their time, their vital forces, and their life to the bureaucracy, which disposes of them according to its interests." The bureaucracy uses the same basic methods as the private capitalist West to increase the amount of value it extracts and reduce the workers' share as well as whatever shreds of autonomy that might exist in the workplace through management techniques and the technicization of work.

That the system is called socialism means nothing. Rather, the *content* of the society — hierarchy, domination, alienation, and production — and not its formal integuments, is key. It is equally important to speak of the content of capitalism in a cultural mode, not only narrowly in terms of the work relation. Most importantly and most broadly, and as Castoriadis argues,

> The Russian regime is part of the socio-historical universe of capitalism because the magma of social imaginary significations [or ideology] that animate its institutions and are realized through it is the very thing that is brought about in history by capitalism. The core of this magma can be described as the unlimited expansion of 'rational' mastery. It is, of course, a question of a mastery that is mostly illusory, and of an abstract pseudo-'rationality.' This imaginary signification constitutes the central juncture of ideas that become effective forces and processes dominating the functioning and development of capitalism: the unlimited expansion of the productive forces; the obsessive preoccupation with 'development,' pseudo-rational 'technical progress,' production and the 'economy'; 'rationalization' and control of all activities; the increasingly elaborate division of labor, universal quantification, calculation and 'planning'; organization as an end in itself, etc. Its correlatives are the institutional forms of the enterprise, the bureaucratic-hierarchical Apparatus, the modern State and Party, etc. Many of these elements — institutional significations and forms — are created in the course of historical periods that ante-date capitalism. [Here Lewis Mumford's description of the anticipations of modern capital in the ancient slave state megamachines comes to mind.

— D.W.] But it is the bourgeoisie that, during its transformation into a capitalist bourgeoisie, changes their function and reunites them to the signification of the unlimited expansion of 'rational' mastery (explicitly formulated since Descartes, and always central to Marx, so that his thinking always remains anchored in the capitalist universe). . . . ("The Social Regime in Russia," *Telos* 38, Winter 1978-79)

Clearly, capitalism is not the unidimensional phenomenon that both left and right would have it be. It emerged from its "classical" origins not only as the growing power of the bourgeoisie universally to impose trade and exchange through contractual labor, but was also inextricably linked to the cult of reductive rationality and efficiency, the rise of science and technology, the growth of the centralized state, and the materialization and quantification of culture.

Capitalism is therefore accordingly an "immense accumulation of commodities" but also and more importantly, what lies behind it: the social relations that make accumulation possible. To paraphrase Jacques Camatte, capital is not a mode of production as Marx put it but a mode of being. (*The Wandering of Humanity*, 1975; see also Fredy Perlman, *The Reproduction of Daily Life*, 1972.) This mode of being, shared by socialism and capitalism, stands in sharp contrast to all forms of communities, in contrast to all vernacular, subsistence societies that preceded it, in which the fundamental motives were not economic and instrumental but communal, cultural, and spiritual (though, again, it was anticipated in those early class societies where relations between kin — or for that matter, between enemies — became relations between strangers based on economic exchange).

Capitalism began by replacing subsistence economies (in fact, noneconomic societies) with the market. Economic relation and trade, "at best a subordinate feature of life," in the words of Karl Polanyi, became central. "The mechanism which the motive of gain set in motion was comparable in effectiveness only to the most violent outburst of religious fervor in history," he argues. "Within a generation the whole human world was subjected to its undiluted influence." (*The Great Transformation*, 1957)

Markets, the state and eventually industrialism all grew together as interlocking aspects of the same social system. Though markets existed before the rise of capitalism, as Polanyi reveals, such markets were "essentially ... neighborhood markets" that "nowhere showed any sign of reducing the prevailing economic system [i.e., autonomy and subsistence] to their pattern." In fact, "Internal trade in Western Europe was actually created by the intervention of the state." The same was true with industrialism, which had to be imposed on the common people, whose response to the emergent factory system was civil war, the burning of factories and destruction of machines. The central authorities had to send in tens of thousands of troops to impose the industrial capitalist order. (See E.P. Thompson's *The Making of the English Working Class*, 1963.)

Another key ingredient of this new social system was the violence and theft carried out in the original accumulation — the despoliation of the traditional commons in Europe, the kidnapping and enslavement of Africans, and the conquest of America, Australia, and Asia. The massive, brutal plunder that paid for the industrialization of Europe and North America exemplifies the necessity for capital always to have a super-exploited colony and sacrifice zone. It is the exploitation of labor and the looting of nature that bring accumulation or profit, which in turn serves to reproduce social power. The creation of wealth required the creation of scarcity — a process going on today, for example, at the frontiers of capitalist development/colonization in those small subsistence cultures now under attack, be it from market expansion through the invasion of such cultures by commodities or from state capitalist megatechnic projects that displace whole cultures altogether.

For tribal and village peoples, the traditional household economies characterized by the absence of commodities and institutional outputs (and identified as "poverty" and "underdevelopment" by development bureaucrats) is actually abundance; while the wealth brought by capitalist investment, industrial development, and bureaucratic institutionalization leads the vast majority to destitution and misery. "More commodities and more cash mean less life," writes Indian ecofeminist Vandana Shiva, "in nature (through ecological destruction) and in society (through denial of basic needs)." The contemporary world starvation crisis is the result, but its roots lie in the original enclosure movement, the slave trade, and the early colonial expansions of modern capital's emergence. (See Vandana Shiva, *Staying Alive: Women, Ecology and Development*, 1989; Ivan Illich, *Tools for Conviviality*, 1973, and *Shadow Work*, 1981; Sylvia Wynter, "Ethno or Socio Poetics," in *Alcheringa: Ethnopoetics*, edited by M. Benamou and J. Rothenberg, 1976.)

The state has always played a central role in capitalist development, but particularly after the mid-nineteenth century, by which time, according to James Petras, all cases of the early states of national capitalist development "involved large-scale state investments in most if not all the essential areas of the economy for varying periods of time." This is partly because by that time world capital had achieved a different scale and character from the original capitalist accumulations in Europe. No country could construct a solid national capital without a statist strategy.

In the colonial world of weaker nations and old empires left behind by advanced capitalist countries, a feeble, vacillating native bourgeoisie (what

Petras calls a "lumpen bourgeoisie") served as middlemen for international capital, administering their nations as permanent sacrifice zones for the colonial powers. In such nations it was the thin middle class (petty bourgeois) layer that produced the Jacobin elites capable of leading national independence wars to create a nationalized capital under the aegis of the post-revolutionary state. Sometimes these countries developed mixed economies (Mexico in the first decades after the revolution) and sometimes they developed bureaucratic, nationalized property forms (U.S.S.R., China). These nationalist independence struggles usually established a one-party state, state ownership and planning in key industrial sectors, and socialist (populist) rhetoric and ideology. While Petras considers only so-called radical nationalist states, who used "socialist forms" to accomplish capitalist ends, "namely, the realization of profit within a class society," the description also fits the socialist bloc, where a class society realizes profit (by extracting surplus value) for the state and for the projects and the privileges of the ruling bureaucratic caste or class. ("State Capitalism in the Third World," in Petras, *Critical Perspectives on Imperialism and Social Class in the Third World*, 1978)

Thus we see the educated, middle class (and in a certain sense, declassé) leaders of (usually marxist) cadre parties using marxist discourse to carry the capitalist project of industrial development, commodity production, and the accumulation of value to those places it had not previously been able to penetrate fully. Using socialist ideology, these leaders laid the foundations for capitalism, expropriating not only the old classes but the traditional commons, and creating internal colonies (in regions inhabited by ethnic minorities, in gulag slave labor camps, and by super-exploitation of the workers for the "socialist fatherland"), to play the role that external colonies and slavery had played for the first wave of private capitalist nations. The marxists were firm believers in the "magma" (to use Castoriadis' term) of capitalist ideology. Rejecting secondary qualities of capital (private property forms characteristic of other times and other countries), they embraced the ideology of development, industry, production, technology, and "rational mastery." To them capitalism was revolutionary and progressive because it shattered the traditional bonds that their sense of colonial inferiority (and let us be fair: their outrage at capitalist injustices) led them to reject as "backward." But socialism was even better because it could deliver what bourgeois society had only promised.

The project to liberate the "means of production" from the private capitalist fetters and thus to expand productive forces made marxism, as Jacques Camatte has noted, "the authentic consciousness of the capitalist mode of production." Bourgeois and marxist cadre shared the same false consciousness. "Historical materialism is a glorification of the wandering in which humanity has been engaged for more than a century: growth of the productive forces as the condition *sine-qua-non* for liberation." (Camatte, *The Wandering of Humanity*, Detroit, 1975)

Camatte's collaborator Gianni Collu puts it another way that merits mention. All the critiques of different kinds of capitalism tend to obscure what is most important: "the transition of value to a situation of its complete autonomy." He continues:

> This transition is a movement from value as an abstract quantity arising out of the production of goods to value as an objectified thing in itself, for the sake of which all goods are produced, and in respect to which all human activities are judged. The traditional 'left' (old and new) does not argue against such a system of value but only against the failure of capitalism to overcome the petty squabbles within production and within social relations. They see, in common with the bourgeoisie, that these squabbles prevent the smooth movement of society towards its total domination by value, toward a society in which all things can be evaluated in terms of numbers, where quantity demolishes quality. Since the left questions not the production of value but the way in which value is produced, it shares with the bourgeoisie the same project: making the production of value more and more efficient. ("Transition," 1969, translated and reprinted in *Ideas for Setting Your Mind in a Condition of Dis*ease*, Falling Sky Books, no date)

In the East Bloc an old joke explained that you could prove the East was socialist rather than capitalist because Lenin's picture was on the money. (Even that is now changing. What image will now grace the bank notes — the tsar? A banker? An historic building being dissolved by acid rain? Some animal they are driving into extinction?) Socialism turned out to be a variant of capitalist development, though not a permanent one: the "classic" colonial form may now be restored. In 1917 an old form of capital fell to a new form; in 1991 the new form then fell to yet another. The first transformation soon became a tragedy, the second now turns tragic farce. It doesn't matter who or what is on the money. It's all capital.

4.

"Wheel of the epoch, keep on turning. . . ." — *Andrei Voznesensky*

Despite its status as an old empire and military power, Russia under the tsars was one of those peripheral nations lagging behind in capital development. The tsars began to develop state capitalism in the relative absence of the social classes and culture necessary to foment the process. By importing capital into a nation still mired in an archaic, bureaucratic despotism, where capital was incapable of catching up with the advanced European states, they unleashed the forces that would ultimately unravel their own power.

Yet the social content of the empire was not so easily superseded, even if structures and specific social classes could be substituted. As Karl Wittfogel remarked in his classic *Oriental Despotism: A Comparative Study in Total Power*, "[N]ine months after the fall of the semi-managerial apparatus state of Tsardom, the Bolshevik revolution paved the way for the rise of the total managerial apparatus state of the U.S.S.R."

In Russia, the seizure of power by the Bolsheviks led almost immediately to a state capitalist regime. Lenin, sharing Marx's fetish for the "progressive" development of industrial technology and production, and fearing that the empire might revert to the "Asiatic despotism" of the tsars, consciously set out to create capitalist foundations. Otherwise, he feared, there would be a restoration of the general, bureaucratic state slavery characteristic of the Asiatic despotism that Marx and others had described at different times as a mode of production distinct from slavery and feudalism. (In such a society, production was dispersed, local, and self-sustaining, but political authority was centralized and bureaucratic. Ancient China and Egypt were given as examples of this kind of society.)

In reply to critics within the Bolshevik Party (as well as from outside it) who argued that not socialism but state capitalism was being established, Lenin wrote in 1918, "If we introduced state capitalism in approximately six months' time, we would achieve a great success and a sure guarantee that within a year socialism will have gained a permanently firm hold and will have become invincible in our country." "Soviet power" had nothing to fear from state capitalism, he argued, as it would be "immeasurably superior to the present system of economy." The "sum total of the necessary conditions of socialism" was in fact "large-scale capitalist technique based on the last word of modern science. . . ."

Lenin went even further, calling for piece work production and the application of Taylorism (time study and the rationalization of labor), and he urged the study of "the state capitalism of the Germans to spare no effort copying it." The new state should shrink from nothing in achieving its goals, neither from "the dictatorship of individual persons" nor the employment of "barbarous methods to fight barbarism." Getting the trains running on time so that merchants could make their appointments was to him "a thousand times more valuable than twenty communist resolutions," he said, making him not only the peer of Mussolini but of his free market heirs in today's former workers state. "Socialism," he wrote that same year, "is nothing but state capitalist monopoly made to benefit the whole people." (Quoted in Maurice Brinton, *The Bolsheviks and Workers' Control*, Solidarity/Black & Red, Detroit 1972)

Hierarchic leadership, dictatorial command and one-man management (often in the person of a former owner or manager) was absolutely essential to realize the state capitalist revolution envisioned by Lenin. As Brinton observes, "Within a year of the capture of state power by the Bolsheviks, the relations of production (shaken for a while at the height of the mass movement) had reverted to the classical authoritarian pattern seen in all class societies. The workers as workers had been divested of any meaningful decisional authority in matters that concerned them most."

Trotsky played a central role in this counterrevolution, not only turning the army into a traditional authoritarian and hierarchic structure (for example, restoring the death penalty for disobedience under fire and abolishing the elective choice of officers). He also called for the militarization of the economy and labor, demanding that military deserters and "deserters from labor" be marshalled into punitive battalions and concentration camps. "The working masses cannot be wandering all over Russia," he told a trade union congress. "They must be thrown here and there, appointed, commanded, just like soldiers." (See Robert V. Daniels, *The Conscience of the Revolution: Communist Opposition in Soviet Russia*, New York, 1969.)

In answer to a Menshevik Party opponent who argued, "You cannot build a planned economy in the way the Pharaohs built their pyramids" (an astonishingly prescient phrase, even if it reflected mostly the idea that coercion would be inefficient), Trotsky replied that even chattel slavery had been productive, and that compulsory serf labor was for its time a "progressive phenomenon." (Isaac Deutscher, *The Prophet Armed: Trotsky 1879–1921*, New York 1965). In *Terrorism and Communism*, written from his military train, he argued that not only was compulsory labor necessary, but that it represented "the inevitable method of organization and disciplining of labor-power during the transition from capitalism to Socialism." Compulsion by the state would also "still play, for a considerable period, an extremely prominent part" in this process. (Trotsky, *Terrorism and Communism*, Ann Arbor, 1963) This was not merely one of the irrational consequences of "rational mastery" but the essence of how the state communist systems came to be universally known — as Daniels puts it, an "industrial society organized on military lines."

Daniels points out that the "dilemmas" faced by the communists in 1921 were already anticipated in passing by Engels, who wrote concerning the peasant wars of the Middle Ages that the worst thing for a revolutionary was to win power in an age when his class is not ready. In such conditions, "He is compelled to represent not his party or his class, but the class for whom conditions are ripe for domination. In the interests of the movement itself," Engels continued, such a figure "is compelled to defend the interest of an alien class, and to feed his own class with phrases and promises, with the assertion that the interests of that alien class are their own interests."

"As a capsule analysis of Soviet Russia," comments Daniels, "this would be hard to improve upon. What is the alien class whose interests are defended? This is a complex question, but perhaps the most apt answer is that suggested in many Communist writings of the period — the 'technical intelligentsia.'" Of course, this explicit critique of Marx was made by his anarchist contemporaries, particularly Bakunin, who had predicted that Marx's authoritarian socialism would in fact bring about a new stage of capitalist development. The statist system of Marx and Engels, Bakunin argued, "basing itself on the alleged sovereignty of the so-called will of the people ... incorporates the two necessary conditions for the progress of capitalism: state centralization and the actual submission of the sovereign people to the intellectual governing minority, who, while claiming to represent the people, unfailingly exploits them." Elsewhere Bakunin writes, "The State has always been the patrimony of some privileged class: a priestly class, an aristocratic class, a bourgeois class. And finally, when all the other classes have exhausted themselves, the State then becomes the patrimony of the bureaucratic class and then falls — or if you will, rises — to the position of a machine." Commenting on these passages, John Clark writes:

> Bakunin, having accepted Marx's critique of bourgeois ideology as the theoretical construct which both legitimates and veils the power relations of capitalist society, [was] extending this critique to Marxism as the emerging ideology of a developing social class, a new class whose power is rooted in the growth of centralized planning and specialized technique. On the one hand, this technobureaucratic class absorbs and expands the functions of previous bureaucracies, and utilizes statist ideology, which presents political domination as necessary for social order, to legitimate its existence. But, on the other hand, it incorporates the new hierarchical system of relations developing out of high technology, and legitimates the resulting domination through the ideology of productivity and economic growth. The result is a highly integrated system of planning and control, which can bypass the long process of synthetic rationalization which is necessary to achieve such a level of order and stability in societies where technobureaucratic functions continue to be distributed among competing systems of power and authority. Bakunin's originality consisted in his recognition, at a very early stage, of both the political-bureaucratic

aspects and the scientific-technical side of such a structure, and in his perception of the nature of its legitimating underpinnings. ("Marx, Bakunin and the Problem of Social Transformation," *Telos* 42, Winter 1979-80; also chapters two and three in John Clark, *The Anarchist Moment: Reflections on Culture, Nature, and Power*, Montreal, 1986).

So, for what it is worth now, the anarchists were right about marxism a century and a half before the rest of the world witnessed the collapse of the communist mystique and the lowering of the hammer and sickle from the towers of the Kremlin. Swept into concentration camps and gunned down by the secret police in tsarist-turned-communist dungeons during the early days of the regime, anarchists and other revolutionaries paid for their opposition to Bolshevik tyranny with their lives. From 1917 to 1922 the Bolshevik leadership worked tirelessly to consolidate power and create vertical command structures, setting up the police and military hierarchies, control commissions and bureaucracies, and crushing all opposition, both outside and inside the ruling party.

"How can strict unity of will be ensured?" asked Lenin in April 1918. "By thousands subordinating their will to the will of one ... Today the Revolution demands, in the interests of socialism, that the masses *unquestioningly obey the single will* [emphasis in original] of the leaders of the labor process." In answer to critics of bureaucratization, Trotsky replied in December 1920 that Russia in fact "suffered not from the excess but from the lack of an efficient bureaucracy," according to Deutscher. (This led Stalin to dub Trotsky the "patriarch of the bureaucrats.") By 1921 and the massacre of the Kronstadt rebels, the party was firmly in control — of a chaotic enterprise lurching toward a dictatorship the likes of which not even the party leaders could foresee. (Thus to say that Lenin was entirely single-minded in his authoritarian purpose and consciously foresaw the dictatorship he forged would be to miss the tragic element in historical events — to insist that Dr. Frankenstein understood the consequences of his activity and felt no horror when his monster no longer responded to his directions. That does not absolve the Bolsheviks and their heirs of their crimes — the world has paid a great price.)

Even inside the party there was a growing awareness that the revolution had been defeated. The "technical intelligentsia," in the words of one opposition group, had been brought to power, and the bureaucracy and the New Economic Policy functionaries had become a new bourgeoisie. The New Economic Policy had allowed capitalist market relations to re-emerge in the countryside after the Bolsheviks had effectively destroyed all self-organized peasant communes and rural militias in the interests of maintaining central power under their command. Lenin labelled opposition to those policies "the most serious crime against the party." At the same time that the bureaucracy was being consolidated under their own rule, even the party leaders warned against it. One detects a nagging awareness of the discrepancy between their intentions and the consequences, their alleged ends and means — a recognition that was the crux of the anarchists' critique of authoritarian socialism during the mid-nineteenth century debates and later.

The Bolsheviks admitted that they had created the apparatus from "such materials as we had at hand," as Trotsky said, referring to the hundreds of thousands of tsarist officials hired by the new state to manage and to quell the workers and peasants who balked at the harness prepared for them by their communist liberators. "We took over the old apparatus, and this was our misfortune," confessed Lenin in 1922. Antibureaucratic moves from above — such as expanding the central committee with workers and rank-and-file party members — had the opposite effect of bringing more apparatchiks loyal to the Secretariat (led by Stalin) into positions of power.

As Daniels observes, "By a process of natural selection the key jobs in the party apparatus were filled with the kind of people who performed well in a hierarchical, disciplined organization … 'apparatus men' who carried out orders effectively and were resolute in combatting opposition activities." This group ushered Stalin into power. "It was not as an individual but as the representative, almost the embodiment, of the secretarial machinery that Stalin accumulated power and prepared the ground for his absolute rule."

By 1923 Lenin believed that the bureaucratic state he founded was reverting to the Asiatic despotism he had feared. By then, however, it was far too late for him to do anything about it, even had he been able to transform his authoritarian mode of thinking to see through the process. His party, under his leadership, had wrecked all manifestations of independent revolutionary and communal activity, suppressing and murdering thousands of people in the process.

In an excessively generous essay on Lenin's "moral dilemmas," Isaac Deutscher writes that by 1922, the Bolshevik leader was saying "that often he had the uncanny sensation which a driver has when he suddenly becomes aware that his vehicle is not moving in the direction in which he steers it." "Powerful forces," Lenin declared, "diverted the Soviet Union from its 'proper road.'" (Deutscher, *Ironies of History*, Berkeley, 1966) Lenin's party was, of course, itself one of the powerful forces; but it, too, was compelled by the ideology of an epoch, the epoch of the rise of statified bureaucratic capital.

Lenin was nevertheless wrong to think that the nation state he had founded had sunk back into simple tsardom — wrong, in Wittfogel's estimation, "because it underrated the economic mentality of the men of the new apparatus." They were "not satisfied with ruling over a world of peasants and craftsmen. They knew the potential of modern industry ... The nationalized industrial apparatus of the new semi-managerial order provided them with new weapons of organization, propaganda, and coercion, which enabled them to liquidate the small peasant producers as an economic category. The completed collectivization transformed the peasants into agricultural workers who toil for a single master: the new apparatus state ... We can truly say that the October revolution, whatever its expressed aims, gave birth to an industry-based system of general (state) slavery."

The society created by marxism-leninism was a new hybrid of capitalism and the despotism of the ancient slave states — a kind of state capitalism, though certainly not the only kind, since private Western capitalism has also evolved into state capitalism. Nor can it be described as an inevitable stage of development in a world-historical progression; it was simply a consequence of the conditions that global capital had previously established, and thus an alternative in the development of capital. And yet it was also something more, what Lewis Mumford called "the first attempt to modernize the oppressive megamachine," that would later be followed by the Nazi state and the Allied Powers during the Second World War.

The dictatorship consolidated its power, Mumford argued, by "utilizing the bureaucratic apparatus and the psychological conditioning of the antiquated megamachine" — submission to power and a quasi-religious loyalty to the state and the leader, as well as the suppression of all rival institutions and mass murders of dissidents and independent thinkers. Stalin became a kind of divine king whose "solemn pronouncements on every subject from the mechanism of genetic inheritance to the origins of language were fatuously hailed as the voice of omniscience ... [a tendency which] later became magnified even to the point of gross caricature — if that were possible — in the pronouncements of Mao Tse-tung."

Mumford's characterization of the new megamachine also hints at the "sinister defects of the ancient megamachine" that contributed to its failure: "its reliance upon physical coercion and terrorism, its systematic enslavement of the entire working population, including members of the dictatorial party, its suppression of free personal intercourse, free travel, free access to the existing store of knowledge, free association, and finally its imposition of human sacrifice to appease the wrath and sustain the life of its terrible, blood-drinking God, Stalin himself. The result of this system was to transform the entire country into a prison, part concentration camp, part extermination laboratory, from which the only hope of escape was death ... The fact that Stalin, like Lenin before him, was treated at death to the ancient Egyptian process of mummification and was put on view for public worship, makes the parallel almost too neat to seem anything but contrived ... But so it actually was." (*The Pentagon of Power*, New York, 1970)

5.

"So he had been asleep! Oh, dear what a wonderful dream that was! And why had he wakened? ... The cheerless dawn shed its dull, unpleasant light through his window ... Oh, how disgusting reality was! How could it even be compared with a dream?" — Nicolai Gogol, "Nevsky Avenue" (1835)

"After the thesis, capitalism, and the antithesis, socialism, here is the product of the thesis: the society of plastic." — B. Charbonneau, *quoted in Jacques Ellul's* The Technological System

One can only speculate as to why the Soviet Union collapsed as a political entity now rather than during the crises of the 1930s or the Second World War. Perhaps it was due to an insurmountable tension between the ossified tsarist megamachine inherited by the Bolsheviks and perfected by Stalin, and the modernized megamachine constructed after the war. The old megamachine served as the foundation for a new, more cosmopolitan system and was eventually outgrown by it in a way perhaps analogous to the way in which slavery in the southern U.S. paid for and eventually succumbed to the forces of industrial capitalism in the north. As capital developed in complexity, it burst its own limitations, bringing the political system down with it.

Certainly by the end of the 1980s the regime had become weaker and much more brittle. The hollowness of official ideology and the pervasive corruption left only a thin layer of support among its political retainers and massive discontent among the rest of the population. Rising expectations generated by the commodity/spectacle system of the West, and the failures of state socialism to fulfill its promises, both helped to bring the regime to an impasse between two worlds, two different configurations of capital — just like the one Russian tsardom had faced.

In marxist terms, the experience of soviet socialism meant that generations of brutality, dictatorship, and exploitation were the way the nation had "progressed" from a medieval empire to a state practicing the "capitalist mode of production." The socialist "dictatorship of the proletariat" provided the internal colonies, primary enclosures, and the super-exploitation of certain sectors and populations, as well as the subsequent investments for the early stages of capitalist development.

In his essay on state capitalism in the Third World, Petras argues that the historical experience of state capitalist regimes suggests "that whatever the initial dynamic and innovation, over the long term stagnation, privatization, and external dependence are recurring phenomena. Insertion into the world capitalist market on unequal terms and increasing indebtedness leads to a crisis that proceeds toward the dissolution of statism as a mode of expansion." What is important is that capital continue to expand; the socialist state may have to "wither away" if need be to facilitate the process.

As Fredy Perlman put it, this "police-as-capitalist" road "worked wonders in procuring preliminary capital," but not so well in managing it. (*The Continuing Appeal of Nationalism*, 1985) The commissars were as inept as their tsarist predecessors had been, and stayed afloat only as long as they were able to conquer new sources of preliminary capital accumulation. (The Chinese communists, though perhaps marginally better administrators, are probably in the same situation as the soviets, caught between the old style megamachine and the modern, more flexible fragmented form characteristic of international private capital. As they appropriate the products, techniques, and development strategies of Western capital and enter into joint ventures with it, they are bound to face similar internal contradictions. Only recently, according to an Associated Press report, Chinese Premier Deng Xiaoping warned that the Communist Party will lose control if it fails to embrace a market economy. "If capitalism has something good," he was reported as saying, "then socialism should bring it over and use it.")

This phenomenon was anticipated indirectly by Marx, though in a way quite unlike the actual outcome. In the *Grundrisse* he describes capital as permanently revolutionary: "Just as capital has the tendency on one side to create ever more surplus labor, so it has the complementary tendency to create more points of exchange … i.e., at bottom, to propagate production based on capital, or the mode of production corresponding to it. The tendency to create the world market is directly given in the concept of capital itself. Every limit appears as a barrier to be overcome."

The Soviet Union appeared as the result of the overcoming of such barriers in a manner never considered by Marx (though clearly anticipated by Bakunin). Its unraveling was equally the result of this "constant tearing down," as Marx put it, of "all the barriers which hem in the development of the forces of production, the expansion of needs, the all-sided development of production, and the exploitation and exchange of natural forces." Rather than a simplistic fixation on bourgeois private property relations, Marx's description of expanding capital suggests a broader definition of the phenomenon (a dialectical view, if you will), that studies capital's dynamic movement and evolution — a view necessary to understand the modern world.

The desire for industrial growth and the expansion of needs, and for the exploitation and valorization of nature for exchange, is shared by bourgeois and commissar alike; it is the ideology of the modern world, East and West, left and right, and is explicitly questioned by only a few marginal dissidents and indigenous peoples. When Nikita Kruschev pounded his shoe on the table at the United Nations in 1960 and promised to "bury" the West, he wasn't referring to a different life beyond the commodity system but better delivery — a kind of sputnik of consumption/production that was bound to fail given the relative power of the rival economies and other historical factors.

"The Industrial Revolution was merely the beginning of a revolution as extreme and radical as ever inflamed the minds of sectarians," Polanyi comments, "but the new creed was utterly materialistic and believed that all human problems could be resolved given an unlimited amount of material commodities." Apart from differences in the distribution of goods and services produced to meet expanding needs (including the expanding needs of production), neither Marx nor the systems bearing his name ultimately questioned this impulse. Thus the Soviet Union did not bury the West but rather the chimera of industrial socialism. The increasingly commoditized mass society created by state socialist forms tended to erode these very forms and what little legitimacy they could summon.

In a world dominated by more powerful Western economies, a technobureacracy already conditioned by greed, cynicism, hierarchic thinking, and pragmatic instrumentalism — in other words, the very prerequisites for leadership roles in corporate capitalism — began to be won over, along with disaffected sections of the population as a whole, to the religion of economic gain. This was a way to jettison the unwieldy and hated symbols of the old regime while maintaining privilege and power, at least for the time being. (Nobody wanted to end up like Ceaucescu, after all.) They reached an understanding with IBM, Mitsubishi and McDonald's just as the tsarist factory managers, government bureaucrats and military officers had been recruited by Bolshevism.

Whether or not this caste will be able to evolve into anything other than a neocolonial "lumpen bourgeoisie" that enriches itself by siphoning off value from a new enlarged sacrifice zone to the private capitalist economies remains to be seen, but no other scenario is apparent. Capital must constantly find new colonies and sacrifice zones for super-exploitation. In the former Soviet Union, the sacrifice zone will be the Siberian forests and oil, as well as the "enclosure" of those basic social supports that state socialism (despite its horrible crimes, and like some ancient megamachine civilizations) tended to provide. The people of the new "commonwealth" are going to get the worst of both worlds — a system that combines the most effective forms of accumulation and repression of both Stalin and Thatcher.

Everyone has probably heard a version of the story of the Russian emigré who, when taken to one of the computerized mega-supermarkets in a U.S. suburb, wept. Would he have wept in front of the Detroit jail, where hungry, homeless people line up nightly in hopes of sleeping inside if it is not too full? For every mega-market there are innumerable starving people. Many of the people straining to pull down the commissar state and its monuments were nevertheless moved by the rhythm of the chief commissar's pounding shoe. (Kruschev even loved Disneyland.) But capital never could (and capitalists never intended to) enrich everyone. The entire world can't be like the handful of small, relatively humane capitalist societies like Sweden. Someone has to pay the hidden costs. The people who in desperation welcomed the idea of markets are now being reminded that property was, is, and always will be theft.

In 1918 the Bolshevik Karl Radek warned that the revolution would "rise like a phoenix" if it were smashed by its bourgeois foes; if, however, the revolution itself "lost its socialist character and thereby disappointed the working masses, the blow would have ten times more terrible consequences for the future of the Russian and the international revolution." (quoted in Brinton) He could not have known how prophetic his words were. In a few generations soviet socialism led to conditions in which people would rebel in order to bring about market capitalism, which could end up reducing them to the kind of beggary and hunger that had caused tsarist Russia to explode.

The international counter-revolutionary role of the soviet state is too well-documented to be reiterated here. In the Eastern Bloc itself, however, the brutal form of capital constructed by the marxist-leninist party state ended up creating the necessary conditions to integrate its population fully into global capital, and a more fully modernized megamachine. Like Moses, the party state could not follow its people into the promised land of the commodity. The state was superfluous, an impediment to the smooth circulation and accumulation of value.

As Mumford observed, contrasting the old and new megamachines, "whereas the earlier modes of achieving productivity and conformity were largely external ... those now applied to consumption are becoming internalized, and therefore harder to throw off." When the Berlin Wall came down it was partly because it no longer meaningfully held anyone or anything in or out. The boundaries had already been abolished, and the behemoth imploded.

Though Lenin argued somewhere that socialism was "electrification plus workers' councils," he made electrification his priority. And it was electrification and all that it implies — a mass energy grid, mining, technocratic planning, toxic chemicals, alienated and compartmentalized labor, hierarchy and vertical command, and societal addiction to a mass energy life — that triumphed in the end.

Just as state socialism was a vehicle for capitalism's emergence, it is necessary to understand capitalism as the vehicle for a mass, megatechnic civilization, the nuclear-cybernetic-petrochemical megamachine that is everywhere proving itself quite adaptable to private corporate capital, bureaucratic state agencies, and even workers councils (and perhaps working best in the long run in some combine of the three). The quasi-religious ideology of the epoch, that of mass technological development, is questioned by virtually no one. And no one (with very few exceptions) is managing to halt it anywhere, even temporarily.

It makes no sense to think about capital simply in terms of markets and property forms. It is a culture and a mode of being. This culture corresponds to the violence and separation that destroyed myriad traditional societies, their commons, and their organic, enspirited cosmos. Through conquest and plunder, this planetary multiverse was reduced to the quantitative in social reproduction (commodity society) and consciousness (rationalist-reductionist science), establishing an economic-instrumental civilization on the ruins of the human past. Whether it calls itself capitalist, socialist, democratic, or fascist, its project is essentially the same: the establishment of a megatechnic work pyramid to expand empires (big mafias and small), through the reduction of nature and human communities to an archipelago of sacrifice zones or gulags from which value is extracted for the maintenance and expanded power of the hierarchy.

"The handmill gives you society with the feudal lord; the steam-mill society with the industrial capitalist," wrote Marx in *The Poverty of Philosophy*. What, then, does a global treadmill give you? The bureaucrat, the development consultant, the laboratory scientist, the technician, the worker, the consumer, the agricultural drudge, the starving castoff. A village turned into a factory, a forest turned into a traffic jam, a hearth into a television. A mountain turned into a toxic slag heap.

Capitalism created a technological system that in turn gave a new content to capitalism. As Jacques Ellul has written, "It is not machines that are shipped to all the countries on the earth, it is, in reality, the ensemble of the technological world — both a necessity, if machines are to be usable, and a consequence of the accumulation of machines. It is a style of life, a set of symbols, an ideology." (*The Technological System*, New York, 1980)

"The capitalist system has been swallowed up by the technological system," writes Ellul. But he misses the point: technology and capital are both surpassing their limitations in runaway fashion, but neither has been swallowed by the other. Capital has in fact always been a hybrid, in its early stages most particularly a hybrid of mercantile industrialism and chattel slavery.

Modern techno-capitalism is no less a syncretic hybrid, never abolishing the irrationalities and brutalities of prior hierarchic/class societies, but rather contemporizing and layering them within its structure. No form of misery has been left behind: all coexist in interpenetrating, contradictory, but functioning agglomerations — from the abject slavery of Latin American *fincas* to the electronic sweatshops of Southeast Asia to the military laboratories in semi-feudal theocratic Muslim states to the planning committees of private capitalist utilities in the U.S. It is all capital, with men in suits and uniforms at the helm, unleashing a planetary catastrophe in their insane pursuit of power and imperial glory.

Everywhere they are burning the Amazon; everywhere they are machine-gunning campesinos; everywhere they are raining bombs down on Basra; everywhere they are setting up new gulags; everywhere they are causing Bhopals; everywhere they are deadening the spirit. And people are fighting, but they are mostly fighting each other, shedding blood from behind flags to prop up their own little mafias of men in suits and uniforms. The whole world is a "Yugoslavia with nukes." Our species is not finding its way out of the labyrinth.

6.

"Every time history repeats itself the price goes up." — popular sign, quoted by Joseph Tainter in The Collapse of Complex Societies *(Cambridge and New York, 1988)*

"Make yourself a plan,
One that dazzles you!
Now make yourself a second plan,
Neither one will do."
 — *Bertolt Brecht*

"I want to be a yellow sail,
sailing to the land we're heading for."
 — *Sergei Esenin (1920)*

As I write the concluding section of this essay in mid-February 1992, Russia and Ukraine continue to wrangle over control of the military. The "prison house of nations" that was the Russian empire and then the Soviet Union crumbles, but nationalism and sectarian violence are growing. Forgetting that all nation states are prisons by definition, people grasp at straws, blaming their neighbors for the misfortunes of post-imperial chaos.

People can now be seen selling their personal belongings on street corners to get money for food. (They're "learning the ropes" of entrepreneurial capitalism, comments one Western consultant.) Did they overthrow stalinist tyranny to become another Mexico or Brazil? At least not yet. They haven't stopped resisting.

Will the former soviet empire decline slowly like Byzantium, without nuclear civil war or other horrors? No one can say. Conditions look grim. Yet mutual aid, solidarity, and resistance were able to reemerge after stalinism had done decades of damage; they are not likely to disappear now.

An anthropological critique starting from the long view of the soviet system as a kind of megamachine empire leads to a comparison with others. Even the (so far) partial collapse of the soviet system has implications for the societies of the West. Certainly, this has been understood by the rulers. U.S. Secretary of State James Baker commented in December 1992, "Held together by a single rope, a fall toward fascism or anarchy in the former Soviet Union will pull the West down, too." (*New York Times*, December 13, 1991) A "fall toward anarchy" might indeed be all that can stop the imposition of fascism, and if it affects the U.S., let all the rulers hang by that same rope.

Could the Soviet Union be a bellwether anticipating the failure of development and the bankruptcy of industrialism internationally? What can we learn from the decomposition of a contemporary civilization that might be relevant to us? Wittfogel speaks of a "law of diminishing administrative return" that seems as appropriate to the state socialist bloc as it was to the forms of "Asiatic despotism" he compared. This is a tendency in such despotic empires for equivalent, "and even increased, administrative endeavors [to] cost more than they yield ... The downward movement is completed when additional outlay yields no additional reward whatsoever. We have then reached the absolute administrative frustration point."

In *The Collapse of Complex Societies*, Joseph Tainter attempts to expand this insight into a comparative critique of collapse of ancient civilizations and other complex societies in history. Tainter's perspective seems excessively deterministic and economistic in places, yet his examination of collapse nags provocatively at anyone thinking about megatechnic civilization. "Sociopolitical organizations," he argues, "constantly encounter problems that require increased investment merely to preserve the status quo."

One can agree with Tainter that in megamachines, at least, the necessary investment goes to "increasing size of bureaucracies, cumulative organizational solutions, increasing costs of internal control and external defense. All of these must be done by levying greater costs on the support population, often to no increased advantage." As the costs increase, "the marginal return begins to decline ... Ever greater increments of investment yield ever smaller increments of return ... At this point, a complex society reaches the phase where it becomes increasingly vulnerable to collapse. . . ."

It's hard not to recall the breakdown of soviet bureaucratic despotism in light of this passage. In the top-heavy totalitarian regime, where according to the catechism every cook would manage the state, the state interfered in the kitchen of every cook. The maintenance of managerial rule became more and more costly, organizationally and financially, to the point where it was no longer tenable. A kind of entropy principle was at work: the more loops of inputs and outputs, the more unwieldy the machine, the more energy sacrificed simply to maintain it. As returns diminish, a society that works as a machine breaks down.

Tainter sees collapse as a way for a society to provide some semblance of continuity, if at a lower level: a kind of "Chapter 11" bankruptcy proceeding. A civilization is compelled to cut its losses and scale down. "Societies collapse when stress requires some organizational change." In a situation of declining marginal returns, in which the payoff for increased outputs would be too low, "collapse is an economical alternative ... [and] may be the most appropriate response." In the case of the Soviet Union, the party state was gangrenous and could be cut away, leaving a section of the hierarchy in place. The decline of many of the services provided by the state would also represent a savings for the center (or rather for the balkanized centers now consolidating in the aftermath of breakdown).

While the breakdown of the Soviet Union is not a collapse of the sort described by Tainter, fleeting aspects of collapse are evident. Things fall apart, chaos looms, there are shortages of food and other supplies for the maintenance of civil society. According to one report, "cuts in services, stoppages at factories, delays in deliveries, and salary freezes have been mounting ... There has also been a rise in lawlessness, from running red lights to hijacking, and a breakdown in the old rules of social behavior, from pushing ahead of old people in milk lines to going door-to-door begging for money." (*New York Times*, September 13, 1991)

One would not expect the bourgeois "newspaper of record" to notice the examples of autonomous self-activity and mutualism of groups that must be occurring in parts of the Soviet Union, but there is still enough troubling evidence that the society is adrift. One would hope that in the breakdown of tyranny, elements of communal solidarity would emerge among the former inmates, but so far the picture does look more like a Hobbesian war-of-all-against-all.

This, of course, is the familiar "script," as Tainter puts it, of any collapse, at least in the popular consciousness — social chaos, a grim struggle over meager resources just to survive, the strong preying on the weak —

PART III: AGAINST THE MEGAMACHINE

but this dramatic picture "does contain many elements that are verifiable in past collapses." It is a grim reminder, if the historical record teaches anything, that breakdown is more an outcome of entropy than of the kind of coherence we might seek. And entropy is neither gentle nor pretty.

In the modern world, of course, no nation state can utterly collapse like ancient empires did. The world is now filled with clusters of rival megamachines, and a power vacuum in any area will be filled by the expansion of another. In past examples of this kind of configuration such as the Mycenaeans and the Maya, all the rival civilizations had to suffer mutual collapse. Thus, if socialism in one country was impossible, the same can be said about collapse. A collapse of civilization as we know it today would have to be global and relatively simultaneous.

As unlikely as this prospect may appear, nevertheless, as Tainter concludes, even if global industrialism has not reached the point of diminishing returns, "that point will inevitably arrive ... However much we like to think of ourselves as something special in world history, in fact industrial societies are subject to the same principles that caused earlier societies to collapse." Will the horrors of modern capitalism be equalled or surpassed by its aftermath? Events in the East Bloc only suggest some scenarios. Let us not underestimate the capacity of common people to discover alternatives in time (even if at a great price), and to find a way through the crisis. They have not yet had their say. But one thing must be clear by now: a world made fit for life once more can never come from the failed mystique, revolutionary or otherwise, of more growth and further modernization; and it can come even less from impotent survivalist gestures in the face of breakdown. In the first case, saving industrialism from its own inertia by "democratizing" the treadmill is not only a socialism of fools and a surrender to reconstituted hierarchies, it is ultimately a losing venture. As for digging bunkers at the margins (if they could be found), it is a destiny not worth living — existing on a denuded star when the cosmos of meaning has turned to dust.

Maintaining human decency in the face of whatever comes, affirming a kind of moral and ethical coherence, preserving memory, defending human personhood and all the interconnectedness of the phenomenal world — these thin reeds are all we have. By articulating a coherent refusal of capital and the new megamachine it generated, those who question the grid, the state, and the world they require may make a small opening for others to follow, encouraging practical responses as well as the communal solidarity that represents our only hope for survival.

One way or another, global capitalism will eventually follow its communist rival into collapse, and growth will "grind to a halt," as Ivan Illich predicted fifteen years before Tainter in words that also subtly bring to mind the soviet crisis. This breakdown will be "the result of synergy in the failure of the multiple systems that fed its expansion," he wrote. "Almost overnight people will lose confidence not only in the major institutions but also in the miracle-prescriptions of the would-be crisis managers." The ability of the hierarchy to define and determine "will suddenly be extinguished because it will be recognized as an illusion. . . ."

Again, Illich was talking about both blocs. He argued that such a moment should be "welcomed as a crisis of revolutionary liberation because our present institutions abridge basic human freedom for the sake of providing people [in fact, only some people — D.W.] with more institutional outputs." (*Tools for Conviviality*, New York, 1973) In spite of the dangers, such a devolution may be our only hope of breaking free of the megamachine complex. By shrugging off the onerous burden of treadmill culture, we may consciously choose the "appropriate response" of collapse, and find ways to let it be a disaster for capital but an adventure for ourselves.

This means, without exception and without any hesitation on our part, the abolition of all empires, of a world of sacrifice zones, drudgery, penury, and the toxic cornucopia of commodity society. It means the renewal of subsistence cultures, which still hang on in villages, among tribal peoples struggling to survive, and even among people finding practical responses in the fissures and cracks of civilization. It means making a life that is slower, quieter, and more contemplative. It means revivifying an aesthetic not of the assembly line but of the forest, and restoring a life that can hear what the natural world is telling us, what we once knew long ago and have forgotten as the urban labyrinth grew up around us and enclosed us.

Megatechnic capital may, of course, find a way to suffocate entirely what is humane in us before it reaches its inevitable limits and implodes under its own inertia. There are laboratories and think tanks working around the clock to do just that, even if they have called this eclipse our ultimate "liberation."

So far, though, we are still alive, and some of us still know who we are. Life's adventure cannot be found at control panels or desks, or in digging the foundations for the work pyramid, or building higher stories in its edifice. Nor is it to be found consuming the laboratory chow of McDonaldization at the petrochemical banquet table, or running on its treadmill to nowhere. It is with the fabric of the living world, the universe itself. We are living an aberration, a nightmarish turn from our true journey. Let all the empires crumble. It is time we rejoined the dance.

(1992)

AGAINST THE MEGAMACHINE

"Industrialism is, I am afraid, going to be a curse for mankind ... To change to industrialism is to court disaster. The present distress is undoubtedly insufferable. Pauperism must go. But industrialism is no remedy. . . ." — Gandhi

How do we begin to discuss something as immense and pervasive as technology? It means to describe the totality of modern civilization — not only its massive industrial vistas, its structural apparatus; not only its hierarchy of command and specialization, the imprint of this apparatus on human relations; not only "the humble objects," which "in their aggregate ... have shaken our mode of living to its very roots," as Siegfried Giedion has written; but also in that internalized country of our thoughts, dreams and desires, in the way we consciously and unconsciously see ourselves and our world.

Questioning technology seems incoherent in the modern world because, invisible and ubiquitous, it defines our terrain, our idea of reason. You cannot "get rid of technology," you cannot "destroy all machines"; we are dependent upon them for our survival. In any case, the story goes, technology has always been with us. When an ape pries termites out of a tree with a twig, that, too, is supposed to be technology. Everything changes, and yet stays the same. Plugging into a computer is no more than an improvement on prying termites out of bark. Therefore, one is expected never to discuss technology as a totality but only specific styles or components of technology, which are to be embraced or discarded according to the criteria of the technological religion: efficiency, velocity, compatibility with the entirety of the aggregate.

No one denies that different modes of life existed; but they have been, or are rapidly being, forgotten. Hence the idea they must have been defective, backward, underdeveloped, and eventually surpassed by progress. You can't "go back," "return to the past" — *"you can't stop progress."* When mercantile capitalism emerged, the individualistic, entrepreneurial spirit was thought the essence of human nature. Even non-western and indigenous societies came to be judged mere preparatory stages of modern market society. As mechanization took command, humanity was seen fundamentally as the "tool user," *Homo faber.* So ingrained was this notion of human nature that when the paleolithic cave paintings at Altamira were discovered in 1879, archeologists considered them a hoax; Ice Age hunters would have had neither the leisure (due to the "struggle for existence") nor the mental capacity (since sophistication is demonstrated first of all by complex technical apparatus) to create such graceful, visually sophisticated art.

Taking the part for the whole — ignoring the complex languages, symbolic exchange, rituals, and dreamwork of diverse peoples, while fetishizing their technics — this ruling idea continues to see all cultural evolution as only a series of advances in technical activities. There is never any suspicion of qualitative difference; the mathematics, techniques, and technical implements of early peoples are seen only as incipient versions of modern cybernetics, rational mastery, and industrial apparatus.

Technology is a way of life

To define technology as any and every technical endeavor or artifact, to think of it as the means by which human beings do everything from picking fruit to firing missiles into space, is to render the word meaningless. This ideology can make no sense of the dramatic changes that have occurred in life; it conceals the fact that technology has become a way of life, a specific kind of society. It assumes that a society in which nearly every sphere of human endeavor is shaped by technology is essentially the same as a society with a limited, balanced technics embedded in the larger constellation of life.

Just as capital has been reductively confused with industrial apparatus and accumulated wealth, when it is more importantly a set of social relations, so has technology been reduced to the image of machines and tools, when it, too, has become a complex of social relations — a "web of instrumentality," and thus a qualitatively different form of domination. Technology is capital, the triumph of the inorganic — humanity separated from its tools and universally dependent upon the technological apparatus. It is the regimentation and mechanization of life, the universal proletarianization of humanity and the destruction of community. It is not simply machines, not even mechanization or regimentation alone. As Lewis Mumford pointed out in *Technics and Civilization*, these phenomena are not new in history; "what is new is the fact that these functions have been projected and embodied in organized forms which dominate every aspect of our existence." (Thus critics of technology are commonly accused of being opposed to tools, when in reality modern industrial technology destroyed human-scale tools, and in this way degraded human labor.)

The constellation of terms related to the Greek root *techne* (meaning art, craft or skill) has changed over time. Words such as *technique, technics*, and *technology* tend to overlap in meaning. They are not static, universal, neutral terms, as a simple dictionary definition might suggest; they reflect actual social relations as well as a process of historical development.

In his *Autonomous Technology: Technics-out-of-Control as a Theme in Political Thought*, Langdon Winner observes that the once limited, specific meaning of the word *technology* as "a 'practical art,' 'the study of the practical arts,' or 'the practical arts collectively,'" has in the twentieth century come to refer to an unprecedented, diverse array of phenomena. The word now "has expanded rapidly in both its denotative and connotative meanings" to mean "tools, instruments, machines, organizations, methods, techniques, systems, and the totality of these and similar things in our experience" — a shift in meaning that can be traced chronologically through successive dictionary definitions.

There is no clean division between what constitutes technique (which in its earliest usage in French meant generally a certain manner of doing something, a method of procedure), a technics which is limited and culture-bound, and a technological system which tends to swallow up every activity of society. A provisional definition of terms might be useful, describing *technique* as that procedural instrumentality or manner in which something is done, whether spontaneous, or methodical, which is shared by all human societies but which is not necessarily identical in its motives or its role in those societies; *technics* as technical operations or the ensemble of such operations using tools or machines — again, not necessarily identical from society to society, and not necessarily either methodical or spontaneous; and *technology* as the rationalization or science of techniques, an idea close to the dictionary definitions — the geometric linking together, systematization and universalization of technical instrumentality and applied science within society. This last definition underscores technology's emergence as a system, hence as an autonomous power and social body. While such definitions may not be perfect, they make it possible to explore better the complex nature of the technological phenomenon and modern civilization's intrinsically technological codes.

A certain procedural instrumentality is shared by a painter applying paint to a canvas (or cave wall), a farmer planting seeds, and an electronics technician testing the strength of some metal in a nuclear device. That doesn't make the character of their activities identical. As Jacques Ellul observes in *The Technological Society*, "It is not ... the intrinsic characteristics of techniques which reveal whether there have been real changes, but the characteristics of the relation between the technical phenomenon and society." Ellul uses the French word *technique* in a way which overlaps with the use of "technics" and "technology" in this essay, and which he defines as "the totality of methods rationally arrived at and having absolute efficiency (for a given stage of development) in every field of human activity."

Whereas previously limited, diversified, local technics bore the stamp of the culture and the individuals from which they emerged, technology now changes all local and individual conditions to its own image. It is gradually creating a single, vast, homogeneous technological civilization which smashes down "every Chinese wall," and generating a dispossessed, atomized and de-skilled human subject more and more identical from Greenland to Taiwan.

A world of means

The wide diversity of primal and archaic societies is evidence that though these societies can be said to share a basic level or repertoire of techniques and tools (containers, horticultural and gathering techniques, food preparation, weaving, etc.), each manifestation is unique, independent, culture-bound, kinship-bound. Neither technique in general nor specific technical activities or objects entirely determines how these societies live.

"Because we judge in modern terms," argues Ellul, "we believe that production and consumption coincided with the whole of life." But in traditional societies "technique was applied only in certain narrow, limited areas ... Even in activities we consider technical, it was not always that aspect which was uppermost. In the achievement of a small economic goal, for example, the technical effort became secondary to the pleasure of gathering together ... The activity of sustaining social relations and human contacts predominated over the technical scheme of things and the obligation to work, which were secondary causes." Technical activity played a role in these societies, he argues, "but it had none of the characteristics of instrumental technique. Everything varied from man to man according to his gifts, whereas technique in the modern sense seeks to eliminate such variability."

As society changed, the notion of applied science emerged as a central motivating value, along with an unquestioning allegiance to quantification, time-keeping, progressive mechanization and ever increasing, ever accelerating production — reflecting not simply a change in technical means but an entire new world of meaning and means. The accompanying religious impulse — the worship of technical prowess, the fascination with technical magic linked to the crude, materialist pragmatism of efficiency of means — tended to conceal the meaning of technology as a system. Ellul: "The techniques which result from applied science date from the eighteenth century and characterize our own civilization. The new factor is that the multiplicity of these techniques has caused them literally to change their character. Certainly, they derive from old principles and appear to be the fruit of normal and logical evolution. However, they no longer represent the same phenomenon. In fact technique has taken substance, has become a reality in itself. It is no longer merely a means and an intermediary. It is an object in itself, an independent reality with which we must reckon."

According to the official religion, technology, rooted in a universal and innate human identity, is paradoxically somehow no more than a simple tool or technique like all previous tools and techniques, a static object which we can manipulate like a hammer. But society has become more and more the sum of its own technical organization (notwithstanding the dysfunctional imbalances which are the residues of the collapse of archaic societies and of uneven development). People have lost their traditional techniques and become dependent upon an apparatus: mass production produces masses. Technology is not a tool but an environment — a totality of means enclosing us in its automatism of need, production and exponential development.

As Langdon Winner argues, "Shielded by the conviction that technology is neutral and tool-like, a whole new order is built piecemeal, step by step, with the parts and pieces linked together in novel ways — without the slightest public awareness or opportunity to dispute the character of the changes underway." What results is a form of social organization — an interconnection and stratification of tasks and authoritarian command necessitated by the enormity and complexity of the modern technological system in all of its activities. Winner observes, "The direction of governance flows from the technical conditions to people and their social arrangements, not the other way around. What we find, then, is not a tool waiting passively to be used but a technical ensemble that demands routinized behavior."

No single machine, no specific aspect of technology is solely responsible for this transformation. Rather, as Ellul puts it, it is the "convergence ... of a plurality, not of techniques, but of systems or complexes of techniques. The result is an operational totalitarianism; no longer is any part of man free and independent of these techniques." A process of synergism, a "necessary linking together of techniques," eventually encompasses the whole system. One realm of technology combines with another to create whole new systems at a rapid rate. The many previously unanticipated "spin-off" developments, for example in fields like cybernetics and genetics, make this description of synergy clear.

A depopulated world of matter and motion

Technology has replaced the natural landscape with the dead, suffocating surfaces of a modern technopolis, a cemetery of "bounded horizons and reduced dimensions." Space has undergone an "inverse revolution." Time, too, since the rise in the use of the weight-driven clock, is bounded and quantified. "The clock, not the steam engine," writes Lewis Mumford in *Technics and Civilization*, "is the key machine of the modern industrial age." With the clock, "Time took on the character of an enclosed space."

The quantification of knowledge and experience takes place on several levels — in the rise of standardized weights and measures, which accompanies the rise of the centralized state; in the spread of clocks and time-keeping; in the "romanticism of numbers," which accompanies the rise of the money economy and its abstract symbols of wealth; in the new scientific methods foreseen by Galileo, confining the physical sciences to the so-called "primary qualities" of size, shape, quantity and motion; and in the methods of capitalist book-keeping and the reduction of everything to exchange value. "The power that was science and the power that was money," writes Mumford, "were, in the final analysis, the same kind of power: the power of abstraction, measurement, quantification."

"But the first effect of this advance in clarity and sobriety of thought," he continues, "was to devalue every department of experience except that which lent itself to mathematical investigation ... With this gain in accuracy went a deformation of experience as a whole. The instruments of science were helpless in the realm of qualities. The qualitative was reduced to the subjective: the subjective was dismissed as unreal and the unseen and unmeasurable non-existent ... What was left was the bare, depopulated world of matter and motion: a wasteland."

Did new technologies and time-keeping spur early capitalist mercantilism, or was the reverse the case? In fact, technical growth and capitalism went hand in hand, bringing about the technological civilization of today. This system expands both by the impulse of economic accumulation and by the mechanization and "rationalization" of all life according to normative, technical criteria. Both processes reduce a complex of human activities to a series of quantifiable procedures. Neither formal, juridical ownership of the apparatus, nor the characteristics of specific machinery or particular materials used in production, is determinative. Rather, modern urban-industrial civilization is a socially regimented network of people and machines — an industrialized production-commodity culture which tends toward the absolute destruction of local communities and technics, and the penetration of the megatechnic system into every aspect of life.

Ellul writes, "When André Leroi-Gourhan tabulates the efficiency of Zulu swords and arrows in terms of the most up-to-date knowledge of weaponry, he is doing work that is obviously different from that of the swordsmith of Bechuanaland who created the form of the sword. The swordsmith's choice of form was unconscious and spontaneous; although it can now be justified by numerical calculations, such calculations had no place whatsoever in the technical operation he performed." Technology transforms swordmaking into a more efficient, more rationalized industrial process (or dispenses with it altogether for more "advanced" modes), and all the swordsmiths into factory hands.

In the factory we see the process of mechanization at its height. Siegfried Giedion comments in *Mechanization Takes Command*, "Mechanization could not become a reality in the age of guilds. But social institutions change as soon as the orientation changes. The guilds became obsolete as soon as the rationalistic view became dominant and moved continually toward utilitarian goals. This was the predestined hour for mechanization." Similarly, Murray Bookchin argues in *Toward an Ecological Society*, "Of the technical changes that separate our own era from past ones, no single 'device' was more important than ... the simple process of rationalizing labor into an industrial engine for the production of commodities. Machinery, in the conventional sense of the term, heightened this process greatly, but the systematic rationalization of labor in ever-specialized tasks totally demolished the technical structure of self-managed societies and ultimately of workmanship, the self-hood of the economic realm ... The distinction between artisan and worker hardly requires elucidation. But two significant facts stand out that turn the transformation from craft to factory into a social and characterological disaster. The first fact is the dehumanization of the worker into a mass being; the second is the worker's reduction into a hierarchical being." (The process was hardly "simple," but Bookchin's description of the emerging factory suggests the possibility of critiquing technology without opposing tools or technics altogether.)

Technology is not "neutral"

The common notion of technology's "neutrality" does not recognize that all tools have powerful symbolic content, are suggestive models for thought and action which affect their users. More importantly, the idea of neutrality fails to see that massification and accelerated, synergistic integration of technology would engender corresponding human structures and modes of thought and experience. Culture and technology interact dynamically, each spurring transformations in the other.

Technology is not neutral because it brings with it its own rationality and method of being used. A network of computers or a steel mill cannot be used variously like a simple tool; one must use them as they are designed, and in coordinated combination with a network of complex support processes without which their operation is impossible. But design and interrelated dependencies bring manifold unforeseen results; every development in technology, even technical development which seeks to curb deleterious technological effects, brings with it other unpredictable, sometimes even more disastrous effects. The automobile, for example, was seen as simply a replacement for the horse and carriage, but mass production techniques combined with Ford's new conception of mass distribution gave the automobile a significance no one could foresee. Ford's revolution actually came at the end of a long period of technical preparation. Mass assembly line production and interchangeability of parts dated back to the end of the eighteenth century; by the end of the nineteenth century the process of mechanization was relatively stabilized, and produced a rise in expectations (reflected in the popularity of the great international expositions on industry) which created the terrain for the automobile's enthusiastic reception as an object of mass consumption. The expanding role of the state was also critical, since it was only the state which would have the means to create a national automobile transportation system.

The automobile is thus hardly a tool; it is the totality of the system (and culture) of production and consumption which it implies: a *way of life*. Its use alone makes its own demands apart from the necessities inherent in production. Nor could a highway system be considered a neutral instrument; it is a form of technical giantism and massification. Considering the automobile, who can deny that technology creates its own inertia, its own direction, its own cultural milieu? Think how this one invention transformed our world, our thoughts, images, dreams, forms of association in just a few generations. It has uprooted communities, undermined farmlands, contributed to vast changes in our dietary habits, shifted our values, contaminated our sexual lives, polluted our air both in its manufacture and use, and created a generalized ritual of sacrifice on the assembly line and on the road.

But the automobile is only one invention, if a key one, of thousands. Who would have thought that within just a few decades of the invention of television millions of human beings would spend more time in front of the cathode ray tube than in almost any other waking activity, deriving their very sense of reality from it? Who would have thought that the world would become a radioactive nightmare "wired for destruction" within a few years of the Manhattan Project? And who can say what emergent technologies have in store for us?

In this light, it is much more important to analyze the distinctions between, say, a spear and a missile, than to concentrate on their common traits. It is important to ask *what kind of society they reflect — and help to bring about.* In the first case we see a hand tool made locally with a specific, unique and limited technique, and that technique embedded in a culture. Each tool is unique and reflects the individuality of its user or maker. In the latter case we see an entire social hierarchy, with an extremely complex division of labor. In such an alienated, compartmentalized, instrumental system, each functioning member is isolated by complex social and procedural opacity, and thus blind to the overall process and its results.

In the first case the creator works directly with the materials, which is to say, in nature. In the second case, the worker is alienated from the materials of nature. Nature is not only depleted and destroyed by exploitation and objectification, by the inevitable destruction to be unleashed by the instrument, but, as Ellul observes, "by the very establishment of technology as man's milieu." In the case of the spear, human limits are implied (though human beings could choose to organize themselves as a machine to do greater destruction, as they did in the ancient state military machines). In the case of the missile, however, the organization of human beings as a machine, as a network of production and destruction, is fundamental to what is produced, and the only limit implied is that attained with the ultimate annihilation of the human race by its technology. If there is an underlying perversity in all instruments of violence or war, whether primitive or technological, we can see that in the former the kind of war which takes place is a limited, personal, sporadic activity, which, along with peace-making, gift exchange and intermarriage, is a moment in a network of reciprocity tending toward the resolution of conflicts. The missile production — which *begins* at the point where community dissolves and the military phalanx is first organized — is an unlimited, depersonalized, institutional system which now magnifies human destructiveness to the point of omnicide.

The convergence of social hierarchies and their ever more powerful and all-encompassing tools renders the distinction between capital and technology at least problematic. Both terms are metaphors — partial descriptions which represent the modern organization of life. The state is an apparatus of administrative technique which cannot be separated from the corporate organizations of centralized, technological hierarchy. Economic planning and the market are submerged in technique, technique in both bureaucratic planning and the chaos of the market. Technological automatism and remote control, standardization and mass propaganda are leaving classical bourgeois society behind; it has therefore become crucial to look at the nature of the mass society which only mass technics could have generated.

The myth of a technology separate from its use assumes that means are simply instruments — factories, supertankers, computer networks, mass agrosystems — and not that *universe of means*: the daily activities of the people who participate in these systems. It fails to understand that such ubiquitous means themselves eventually become ends, requiring their inevitable characterological internalization in human beings — in other words, that human beings must obey and thus become the slaves of their mechanical slaves. As Lewis Mumford warned in *The Pentagon of Power,* "It is the system itself that, once set up, gives orders." This "self-inflicted impotence" is "the other side of 'total control.'"

Technology — systematized, "rationalized" mass technics — is more than the sum of its parts; this totality undermines human independence, community and freedom, creating mass beings who are creatures of the universal apparatus, standardized subjects who derive their meaning from the gigantic networks of "mass communication": a one-way barrage of mystification and control. Even those ostensibly directing the machines are themselves its creatures, each one isolated in a compartment of the giant, opaque hive, so such "control" is ambiguous. The conspiratorial notion of "technocracy" is inadequate, if not entirely outmoded. The blind, centrifugal complexity of the system defies conscious control, coming more and more to resemble a locomotive with no throttle hurtling toward an abyss.

A fundamental mutation has occurred

It is now a familiar truism that modern technologies diversify experience. But mechanization has in many ways narrowed our horizons by standardizing our cultures into a global techno-monoculture. This is evident in the mechanization of agriculture, one example being the cultivation of fruit trees. As Giedion points out, "The influence of mechanization ... leads to standardization of the fruit into few varieties ... We have seen an orchard of 42,000 Macintosh trees; and the apples were so uniform that they might have been stamped out by machine."

Such standardization was not always the case. Giedion mentions a noted landscape architect of the first half of the nineteenth century who lists 186 varieties of apple and 233 varieties of pear for planting by arborists, and who for the keeper of a small orchard recommends thirty different kinds of apple "to ripen in succession." He adds, "The large red apple, which attracts the customer's eye, is especially favored, and bred less for bouquet than for a resistant skin and stamina in transit. The flavor is neutralized, deliberately, it would seem." Giedion's example seems quaint today as transnational corporations maneuver to take control of world seed and genetic material, and a multitude of localized varieties are replaced by agricultural monoculture.

With modern communications technology, another fundamental mutation has occurred or is occurring. The media have usurped reality itself. After Jorge Luis Borges, Jean Baudrillard takes as his metaphor for this state of affairs the fable of a map "so detailed that it ends up covering the territory." Whereas with the decline of the Empire comes the deterioration of the map, tattered but still discernible in some remote places, "this fable has come full circle for us," writes Baudrillard, "and if we were to revive the fable today, it would be the territory whose shreds are slowly rotting across the map. It is the real, and not the map, whose vestiges subsist here and there, in the deserts which are no longer those of the Empire, but our own." (*Simulations*)

Since the emergence of mechanization, with the invention of the telegraph perhaps as a representative point of departure, communication has been degraded from a multifaceted, ambivalent, contextually unique and reciprocal relationship between human beings to an abstract, repetitive and homogenized "message" passing between a unilateral transmitter and a passive receiver. It is this one-dimensional transmission which is the starting point of the mass media and computers. The simulated, ostensibly "interactive" response that such technology allows has little or nothing in common with genuine human communication.

But the discourse has shifted — reality has come to resemble this model. As Ellul remarks in *The Technological System*, "It is the technological coherence that now makes up the social coherence." Previously the forces of domination were never able to gain hegemony over all of society; people maintained forms of solidarity and communal discourse which resisted and excluded power (village, religious and neighborhood communities, proletarian culture, bohemianism, for example, which continue to exist in pockets only in extremely attenuated form). The preeminence of technology, particularly meaning-creating "communication" technology, changes this, and all of human intercourse tends to be restructured along the lines of this petrified information and its communication. Seven hundred and fifty million people now watch the same televised sporting event one evening and spend the next day talking about it.

According to the disciples of mechanization, the exponentially expanding volume of artistic, intellectual, and scientific production — of films, recordings, books, magazines, gadgets, scientific discoveries, art, web sites, all of it — implies that subtle human values and a plenitude of meaning and well-being are accumulating at a tremendous rate, that we can now experience life more rapidly, in greater depth, and at a greater range. As a journalist comments, "If the average person can have access to information that would fill the Library of Congress or can control as much computing power as a university has today, why should he be shallower than before?" (Paul Delany, "Socrates, Faust, Univac," *New York Times Book Review*, March 18, 1984) Electronic communications are even said to enhance human values based on family, community and culture. Writes Marshall McLuhan in *The Medium is the Message*: "Our new environment compels commitment and participation. We have become irrevocably involved with, and responsible for, each other."

Of course, such computer power is not available in any significant way to most people. But this is secondary. More importantly, two realities — human meaning and mediatization, the territory and the map — are incommensurable, and cannot long coexist. The media undermine and destroy meaning by simulating it. We are no longer merely victims of a powerful, centralized media; we are that and more. We are in a sense becoming the media. Baudrillard writes in *Simulations* that we are "doomed not to invasion, to pressure, to violence and to blackmail by the media and the models, but to their induction, to their infiltration, to their illegible violence." In such a world, choice is not much different from switching tv channels. The formative experience of using information will tend to be the same everywhere.

A person participates in this structure by parroting the code. Only the Machine, the Master's Voice, actually speaks. The parasite must finally consume its host, the model be imposed once and for all. When computer enthusiasts brag that communications technology has increased the density of human contact, they turn the world on its head, describing an artificial world in which human contact has no density it all. Individuality itself becomes a commodity or function, manufactured and programmed by the system. One participates in mass society the way a computer relay participates in the machine; the option remains to malfunction, but even rebellion tends to be shaped by the forms technology imposes. This is the individuality toward which computerized life drifts: a narcissistic, privatized, passive-aggressive, alienated rage, engaging in a sado-masochistic play far removed from the consequences of its unfocused, destructive impulses.

Meaning has been reshaped

Information, now emerging as a new form of capital and wealth, is central to the new "hyperreality." While the demand for information, the "democratic" distribution of "facts" is the battle cry of those outsiders who struggle to recapture the machinery of media from the centralized institutions of power, it is at least in part the nature of the fact — and finally of masses of facts transmitted on a mass scale as information — which lies behind the problem of the media.

Not that facts have no reality at all, but they have no intrinsic relation to anything: they are weightless. The fact is a selection, hence an exclusion. Its simplification mutilates a subtle reality which refuses to be efficiently packaged. One set of facts confronts another, orchestrated as propaganda and advertising. The fact achieves its ultimate manifestation in trivia and in statistics, to which society is now addicted. Ellul writes in *Propaganda: The Formation of Men's Attitudes*, "Excessive data do not enlighten the reader or listener, they drown him." People are "caught in a web of facts." Whatever specific message is transmitted by the media, the central code is affirmed: meaning must be designed and delivered. "Everywhere," writes Ellul in language evocative of Orwell or Wilhelm Reich, "we find men who pronounce as highly personal truths what they have read in the papers only an hour before. . . ." The result is an amputated being — "nothing except what propaganda has taught him."

The information in which industrial capitalism trades is not neutral; *meaning itself has been reshaped.* The scope of thought is bounded by the computer and its clarity can only be of a certain kind — what a fluorescent lamp is, say, to the entire light spectrum. Rather than increasing choices, the technology imposes its own limited range of choice, and with it the diminishing capacity to recognize the difference. (Thus a person staring at a computer screen is thought to be engaged in an activity as valuable as, even perhaps superior to, walking in the woods or gardening. Both are thought to be gathering or making use of "information.")

Equally naive is the idea that the "information field" is a contested terrain. The field itself is in reality a web of abstract, instrumentalized social relations in which information expands through alienated human activity, just as the system of value reproduces itself through the false reciprocity of commodity exchange. It therefore constitutes subtle relations of domination. Be they critics or promoters, most writers on technology see this information field as an emerging *environment of human discourse.*

Even the desire to transform society through "democratic" access and "rational" selection tends to be colonized as a media message, one competing set of facts among many. In a world dominated by loudspeakers, where political action is reduced to the pulling of lever A or lever B, nuance is lost. In the media, what moves the receiver is not so much truth, or nuance, or ambivalence, but technique. And technique is the domain of power, gravitating naturally toward established ideology — the domain of simulated meaning. Real meaning — irreducible to a broadcast — disintegrates under such an onslaught. As Nazi leader Goebbels remarked, "We do not talk to say something, but to obtain a certain effect." People predisposed to accept such counterfeit as reality will follow the lead of the organization with the biggest and best loudspeakers, or succumb, resigned, to the suspicion that nothing can be knowable, and nothing can be done.

The media: capital's global village

The alienated being who is the target of Goebbels' machinery can now most of all be found in front of a television set — that reality-conjuring apparatus which is the centerpiece of every modern household, the emblem of and key to universality from Shanghai to Brooklyn. Everywhere people now receive television's simulated meaning, which everywhere duplicates and undermines, and finally colonizes what was formerly human meaning in all its culture-bound manifestations.

People and events captured by communications media, and especially by television, lose what Walter Benjamin called their aura, their internal, intersubjective vitality, the specificity and autonomous significance of the experience — in a sense, their spirit. Only the external aspects of the event can be conveyed by communications media, not meaning or experiential context. In his useful book, *Four Arguments for the Elimination of Television*, Jerry Mander describes how nature is rendered boring and two-dimensional by television, how subtle expressions of emotion become incoherent — for example, how the ceremonies of a group of tribal people, or their subtle motives for protecting a sacred place, are lost when captured by the camera and embedded in a context of televised images.

Although television, through its illusion of immediacy and transparency, seems to represent the most glaringly destructive example of the media, the same can be said of all other forms. The cinema, for example, generates social meaning through the so-called content of the film (as manipulation) and through the act of film-going itself (as alienation) — a spectacularized social interaction mediated by technology. In a movie theater, modern isolation is transposed by the passive reception of images into the false collectivity of the theater audience (which can also be said of modern mass sporting events). As in modern social life itself, like all media, film-going is "a social relation mediated by images," as Guy Debord described modern spectacular society in *The Society of the Spectacle*. (Nowadays the sheer *quantity* of films, the act of frequent film-viewing, either on videos or in movie theaters, also has its troubling effect on human sensibilities.)

But it is no longer a question of the loss of aura in art and drama. Modes of being are expanded and imploded by their constant surveillance. Today one can experience emotions and drama every day for the price of a ticket. But how can these emotions and human values resist trivialization and ironic inversion when they are not grounded in anything but the mechanical transmission of images exchanged as a commodity? When hundreds of media outlets provide any image, any titillation, any pseudo-experience to the point of utter boredom? We surveil ourselves, luridly, as on a screen.

And isn't it also obvious that electronic media works best at duplicating high contrast, rapid, superficial and fragmentary images — which is precisely why the new cultural milieu is overwhelmingly dominated by rapid channel-switching, frenetic computer games, the speed of machines, violence and weapons, and the hard-edged, indifferent nihilism of a degraded, artificial environment? The technofascist style prevalent today, with it fascination with machines, force and speed, works well in the media, until there is no separation between brutalization by power and a internalized, "self-managed" brutalization.

A sky reminds us of a film; witnessing the death of a human being finds meaning in a media episode, replete with musical score. An irreal experience becomes our measure of the real: the circle is completed. The formation of subjectivity, once the result of complex interaction between human beings participating in a symbolic order, has been replaced by media. Some argue that this makes us free to create our own reality — a naive surrender to the solipsism of a mirrored cage. Rather, we are becoming machine-like, more and more determined by technological necessities beyond our control. We now make our covenant with commodities, demand miracles of computers, see our world through a manufactured lens rather than the mind's eye. One eye blinds the other — they are incommensurable. I think of a photograph I saw once of a New Guinea tribesman in traditional dress, taking a photograph with an instamatic camera. What is he becoming, if not another cloned copy of what we are all becoming?

The fact that everyone may someday get "access" to media, that we have all to some degree or another become carriers of media, could be the final logic of centralization spinning out of orbit — the final reduction of the prisoners to the realization that, yes, they truly *do* love Big Brother. Or the realization that nature does not exist but is only what we arbitrarily decide to organize, or that we do not experience a place until we have the photograph. The age of the *genuine imitation*. The paleolithic cave walls are redone to protect the originals which themselves are shut forever — these imitations are "authentic," of course, but the spirit of the cave has fled. Even the copies will inevitably become historical artifacts to be preserved; this is "art," do you have your ticket, sir? There is no aura. For an aboriginal tribal person, the mountain speaks, and a communication is established. For the tourist, it is domesticated, desiccated — a dead image for the photo album.

Though print media are being eclipsed by television and computers, they now function similarly, with their spurious claim to "objectivity," their mutilating process of selection and editing, their automatic reinforcement of the status quo, their absolute accumulation. The greater the scope, the more frequent the publication, the more newspapers and magazines in particular impose their model of fragmented, ideologized reality. While the corporate (and in some places the state) press functions as part of a Big Lie apparatus, it distorts the information it transmits both in the content and in the context in which it presents it. Newspaper-reading and addiction to news in general have become another version of the imperial circus, a kind of illiteracy which makes people as much the creatures of rumor and manipulation (through advertising and public relations) as they were prior to modernization and the rise of a public education system which was supposed to make informed citizens of them. In fact, as the techniques and scope of media have expanded, people have tended to become more manipulated than ever.

Ellul writes, "Let us not say: 'If one gave them good things to read ... if these people received a better education ...' Such an argument has no validity because things just are not that way. Let us not say, either: 'This is only the first stage'; in France, the first stage was reached half a century ago, and we still are very far from attaining the second ... Actually, the most obvious result of primary education in the nineteenth and twentieth centuries was to make the individual susceptible to propaganda."

But how do people confront centralized power, with its machinery of deceit, without resorting to media? Even those who oppose totalitarianism need to marshal information to spread their ideas, win and inform their allies. Yet people's capacity to resist the structures of domination is undermined by the overall effect of media. Can we possibly defeat the empire in a penny-ante game of facts when a single pronouncement by that media image called a "President" — say, that this week's enemy nation is "terrorist" and must be destroyed — drowns out the truth? If people can be moved to resist domination only by means of mass media, if they can only be directed to resist as they are now to obey, what can this portend for human freedom? The "global village" is capital's village; it is antithetical to any genuine village, community or communication.

A revolution in human response

Technology transmutes our experience — won't it also result in undermining our very organism, rather than continually improving upon it, as it promises? In a wisecracking, hucksterish tone, one celebratory popularization of the new technologies, *The Techno/Peasant Survival Manual*, describes an electrode helmet hooked up to a microcomputer capable of analyzing and measuring the activity of the human brain, "studying its electrical output in units of 500 milliseconds ... With this ability to quantify human thought, the technocrats are not only learning how we think, they are in the process of challenging our very definitions of intelligence."

Of course, computers say little or nothing about how people think, because human thought is not quantifiable or reducible to computer operations. What *is* happening is that fundamental attitudes are changing, and with them, a definition of something the technocratic structure cannot really comprehend without transmuting its very nature. New communications environments socialize people in ways far different from age-old customs and modes in which they once learned to think, feel and behave like human beings; thus, technological structures are "revolutionizing" human response by forcing life to conform to the parameters of the machines. This quantification will reshape thought, which is potentially mutable; it will become "true" by force, as the railroad became more true than the buffalo, and the sheep enclosure more true than the commons.

Even the shape of the child's developing brain is said to be changing. Children were formerly socialized through conversation in an intimate milieu; now, in the typical family living room with its television shrine, the areas of the child's brain once stimulated by conversation are increasingly developed by passively consuming the visually exciting (but kinesthetically debilitating or distorting) images of tv and video games. No one can say exactly what this means, though at a minimum, increased hyper-activity and decreased attention span may be two consequences. (Instead of urging caution, the education philosopher I heard relate this disturbing story went on to propose *more* computer- and video-based "interactive" technology in schools to teach this changing child.)

What can conform to the computer, what can be transmitted by the technology, will remain; what cannot will vanish. That which remains will also be transformed by its isolation from that which is eliminated, and we will be changed irrevocably in the process. As language is reshaped, language will reshape daily life. Certain modes of thinking will simply atrophy and disappear, like rare, specialized species of birds. Later generations will not miss what they never had; the domain of language and meaning will be the domain of the screen. History will be the history on the screens; any subtlety, any memory which does not fit will be undecipherable, incoherent.

Our total dependence on technology parallels our dependence on the political state. New technologies, "interfaced" with the technical-bureaucratic, nuclear-cybernetic police state, are creating a qualitatively new form of domination. We are only a step away from the universal computerized identification system. Technology is already preparing the ground for more pervasive forms of control than simple data files on individuals. As forms of control such as total computerization, polygraph tests, psychological conditioning, subliminal suggestion, and electronic and video eavesdropping become part of the given environment, they will be perceived as natural as superhighways and shopping malls are today.

But while there is reason for concern about computer threats to privacy, a deepening privatization, with a computerized television in every room as its apotheosis, makes the police almost superfluous. Eventually computer technology may have no need of the methods it employs today. According to Lewis M. Branscomb, Vice President and Chief Scientist of IBM, the "ultimate computer" will be biological, patterned on DNA and cultivated in a petri dish. "If such a computer could be integrated with memory of comparable speed and compactness, implanted inside the skull and interfaced with the brain," the Diagram Group authors of *The Techno/ Peasant Survival Manual* enthuse, "human beings would have more computer power than exists in the world today." Genetic engineering, cloning, integrating the human brain into cybernetic systems — is there any doubt that these developments will render human beings obsolete just as industrial technology undermined earlier human communities? There may no longer be any need to monitor an anarchic, unruly mass, since all the controls will be built in from the start. The "irrational" aspects of culture, of love, of death will be suppressed.

Mechanization penetrates every province

If technology is effective in creating, directly or indirectly, ever more powerful modes of domination in its wake, it is not nearly as successful when used to curb its own development and the conflicts, devastations and crises which ensue. It suppresses "irrationality," which then takes its revenge in the greater irrationalities of mass technics. (One can only imagine what manner of disaster would follow an absurd attempt to "interface" a computer with a human brain.) According to the technocrats, technology can be curbed and made to serve human needs through "technology assessment." "Futurist" Alvin Toffler (*futurist* being a euphemism for high-paid consulting huckster) argues, for example, that it is "sometimes possible to test new technology in limited areas, among limited groups, studying its secondary impacts before releasing it for diffusion."

Toffler's reification of technology into a simple system used in an isolated area, at the discretion of experts and managers, fails to understand how technology transforms the environment, and most importantly, how it is already trapped within its own procedural inertia. Clearly, the new technologies appearing everywhere simultaneously cannot be isolated to study their effects — the effects of the whole system must be taken into account, not the laboratory effects of an isolated component. Laboratory experiments on a given geographical area or social group performed by a powerful, bureaucratic hierarchy of technicians and managers are themselves technology and carry its social implications within them.

Discussing the mechanization of bread baking, Giedion shows how technology, becoming trapped within its own instrumentality and centered on the hyperrationality of procedure, not only shifts an activity beyond the control of individuals, but ultimately undermines the very ends it started out to accomplish. He asks, how did bread, which was successfully produced locally and on a small scale, succumb to large mechanization? More importantly, how was it that public taste was altered regarding the nature of the "staff of life," which had changed little over the course of centuries, and which "among foodstuffs ... has always held a status bordering on the symbolic"?

Mechanization began to penetrate every province of life after 1900, including agriculture and food. Since technology demands increasing outlays and sophisticated machinery, new modes of distribution and consumption are devised which eclipse the local baker. Massification demands uniformity, but uniformity undermines bread. "The complicated machinery of full mechanization has altered its structure and converted it into a body that is neither bread nor cake, but something half-way between the two. Whatever new enrichments can be devised, nothing can really help as long as this sweetish softness continues to haunt its structure."

How taste was adulterated, how "ancient instincts were warped," cannot be easily explained. Again, what is important is not a specific moment in the transformation of techniques, nor that specific forms of technology were employed, but the overall process of massification by which simple, organic activities are wrested from the community and the household and appropriated by the megamachine. Bread is the product of a large cycle beginning with the planting of wheat. Mechanization invades every sector of the organic and undermines it, forever altering the structure of agriculture, of the farmer, of food. Not only is bread undermined by mechanization; the farmer is driven from the land. Giedion asks, "Does the changing farmer reflect, but more conspicuously, a process that is everywhere at work? ... Does the transformation into wandering unemployed of people who for centuries had tilled the soil correspond to what is happening in each of us?"

The Diagram Group gushes, "Technology ... will change the quality, if not the nature, of everything. Your job and your worklife will not be the same. Your home will not be the same. Your thoughts will not be the same ... We are talking about an increase in the rate of innovation unprecedented in human history, what some scientists are now calling spiral evolution." Says Robert Jastrow, Director of NASA's Goddard Space Institute: "In another 15 years or so we will see the computer as an emergent form of life."

Over a hundred years ago, Samuel Butler expressed the same idea as satire in his ironical utopian novel *Erewhon*, lampooning the positivist

popularization of Darwinism and the widespread belief that mechanization would usher in paradise, and suggesting that the theory of evolution
was also applicable to machines. "It appears to us that we are creating our
own successors," he wrote. "We are daily adding to the beauty and deli-
cacy of their physical organization; we are daily giving them greater power
and supplying by all sorts of ingenious contrivances that self-regulating,
self-acting power which will be to them what intellect has been to the human race." No longer does Butler's humor seem so humorous or far-fetched.
What begins as farce ends as tragedy. Perhaps humanity will find itself
even further reduced from being a mere appendage to the machine to a
hindrance.

Only the circuitry acts

Nowhere do we see this possibility more clearly than in the emerging
biotechnology, the latest frontier for capital, which reduces the natural world
to a single monolithic "logic" — capital's logic of accumulation and control. As Baudrillard puts it in *Simulations*, "that delirious illusion of uniting
the world under the aegis of a single principle" unites totalitarianism and
the "fascination of the biological ... From a capitalist-productivist society
to a neo-capitalist cybernetic order that aims now at total control. This is
the mutation for which the biological theorization of the code prepares the
ground."

"We must think of the media as if they were ... a sort of genetic code
which controls the mutation of the real into the hyperreal," writes
Baudrillard. The destruction of meaning in the media foreshadows the can-
nibalization by capital of the sources of life itself. The "operational configuration," "the correct strategic model," are the same: life defined by information, information as "genetic code," no longer necessarily "centralized"
but molecular, no longer exactly imposed but implanted — a "genesis of
simulacra," as in photography, in which the original, with its human aura,
its peculiar irreducibility to this technocratic-rationalist model, vanishes
— or is vanquished.

In another context, Frederick Turner (not to be confused with the
author of *Beyond Geography*) writes in what can only be described as a
techno-spiritualist/fascist manifesto ("Technology and the Future of the
Imagination," *Harper's*, November 1984), that " our silicon photograph [or
circuit] doesn't merely represent something; it does what it is a photograph of — in a sense it is a miraculous picture, like that of Our Lady of
Guadalupe: it not only depicts, but does; it is not just a representation, but
reality; it is not just a piece of knowledge, but a piece of being; it is not just
epistemology but ontology."

What the Great Chain of Being was for medieval society, and the clock-like universe for the mechanical-industrial revolution, the genetic code, the molecular cell, and the clone or simulacrum are for the Brave New World looming today. The invasion by capital into the fundamental structures of life can only result in dangerous homogenization in the service of "total control," and, inevitably, the collapse of complex life systems on this planet. Once more the enemy hides behind a "humane" cloak — this time not religious salvation, nor simply progress or democracy, but the conquest of disease and famine. To challenge this further manifestation of progress, according to the ruling paradigm, is to oppose curing disease, to turn away from the hungry. Once again only technology and its promise — a totally administered world — can supposedly save us. And once more, it all makes "perfect sense" because it corresponds to the operational configurations of the culture as a whole.

If engineered genetic material corresponds to the silicon photograph, a proper response might be learned from Crazy Horse, the Oglala mystic of whom no photograph was ever taken, who answered requests to photograph him by saying, "My friend, why should you wish to shorten my life by taking from me my shadow?" Now all our shadows are in grave danger from more ferocious "soul catchers," sorcerers and golem-manufacturers, ready to unleash a final paroxym of plagues.

Or is the ultimate plague a nuclear war? Modern technological development has always been embedded most deeply in expanding war and competing war machines. As propagandists lull us to sleep with promises of cybernetic technotopia, other technicians study readouts for their attack scenarios. Ultimately, it makes no difference whether a final war (or series of wars) is initiated by system errors or by the system's proper functioning; these two possible modalities of the machinery represent its entire range. No computer warns of impending annihilation — the life force is not, and cannot be programmed into them. And just as human society is tending to be reduced to the circulation of reified information, so is it falling under the sway of a bureaucratic apparatus which has turned the "unthinkable" — nuclear megacide, ecological collapse — into business-as-usual. No human considerations influence its imperative or momentum; no dramatic descriptions of the consequences of its unremarkable, everyday acts appear in the readouts. No passion moves the technicians from their course. As the archetypical nuclear bureaucrat Herman Kahn once wrote (in *Thinking the Unthinkable*), "To mention such things [as nuclear holocaust] may be important. To dwell on them is morbid, and gets in the way of the information." Where the discourse is curtailed to less than a shadow, so too are human beings. Only the circuitry acts; human response is suffocated.

Technology refused

Skepticism toward progress is typically dismissed as dangerous, atavistic and irrational. In *The Existential Pleasures of Engineering*, one professional apologist for technology, Samuel C. Florman, writes, "[F]rightened and dismayed by the unfolding of the human drama in our time, yearning for simple solutions where there can be none, and refusing to acknowledge that the true source of our problems is nothing other than the irrepressible human will," people who express luddite worries "have deluded themselves with the doctrine of anti-technology." The increasing popularity of such views, he insists, "adds the dangers inherent in self-deception to all of the other dangers we already face."

While indirectly acknowledging the significant dangers of mass technics, Florman apparently feels that declining technological optimism is responsible for technology's ravages, rather than being a symptom or consequence of them. The "other dangers we already face" — dangers which of course are in no way to be blamed on technology — are simply the result of "the type of creature man is." Of course, the "type of creature man is" has made this dangerous technology. Furthermore, Florman's reasoning coincides with the attitudes and interests of this society's political, corporate and military elites. "So fast do times change, because of technology," intones a United Technologies advertisement, "that some people, disoriented by the pace, express yearning for simpler times. They'd like to turn back the technological clock. But longing for the primitive is utter folly. It is fantasy. Life was no simpler for early people than it is for us. Actually, it was far crueler. Turning backward would not expunge any of today's problems. With technological development curtailed, the problems would fester even as the means for solving them were blunted. To curb technology would be to squelch innovation, stifle imagination, and cap the human spirit."

It doesn't occur to these publicists that curbing technology might itself be an innovative strategy of human imagination and spirit. But to doubt the ideology of scientific progress does not necessarily signify abandoning science altogether. Nor does a scientifically sophisticated outlook automatically endorse technological development. As another possibility, Ellul points to the ancient Greeks. Though they were technically and scientifically sophisticated, the Greeks

> were suspicious of technical activity because it represented an aspect of brute force and implied a want of moderation … In Greece a conscious effort was made to economize on means and to reduce the sphere of influence of technique. No one sought to apply scientific thought technically, because scientific thought corresponded to a conception of life, to wisdom. The great preoccupation

of the Greeks was balance, harmony and moderation; hence, they fiercely resisted the unrestrained force inherent in technique, and rejected it because of its potentialities.

One could argue that the convenience of slavery explains the anti-technological and anti-utilitarian attitudes of the Greeks. While slavery as a system was certainly related — among a multitude of factors — to the low regard in Greek culture for manual labor and the lack of utilitarian values among its elites, to reduce a cultural outlook to a single factor is absurd. One could just as easily claim that the philosophical quest, the notion of tragedy, and other cultural aspects were the results of slavery. But slavery has existed in many societies and cultures, including the expanding industrial civilization of the United States. That the Greeks could have a scientific outlook without a technological-utilitarian basis proves, rather, that such a conception of life is possible, and therefore a science without slavery and without mass technics is also possible.

Defenders of scientific rationality usually paint themselves in Voltairian hues, but it is they who rely on outmoded formulas which no longer (and perhaps never did) correspond to reality. The contemporary scientism of the great majority, with its mantra that progress is unstoppable and its weird mix of mastery and submission, is little more than an accumulation of unsubstantiated platitudes — the general theory of this world, its logic in a popular form, its moral sanction, its universal ground for consolation and justification. As technological optimism erodes, its defenders invoke a caricature of the Enlightenment to ward off the evil spirits of unsanctioned "irrationality."

Yet what modern ideology stigmatizes as irrational might be better thought of as *an alternative rationality or reason.* In the eighteenth century, a Delaware Indian who came to be known as the Delaware Prophet, and whose influence on the Indians who fought with Pontiac during the uprising in 1763 is documented in Howard Peckham's *Pontiac and the Indian Uprising*, "decried the baneful influence of all white men because it had brought the Indians to their present unhappy plight. He was an evangelist, a revivalist, preaching a new religion. He was trying to change the personal habits of the Indians in order to free them from imported vices and make them entirely self-dependent. He gave his hearers faith and hope that they could live without the manufactures of the white men."

This critic of technology wasn't worrying about possible future effects of the manufactured products bestowed by traders on his people, he was announcing the *actual* decline of native communal solidarity and independence. Pontiac quoted the Delaware Prophet to his followers in April 1763 as saying, "I know that those whom ye call the children of your Great Father supply your needs, but if ye were not evil, as ye are, ye could surely do without them. Ye could live as ye did live before knowing them ... Did ye not live by the bow and arrow? Ye had no need of gun or powder, or anything else, and nevertheless ye caught animals to live upon and to dress yourself with their skins. . . ."

"Primitive fears"

Such insights, and particularly any reference to them now, are usually dismissed as romantic nostalgia. "It took time and experience," writes that well-known devotee of industrialism, Marx, "before the workpeople learnt to distinguish between machinery and its employment by capital, and to direct their attacks, not against the material instruments of production, but against the mode in which they are used." (*Capital*) But despite the historical justifications of marxist and capitalist alike, both the mode and the increasingly ubiquitous machinery managed in time to domesticate the "workpeople" even further, transforming them as a class into an integral component of industrialism.

Perhaps they should have been good marxists and gone willingly into the satanic mills with the idea of developing these "means of production" to inherit them later, but their own practical wisdom told them otherwise. As E.P. Thompson writes in his classic study, *The Making of the English Working Class*, "despite all the homilies ... (then and subsequently) as to the beneficial consequences" of industrialization — "arguments which, in any case, the Luddites were intelligent enough to weigh in their minds for themselves — the machine-breakers, and not the tract-writers, made the most realistic assessment of the short-term effects ... The later history of the stockingers and cotton-weavers [two crafts destroyed by industrialization] provides scarcely more evidence for the 'progressive' view of the advantages of the breakdown of custom and of restrictive practices. . . ."

Thompson is correct in assessing the basic rational practicality of the luddites, who resisted so fiercely because they had a clear understanding of their immediate prospects. But it's clearer now that they also anticipated, as well as anyone could in their time and place, the eventual, tragic demise not only of vernacular and village society but of the classical workers movement itself, along with its urban context — to be replaced by an atomized servitude completely subject to the centrifugal logic and the pernicious whims of contemporary urban-industrial, market-dominated, mass society. The romantic reaction against mechanization and industrialism has also been maligned, and must be reappraised and reaffirmed in light of what has come since. No one, in any case, seriously argues a literal return to the life of ancient Greeks or eighteenth century Indians. But the Greek emphasis on harmony, balance and moderation, and the Indians' stubborn desire to resist dependence, are worthy models in elaborating our own response to these fundamental questions. At a minimum, they make it reasonable for us to challenge the next wave, and the next, and the next — something the ideologies of scientism and progress have little prepared us to do.

If some tend to look to previous modes of life for insights into the changes brought about by modern technology and possible alternatives to it, others dismiss the insights of tribal and traditional societies altogether by bringing up those societies' injustices, conflicts and practices incomprehensible to us. No society is perfect, and all have conflicts. Yet modernization has in fact superseded few age-old problems; for the most part it has suppressed without resolving them, intensified them, or replaced them with even greater ones.

Traditional societies might have resolved their own injustices or done so through interaction with others without causing vast harm to deeply rooted subsistence patterns; after all, ancient injustices have social and ethical bases and are not a function of the relative level of technical development. But modernizing missionaries have for the most part only succeeded in bursting traditional societies and laying the basis for dependency on mass technics. In the end the natives are "converted" to democracy, or to socialism, at the point of a gun. When the process is completed — no democracy, no socialism, and no natives. The impulse to dissect and improve small, idiosyncratic, subsistence societies, to turn them into modern, secular, industrial nation-states — be it from the optic of universal (western) reason, or the dialectic, or "historical necessity" — results in monocultural conquest and integration into global industrial capitalism.

The related dogma that "underdeveloped" societies were in any case fatally flawed, and therefore poised to succumb not only derives its strength from a pervasive sense of powerlessness to preserve former modes of life and communities, no matter what their merits; it also provides ongoing justification for the obliteration of small societies still coming into contact with urban-industrial expansion. It is a species of blaming the victim. But their demise is more readily explained by the tecnical, economic and military might of the invading civilization and its power to impose relations of dependence. As Francis Jennings observes in *The Invasion of America* (to provide one example), it was not the defects in indigenous North American societies that caused them to be undermined by European mercantile civilization, but (at least in part) their *virtues*. Their gift economy, Jennings writes, made it impossible for them to understand or conform to European business practices. Their culture allowed them to become traders, but they could never become capitalists. "[I]n a sense one can say that the Indians universally failed to acquire capital because they did not want it."

The indigenous refusal of economic relations — neither wholly rational nor irrational, neither wholly conscious nor unconscious, but a dialectical interaction between these polarities — parallels the ancient Greeks' refusal of technology. Their notions of life were utterly foreign to the economic-instrumental obsession by which modern civilization measures all things. And in the case of the Indians, because of the overwhelming power of the invaders, they succumbed — as societies, cultures, languages, innumerable subsistence skills and subtle ecological relationships continue to crumble. Thus in a sense the luddites remain the contemporaries of ranchers in Minnesota who felled power line pylons built across their land in the 1970s, and the anti-development, anti-toxics and anti-nuclear movements that have flourished at the end of the twentieth century. The Delaware Prophet is the contemporary of the Waimiri Atroari people in Brazil, who consistently fought invasions by missionaries, Indian agents, and road-building crews in the 1960s and 1970s, and of Indians in Quebec fighting the Canadian government for their lands since the increase of oil and gas exploration there.

In Quebec, a Montagnais Indian, speaking for all, testified, "Our way of life is being taken away from us." The Montagnais had been "promised that with houses and schools and clinics and welfare we could be happy." But the promise was not fulfilled. "Now we know it was all lies. We were happier when we lived in tents." No cheerful bromide about the ultimate benefits of progress can respond adequately to this somber recognition.

Technology out of control

Devouring the otherness of the past has not saved modern civilization from deepening crisis. The civilization that promised to abolish all previous forms of irrationality has created a suicidal, trip-wire, exterminist system. Technological runaway is evident; we do not know if we will be destroyed altogether in some technologically induced eco-spasm, or transmuted into an unrecognizable entity shaped by genetic, cybernetic and pharmacological techniques. The managerial notion of "technology assessment" by which technocrats try to rationalize technological growth is comparable to attempting to stop a car careening out of control by referring to the driver's manual. Technology's efficiency is inefficient, its engineering obtuse and myopic.

The highly divided, centrifugal nature of the technical-bureaucratic apparatus undermines its own planning, making it chaotic. Each technical sector pursues its own ends separate from the totality, while each bureaucracy and corporate pyramid, each rival racket, pursues its own narrow social interest. There is never enough information to make proper decisions; the megamachine's complicated, multiple inputs undermine its own controls and methods. A computer coughs in some air-conditioned sanctum, and thousands, perhaps millions, die. Knowledge is undermined by its own over-rationalization, quantification and accumulation, just as bread is negated by its own standardization. Who can truly say, for example, that they are in control of nuclear technology? Meanwhile the system speeds along at an ever faster pace.

Even defenders of technology admit that it tends to move beyond human control. Most counter that technology is not the problem, but rather humanity's inability to "master" itself. But humanity has always grappled with its darker side; how could complex techniques and dependence on enormously complicated, dangerous technological systems make the psychic and social challenge easier? Even the question of "self-mastery" becomes problematic in the face of the changes wrought in human character by technology. What will define humanity in a hundred years if technology holds sway?

In *The Conquest of Nature: Technology and Its Consequences*, R. J. Forbes argues that while "it is possible to see a tendency in the political-technological combination to take on a gestalt of its own and to follow its own 'laws,'" we should rely on "the inner faith of the men who make the basic inventions." That scientific-technological rationality must finally rely on an undemonstrated faith in its ability to harness demons it wantonly unleashes — a faith in technicians already completely enclosed in their organizations and practices — is an irony lost on Forbes. We have relied on their "inner faith" for too long; even their best intentions work against us.

"There are no easy answers," announces an oil company advertisement. "Without question, we must find more oil. And we must learn to use the oil we have more efficiently. So where do we start?" *Without question* — such propaganda promotes the anxiety that we are trapped in technology, with no way out. Better to follow the program to the end. An IBM ad says, "Most of us can't help feeling nostalgic for an earlier, simpler era when most of life's dealings were face-to-face. But chaos would surely result if we tried to conduct all of our dealings that way today. There are just too many of us. We are too mobile. The things we do are too complex — and the pace of life is too fast."

A technological culture and its demands serve to justify the technology which imposes them. Those who doubt are cranks, while the calm, reasoned logic of military strategists, technical experts, bureaucrats and scientists is passed off as wisdom. Thus, during the 1979 partial meltdown at the Three Mile Island nuclear power plant in Harrisburg, Pennsylvania, at the moment in which it was unclear what was going to happen to the bubble in the reactor container, a typical headline read, "Experts Optimistic." Aren't they always? "Without question, we must find more oil," and create more energy, mine more minerals, cut more trees, build more roads and factories, cultivate more land, computerize more schools, accumulate more information ... If we accept the premises, we are stuck with the conclusions. In the end, technology is legitimated by its search for solutions to the very destruction *it* has caused. What is to be done with chemical and nuclear wastes, ruined soils and contaminated seas? Here the technicians insist, "You need us." But their "solutions" not only naturalize and prolong the original causes of the disaster, they tend to aggravate it further. To decline to join the chorus is to seek "easy answers."

True, there are no easy answers. But we can at least begin by questioning the idea of technology as sacred and irrevocable, and start looking at the world once more with human eyes and articulating its promise in human terms. We must begin to envision the radical deconstruction of mass society.

Toward an epistemological luddism

I recognize the contradictions in even publishing this essay. I am not sure how to move beyond the code; in order to do so, with tremendous ambivalence and doubt, I partake in it in a limited, awkward, conditional way. It is an act of desperation. Perhaps to some degree it is a question of orientation; I think it fair to distinguish between using established technical means to communicate out of pragmatic necessity, and volunteering to help construct the latest means. We need the courage to explore a process of change in our thinking and practice — to learn how we might become less dependent on machines, less linked to "world communications," not more.

Of course, one can't wish mass society away; a simplistic, monolithic response to the daunting technical problems confronting us, added to the social crisis we are experiencing, would be pointless and impossible. But it is the technological system which offers "easy answers" — starting with unquestioning surrender to whatever sorcery it dishes up next. We *can* respond without accepting its terms. We *can* swim against capital's current. Abolishing mass technics means *learning to live in a different way* — something societies have done in the past, and which they can learn to do again. We have to nurture trust, not in experts, but in our own innate capacity to find our way.

In *Autonomous Technology*, Langdon Winner suggests that a possible way to halt the decaying juggernaut would be to begin dismantling problematic technological structures and to refuse to repair systems that are breaking down. This would also imply rejecting newly devised technological systems meant to fix or replace the old. "This I would propose not as a solution in itself," he writes, "but as a method of inquiry." In this way we could investigate dependency and the pathways to autonomy and self-sufficiency. Such an "epistemological luddism," to use Winner's term, could help us to break up the structures of daily life, and to take meaning back from the meaning-manufacturing apparatus of the mass media, renew a human discourse based on community, solidarity and reciprocity, and destroy the universal deference to machines, experts and information. Otherwise, we face either machine-induced cataclysm or mutilation beyond recognition of the human spirit. For human beings, the practical result will be the same.

For now, let us attend to first things first — by considering the possibility of a conscious break with urban-industrial civilization, a break which does not attempt to return to prior modes of refusal (which would be impossible anyway), but which surpasses them by elaborating its own, at the far limits of a modernity already in decay. We begin by annunciating the possibility of such a decision — a very small step, but we begin where we can. A new culture can arise from that small step, from our first awkward acts of refusal to become mere instruments. Of course, such a culture wouldn't be entirely new, but would derive its strength from an old yet contemporary wisdom, as ancient and as contemporary as the Delaware prophet and the Chinese philosopher Chuangtse, who said: "Whoever uses machines does all his work like a machine. He who does his work like a machine grows a heart like a machine, and he who carries the heart of a machine in his breast loses his simplicity. It is not that I do not know of such things; I am ashamed to use them." When we begin listening to the heart, we will be ashamed to use such things, or to be used by them.

(1981–1985/1997)

THE SNOWMOBILE REVOLUTION: NOTES ON TECHNOLOGICAL INVASION

 The unquestioned authority of the technological way of life in the modern world of the West derives much of its power from the fact that the destructive effects of its emergence are no longer apparent to those who now live entirely within its shadow. Memory is short, and most people do not long for what they cannot remember. But a look at emerging industrialism and the rise of technological civilization shows that even though these forces grew gradually in the western milieu which gave birth to them, the results were fatal to human community.

How much clearer this is then, and how flimsy the argument based on the universal amnesia that declares the neutrality of technology, when one considers the technological invasion of so-called "precapitalist" societies. Entire societies collapse overnight under the onslaught of relocation, industrialization, clock time, television, guns, motorcycles; the "old ways" are burst not only by massive, dramatic changes but by the little things which leak into a culture from industrial capitalism. Eventually the culture and the people are destroyed; the physical survivors become proletarians of the technological civilization, usually at its very bottom rungs. As Jacques Ellul writes in *The Technological Society*, "Technical invasion does not involve the simple addition of new values to old ones. It does not put new wine into old bottles; it does not introduce new content into old forms. The old bottles are being broken."

The Bikini islanders

An extreme example of this process can be seen in the relocation of the Bikini Islanders from their atoll in 1946 by the United States government in order to use the area for nuclear weapons tests. The Bikinians had already suffered cultural crisis from many sources, including Japanese military conquest and the conversion of the islanders to Christianity by missionaries. In 1946, the U.S. Navy convinced the Bikinians that they should sacrifice their island for the good of all humanity, using the Bible to compare them to the Israelites, "who the Lord saved from their enemy and led them to the Promised Land." The Bikinians, awed by the power of their American sponsors and accustomed to the authority imposed by outsiders, consented to abandon their homeland.

In "Relocation and Technological Change in Micronesia" (in *Technology and Social Change*, edited by H. Russell Bernard and Pertti J. Pelto), Robert Kiste describes the deculturization of the Bikini islanders. The Bikinians were first moved to the uninhabited island of Rongerik, but it was unlike their home and they could not adjust. New ecological conditions and government intervention demoralized the people. Houses and canoes deteriorated for lack of raw materials. Their traditional forms of association, work and distribution were destroyed by a committee form of delegation and authority.

Rationing was implemented, and the Bikinians were reduced to starvation. After two years at Rongerik, they were moved once again to Kwajalein where they were fed, housed and clothed by the military, which contributed to a growing sense of dependence and inferiority. Some were put to work, and many came to like the soft drinks, ice cream, candy and Hollywood movies which they were offered by the Americans. When a permanent location was found for them on Kili (all of the islands are in the Marshall islands), their canoes had deteriorated to such a degree that they were left behind. Primarily a fishing people (who had done some minimal agricultural activity), the Bikinians were completely cut off from their former way of life. Kili was not even appropriate for fishing, with heavy seas, few marine resources, no lagoon or sheltered fishing area, and no protective anchorage for vessels. The Bikinians had to change their entire way of life if they were going to survive on Kili. Attempts to engage in agriculture were only minimally successful, in part because of the traditional lack of interest in such work, and also because the islanders received assistance and a trust fund from the U.S. government. When in the 1950s the houses on the island needed repairs, rather than using pandanus leaf thatch, their original material on Bikini (which in any case was relatively scarce on Kili), they had come to prefer imported building materials and demanded supplies.

Their outbursts of dissatisfaction were generally accompanied by demands for an increase in their trust fund, along with demands to return home. "The past at Bikini," writes Kiste, "became something of a Golden Age in the stories told by the elders." A song reflecting their longing for Bikini was composed:

Nothing can be right for me, I cannot be happy.
As I sleep on my sleeping mat and pillow, I dream about my
atoll and its beloved places.
When in dreams I hear the sounds I once knew my memories
make me "homesick."
It is then that nostalgia overwhelms me and makes me weep
because it is more than I can stand.

The Government has begun to return the various peoples of the atolls to their homelands, and already the problem of radiation contamination is beginning to be noted. But even if the radiation could be cleaned up and the atoll restored to its original state, the people have been changed. A whole generation grew to maturity during the diaspora, and the old ways and the old skills have more or less disappeared. Technological civilization cannot put back what it has taken away.

The snowmobile revolution

A less extreme example is that of the "snowmobile revolution" above the arctic circle, among Lapps (Sami), Eskimos and other northern peoples. "In places where the snowmobile has been integrated into major parts of the economic system, significant changes are occurring in practically all aspects of culture," write Pertti J. Pelto and Ludger Muller-Wille in the same book. We will concentrate on the Skolt Lapps.

Snowmobiles were first introduced into Finland in 1961-62, and within a year, westernized people such as schoolteachers and forest rangers began buying them. Later, wealthier Lapp reindeer herdsmen bought snowmobiles, initiating a trend in which increasing numbers of herdsmen purchased the machines and sold their previously indispensable draught reindeer to Finns who wanted the animals for racing. (A parallel trend occurs when Eskimos sell their dogs to Canadians who want them for racing.)

The introduction of snowmobiles rapidly changed the lives of Lappish people, immediately affecting the character of the traditional annual reindeer roundup. The age-old methods of herding were abandoned in favor of the quicker method of stampede herding with snowmobiles. The early owners of the vehicles derived tremendous economic advantages, but the normal rhythms of the seasonal roundup were so disrupted that the fertility and population of the herds plummeted sharply. As more herders were forced to buy machines to keep up with the new herding methods and as the herds shrank, the advantages enjoyed by the earliest owners diminished.

But the situation of those who purchased machines later was even worse. Many were forced to sell their stock and eventually gave up herding altogether. "Because the later purchasers are poorer in reindeer herds, material goods, wage incomes and nearly every other economic index, they would appear to be in further economic jeopardy now than they were before the snowmobile revolution," write the authors. Here one discerns that it isn't simply a question of a single technology, but a complex of techniques and social relations which have become more and more prevalent among the Lapps.

But something else has taken place in the course of these events. The snowmobile has passed from being "simply" an innovation, to being an advantage for a small group, eventually to a generalized phenomenon, and finally to a necessity for survival. "Economic activities have become enormously speeded up in Lapland," write Pelto and Muller-Wille, "especially in reindeer herding, and each individual is locked into a very complex association system in which he does not have the possibility of setting his own work pace. This lesson was brought home when we interviewed the most traditional herdsman of the Skolt Lapp community in Sevettijarvi. He told us that he dislikes the snowmobiles, but next year (1968) he must purchase one in order to get around to all the roundups and other important herding events. Those men who cannot buy snowmobiles appear to be at a serious disadvantage under present conditions ... Each individual reindeer herder is practically forced to acquire a machine, just to keep up."

In a subsequent book, *The Snowmobile Revolution: Technology and Social Change in the Arctic*, Pelto observes that distinct groups of "winners" and "losers," a class society, has emerged from the process of technological invasion among the Lapps. Those who adapt best to the new technology and to the necessities of the new money economy have become the most powerful group in the society, while those who cling to the old ways end up "unemployed" (a status unknown before the advent of technology). Without herds, they are eventually forced to become wage laborers. Langdon Winner, discussing Pelto's research in his book *Autonomous Technology*, writes, "The development of a more complex system of socioeconomic differentiation was accompanied by the rise of 'needs' associated with a more modern style of life — washing machines, household gas, telephones, and chain saws. How successfully a Skolt adapted to the snowmobile determined, by and large, his access to these goods. Hence, what had previously been a highly egalitarian society became inegalitarian and hierarchical almost overnight."

The ecological impact of snowmobiles has become well known in the last few years. In Finland, for example, hunters using snowmobiles wiped out most of the bear population in a single season. Other aspects of the snowmobile besides the massive decimation of animal life are the noise pollution, the accumulations in junkyards of worn out machines, air pollution from the combustion engines, and the overall impetus it gives to the commodity production and consumption cycle of urban industrialism. But it is also taking its toll on the Lapps and other northern peoples and their cultures. The comment is frequently made, by snowmobile owners and nonowners alike, that "those machines are eating the reindeer." As the reindeer go, so go the Lapps. Their growing technological and economic dependence on civilization assure their integration into it and their cultural annihilation. As they forget their old skills and former modes of life, they will simply become shattered fragments and victims of capital. They will become like us, alienated "modern citizens."

A note on anthropology

As anthropologists have come to realize the unprecedented manner in which people's lives have been changed by technological invasion, they have, in the fashion of all academics, turned the study of this process into a professional exercise. Of course, by the time they arrive, the victims of invasion have already undergone precipitous transformations, so one cannot be exactly sure what it is they are trying to accomplish apart from research for its own sake. They usually discover commonplaces which were obvious from the beginning — e.g., that technology is changing everything in "uncertain" ways — and conclude by proposing further unending studies of the process. To begin to oppose technology would be unthinkable for them since technological civilization is the wave of the future, and to oppose it would in any case upset their precious "objectivity."

Editors Pelto and Bernard of *Technology and Social Change*, for example, write that "some tales of technical modification can be real horror stories." But, they maintain, "Because few of us would prefer to give up our 'civilized' comforts to return to a hunting and gathering existence, it would be fatuous to assert that all technological change throughout history has been bad." But the question is not our return to modes which have been destroyed — whoever "we" think we are — but the contemporary destruction of these modes where they remain, what the process of this civilization means, and whether or not there are possibilities outside this form that all human life is taking.

Technology's effects "are not at all clear yet," they claim, since "the long-range effects of snowmobile ownership and use have not been played out ... On-going research throughout the next few years — in several different locations — is essential for an evaluation of the full impact of snowmobiles on arctic populations." One can only wonder why they would bother. The results are transparent. The anthros will get grants and fellowships to study the integration of the arctic peoples into the modern, undifferentiated way of life. But they will eventually study themselves out of a meal ticket since no one will be interested in knowing the culture of a third-generation tribal who works in a gas station and gets his ideas from national television. The anthros will either disappear along with the "quaint" peoples they study or become engineers of social control and technicians of psychological conditioning.

Anthropology could instead begin from the beginning — turn away from its quantification of human experience, and move toward an open critique of the society which engendered it. That would mean breaking with the official ideology of scientific objectivity and technological progress, and putting an end to the cannibalistic mania for research. Anthropologists might cease to act as the agents of empire, and get on with the business of relearning (if it is possible) how to live on this earth. The physicians, in other words, must heal themselves. Of course, they would no longer be anthropologists, but like the rest of us, mere human beings.

(1981)

THE LANGUAGE OF DOMESTICATION & THE DOMESTICATION OF LANGUAGE

"As progress and technology transform our way of life and our physical surroundings," writes Marilynn Rashid, "they eat away at our language, enfeeble our spirit. ..."[1] (See page 157 for endnotes.) In his book, *Shadow Work* (Marion Boyers, 1981), Ivan Illich describes language as one of the earliest areas of human competence — a cultural commons and focal point of shared meaning — to come under attack from church and state, and later from advancing technology and bureaucratic institutionalization. Illich argues that by undermining the "vernacular" domain in language, technics, and other areas of human activity, these forces of authority destroy self-sufficiency and freedom, making us all wards of the state and disabling professional institutions.

The vernacular is commonly understood to signify local, unschooled, colloquial language, but Illich attempts to restore it to its former, fuller meaning. "We need a simple adjective," he explains, "to name those acts of competence, lust, or concern that we want to defend from measurement or manipulation from Chicago Boys and Socialist Commissars. The terms must be broad enough to fit the preparation of food and the shaping of language, childbirth and recreation," but must be clearly distinguished from unpaid labor and hobbies which represent the "shadow work," that other side of industrial labor, in modern society.

Domain conquered by pedagogues

In Rome the term *vernacular* was employed up until about 600 CE "to designate any value that was homebred, homemade, derived from the commons." Such a term was "opposed to what was obtained in formal exchange," and represented a culture based on "sustenance derived from reciprocity patterns embedded in every aspect of life, as distinguished from sustenance that comes from exchange or from vertical distribution."

Illich contrasts such a vernacular society with contemporary commodity-intensive society, which shatters these reciprocity patterns and modes of self-sufficient subsistence and mutual aid, replacing them with wage work and its twin, unpaid shadow work (such as housework, education, even hustling). Equally, it breaks up household and community economies with market economics; undermines autonomy and independence with dependence, medicalization and welfare; and replaces self-created, reciprocally generated language and knowledge with the professionally mediated language and information of the schoolroom, government office, data bank, and mass media. *Shadow Work* actually treats several aspects of this process, though I will limit myself here to its treatment of language.

What originally drew me to Illich's book was his treatment of the Andalusian Renaissance humanist Antonio de Nebrija, author in 1492 of the first grammar in Spanish, and in fact in any Romance language. I had been reading about the history and evolution of the Spanish language, and a friend recommended Illich's book for its lucid treatment of language as a domain conquered by pedagogues, just as the New World was being conquered by adventurers and missionaries.

As Illich suggests, there is a fascinating parallel between Nebrija and his contemporary, Columbus. Both petition the Queen of Spain to embark on projects of exploration and conquest — Columbus arguing for geographic expansion, Nebrija for a cultural and linguistic expansion. She resists both, finally consenting to the dream of the navigator (for such conquest was more understandable to a monarch of that time) and rejecting that of the scholar.

Illich observes, "Columbus proposes only to use the recently created caravels to the limit of their range for the expansion of the Queen's power in what would become New Spain," whereas "Nebrija is more basic — he argues the use of his grammar for the expansion of the Queen's power in a totally new sphere: state control over the kind of sustenance on which people may draw every day." This opening salvo in the state's war against subsistence values — replacing the vernacular with taught "mother tongue," an invention of clerics and pedagogues in the service of church and state — represents "the first invented part of universal education."

In his introduction to his *Gramática castellana* (Castilian Grammar), which is also his petition to Queen Isabella, Nebrija reveals his consciously political and imperial outlook, calling for a new society and empire over the fragmenting vernacular society and the territories to be conquered. He intuits, with the conquest (also in 1492) of Granada, the last Moorish kingdom on the Iberian peninsula, that Spain is on the threshold of empire — hence anticipating the conquests of the New World even before Columbus set eyes on its shores.

Nebrija's linguistic authoritarianism was marked early. He even left Spain for Italy as a youth not only because he was drawn to the new Renaissance orientation there but because he detested the linguistic anarchy and the lack of Latin spoken in his homeland. His biographer, Felix Olmedo, wrote that upon his return in 1470, "he saw himself as coming to battle against barbarism."

Nebrija returned to a Spain in the process of national organization and Renaissance. The first steps of geographic expansion and exploration, the spread of humanism, and the growth of commerce all reflected a general phenomenon of social dynamism and growth. The consolidation of national, centralized power was well under way, with the unification of Aragon and Castile (by the marriage of Ferdinand and Isabella), ecclesiastic reorganization and the establishment of the Inquisition, and the conquest of Granada and expulsion of thousands of Jews and Muslims. Many privileges and forms of authority previously belonging to the nobility, the military orders, the municipalities and the municipal *cortes* were being incorporated by the Crown, which backed up its power throughout the peninsula with the organization of a national police, the *Santa Hermandad*, or "Sacred Brotherhood."

Nebrija's notion of a regulated national language is timely, then, though his idea of the intimate relationship between language and empire is not original. Alfonso the Wise (1221-84) had already had such an outlook, bringing together Hebrew, Arabic and Latin scholars to translate works of Classical Antiquity and the *fueros* or Iberian laws into Castilian. Another scholar and contemporary of Nebrija, the Aragonese Gonzalo García, wrote prior to Nebrija, "Language, commonly, more than other things, follows empire … since the word should be like money … which is refused in none of the lands of the Prince who has coined it." This notion of language as an object of commerce in the service of state power, with the standardization necessary for its exchange, is central to the tremendous evolution which the entire European continent undergoes from the late Middle Ages through the emergence of industrial capitalism.

This process is seen in every domain of life, reflected for example in the new concept of artistic perspective, in which the symbolic relationship between objects becomes a visual, mathematical function. The graphic representation of movement by the French theologian Nicolas Oresme (1320?-82) and the description of the four "primary qualities" — size, shape, quantity and motion — by Galileo Galilei (1564–1642) represent other examples of this process of objectification and quantification.

The appearance of clock time in the Benedictine monasteries, the standardization of currencies, weights and measures, and the emergence of a money economy long precede industrialization; in fact they prepare the ground for industrial capitalism's pillage of subsistence cultures and forms of traditional social reproduction. This entire progression leads to a total deformation of experience, founded upon instrumental rationality, technical and professional hierarchy and statified power — the pillars of modern industrial civilization.

The sword and the book

Nebrija's desire to instrumentalize and regulate language is part of this long process. Previously, such grammatical regulation, under the concept of *artificio*, was limited to the teaching of learned languages such as Greek and Latin, and had little influence on most people's lives. As Hispanist and philologist Rafael Lapesa has remarked, "It was a novelty to apply it to spoken language, since it was believed that, learned from the lips of one's mother, practice and good sense sufficed in order to speak it properly." By applying such rules to Castilian, Nebrija created a language model, an artificial, reified construction, which would later come to be institutionalized and imposed.

Nebrija's intent is absolutely political: to forge a pact between the sword and the book, as Illich says, "a pact ... of sword and expertise, encompassing the engine of conquest abroad and a system of scientific control of diversity within the kingdom." Referring to Rome, he reminds the Queen that language has always accompanied empire. In answer to her lack of understanding as to the usefulness of a grammar for a tongue everyone speaks without the help of experts, he replies, "Soon Your Majesty will have placed her yoke upon many barbarians who speak outlandish tongues. By this, your victory, these people shall stand in a new need; the need for the laws the victor owes to the vanquished, and the need for the language we shall bring with us." Illich comments, "While Columbus sailed for foreign lands to seek the familiar — gold, subjects, nightingales — in Spain Nebrija advocates the reduction of the Queen's subjects to an entirely new type of dependence. He presents her with a new weapon, grammar, to be wielded by a new kind of mercenary, the *letrado* ... He offers Isabella a tool to colonize the language spoken by her own subjects; he wants her to replace the people's speech by the imposition of the Queen's *lengua* — *her* language, *her* tongue."

Nebrija knows the significance of his proposal: making the regulation of language itself a critical support for the nation state. This new state, Illich continues, "takes from people the words on which they subsist, and transforms them into the standardized language which henceforth they are compelled to use, each one at the level of education that has been institutionally imputed to him. Henceforth, people will have to rely on the language they receive from above, rather than develop a tongue in common with one another." This "radical change from the vernacular to taught language," he concludes, "foreshadows the switch from breast to bottle, from subsistence to welfare, from production for use to production for market. . . ."[2]

Though Nebrija's proposal was not understood by the Queen, his methods were employed in the conquests of America, both in the regulation and investigation of the indigenous languages in order to proselytize the faith, and in the teachings of Spanish to the conquered peoples to bring them into the empire and integrate them into the system of power. But the conquest was also to make its advances in another manner. Its main project was to suppress that situation in which language, in Nebrija's words, had "been left loose and unruly," thus evolving in a few centuries from Latin to the Romance languages. Here he is directly attacking vernacular language in all its diversity, creative liberty, extension and autonomy; thus "dialects" don't even rate as legitimate languages and should be suppressed.

Of course a language, as someone once remarked, is only a dialect with an army. In his attack on linguistic anarchy, Nebrija is the spiritual forefather of Spanish dictator Francisco Franco, who suppressed and prohibited Catalan, Galician and Basque after the 1936–39 Civil War. Language is rightly seen as a potential realm of freedom; because it defies imposed authority, it isn't language but "barbarism," and must (according to the state) be annihilated. In the continuing bloodbath in the Basque region and the rivalry and resentments present throughout the country over regional languages, Spain is still living out the consequences of that brutal war of annihilation.

Like the bureaucrats and aspiring bureaucrats of all totalitarian states (and which of them cannot be truly described as totalitarian?) Nebrija understood that linguistic authority brings with it social control. By subjecting speech to the state and its organs of bureaucratic administration, the maintenance of power can be ensured. Because language is directly linked to social meaning itself, to a people's capacity to define themselves and their world, its instrumentalization undermines this realm of freedom by encoding it into a hierarchy of domination. The human beings subject to it tend to become mere instruments themselves, collaborators in and mouthpieces for their own suppression.

Everyday speech, once a domain of reciprocally created meaning and social cooperation, now becomes, in Illich's words, "the product of design … paid for and delivered like a commodity." And despite the timeworn commonplace of language academics that language cannot degenerate but merely fulfills a changing "need" — from knowing the names of wildflowers and herbs, say, to varieties of automobiles — a language spoken in an increasingly alienated and administered universe obviously undergoes the same process of corruption and degeneration that its speakers experience. As people become things, their language reflects and conspires with their thingification. The cultural commons becomes polluted by capital; like other domains of human autonomy, speech gets stolen, transformed into a power of manipulation, dependence and conformism.

"Taught mother tongue," Illich says, "has established a radical monopoly over speech." And though the vernacular does not necessarily die, it certainly does wither under the onslaught of a manufactured language utilized to prop up the codes of power and powerlessness. "People who speak taught language imitate the announcer of news, the comedian of gag writers, the instructor following the teacher's manual to explain the textbook, the songster of engineered rhymes, or the ghost-written president." Their language "implicitly lies," is created for spectators. "While the vernacular is engendered in me by the intercourse between complete persons locked in conversation with each other, taught language is syntonic with loudspeakers whose assigned job is gab."

As Illich's arguments suggest, linguistic anarchy is a precondition for social liberation. The instrumentalized and standardized codification of language must be transgressed so that a new matrix of autonomous meaning can be engendered. Such a language can only be nurtured into being through a liberatory practice which resists and eventually overthrows the ideological idiom of power and dependency — that suppression of a speech freely given and freely received. As Lautréamont declared, poetry will be made by all.

(1984)

Endnotes

1. Marilynn Rashid, "Newspeak and the Impoverishment of Language" (Winter 1984 *Fifth Estate*).

2. In his essay, "A Family Quarrel," (Spring 1983 *Fifth Estate*), Bob Brubaker mentions in passing the problems in Illich's discussion of human needs, his dependence on such questionable criteria as productivity and counterproductivity for critiquing industrialism. This tends to make Illich "an (anti-) capitalist efficiency expert," Brubaker argues — and, I might add, contributes

to his confusion on technology. In *Toward a History of Needs*, a very worthwhile book, he makes the error of distinguishing between an abstract potentiality for technology and its present uses, blaming its "counter-productivity" on the "radical monopoly" enjoyed by professionals and technocrats, thus falsely separating these social categories from the web of technical-instrumental activities which they incarnate. He ends by defending the "great inventions of the last hundred years, such as new metals, ball bearings, some building materials, electronics," even computers as "in principle ... the hardware that could give an entirely new meaning" to freedom. Illich does not explain how such technological development could be controlled, or who would decide (and how) which of these "great inventions" will be used. In fact, despite this abstract concept of technology, freedom can never be established or guaranteed by "hardware."

ANARCHY & THE SACRED

"O Sariputra, form is here emptiness, emptiness is form; form is no other than emptiness, emptiness is no other than form. . . ." — *the Prajaparamita Sutra, quoted in* Manual of Zen Buddhism, *D.T. Suzuki*

"Wisdom alone is whole and is both willing and unwilling to be named Zeus." — *Herakleitos*

Beyond anarchism?

In an article in the Summer 1987 Fifth Estate *reporting on the June 1987 Minneapolis Anarchist Gathering, I started a discussion on the nature of spirituality and rationality that continues to this day in radical ecological and anarchist circles. I criticized an orthodox "dyed-in-the-wool anarchism with chapter and verse quotations from the 19th century luminaries," calling it "a moribund ideology ... which has little to offer in the way of critique of contemporary forms of domination," and as an example of such dogmatism, I mentioned an incident at the gathering in which a group of anarchosyndicalists picketed a workshop on paganism and anarchy with signs reading, "Say No to All Religion." While describing paganism as "problematic," I emphasized my sympathy for animism and the spiritual wisdom of tribal peoples, but felt it necessary to register my concerns. My comments follow:*

The pagan workshop and my discussions with people who participated in the solstice celebration raised more questions than they answered. There was a marked anti-intellectual attitude that made it difficult to discuss historical paganism and its relation to anarchy. The contrasts pagans made with christianity were frequently simplistic, and they had no answer to the question of how paganism was to avoid authoritarianism except to say that it is a "powerful tool" that could be misused.

The spiritual relationship tribal people have had with the earth had a context, but for modern (detribalized) people, it can be dangerously contrived. Pagan anarchists should consider the problem of charisma, emotional identification, and domination, as well as the myriad pagan-fascist and socially quietistic spiritual movements in the U.S. and Europe before they announce that paganism is "inherently libertarian" and "the essence of anarchy," as one starry-eyed solstice worshiper told me.

As a general, intuitive orientation, animism makes sense, but to refuse to see our actual separation from nature and the problems and responsibilities it raises, to throw away a necessary skepticism, is to reduce the animist insight to an ideology with potentially sinister consequences. (The 19th century anarchist throwbacks who briefly picketed the pagan workshop, however, without even discussing the question with the pagans, were certainly no better in their rationalist positivism. They can't imagine the sacred character of the very land they are trodding on; they need to take at least a year off, get out in the woods, and read some good books about primal peoples.)

Someone suggested putting together a discussion around the theme "Beyond Anarchism," which might have led in an interesting direction. I believe in the need for a new revolutionary discourse based on the history of revolutionary movements, a critique of technological civilization and instrumentalism, and a visionary recognition of our primal roots. But that is as yet too much to expect of the anarchist movement, and may always be.

Nevertheless, the wide variety of anarchist views comes with the territory, and underlies both the movement's strengths and its weaknesses. The classical anarchist movement was eclipsed once and for all in the 1930s with the defeat of the Spanish Revolution, and it's not about to be revived. As George Woodcock writes in the epilogue to his history of anarchism, "Lost causes may be the best causes — they usually are — but once lost they are never won again."

But, he continues, "ideas do not die ... And when we turn to the anarchist idea, we realize that it is not merely older than the historical anarchist movement, but it has also spread far beyond its boundaries." Anarchism as ideology is, like all isms, a wasm. But anarchy lives, and an anarchist orientation is critical to a struggle for human liberty. In fact, a generalized anti-authoritarian orientation is playing a role in the wider radicalization that has begun to sweep this country since 1980, particularly though not exclusively among young people. It can play a healthy role in overcoming the errors made in the past, as in the 1960s, in succumbing to authoritarian politics, reformism, spiritual quietism, and social passivity.

As a general perspective, anarchy can shift the current radicalization toward a more liberatory position by its intransigent vision of freedom and its rejection of hierarchy and all forms of domination. By renewing and deepening a vision that includes past forms of freedom (anarchies) and contemporary forms of revolt, we can move beyond ideology towards genuine radical transformation and egalitarian human communities. But anarchists must critically view their own counter-culture, history, and current trajectory. If we can, we may assist in opening up the whole of society in a way that can take it all, as somebody once said, beyond the point of no return. . . .

The anarchist vision must evolve

In the Spring 1988 FE, anarcho-syndicalist Jon Bekken responded, "[I was] one of the '19th century anarchist throwbacks who briefly picketed the pagan workshop' at the Gathering ... [Watson] apparently took offense at our 'rationalist' ideas ... and at our decision not to attend the pagan workshop in order to discuss the merits of superstition and romantic nostalgia for the days when we lived in caves. . . ." Bekken continued that according to my argument, "anything more thoughtful than an inchoate spirit of rebellion becomes 'ideology.'" I was also guilty of ignoring the working class, "which has no place in [a] neoprimitivist vision. . . ." And he concluded, "Just what do you have to offer that goes 'beyond anarchism,' that's more contemporary than our idea of building a self-managed, stateless society?" Part of my reply follows:

The anarchist vision, if it is to remain true to its own spirit, must evolve and grow. Otherwise, we are left with the brittle shell of a century-old ideology — the anarchism of ideologues. Jon Bekken unwittingly provides an example of what I am talking about, accusing me of opposing "rationality," an ambiguous and problematic word, when it was specifically his positivist rationalism I attacked (since what constitutes genuine rationality is at least open to debate). His dismissal of the contemporary rediscovery of humankind's original anarchies reflects his ignorance of critical advances that have taken place in anthropological literature over the last twenty years, that have merged with an anarchist and communitarian perspective to open up whole new areas of discussion of modern civilization, human community, and the nature of hierarchical power.

Bekken asks how we might go "beyond anarchism." One area where classical anarchist writings fall short of understanding contemporary forces of domination, and therefore, the sources of liberty, is in the question of technology and science. There are definitely contradictory currents within anarchism regarding technology, but it is fair to say that the dominant perspective has been productivist and scientist in its uncritical acceptance

of technological development. As in marxian socialism, scientific-technological development is perceived as a liberating force.

Kropotkin, for example, wrote in *An Appeal to the Young*, "It is now no
longer a question of accumulating scientific truths and discoveries ... We
have to make science no longer a luxury but the foundation of every man's
life." Bakunin argued, "We recognize then the absolute authority of science ... Outside of this only legitimate authority, legitimate because it is
rational and is in harmony with human liberty, we declare all other authorities false, arbitrary and fatal." Proudhon, too, stressed the "need for
centralization and large industrial units. . . ."

These affirmations of the mass technological development undertaken
by capital itself reveal little recognition of mass technics as an emergent
social system. Though there were some early manifestations of a technological critique in the nineteenth century, it would take another fifty to
seventy-five years of capitalist development for a rounded critique to appear, in the post-World War II appraisals of technology in historical and
sociological literature, in particular Lewis Mumford's insights into the industrial megamachine that grew out of world war and the convergence of
nuclearism, mass war techniques and cybernetic planning. This new mode
of society, Mumford realized, reiterated in many ways the ancient slave
states, and would have consequent effects on human community and
personhood which would spell even greater dangers for human freedom.

Ideological anarchists, especially the syndicalists, haven't read Mumford;
they have their noses stuck in Bakunin, who when he was at his worst,
described the modern megamachine in the most positive terms. Writing
on workers' cooperatives, he argued, "one can only guess at the immense
development which surely awaits them and the new political and social
conditions they will generate. It is not only possible but probable that they
will, in time, outgrow the limits of today's counties, provinces, and even
states to transform the whole structure of human society, which will no
longer be divided into nations but into industrial units."

Anarchist writer Daniel Guérin adds, commenting on this passage, that
"these would then 'form a vast economic federation' with a supreme
assembly at its head. With the help of 'world-wide statistics, giving data as
comprehensive as they are detailed and precise,' it would balance supply
and demand, direct, distribute and share out world industrial production
among the different countries so that crises in trade and employment,
enforced stagnation, economic disaster, and loss of capital would almost
certainly entirely disappear." (Guerin, *Anarchism*) This technocratic-
cybernetic vision has nothing in common with an authentic libertarian society. As Eugene Schwartz remarks in his book, *Overkill: The Decline of*

Technology in Modern Civilization, "Cybernetics is for automata, and the planned society is a prelude to the universal concentration camp."

Because they have not looked critically at the emergent technological order, anarcho-syndicalists do not comprehend the contemporary forces of domination. Joseph Weizenbaum's important book, *Computer Power and Human Reason,* reveals the fallacy of such uncritical attitudes towards technology. Tools and machines are not mere instruments, he argues, "they are pregnant symbols in themselves ... A tool is a model for its own reproduction and a script for the re-enactment of the skills it symbolizes ... [it] thus transcends its role as a practical means towards certain ends: it is a constituent of man's symbolic re-creation of his world."

Modern technological civilization has come to undermine and reshape culture and meaning. As Max Horkheimer wrote in *The Eclipse of Reason* on the outcome of the positivist philosophy shared by many anarchists, "concepts have become 'streamlined,' rationalized, labor-saving devices ... in short, made part and parcel of production. Meaning has become entirely transformed into function ... only one authority, namely, science, conceived as the classification of facts and the calculation of probabilities," can now be recognized. A very interesting closing of the circle started by Bakunin's genuflection to science.

At least one can say for the pagans that their symbolic connection to the world starts with nature and not the machine and the factory so worshipped by the syndicalist, which is why syndicalists are so threatened by their intuition of the sacred in the living world. As Jacques Ellul observed in *The Technological Society,* "[T]here is nothing spiritual anywhere. But man cannot live without the sacred. He therefore transfers his sense of the sacred to the very thing which has destroyed its former object: to technique itself. In the world in which we live, technique has become the essential mystery. . . ." And further on he comments, "Technique is the hope of the proletarians; they can have faith in it because its miracles are visible and progressive. . . ."

Science based on faith

This religious fervor will have nothing to do with any remanifestation of the old nature religions. It is imperative for those who share in this complex mystique of western civilization to deny absolutely any legitimacy of the lifeways or visions of our primal ancestors. But in some sense inaccessible to scientific-instrumentalist rationalism, the natural world is our mother and living beings our cousins, and in this sense they have spirit and participate in a reciprocal communication and symbiosis with us (in fact ecological science has essentially confirmed this notion of interrelatedness). Anarcho-syndicalists, like the liberal statists Paul Feyerabend critiques in *Science in a Free Society,* "regard rationalism (which for them coincides with science) not just as one view among many, but as a basis for society. The freedom they defend is therefore granted under conditions that are no longer subjected to it. It is granted only to those who have already accepted part of the rationalist (i.e. scientific) ideology." For them, "The excellence of science is assumed, it is not argued for. Here scientists and philosophers of science act like the defenders of the One and Only Roman Church acted before them: Church doctrine is true, everything else is Pagan nonsense ... the assumption of the inherent superiority of science has moved beyond science and has become an article of faith for almost everyone." Science has become an integral component of society, just as the church was. "Of course, even where church and state are carefully separated, science and the state are completely integrated."

But the ideology of scientific objectivity is itself based on faith, on an irrational dogma that by posing as the only valid form of knowledge not only mystifies its own ideological foundations and leap of faith, but corrodes the possibility for a free discourse about the world in the way that Bekken's crude call to expel pagans from the anarchist gathering did. This scientism, as Weizenbaum argues, is itself "an elaborate structure built on piles that are anchored, not on bedrock as is commonly supposed, but on the shifting sand of fallible human judgment, conjecture, and intuition."

Weizenbaum notes that the scientific demonstrations the average person accepts on faith are themselves "fundamentally acts of persuasion." But, "infected with the germ of logical necessity," they claim to describe how things "actually are" and *must be.* "In short, they convert truth to provability," and reduce reality. "Belief in the rationality-logicality equation," he says, "has corroded the prophetic power of language itself."

Because anarchists question and confront all forms of authority and do not reduce the social question to one of class domination and exploitation as do marxists and syndicalists, they have always looked at the whole human being and the whole society, and explored other areas of domination and autonomy ignored by classical liberal and socialist perspectives. Anarchists should be receptive both to a technological critique in a world increasingly determined by technology, and to ancient animist visions of interrelatedness and natural reciprocity and symbiosis: after all, these latter sensibilities are suggested in the best passages of Kropotkin's *Mutual Aid.*

One can in fact rediscover a classical anarchist critique of technology if one looks carefully, for example Bakunin's very suggestive criticism of Marx's statism and support for material and economic development, in his prescient comment that "finally, when all the other classes have exhausted themselves, the State then becomes the patrimony of the bureaucratic class and then falls — or if you will, rises — to the position of a machine." (See John Clark's essay "Marx, Bakunin, and Social Transformation," in his book, *The Anarchist Moment.*) The editor of the anarchist journal *Man!*, Marcus Graham, was also accurate in his appraisal of the anarchist tradition as far back as 1934, when he wrote that "the future will prove Kropotkin, from an Anarchist point of view, has, in accepting thus the machine [as an instrument of human liberation], made one of the gravest errors. Such an attitude was perfectly logical for the Marxian school of thought, but certainly not for the Anarchist."

Anarchism not a program

Interestingly, liberal historian Irving L. Horowitz points out in his book, *The Anarchists*, that the marxists had an advantage over the anarchists, since marxists put their faith in developing technology, while anarchists "never confronted," except in the later stages of the classical movement, "the problems of a vast technology," but rather ignored them by calling for a society "that was satisfying to the individual producer rather than feasible for a growing mass society ... The anarchist literature contains a strong element of nostalgia, a harkening back to a situation where workshops were small, where relationships were manageable, where people experienced affective responses with each other. Technology and the material benefits of science were never seriously entertained by the anarchists except in a ministerial contempt for that which destroys the natural man."

Considering the anarchist quotes above, Horowitz's argument is not entirely accurate, yet his reasoning is similar to Bekken's attack on neo-luddism and neo-primitivism as mere nostalgia for the stone age. Anarchism itself is not valid in Horowitz's view because it has not kept pace with technological progress. "We are in a technological era that is qualitatively different, that brings forward entirely new forms of social behavior and social existence. Much as we prefer not to breed fragmented specialists, it is impossible to envision the era of hydrogen power and mass electrification in terms of simple, spontaneous association of individual craftsmen. The forms of technology moving from craft to a network of minutely separated functions have, therefore, tended to undermine the idea of the anarchist Everyman."

Horowitz's argument is compelling, but it is posed backwards. Technology has certainly transformed the world, but the question is not whether the anarchist vision of freedom, autonomy, and mutual cooperation is any longer relevant to mass technological civilization. It is more pertinent to ask whether freedom, autonomy, or human cooperation themselves can be possible in such a civilization.

I don't think that they can, which is why the anarchist vision does remain "more relevant than ever," but not exactly for the reasons the syndicalists believe. Considering that critics of anarchism recognize an anti-technological current in it, and that this critique can be found in the tradition itself if one reads carefully and critically, perhaps luddism is closer to the genuine anarchist tradition, particularly in its capacity to evolve and to confront the evolving forms of domination, than the anarchist militants who wear the word on their sleeves.

Despite Bekken's contempt for the growing interest in the lives and visions of primal peoples, that interest too resides in the anarchist tradition. As Alex Comfort writes in the introduction to Harold Barclay's *People Without Government*, "The challenge 'go run a modern state like a pygmy village and see what happens' misses the rather unusual cast of mind which anarchists seek to impart. Unlike Marxism or democratic capitalism which are institutionalized theories, the rejection of authority as a social tool is an attitude, not a program. Once adopted it patterns the kinds of solutions we are disposed to accept."

The growing reassessment of our primal, animist roots suggests that an authoritarian hierarchical and instrumentalist civilization brings with it an authoritarian, unitary, homogenized and instrumental form of knowledge. The rationalist wants to suppress the otherness of nature and spirit, to reduce nature to a passive object for domination and to banish spirit altogether. But, as poet Antonio Machado has written, this other "refuses to disappear; it subsists, it persists; it is the hard bone on which reason breaks its teeth."

Yet as the repressive, pathological and destructive character of instrumental civilization is more and more apparent to everyone, this primal other is reasserting itself, leading to what Jamake Highwater has called "a variety of attempts to regain contact with the roots of traditions which, viewed by progressive thinkers as old-fashioned and obsolete, have slipped into oblivion … From the polysynthetic metaphysics of nature envisioned by primal peoples, from a nature immediately experienced rather than dubiously abstracted, arises a premise that addresses itself with particular force to the root causes of many contemporary problems, especially to our so-called ecological crisis." (*The Primal Mind: Vision and Reality in Indian America*) Highwater cites Joseph Epes Brown, author of many books of Amerindian spiritual traditions: "It is perhaps this message of the sacred nature of the land that today has been most responsible for forcing the Native American vision upon the mind and consciousness of the non-Indian."

How to move beyond anarchism? I think Epes Brown's remark suggests a general orientation. A vision of human liberation and a cooperative, nonhierarchical society will go nowhere if it does not reject the present technological, social, and economic structures of life, and unless it is linked to a renewal of the sacredness of nature, its interrelatedness, and our connectedness to it. If we cannot see the spirit that resides in the natural world, we cannot fully envision the ineffable human spirit of liberty that has motivated the anarchist project — before it was called "anarchist" — from the beginning of class societies. A society operating under an abstracted, rationalized and instrumentalist relationship to the natural world only recreates such relations between human beings; the domination of nature and the domination of human beings originated together, and it is together that they must be abolished.

Nevertheless, pagans and spiritual anarchists should remember that attempts by detribalized moderns to renew primal traditions through modern ritual and other extrarational methods do contain dangers that cannot be dismissed (and which even pagans acknowledged). A certain measure of skepticism and self-restraint is useful. The ancient slave states, with their combination of political and priestly power, make clear to us that a sense of the sacred, even of the sacred in nature, can be and has been manipulated for authoritarian purposes.

A defense of spirituality

Another letter in the Spring 1989 FE from Lev Chernyi, editor at that time of Anarchy: A Journal of Desire Armed, *took up the discussion, arguing that while he was "no particular fan" of the anarcho-syndicalism represented so far in the debate, the "Say No to All Religion" idea was worth exploring, and the "pro-spiritual stance … worth a more critical examination."*

He wrote: "Why is it not obvious that this 'religious,' 'spiritual,' 'sacred' 'faith' in technological rationality is a direct, though nominally inverted, continuation of the traditions of religious alienation in which it was incubated and from which it was born. For me, the continuities between religion and scientific ideologies are more significant than their differences. Why reject scientific ideology only to embrace the idiocies of religion, spiritualism and the sacred? Isn't it clear that your criticisms of the reification and worship of technique no less imply the importance of a critique of the reification and worship of nature?

"[A] defense of the spiritual and the sacred … seems to have no justification save the close association these concepts have established with the anthropology of primitive societies. Must we uncritically adopt the cultural mistakes of the primitives in a package deal along with all that is more valuable and worthy of our emulation? Can't we realize that if our "more advanced" stage of human culture has become as fucked up as it has, that it is highly likely that its "more primitive" stages — even before the first hints of ecological catastrophe and institutionalized hierarchies — probably had their flaws too?

"The concept of the sacred is the foundation for all religion, spiritualism, ideology, worship, faith, belief. It logically (and inevitably) implies the existence of the profane. And though it may be transmuted into many other dualities — good and evil, spirit and matter, god and devil — they all perform the same insidious function of dividing our naturally whole experience of our world into two rather arbitrary conceptual spheres. The idea of the sacred is a conceptual fetishization, a reification of certain aspects of what we might otherwise more clearly see as the unity of our experience. Why not just jettison it in favor of a truly holistic and non-dualist perspective?"

Another correspondent, "Feral Faun," wrote that since the word "sacred" means "separated, set apart" and usually specifically "set apart for a religious or other special purpose," a "truly radical ecological viewpoint would, thus, utterly reject the concept of sacredness, pointing out that no being has a truly separate existence — we are all connected — so nothing is sacred.

"It was the Judeo-Christian concept that humans were sacred — separated from and placed above all other beings — that was one of the main ideological justifications of the rape of the earth. There is evidence that the concept of the sacred played a major role in the development of property and exchange, authority, sex roles, work, agriculture and the domestication of animals. In other words, it is a major source of this alienated civilization." The idea that some deep ecologists and others have maintained "that everything is sacred," he added, "is both blatantly untrue (everything is not 'set aside for a special purpose') and, like all such glittering generalities, meaningless. It tells us nothing. It is just as meaningful, and more true, to say nothing is sacred. It cannot be an abstraction like 'sacredness' which motivates our defense of the earth, but our own very real, personal love for the natural wild beings we interact with. Otherwise, we will fall into absurd moralism and dogmatism. . . . "

My reply follows:

Lev Chernyi argues that the notion of the sacred that has been transferred to technology is "a direct, though nominally inverted, continuation of ... religious alienation. . . ." To the degree that this is true, it is because science and industrialism grew out of a culture whose religious experience was already cut off from deeper spiritual realities. While he and I agree that scientific materialism is itself a dogmatic faith (at least for most people, including the practitioners of science), on what other basis but empiricism and science does the modern atheist reject the "idiocies" of the sacred in all its manifestations?

To say, further, that the intuition of the sacred is false because the world is simply what it is, is to overlook that the world is also *not* what it is. The christian civilization that created industrialism had lost sight of this insight, but it was understood in most archaic, and particularly primal, societies.

"From one point of view all those divinities exist," a Tibetan lama told a visitor, "from another they are not real." And a Tantric text puts it, "All of these visualized deities are but symbols representing the various things that occur on the Path." (quoted in Joseph Campbell's *The Hero with a Thousand Faces*) In an essay on the role of clowns in Native American cultures, Barbara Tedlock tells the story of a white man cured by a Navajo healer during a Red Ant ceremony, who asked "whether he really had red ants in his system. The curer told him, 'No, not ants, but *ants*. We have to have a way of thinking strongly about disease.'" (Dennis and Barbara Tedlock, *Teachings from the American Earth*)

Are the ants real, and the *ants* an illusion? Is something someone tells you in a dream less real than what is told you in waking life, even if what you hear in the dream has such an effect upon you it changes your life? Lev is confusing ants and *ants*, but primal peoples don't seem to do so. "The Sanema Indians told the anthropologist Johannes Wilbert that their shamans could fly, or at least walk one foot above the ground," reports Hans Peter Duerr in his luminous book, *Dreamtime: Concerning the Boundary Between Wilderness and Civilization*. "Naively, the scientist answered that after all, he could see that the shamans ran around like anybody else. Whereupon the Indians countered, 'The reason for that is that you do not *understand*' ... Put differently, one might say that the Indians knew that the ethnographer had not the faintest notion what the word 'flying' meant in shamanistic context, because he supposed that one could only fly like a bird or like a Pan Am pilot."

If anything characterizes civilization's "magical rationalism (to use a term that reflects what I was trying to say previously), it is an intense fear of such flying combined with a pathological, earth-destroying desire to simulate it with a physical apparatus. This society has forgotten what the shaman knows, and what the popular song reminds us, that thinking is the best way to travel. Shamanistic flight becomes less and less possible in a world in which living nature is reduced to dead objects — resources or commodities — and from which spirit is banished: a world in which nothing is sacred. The need to fly remains, of course, hence Pan Am and the space shuttle. Technology rules in such a world because no other meaning remains other than blind instrumentalism and procedural nothingness.

In primal societies, on the other hand, technique was kept to its proper dimensions by making it more a question of experimentation *in order to see,* confirming Mircea Eliade's definition of shamanism in his book by that name as a "technique of ecstasy." Such experimentation is found, to give some extreme examples, among the Innuit, who advise the spiritual explorer, "Go to a lonely place and rub a stone in a circle on a rock for hours and days on end," or, "Let the person who wants a vision hang himself by his neck. When his face turns purple, take him down and have him describe what he's seen." (cited in *Shaking the Pumpkin: Traditional Poetry of the North American Indians*, edited by Jerome Rothenberg)

A fundamental solidarity of life

Chernyi sees no justification for the affirmation of the sacred "save for the close association" between this perspective and primal societies — an enormous exception! These societies were saturated in myth, saturated in the sacred; we cannot approve their sense of kinship and community, their reciprocity and communism, their stateless anarchy, their sensitive integration with the natural world, and then dismiss their profound sense of the sacredness of nature and the cycles of life as "cultural mistakes." As Eliade observes in *The Myth of the Eternal Return*, in such societies, "every act which has a definite meaning — hunting, fishing, agriculture, games, conflicts, sexuality — in some way participates in the sacred ... the only profane activities are those which have no mythical meaning, that is, which lack exemplary models." All meaningful acts, therefore, connect humans with the nonhuman other, the sacred. And as Ernst Cassirer has written, basic mythic conceptions and acts "are not mere products of fantasy which vapor off from fixed, empirical, realistic existence, to float above the actual world like a bright mist; to primitive consciousness they present the *totality* of Being. The mythical form of conception is not something super-added to certain definite *elements* of empirical existence; instead, the primary 'experience' itself is steeped in the imagery of myth and saturated with its atmosphere." (*Language and Myth*)

Does the intuition of the sacred signal a reification of nature as it "really" is, or is it a question of the metaphorical, analogical forms of thought that characterize this intuition? Is the idea of the sacred a mystique that conceals an essential "unity of ... experience," or is it a way through this remarkable and problematic phenomenon called mind, of connecting with and apprehending the world? Is sacred myth a lie, or as Joseph Campbell puts it in *The Hero with a Thousand Faces*, "the secret opening through which the inexhaustible energies of the cosmos pour into human cultural manifestation"? Is it certain that the notion of the sacred is the direct source of alienated religion and abstract science, or could alienated religion itself be a simulation of the original notion, with this ambivalence between ants and *ants* suppressed, in order to legitimate a nascent leviathan and its breach of the reciprocal gift and symbolic cycles? And with the passing of so many generations of slaves, couldn't this religion have become a pillar of authoritarian conditioning, a spectral image of that which it replaced?

Why do we suffer when someone cuts down an ancient tree? Is it because "resources" are being wasted, or because we think the tree-cutter is making an obscene profit, or is it for aesthetic reasons? Or is there some level of meaning, connection, kinship, that has a spiritual, sacred character, a personhood? How about if someone cuts down our parents? Does a spirit reside within the people and the trees, or are they just loops of geobiochemical processes? The impoverished optic of scientific rationalism dismisses this spirit, this *orenda*, this *manitu*, this Mighty Something or Great Mysterious as superstitious idiocy. Similarly, the ethnographer congratulates himself for knowing that the vision of the *bruja* is "really" only a hallucination caused by pharmacological substances. Commenting on this mentality, Duerr writes, "What is *real*, the scientists say, must *pass our tests*." Of course to pass our tests this reality must be commensurable to our experiments, must fit into our laboratory. By that time it no longer matters. Duerr quotes a Haitian proverb: "The spirits leave the island when the anthropologists arrive."

Yet for the primal or archaic person, as Eliade points out, "It is the experience of the sacred — that is, an encounter with a transhuman reality — which gives birth to the idea that something really exists." (*Myth and Reality*) And as Robin and Tomia Ridington write in an essay on shamanism in the Tedlock book, myths "do not give meaning to life but rather disclose the meaning that is its intrinsic property." "The shaman does not really fly up and down, but inside to the meaning of things." One might ask, if the sacred has a symbolic dimension, why not go past it to a direct experience of reality? Duerr answers, "What the sorcerer is concerned with is to demonstrate to the anthropologist that there is a range of reality which his armour-plated culture usually forbids him to enter, and even more importantly, to recognize as reality." While the rationalist may try to stand back from events to see an "objective" view, the shaman *participates* in them.

In *An Essay on Man*, Ernst Cassirer points out that this dual reality with which the primal person lives and which civilization tries to suppress, actually does represent a more fundamental unity. The primal person, he writes, does not approach reality "with merely pragmatic or technical interest ... His view of nature is neither merely theoretical nor merely practical: it is sympathetic ... Primitive man by no means lacks the ability to grasp the empirical differences of things. But in his conception of nature and life all these differences are obliterated by a stronger feeling: the deep conviction of a fundamental and indelible solidarity of life that bridges over the multiplicity and variety of its single forms. He does not ascribe to himself a unique and privileged place in the scale of nature. The consanguinity of all forms of life seems to be a general presupposition of mythical thought." Commenting on this passage, Jamake Highwater remarks that for Native Americans, this solidarity of life "is an expression of kinship and not a conviction of unity." In such a way, it does not impose any single vision, but rather "a multiverse of possibilities."

What can it mean for us to ferret out the "flaws" of primal society and its vision, flaws that may have existed, we are told, "even before the first hints" of hierarchy and ecological destruction? Such a search probably says more about our society than it does about theirs. Or perhaps nature, too, has its flaws, flaws which existed even before a hint of the appearance of this problematic, tricksterish figure, humanity. And can we even use the word "stage" (even qualified by putting quotation marks around the obviously mechanistic and eurocentric idea of "primitive" and "advanced" stages), given the long continuity and stability of such societies — some ninety nine percent of human existence — in contrast with our eyeblink of history? Can we assume that the sacred as it existed for someone like Black Elk or a Tungus shaman led "directly" to what it came to mean to born-again christians, reactionary mullahs, and NASA technocrats? Couldn't it be that there was instead a reversal of magnetic poles in primitive society, that led to the rupture and to state society, with causes that may be beyond available evidence and our ability to uncover? Isn't the notion of a fatal flaw or first cause something we bring to this question from *our* world?

Matters of interpretation

Our world has been desacralized, even though we are plagued by "magical rationalism" and technolatry, so it is difficult for us to comprehend a sacred vision free of alienated and manipulative aspects. It is because our civilization has suppressed the balance between ants and *ants*. The world of ants has been degraded to energy and resources: the world of *ants* has been burned at the stake. Yet the sacred persists, either as a revenge on its own repression, as the quote from Ellul suggests, or as an opening for us to experience that mysterious other in nature and in ourselves. The Teton Sioux bear singer sings,

> *my paw is sacred*
> *all things are sacred.*

It is not a logical absurdity, as Feral Faun argues, that everything is sacred. It depends, for one thing, on how we define *everything*.

The dualities that Lev derides may also be a matter of interpretation. As Stanley Diamond writes in his essay "Job and the Trickster" (in his *In Search of the Primitive)*, the structure of civilization is reflected in deep, deterministic, unyielding dualities of good and evil. Ambivalence, which among primal peoples allowed freedom to express itself fully and openly (for example, through the tradition of clowns who mock sacred ceremonies with impunity, and who thus play an important role in reminding people of ambivalence and mythic duality), is suppressed in civilization.

Among primitive peoples, Diamond writes, "all antinomies are bound into the ritual cycle. The sacred is an immediate aspect of man's experience. Good and evil, creation and destruction — the dual image of the deity as expressed in the trickster — are fused in the network of actions that define primitive society. Therefore moral fanaticism, based as it is on abstract notions of pure good, pure evil and the exclusive moral possibility or fate of any particular individual — what may be called moral exceptionalism — is absent among primitive people. In primitive perspective, human beings are assumed to be capable of any excess. But every step of the way, the person is held to account for those actions that seriously threaten the balance of society and nature."

The clown underscores this refusal of absolute dualities. In Native American societies, the clown lived a life of reversals, throwing every custom and even notions of common sense into question; once recognized as such a person, the clown was considered special and thus protected. Clowns would wear heavy clothing in the hot summer and go nearly naked in the winter, complaining about the cold in the summer and the heat in the winter. Every experience was *derealized*, to use the surrealist term, by the clown, in what has been called a "burlesque of the sacred." Diamond notes, referring to this cultural mode, that one "can hardly imagine" such mockery "taking place, at, let us say, a modern patriotic ceremony; in this sense all state structures tend toward the totalitarian. But, among primitives, sacred events are frequently and publicly caricatured, even as they occur."

According to Barbara Tedlock, "the Navajo clown who reveals sleight-of-hand tricks [thus causing the people to laugh at the shamans] is in effect reminding the people that these tricks are not in themselves the power which cures them, but are instead a symbolic demonstration of power which is itself invisible."Another writer on the Navajos observes that although Navajo belief "stresses the dichotomy of good and evil, it does not set one off against the other. It rather emphasizes one quality or element in a being which in different circumstances may be the opposite. Sun, though 'great' and a 'god,' is not unexceptionally good ... Similarly, few things are wholly bad ... Thus evil may be transformed into good; things predominantly evil, such as snake, lightning, thunder, coyote, may even be invoked. If they have been the cause of misfortune or illness, they alone can correct it ... In short, definition depends upon emphasis and context, not upon exclusion." (Reichard's *Navajo Religion*, quoted in *Technicians of the Sacred*)

Tedlock tells the Acoma tale of the first clown, who, interestingly, "'was different from the other people because he knew something about himself' ... and since he was not 'afraid of anything,' nor did he 'regard anything as sacred,' he was 'to be allowed everywhere.'" Even an irreverent, nonbelieving prankster found a place in such a community. The contrast with repressive world religions is stark, though the clown tradition existed even into the late Middle Ages in christian Europe, which should prevent us from painting even that period in unambiguous black and white. Remember that such paint was mixed by eighteenth century *philosophes* and nineteenth century positivists. The rigid dualities that Chernyi protests do not appear to come from that constellation of sacred beliefs we see among primal peoples; rather, they seem to be part of the process by which the Old Ways are suppressed.

This is not to argue that we should mechanistically copy the ways of primal peoples; we are who we are and can do nothing but start from our own historical experience. But I think the growing recognition of the sacredness of the living earth, of the personhood of the sky, land and waters, of our familial and emotional connection to the rest of creation, is a fundamental element in finding our place in the natural world and re-establishing a proper balance with it. It is integral, I think, to what Lewis Mumford called that "profound and ultimately planet-wide re-orientation of modern culture" that it will take to turn the present exterminist onslaught around. Obviously, we need to act with humility. We can't pretend to have some spiritual program or a new religion; it would be ludicrous and manipulative and end up a horrible simulation of the forms of primal animism without any of their content. But a dramatic renewal of identification with the earth and revulsion against an instrumental relationship with it seem necessary to break through this civilization and create a new culture.

The situationist image of people making a revolution to realize their own desires is incomplete; they must also establish a community with the rest of life. As Theodore Roszak writes in *Where the Wasteland Ends*, "Until we find our way once more to the experience of transcendance, until we feel the life within us and the nature about us as sacred, there will seem to be no 'realistic' future other than more of the same: a single vision and the artificial environment forever and ever, amen."

> *"It may be that some little root of the sacred tree still lives. Nourish it, then, that it may leaf and bloom and fill with singing birds."*
> — *Black Elk*

(1989)

THE FAILURE OF CIVILIZATION & THE FAILURE OF NOAM CHOMSKY

The failure of civilization: it has been given some eight thousand years to prove itself a superior mode of life to the ninety nine plus percent of previous human existence, primarily in tribal, communal, mostly egalitarian societies. Has the transformation to complex civilizations made the species more peaceable, more communal, more egalitarian, or has it had the opposite effect? Let us consider not civilization's ideal, but rather what might be termed "real-existing" civilization.

None of the original problems of life — none of the questions posed before the immensity of the cosmos by ancient Greeks and Chinese, by the prophets, by shamans and seers of primal societies, by contemplatives and social-cultural revolutionaries and visionaries — have been resolved by civilization. Civilization has only managed to give the dark side of our nature access to push-button massacres and alienation, threatening now, with all its tools and toys, to "resolve" its problems and all fundamental questions of existence once and for all by the final eclipse of humanity and the natural habitat in which we have evolved.

"Has civilization failed?" should be the starting point for meaningful discourse on where we find ourselves along the continuum of our real (natural, species) history. But there is enormous denial on this matter, coming most of all from civilization's most dedicated reformers. Reform of civilization could arguably be our only real option; we should not dismiss without serious consideration the compelling possibility of biological irreversibility (and its parallel in cultural irreversibility) as a paradigm for our mono/cultural destiny so far. Everything seems to go downhill. But let us at least have the courage and the honesty (with ourselves) to admit that civilization has brought no ultimate good to our species, has failed to deliver what dubious promises it offered, while in planetary terms has proved an unmitigated disaster.

This is in a sense where a group of people around the publication *Anarchy: A Journal of Desire Armed* attempted to begin with celebrated left libertarian writer (and one-man anti-imperial truth squad) Noam Chomsky when they interviewed him briefly before a speaking engagement in Columbia, Missouri. (*Anarchy,* Summer 1991) We owe them our praise and gratitude for opening the dialogue, even if the results were so disappointing. It was an interesting idea to ask Chomsky about issues other than what we normally expect from him, particularly given the energy such discussions have taken up in the anarchist/anti-authoritarian milieu.

But judging from the interview, Chomsky was very negative and close-minded about the discussion, refusing to even consider it as a valid area of dialogue or to recognize any distinction in the terminology describing civilization (complex, hierarchic, megatechnic societies) and primal and vernacular communities. To Chomsky, all human cultures are civilizations (so much for linguistic subtlety), from gatherer-hunters to modern capitalism. "Civilization has many aspects," he told the people from the Columbia Anarchist League. "It doesn't mean anything to be for it or against it," as if it were a simple for/against formula that we have been elaborating.

Is technology neutral?

Chomsky may be forgiven for his unfamiliarity with what the *Fifth Estate* has tried to elaborate over the last decade or so — he's a busy man, and he does very important work. But he also appears to know nothing about the insights of critical anthropology (writers such as Sahlins, Clastres, Diamond) or the critique of technology (an enormous literature including critical work by his MIT colleague Joseph Weizenbaum and former colleague Langdon Winner, but including people like Ivan Illich, Jacques Ellul, and someone of the stature of Lewis Mumford, who laid groundwork for the possibility of a critique of civilization based on its technical, and by implication, its social relations). Chomsky appears to know little about any of this.

For example, he relativizes oppression by claiming it existed in all civilizations (by which he means societies). "Some of the worst forms of oppression and brutality are in pretechnological societies," he argues, repeating modern civilization's standard dogma. Thus the presence of so-cial conflict or oppression in other societies not only silences discussion of primal and vernacular cultures and their values but mystifies the impor-tant distinctions that critical anthropologists and others have made between direct, highly idiosyncratic social relations in small societies and the kind of systemic (and alienated), institutionalized violence and oppression in hierarchic societies. Here Chomsky reveals himself to be much more of a marxist (and a rather conventional one at that) than an anarchist.

When the technology discussion really starts heating up, the good professor declares it all entirely neutral. "A libertarian society," he tells us, "would want to make use of the most advanced technology there is, and in fact would want to advance it further. Take a real contemporary technol-ogy like, say, information processing technology. You know, that can be used for oppression; it can be used for liberation. . . ." There is not even a shred of criticality here — no influence of Mumford (or perhaps Schumacher), nothing of a writer like Bookchin (who lies somewhere be-tween us and Chomsky), not even a healthy dash of Emerson or Thoreau! Nope, everything "depends on the social institutions in which [technol-ogy] exists." Even robotics: "Robotics itself is neutral."

Unquestioning affirmation of civilization

What is so disappointing is Chomsky's arrogant certainty that tech-nics itself could never become systemic, culture-forming, not only being shaped by but eventually shaping the institutions that engender and ad-minister it; or that technology might possibly have inertial aspects that synergize with the social environment, that it might come to shape mean-ing, that it might complicate or even ultimately undermine our possibili-ties for a liberatory society. And nothing about tribal societies is allowed in the discussion of models for freedom if any examples of oppression and brutality can be found in any of them. There is not the slightest suspicion in this normally skeptical thinker that there might be more to "information processing technology" — let alone information processing or even infor-mation — than pragmatically meets the eye within present circumstances. (I suspected that Chomsky's position on technology might be less than enlightened when I read, in *The Chomsky Reader* — a generally excellent book, by the way — that he has been "in an electronics laboratory for the last thirty years" — a punishment!)

For such a brilliant critic of empire to have failed to study technics more profoundly is perhaps understandable, though very unfortunate. But to affirm so authoritatively all the shibboleths of technological civilization is horrid. It marginalizes not only what we have attempted to do, but the greens and anti-development movements in the Third World, native peoples and radical ecologists of all kinds. For Chomsky, civilization's cardinal rule that more is better, bigger is better, faster is better, more complicated is better, and all the rest, goes entirely unquestioned. "Automobiles, robotics, or information processing, there you have a liberatory technology," he chided his anarchist interviewers, and then the final, predictable reckoning: "The only thing that can possibly resolve environmental problems is advanced technology. . . ." Full steam ahead; forgive us if we choose to disbelieve the assurances of the faithful.

Long life to Chomsky in his courageous, relentless, single-minded (and sometimes seemingly single-handed) battle against the Big Lie. His books are invaluable in disseminating historical truth in order to combat the imperial propaganda machine. As my friend Dolores told me, "Hey, he's still worth reading — nobody's perfect."

But in other matters, such as a more fundamental critique of modern civilization, of what capital engendered on a global scale — megatechnics, cybernetic alienation, and weapons of mass destruction that not only come in the form of bombs and warships and the like but also in the form of conveniences, scientific efficiency, and progressive rationalization — he's pretty hopeless. Too bad. Another painful example of how impoverished real prospects for freedom remain.

(1991)

A HUMBLE CALL TO SUBVERT
THE HUMAN EMPIRE

I've been thinking about how an optimistic, problem-solving attitude can conceal a deeper hopelessness ever since I ran across the following news item: in 1995 India's Environment Ministry moved to protect Indian butterfly and moth species under the government's Wildlife Act to prevent smuggling of the insects. The measure came after two German tourists were caught trying to leave the country with 15,000 preserved butterflies and moths in their luggage.

Should we feel relief at attempts to plug one of the myriad leaks in nature's troubled reservoir, that some are grappling with a grave issue most of us did not even suspect existed? Or numb grief, knowing the guardians cannot block every gate, nor stanch every hemorrhaging wound? "Man the exterminator has designs on everything that lives," the misanthropic philosopher E.M. Cioran once quipped. "Soon we will be hearing about the last louse." Those two smugglers exemplify a short-term, narrow self-interest driving both individuals and international institutions toward the abyss. But they were only the ones who happened to be intercepted, and thus a guarantee there are more — fifty, perhaps a hundred more. In a world where human beings are the measure of all things and sole repository of value, where every unique manifestation of life has become merchandise, rare butterflies will have little chance of living out their own evolutionary destiny.

Sadly, collectors are also only one factor, probably a lesser one, in the demise of butterflies, greatly overshadowed by macrocosmic insults like dam construction, logging, agriculture and the use of biocides, urban and industrial development, and other disruptions of butterfly habitat. And as a single moth goes, so may a flower, and with the moth and flower, other members of a small and complex community of life utterly indivisible, and invisible to us.

Those moths and butterflies that do eventually succumb will join an accelerating *danse macabre* of extinction brought about by a single clever species during the last few centuries, and most acutely in the last few decades. Some victims are already gone: great auk, passenger pigeon, woodland bison, Eskimo Curlew, Dodo (and with it a plant dependent for its germination on the passage of its seed through the Dodo's digestive tract). Others are sliding irrevocably toward the chute: rhinoceros, elephant, tiger, piping plover, and other creatures that are vanishing before we even know of them. Like the auk, so utterly extinguished by the mid–1800s that some thought it apocryphal, these beings may one day be considered fabulous not only figuratively but in the precise sense of the unicorn, because there will be little difference in the minds of our grandchildren whether they once lived or were whimsy.

It's easy to find scientists and lay people who consider this sense of loss mere sentimentality unworthy of our status as "the lords and possessors of nature," to repeat Descartes' unhappy phrase. After all, extinction is natural and inevitable, they are quick to remind us. According to this argument, trying to save species that have lost the competition between the "fit" and "unfit" is an attempt to turn back an inexorable clock; there is little room for such beautiful losers in the ongoing march of human progress.

Extinction is indeed as natural as the death of an individual. But in the present case countless species are not simply disappearing randomly; whether the process is entirely premeditated or not, human beings and institutions are actively making choices which bring about their demise. The Worldwatch Institute reports that three fourths of the world's bird species are declining in population or threatened with extinction. One in four mammals is threatened. Virtually all species of wild cats and most bears are declining seriously, and more than two thirds of the world's 150 primate species are threatened. Peter Raven, Director of the Missouri Botanical Garden and a conservation biologist of international reputation, estimates that as ecosystems are converted to agricultural and pastoral purposes in the next twenty to thirty years, the rate of extinction of plant and animal land species will go from several per day to *several hundred per day*. Nearly all contemporary extinctions are due directly or indirectly to human activities — development, deforestation, contamination, hunting and the introduction of aggressive exotic species into new habitats.

Rising human population is widely considered to be the single underlying cause of the contemporary die-off along the bulldozer's blade and chainsaw's teeth. Ecological meltdown is typically represented by a landless peasant slashing the forest with his machete, or a tribal woman carrying a bundle of sticks on her head — and a hungry child on her back.

To be sure, the well-known ascending J-curve of rising human numbers, accompanying the vertiginous obliteration of innumerable other species, leaves a stunning impression. At present growth rates, world population is estimated to reach 8.9 billion by the year 2030, and level off at 11.5 billion around 2150 — an unprecedented rise in human numbers of more than ten times in two hundred years. Yet sheer numbers do not explain the current mass extinction spasm; population growth is one increasingly aggravating factor in a constellation of causes. We need to look beyond the numbers at social structures, an energy- and commodity-intensive development model, and the social and historical causes of extreme poverty.

For example, while they comprise only 25 percent of the world's population, advanced industrial nations account for 75 percent of energy use and consume 85 percent of all forest products. U.S. per capita energy consumption is some 250 times greater than that of many poor countries, suggesting that daily life in the North contributes far more to ecological destruction than population growth in the South (though growing middle classes in the South are having a similar impact there). On a global scale, according to one U.S. official, the impact of the world's poorest people is "probably more akin to picking up branches and twigs after commercial chain saws have done their work."

The biological notion of carrying capacity — essentially the maximum number of a species that a habitat can indefinitely support — is complicated enough for there to be wide divergence of opinion whether or not the planet can adequately support such human numbers (though there are copious signs that our ability to feed ourselves is declining due to abuse and over-exploitation of our food sources). There is adequate evidence that the reason people are presently starving is not because our numbers have surpassed carrying capacity. But even if some believe we can provide a decent life to two or three times the number of people now living, no thoughtful person could possibly doubt the disastrous effect such numbers will inevitably have on other species, other than those which easily adapt or which we find useful to us. Calculating our maximum load is terribly misguided if we feel any sense of responsibility for those other beings most certainly being obliterated as we struggle to keep up.

Even thinking only of our own offspring and not of those of other beings, how many people the earth can support is still the wrong question; we also need to consider *what kind* of life we want to lead — crowded into the urbanopolis, the landscape entirely marshaled to meet our ever-expanding needs, or in community with other species in a green world something like the one in which we evolved. The latter planet will make it possible for all species — and thus, wilderness and diverse land and ocean habitats — to flourish. That will be the best world for us, too, but common sense makes clear that it will necessitate fewer of us.

There is a "nature-red-in-tooth-and-claw" idea that human depredation and consequent mass extinction are entirely natural. According to this view, even Paleolithic humans, being an intrinsically murderous lot, carried out their share of mass extinctions (for example, supposedly wiping out many large mammals in North America). Yet there is little hard evidence, and much reason to doubt — except in the most obvious cases of extinction on islands like that of the flightless Moa of New Zealand/Aotearoa, for example — that mass extinctions were caused by prehistoric foragers and hunters. Farley Mowat, in his book, *Sea of Slaughter,* provides a dizzying description of the carnage perpetrated on the animals of the North American eastern seaboard by Euroamerican explorers and entrepreneurs. He notes that the great auk coexisted with human hunters for millennia before succumbing in a couple of hundred years to the mechanized, market-driven empire that was only the quaint precursor to ours.

Ultimately, we can remain agnostic about whether or not our distant ancestors foolishly fouled their nest. It is pretty much irrelevant to the reality we face now: an immensely brutal, and thoroughly anthropocentric civilization is presently ravaging the earth, ostensibly in our human interest. The scale and scope of the devastation is unprecedented in the history of our species. This civilization's arrogance is evident in our scientific tradition's urge to expand what Francis Bacon called "the empire of man." It has more archaic sources, too. The Judeo-Christian biblical edict granted us "dominion over the fish of the sea, and over the fowl of the air, and over the cattle, and over all the earth, and over every creeping thing that creepeth upon the earth." Now many animals mentioned in the Bible are going the way of the Dodo — Jonah's whale, the Persian Wild Ass on which Jesus rode into Jerusalem, the Nubian Ibex, the Arabian oryx which Isaiah tells us was trapped in nets, and others. Human dominion has done these creatures little good; most have fallen forever into out nets.

The image of a human imperium oppressing the rest of nature is metaphor, but not merely so; it conforms to an actual pattern of imperial conquest, plunder, eventual exhaustion and collapse. Our century has given a privileged layer of humanity an industrially organized life more opulent, more wasteful (yet still more frenetic, alienated and oppressive) than that of any ancient hierarch. We've transformed the earth into a giant mine and waste pit, its forests and meadow lands into enormous feed lots for billions of stock animals, its waters into cesspools devoid of life, its skies into orbiting junkyards of contaminated rocket debris. The world's tallest mountains are littered with expedition trash, and ships at sea do not go a single day without seeing plastic garbage. Giant nets thirty miles long drag the oceans, killing millions of sea creatures, including birds and mammals, many of them simply thrown overboard.

The whole planet has become a war zone for every other thing that creepeth upon the earth, generating a bio-crisis not just for individual species, but for whole webs of life. Human beings are now altering the basic physiology of the planet. Industrial smog can be found everywhere over the oceans, and weather patterns have been so dramatically affected that climatologists now discuss the phenomenon of "climate death." Industrial contamination is pervasive, even in the fat cells of Antarctic penguins, and the rain is not only acid but toxic. Whether industrialism warms or cools the atmosphere, its unprecedented chemical experiment threatens to reconfigure life in ways barely imaginable, but undoubtedly for the worse.

All empires turn out to be relatively short-lived enterprises that finally betray their own subjects. Despite their enormous cost to the rest of life, modern civilization's demands on the planet have engendered a mode of life that fails to meet even the barest essentials of one fifth of humanity, or to satisfy fundamental psychic needs of the rest. However many preserved exotic butterflies the privileged may be able to purchase for a time, progressive "humanization" of the planet dehumanizes the very people it purports to serve. And we too have fallen into the nets, as our genes are mapped, and some deemed useless "junk DNA" — like the animals discarded from fishing vessels as economically worthless. The earliest stages of tampering are underway, as the empire prepares to be fully internalized. Our very anthropocentrism may be our own undoing, with our relentless religion of economic-technical instrumentalism proving useless to prevent it.

Pragmatic self-interest alone should teach us that we must change before nature exacts inevitable revenge. And nothing can be done, North or South, without social strategies that create institutions to provide practical alternatives, and thus opportunities for people to change. Yet meaningful subversion of the "empire of man" requires more than enlightened self-interest or even social justice. It means real transformation — a cultural practice neither anthropocentric nor simply "ecocentric," but perhaps *polycentric*. It requires a way of living that considers *all life* a larger community deserving of our solidarity. In the process, people may discover that limiting our numbers and consumption — living more simply so that others (human and non-human) may simply live — brings ineluctable rewards of its own. Such a recognition suggests precisely that spiritual dimension missing so dramatically from modern life and its frenzy of accumulation.

For the last few years I have practiced T'ai Chi, an ancient, meditative martial art that names many of its postures for animals such as monkeys, cranes and tigers. I have often wondered what would become of a practice inextricably woven to such creatures when human hubris finally extinguishes them. What will become of our own spirit when inspirited creatures we invoke are gone from our midst? Who — and what — will *we* be? When we realize the life-forms and life-webs we've slaughtered and abused are our own larger self, as many native peoples, radical ecologists and other "counter-traditions" remind us, we will have begun the necessary process of renewal that could make life worth living in the coming centuries.

(1996)

IV.
CIVILIZATION
IN BULK

Illustration by Freddie Baer

Illustration by Johann Humyn Being

CIVILIZATION IS LIKE A JETLINER

Civilization is like a jetliner, noisy, burning up enormous amounts of fuel. Every imaginable and unimaginable crime and pollution had to be committed in order to make it go. Whole species were rendered extinct, whole populations dispersed. Its shadow on the waters resembles an oil slick. Birds are sucked into its jets and vaporized. Every part, as Gus Grissom once nervously remarked about space capsules before he was burned up in one, has been made by the lowest bidder.

Civilization is like a 747, the filtered air, the muzak oozing over the earphones, the phony sense of security, the chemical food, the plastic trays, all the passengers sitting passively in the orderly row of padded seats staring at Death on the movie screen. Civilization is like a jetliner, an idiot savant in the cockpit manipulating computerized controls built by sullen wage workers, and dependent for his directions on sleepy technicians high on amphetamines with their minds wandering to sports and sex.

Civilization is like a 747, filled beyond capacity with coerced volunteers — some in love with the velocity, most wavering at the abyss of terror and nausea, yet still seduced by advertising and propaganda. It is like a DC-10, so incredibly enclosed that you want to break through the tin can walls and escape, make your own way through the clouds, and leave this rattling, screaming fiend approaching its breaking point. The smallest error or technical failure leads to catastrophe, breaking all your bones like egg shells and scattering your sad entrails like belated omens over the runway.

Of course civilization is like many other things besides jets — always things — a chemical drainage ditch, a woodland knocked down to lengthen an airstrip or to build a slick new shopping mall where people can buy salad bowls made out of exotic tropical trees which will be extinct next week. Or perhaps a graveyard for cars, or a suspension bridge which collapses because a single metal pin has shaken loose. Civilization is a hydra. There is a multitude of styles, colors, and sizes of Death to choose from.

Civilization is like a Boeing jumbo jet because it transports people who have never experienced their humanity where they were to places where they shouldn't go. In fact it mainly transports businessmen in suits with briefcases filled with charts, contracts, more mischief — businessmen who are identical everywhere and hence have no reason at all to be ferried about. And it goes faster and faster, turning more and more places into airports, the (un)natural habitat of businessmen.

It is an utter mystery how it gets off the ground. It rolls down the runway, the blinking lights along the ground like electronic scar tissue on the flesh of the earth, picks up speed and somehow grunts, raping the air, working its way up along the shimmering waves of heat and the trash blowing about like refugees fleeing the bombing of a city. Yes, it is exciting, a mystery, when life has been evacuated and the very stones have been murdered.

But civilization, like the jetliner, this freak phoenix incapable of rising from its ashes, also collapses across the earth like a million bursting wasps, flames spreading across the runway in tentacles of gasoline, samsonite, and charred flesh. And always the absurd rubbish, Death's confetti, the fragments left to mock us lying along the weary trajectory of the dying bird — the doll's head, the shoes, eyeglasses, a beltbuckle.

Jetliners fall, civilizations fall, this civilization will fall. The gauges will be read wrong on some snowy day (perhaps they will fail). The wings, supposedly de-iced, will be too frozen to beat against the wind and the bird will sink like a millstone, first gratuitously skimming a bridge (because civilization is also like a bridge, from Paradise to Nowhere). A bridge laden, say, with commuters on their way to or from work, which is to say, to or from an airport, packed in their cars (wingless jetliners) like additional votive offerings to a ravenous Medusa.

Then it will dive into the icy waters of a river, the Potomac perhaps, or the River Jordan, or Lethe. And we will be inside, each one of us at our specially assigned porthole, going down for the last time, like dolls' heads encased in plexiglass.

(1983)

CIVILIZATION IN BULK: EMPIRE AND ECOLOGICAL DESTRUCTION

Having had the privilege of living for a time among stone age peoples of Brazil, a very civilized European of considerable erudition wrote afterwards, "Civilization is no longer a fragile flower, to be carefully preserved and reared with great difficulty here and there in sheltered corners ... All that is over: humanity has taken to monoculture, once and for all, and is preparing to produce civilization in bulk, as if it were sugar-beet. The same dish will be served to us every day."[1] (See page 197 for endnotes.)

Those words were written in 1955. Now that civilization is engulfing the entire planet, the image of the fragile flower has largely wilted. Some of civilization's inmates are remembering that the image was always a lie; other ways of seeing the world are being rediscovered. Counter-traditions are being reexamined, escape routes devised, weapons fashioned. To put it another way, a spectre haunts the heavy equipment as it chugs deeper into the morass it has made: the spectre of the primal world.[2]

Devising escapes and weapons is no simple task: false starts and poor materials. The old paths are paved and the materials that come from the enemy's arsenal tend to explode in our hands. Memory and desire have been suppressed and deformed; we have all been inculcated in the Official History. Its name is Progress, and the Dream of Progress continues to fuel global civilization's expansion everywhere, converting human beings into mechanized, self-obliterating puppets, nature into dead statuary.

The Official History can be found in every child's official history text: Before the genesis (which is to say, before civilization), there was nothing but a vast, oceanic chaos, dark and terrible, brutish and nomadic, a bloody struggle for existence. Eventually, through great effort by a handful of men, some anonymous, some celebrated, humanity emerged from the slime, from trees, caves, tents and endless wanderings in a sparse and perilous desert to accomplish fantastic improvements in life. Such improvements came through the mastery of animals, plants, and minerals; the exploitation of hitherto neglected Resources; the fineries of high culture and religion; and the miracles of technics in the service of centralized authority.

This awe-inspiring panoply of marvels took shape under the aegis of the city-state and behind its fortified walls. Through millennia, civilization struggled to survive amid a storm of barbarism, resisting being swallowed by the howling wilderness. Then another "Great Leap Forward" among certain elect and anointed kingdoms of what came to be called "the West," and the modern world was born: the enlightenment of scientific reason ushered in exploration and discovery of the wilderness — internal (psychic) and external (geographic). In the kingdom's official murals, the Discoverers appear at one end, standing proudly on their ships, telescopes and sextants in their hands; at the other end waits the world, a sleeping beauty ready to awaken and join her powerful husband in the marriage bed of nature and reason. Finally come the offspring of this revolution: invention, mechanization, industrialization, and ultimately scientific, social and political maturity, a mass democratic society and mass-produced abundance.

Certainly, a few bugs remain to be worked out — ubiquitous contamination, runaway technology, starvation and war (mostly at the uncivilized "peripheries"), but civilization cherishes its challenges, and expects all such aberrations to be brought under control, rationalized by technique, re-designed to serve human needs, forever and ever, amen. History is a gleaming locomotive running on rails — albeit around precarious curves and through some foreboding tunnels — to the Promised Land. And whatever the dangers, there can be no turning back.[3]

A false turn

But now that several generations have been raised on monoculture's gruel, civilization is coming to be regarded not as a promise yet to be fulfilled so much as a maladaption of the species, a false turn, or a kind of fever threatening the planetary web of life. As one of History's gentle rebels once remarked, "We do not ride upon the railroad, it rides upon us."[4] The current crisis, occurring on every level, from the ecospheric to the social to the personal, has become too manifest, too grievous, to ignore. The spectre haunting modern civilization, once only a sense of loss, now has open partisans who have undertaken the theoretical and practical critique of civilization.[5]

So we begin by reexamining our list of chapters, not from the point of view of the conquerors but the conquered: the slaves crushed under temple construction sites or gassed in the trenches, the dredged and shackled rivers, the flattened forests, the beings pinned to laboratory tables. What voice can better speak for them than the primal? Such a critique of "the modern world through Pleistocene eyes," such a "geological kind of perspective," as the indigenous authors of the 1977 Haudenosaunee (Iroquois) document, *A Basic Call to Consciousness*, put it, immediately explodes the conquerors' Big Lie about "underdevelopment" and the "brutality" of primal society, their vilification of prehistory.[6]

The lie has most recently been eroded not only by greater access to the views of primal peoples and their native descendants who are presently fighting for survival, but by a more critical, non-eurocentric anthropology willing to challenge its own history, premises and privilege.[7] Primal society, with its myriad variations, is the common heritage of all peoples. From it, we can infer how human beings lived some 99 percent of our existence as a species. (And even a large part of that last one percent consists of the experience of tribal and other vernacular communities that resist conquest and control in creative, if idiosyncratic ways.)

Looking with new/old eyes on the primal world, we see a web of autonomous societies, splendidly diverse but sharing certain characteristics. Primal society has been called "the original affluent society," affluent because its needs are few, all its desires are easily met.[8] Its tool kit is elegant and lightweight, its outlook linguistically complex and conceptually profound yet simple and accessible to all. Its culture is expansive and ecstatic. It is propertyless and communal, egalitarian and cooperative. Like nature, it is essentially leaderless: neither patriarchal nor matriarchal, it is anarchic, which is to say that no archon or ruler has built and occupied center stage. It is, rather, an organic constellation of persons, each unique.

A society free of work

It is also a society free of work; it has no economy or production *per se*, except for gift exchange and a kind of ritual play that also happen to create subsistence (though it is a society capable of experiencing occasional hunger without losing its spiritual bearings, even sometimes choosing hunger to enhance interrelatedness, to play or to see visions).[9] The Haudenosaunee, for example, write that they "do not have specific economic institutions, [or] ... specifically distinct political institutions." Furthermore, the subsistence activities of Haudenosaunee society, "by our cultural definition, [are] not an economy at all."[10]

Primal society's plenitude resides in its many symbolic, personal and natural relationships, not in artifacts. It is a dancing society, a singing society, a celebrating society, a dreaming society. Its philosophy and practice of what is called animism — a mythopoetic articulation of the organic unity of life discovered only recently by the West's ecologists — protects the land by treating its multiplicity of forms as sacred beings, each with its own integrity and subjectivity. Primal society affirms community with all of the natural and social world.

Somehow this primal world, a world (as Lewis Mumford has observed) more or less corresponding to the ancient vision of the Golden Age, unravels as the institutions of kingship and mass society emerge.[11] How it happened remains unclear to us today. Perhaps we will never understand the mystery of that original mutation from egalitarian to state society. Certainly, no standard explanations are adequate.[12] "That radical discontinuity," in the words of Pierre Clastres, "that mysterious emergence — irreversible, fatal to primitive societies — of the thing we know by the name of State," how does it occur?

Primal society maintained its equilibrium and its egalitarianism because it refused power, refused property. Kingship could not have emerged from the chief because the chief had no coercive power over others. Clastres insists: "Primitive society is the place where separate power is refused, because the society itself, and not the chief, is the real locus of power."[13]

It is possible that we could approach this dissolution of original community appropriately only by way of mythic language like the Old Ones would have used. After all, only a poetic story could vividly express such a tragic loss of equilibrium. The latent potentiality for power and technique to emerge as separate domains had been previously kept at bay by the gift cycle, "techniques of the sacred," and the high level of individuation of society's members.

Primal peoples, according to Clastres, "had a very early premonition that power's transcendence conceals a mortal risk for the group, that the principle of an authority which is external and the creator of its own legality is a challenge to culture itself. It is the intuition of this threat that determined the depth of their political philosophy. For, on discovering the great affinity of power and nature, as the twofold limitation on the domain of culture, Indian societies were able to create a means for neutralizing the virulence of political authority."[14]

This, in effect, is the same process by which primal peoples neutralized the potential virulence of technique: they minimized the relative weight of instrumental or practical techniques and expanded the importance of techniques of seeing: ecstatic techniques. Thus, the predecessor of kingship is not to be found in the shaman either. The shaman is, rather, as Jerome Rothenberg puts it, after Eliade, a "technician" of ecstasy, a "protopoet" whose "technique hinges on the creation of special linguistic circumstances, i.e. of song and invocation."[15]

Technology, like power, is in such a way refused by the dynamic of primal social relations. But when technique and power emerge as separate functions rather than as strands inextricably woven into the fabric of society, everything starts to come apart. "The unintended excrescence that grows out of human communities and then liquidates them," as Fredy Perlman called it, makes its appearance.[16] A sorcery run amok, a golem-like thingness that outlives its fabricators: somehow the gift cycle is ruptured; the hoop, the circle, broken.

The community, as Clastres puts it, "has ceased to exorcise the thing that will be its ruin: power and the respect for power." A kind of revolution, or counter-revolution, takes place: "When, in primitive society, the economic dynamic lends itself to definition as a distinct and autonomous domain, when the activity of production becomes alienated, accountable labor, levied by men who will enjoy the fruits of that labor, what has come to pass is that society has been divided into rulers and ruled, masters and subjects ... The political relation of power precedes and founds the economic relation of exploitation. Alienation is political before it is economic; power precedes labor; the economic derives from the political; the emergence of the State determines the advent of classes."[17]

The emergence of authority, production, and technology are all moments within the same process. Previously, power resided in no separate sphere, but rather within the circle — a circle that included the human community and nature (nonhuman kin). "Production" and the "economic" were undivided as well; they were embedded in the circle through gift sharing, which transcends and neutralizes the artifactuality or "thingness" of the objects passing from person to person. (Animals, plants, and natural objects being persons, even kin, subsistence therefore is neither work nor production, but rather, gift, drama, reverence, reverie.) Technique also had to be embedded in relations between kin, and thus open, participatory, and accessible to all; or it was entirely personal, singular, visionary, unique and untransferable.

Equilibrium exploded

The "great affinity of power and nature," as Clastres puts it, explains the deep cleft between them when power divides and polarizes the community. For the primal community, to follow Mircea Eliade's reasoning, "The world is at once 'open' and mysterious ... 'Nature' at once unveils and 'camouflages' the supernatural, [which] constitutes the basic and unfathomable mystery of the World." Mythic consciousness apprehends and intervenes in the world, participates in it, but this does not necessitate a relation of domination; it "does not mean that one has transformed [cosmic realities] into 'objects of knowledge.' These realities still keep their original ontological condition."[18]

The trauma of disequilibrium exploded what contemporary pagan feminists have called "power within" and generated "power over." What were once mutualities became hierarchies. In this transformation, gift exchange disappears; gift exchange with nature disappears with it. What was shared is now hoarded: the mystery to which one once surrendered now becomes a territory to be conquered. All stories of the origins become histories of the origins … of the Master. The origin of the World is retold as the origin of the State.

Woman, who through the birth process exemplifies all of nature and who maintains life processes through her daily processes of nurturance of plants, animals and children, is suppressed by the new transformer-hero. Male power, attempting to rival the fecundity of woman, simulates birth and nature's fecundity through the manufacture of artifacts and monuments. The womb — a primordial container, a basket or bowl — is reconstituted by power into the city walls.

"Thus," as Frederick W. Turner argues in *Beyond Geography: The Western Spirit Against the Wilderness*, "the 'rise to civilization' might be seen not so much as the triumph of a progressive portion of the race over its lowly, nature-bound origins as a severe, aggressive *volte-face* against all unimproved nature, the echoes of which would still be sounding millennia later when civilized men once again encountered the challenges of the wilderness beyond their city walls."[19]

No explanation and no speculation can encompass the series of events that burst community and generated class society and the state. But the result is relatively clear: the institutionalization of hierarchic elites and the drudgery of the dispossessed to support them; monoculture to feed their armed gangs; the organization of society into work battalions; hoarding, taxation, and economic relations; and the reduction of the organic community to lifeless resources to be mined and manipulated by the archon and his institutions.

The "chief features" of this new state society, writes Mumford, "constant in varying proportions throughout history, are the concentration of political power, the separation of classes, the lifetime division of labor, the mechanization of production, the magnification of military power, the economic exploitation of the weak, and the universal introduction of slavery and forced labor for both industrial and military purposes." In other words, a megamachine made up of two major arms, a labor machine and a military machine.

The crystallization of a fluid, organic community into a pseudo-community, a giant machine, was in fact the first machine, the standard definition of which, Mumford notes, is "a combination of resistant parts, each specialized in function, operating under human control, to utilize energy and perform work. . . ." Thus, he argues, "The two poles of civilization are mechanically-organized work and mechanically-organized destruction and extermination. Roughly the same forces and the same methods of operation [are] applicable to both areas." In Mumford's view, the greatest legacy of this system has been "the myth of the machine" — the belief that it is both irresistible and ultimately beneficial. This mechanization of human beings, he writes, "had long preceded the mechanization of their working instruments ... But once conceived, this new mechanism spread rapidly, not just by being imitated in self-defense, but by being forcefully imposed. . . ."

One can see the differences here between the kind of technics embedded in an egalitarian society and technics-as-power or technology. As Mumford argues, people "of ordinary capacity, relying on muscle power and traditional skills alone, were capable of performing a wide variety of tasks, including pottery manufacture and weaving, without any external direction or scientific guidance, beyond that available in the tradition of the local community. Not so with the megamachine. Only kings, aided by the discipline of astronomical science and supported by the sanctions of religion, had the capacity of assembling and directing the megamachine. This was an invisible structure composed of living, but rigid, human parts, each assigned to his special office, role, and task, to make possible the immense work-output and grand designs of this great collective organization."[20]

Civilization as labor camp

In his intuitive history of the megamachine, Fredy Perlman describes how a Sumerian "Ensi" or overseer, lacking the rationalizations of the ideology of Progress which are routinely used to vaccinate us against our wildness, might see the newly issued colossus:

"He might think of it as a worm, a giant worm, not a living worm but a carcass of a worm, a monstrous cadaver, its body consisting of numerous segments, its skin pimpled with spears and wheels and other technological implements. He knows from his own experience that the entire carcass is brought to artificial life by the motions of the human beings trapped inside, the zeks who operate the springs and wheels, just as he knows that the cadaverous head is operated by a mere zek, the head zek."[21]

It is no accident that Fredy chose the word *zek*, a word meaning gulag prisoner that he found in Solzhenitsyn's work. It was not only to emphasize that civilization has been a labor camp from its origins, but to illuminate the parallels between the ancient embryonic forms and the modern global work machine presently suffocating the earth. While the differences in magnitude and historical development are great, essential elements shared by both modern and ancient systems — elements outlined above — position both civilizations in a polarity with primal community. At one end stands organic community: an organism, in the form of a circle, a web woven into the fabric of nature. At the other is civilization: no longer an organism but organic fragments reconstituted as a machine, an organization; no longer a circle but a rigid pyramid of crushing hierarchies; not a web but a grid expanding the territory of the inorganic.

According to official history, this grid is the natural outcome of an inevitable evolution. Thus natural history is not a multiverse of potentialities but rather a linear progression from Prometheus' theft of fire to the International Monetary Fund. This ideology dismisses a million and more years of species life experienced in organic communities as a kind of waiting period in anticipation of the few thousand years of imperial grandeur to follow. The remaining primal societies even now being dragged by the hair into civilization's orbit along its blood-drenched frontier are dismissed as living fossils ("lacking in evolutionary promise," as one philosopher characterized them), awaiting their glorious inscription into the wondrous machine.[22]

Thus, as Fredy Perlman argued, imperialism is far from being the last stage of civilization but is embedded in the earliest stages of the state and class society. There is always a brutal frontier where there is empire and always empire where there is civilization. The instability and rapidity of change as well as the violence and destructiveness of the change both belie empire's claim to natural legitimacy, suggesting once more an evolutionary wrong turn, a profoundly widening disequilibrium.

The frontier expands along two intersecting axes, centrifugal and centripetal. In the words of Stanley Diamond, "Civilization originates in conquest abroad and repression at home. Each is an aspect of the other."[23] Outwardly, empire is expressed geographically (northern Canada, Malaysia, the Amazon, etc.; the ocean bottoms, even outer space) and biospherically (disruption of weather and climate, vast chemical experiments on the air and water, elimination and simplification of ecosystems, genetic manipulation). But the process is replicated internally on the human spirit: every zek finds an empire in miniature "wired" to the very nervous system.[24]

So, too, is repression naturalized, the permanent crisis in character and the authoritarian plague legitimated. It starts with frightened obedience to the archon or patriarch, then moves by way of projection to a violent, numbed refusal of the living subjectivity and integrity of the other — whether found in nature, in woman, or in conquered peoples.

At one end of the hierarchic pyramid stands unmitigated power; at the other, submission mingles with isolation, fragmentation and rage. All is justified by the ideology of Progress — conquest and subjugation of peoples, ruin of lands and sacrifice zones for the empire, self repression, mass addiction to imperial spoils, the materialization of culture. Ideology keeps the work and war machines operating.

Ultimately, this vortex brings about the complete objectification of nature. Every relationship is increasingly instrumentalized and technicized. Mechanization and industrialization have rapidly transformed the planet, exploding ecosystems and human communities with monoculture, industrial degradation, and mass markets. The world now corresponds more closely to the prophetic warnings of primal peoples than to the hollow advertising claims of the industrial system: the plants disappearing and the animals dying, the soils denuded along with the human spirit, vast oceans poisoned, the very rain turned corrosive and deadly, human communities at war with one another over diminishing spoils — and all poised on the brink of an even greater annihilation at the push of a few buttons within reach of stunted, half-dead head-zeks in fortified bunkers. Civilization's railroad leads not only to ecocide, but to evolutionary suicide.

Every empire lurches toward the oblivion it fabricates and will eventually be covered with sand. Can a world worth inhabiting survive the ruin that will be left?

(1991)

Endnotes

1. Claude Lévi-Strauss, *Tristes Tropiques* (1961, New York: Atheneum, 1971), p. 39.
2. The word "primal" has replaced its relative "primitive." Both words, according to Stanley Diamond, derive from "the presumptive proto-Indo European root *pri*," and mean "before," or "earliest, original, primary." Diamond defines primitive as referring to "widely distributed, well-organized institutions that had already existed just prior to the rise of ancient civilization; it does not imply historically an inchoate time of cultural origins nor psychiatrically the period when supposed primary processes were directly expressed." Thus Diamond accepts the word and tries "to define it further" within its proper context as "signifying a prior state of affairs, a relative sense of origins. . . ." See "The Search for the Primitive," in *In Search of the Primitive* (1974; New Brunswick and London: Transaction Books, 1981), pp. 123-129.
3. As mass technics get closer to the brink, its defenders become even more shrill. The New Canaan is just around the corner, we are assured, sometimes in optimistic tones, other times in the grim voice of Necessity. Whatever the outcome, we cannot "go back." In any case, the argument goes, science and technology have provided in the nick of time the very (and only) tools it will take to resolve the interlocking crises they have produced. Any other perspective on technological domination is dismissed as "regressive" and a

"technophobic" desire to go back to the stone age. This is argued by both corporate engineers and leftist/syndicalist critics of capitalism. For discussions of this ideology, see Langdon Winner's *Autonomous Technology: Technics-Out-of-Control as a Theme in Political Thought* (Cambridge: MIT Press, 1977), pp. 238-251, and Joseph Weizenbaum's *Computer Power and Human Reason* (San Francisco: Freeman, 1976), p. 31.

4. Thoreau, *Walden* (New York: Bantam Books, 1982), p. 174.

5. In *The Old Ways* (San Francisco: City Lights, 1977), Gary Snyder comments, "To combat cultural genocide one needs a critique of civilization itself." ("The Politics of Ethnopoetics," p. 20) Many radical anthropologists, ecologists, and historians have begun to elaborate this critique, from indigenist, feminist, anti-authoritarian, and radical socialist perspectives.

6. *Basic Call to Consciousness* (1978, pp. 69-70). Available from *Akwesasne Notes,* Mohawk Nation, via Rooseveltown, NY 13683.

7. By *privilege*, I mean its social-economic privilege as an activity most generally of colonial and neocolonial elites in relation to conquered peoples, but also its ideology of a privileged epistemological position in relation to the cultures it claims to study objectively. As Pierre Clastres has noted, "Ethnology ... wants to situate itself directly within the realm of universality without realizing that in many respects it remains firmly entrenched in its particularity, and that its pseudo-scientific discourse quickly deteriorates into genuine ideology. (Some assertions to the effect that only Western civilization is able to produce ethnologists are thereby reduced to their true significance.)" *Society Against the State* (New York: Zone Books, 1987), p. 17.

8. See Marshall Sahlins, *Stone Age Economics* (Chicago: Aldine, 1972). In the *Basic Call,* the authors write, "Our people live a simple life, unencumbered by the need of endless material commodities. The fact that their needs are few means that all the peoples' needs are easily met. ..." (p. 68).

9. Arguing that "it is value, not a series of needs, which is at the basis of culture," Dorothy Lee demonstrates that the "utilitarian calculus" characteristic of modern civilization does not apply universally. For example, "though a laborer on a New Guinea plantation needs a minimum diet of seven pounds of yams, plus a stated amount of meat, an Arapesh in his own hamlet, working in his fields, climbing up and down steep mountain sides, working hard at ceremonials, can live a meaningful life and procreate healthy children on three pounds of yams a day, and almost no meat." For the Arapesh "multiplies his exertions and minimizes his subsistence so as to achieve a maximum of social warmth." The Trobrianders studied by Malinowski chose to grow yams rather than taro, even though the latter provided more calories for less effort, and furthermore, grew them to give them away. Frequently, they would not even be eaten. The social connectedness is the motivation, not caloric intake. *Freedom and Culture* (New York: Prentice Hall/Spectrum, 1959), pp. 70-77; 89-104.

The ethnographic and historical literature is abundant with examples of primal peoples going without food to enhance their relations or to achieve visions. See further discussion on scarcity in my *Beyond Bookchin: Preface for a Future Social Ecology* (Detroit and New York: Black & Red/Autonomedia, 1996), pp. 103-9, and "Deep Ecology & Environmental Philosophy: On the Ethics of Crisis and the Crisis in Ethics," below, footnote 32.

10. *Basic Call...*, p. 98.

11. Lewis Mumford, *Technics and Human Development* (New York: Harcourt, Brace, Jovanovich, 1967), p. 181. In Hesiod's *The Work and the Days*, we read of the Golden Age: "They lived as if they were gods,/ their hearts free from all sorrow,/ by themselves, and without hard work or pain.../ They took their pleasure in their festivals,/ and lived without troubles./ When they died, it was as if they fell asleep./ All goods were theirs./ The fruitful grainland/ yielded its harvest to them/ of its own accord. . . ." (Richard Lattimore translation, University of Michigan Press, 1978). The Chinese sage Chuangtse tells of "the Age of the Perfect Nature," when "the people tied knots for reckoning. They enjoyed their food, beautified their clothing, were satisfied with their homes, and delighted in their customs. Neighboring settlements overlooked one another, so that they could hear the barking of dogs and crowing of cocks of their neighbors, and the people til the end of their days had never been outside their own country. . . ." See "Opening Trunks, or a Protest Against Civilization," in *The Wisdom of China and India*, edited by Lin Yutang (New York: Modern Library, 1942), pp. 671-675.

12. For example, the argument that a growing surplus brought about the state: all evidence shows a thought-out suppression or institutionalized festive sharing or destruction of surplus. As Sahlins points out, the "dominant form of primitive production is under-production. . . ." The same is true of the arguments concerning agriculture and technology. Whether primal societies are "agricultural or preagricultural" they "seem not to realize their own economic capacities. Labor power is underused, technological means are not fully engaged, natural resources are left untapped." This argument does not therefore even indirectly confirm the Hobbesian and Malthusian notions of brutish and penurious primitive life that is a keystone of modern civilization's ideology. "So understood, 'underproduction' is not necessarily inconsistent with pristine 'affluence.' All the people's material wants might still be easily satisfied even though the economy is running below capacity. Indeed, the former is rather a condition of the latter: given the modest ideas of 'satisfaction' locally prevailing, labor and resources need not be exploited to the full." (Sahlins, pp. 49, 41)

Agriculture is commonly blamed. See for example John Zerzan, "Agriculture," in *Elements of Refusal* (Seattle: Left Bank Books, 1988), pp. 63-71, also "Anarchy and Ecstasy" by Hakim Bey in the Winter 1990–1991 *Fifth Estate*. For responses to Zerzan see Bob Brubaker, "Comments on John Zerzan's Critique of Agriculture" (Winter 1988-89 *Fifth Estate*) and my essay, "The Question of

Agriculture" (Spring 1989 *Fifth Estate*). Nevertheless, the ethnographic evidence does not substantiate this idea. As Clastres argues, the diverse relations between and combinations of agriculture and sedentarism, and sedentarism and such activities as hunting, gathering, and fishing, undermine the view that agriculture brought about the state. The movement of societies from gathering-hunting to agriculture and the (less frequent) reverse movement of others "appears to have been affected without changing the nature of those societies in any way ... In other words, as regards primitive societies, a transformation at the level of what Marxists term the economic infrastructure is not necessarily 'reflected' in its corollary, the political superstructure, since the latter appears to be independent of its material base."

In the Americas, for example, "Some groups of hunters-fishers-gatherers, be they nomads or not, present the same socio-political characteristics as their sedentary agriculturist neighbors: different 'infrastructures,' the same 'superstructure' ... Hence, it is the Political break [*coupure*] that is decisive, and not the economic transformation." The technology/surplus/economy/agriculture speculations do not lead to origins, but, rather, beg the question: why would people put on a yoke? (Clastres, pp. 201-202, see also pp. 204-205)

As for population pressures, population growth is much more apparently a result, not a cause, of class society. Furthermore, relatively dense populations have been able to maintain stateless, communal, egalitarian societies. Sahlins writes that it is therefore "evident that current mechanistic explanations from demographic cause — or conversely, the inference of 'population pressure' from an observed economic or political 'effect' — are often oversimplified. In any given cultural formation, 'pressure on land' is not in the first instance a function of technology and resources, but rather of the producers' access to sufficient means of livelihood. The latter clearly is a specification of the cultural system — relations of production and property, rules of land tenure, relations between local groups, and so forth." Thus scarcity caused by "population pressure" is more a consequence of cultural relations since the primal community consistently produces far below its (abstract or scientifically generated) "capacity." (Sahlins, footnote 5, p. 49).

Less standard explanations, for example, Zerzan's idea that symbolization (e.g., the idea of time or language) brought about the original rift with a primordial, ontological unity not only go against our knowledge of primal societies but, more importantly, posit a fetishized unity that suppresses the actual complex interrelations of these societies, ending in a conundrum of origins. See *Elements of Refusal* for these arguments.

13. Clastres, pp. 206, 202, 154.
14. Clastres, pp. 44-45.
15. *Technicians of the Sacred: A Range of Poetries from Africa, America, Asia, and Oceania*, edited by Jerome Rothenberg (Garden City: Doubleday/Anchor,

1969), pp. 423-424. The idea recently raised in the anti-authoritarian milieu that the shaman is the "first specialist" and thus a precursor to the archon (despite their differences, both John Zerzan and Murray Bookchin argue this point), is typical of the unfortunate logic that imposes modern categories of civilization onto contexts to which they do not apply. Thus a person with what might be called special gifts is labelled a specialist, and relations that are unique, informal, and unrepeatable are seen as formalized and professional. It is just as (un)likely that the individual who made the best canoe, who sang remarkably, or was respected for other unique and special talents could become the archon. See the essay "Status Among the Montagnais-Naskapi of Labrador" in Eleanor Burke Leacock's *Myths of Male Dominance* (New York: Monthly Review Press, 1981).

16. Fredy Perlman, *Against His-story, Against Leviathan!* (Detroit: Black & Red, 1983), p. 134.

17. Clastres, p. 198.

18. Mircea Eliade, *Myth and Reality* (New York: Harper Colophon, 1975), pp. 142-143.

19. Turner's use of gender-exclusive terminology is correct: we are talking about civilized men. The *volte-face* he describes is foremost a suppression of woman and is the foundation of patriarchy. He continues, "The sheer visual stimulation of numbers of people living together thanks to human inventiveness must have fostered a burgeoning sense of the efficacy of human willpower — and this is the progenitor of the will to power, of the urge to dominate the land, and of the belief that *all* of nature may ultimately be tamed." Frederick Turner, *Beyond Geography: The Western Spirit Against the Wilderness* (New York: Viking, 1980), pp. 25-6, emphasis in original.

20. Mumford, pp. 188–191.

21. Perlman, p. 27.

22. The comment that an affirmation of primal lifeways is "totally lacking in evolutionary promise" comes from Murray Bookchin's *The Ecology of Freedom* (Palo Alto: Chesire Books, 1982), p. 58. For discussion of this and other problems in Bookchin's work, see my *Beyond Bookchin: Preface for a Future Social Ecology*, chapters 3, 7 and 8.

23. Diamond, p. 1.

24. This image of "wiring" comes from the discussion of Wilhelm Reich in Monica Sjoo and Barbara Mor, *The Great Cosmic Mother: Rediscovering the Religion of the Earth* (San Francisco: Harper & Row, 1987), p. 17. They observe, "Fascism is not a wild 'barbaric' phenomenon that appears suddenly and without reason in the midst of 'civilization.' It is the result of a long conditioning process, and the institutions that do the conditioning are those of 'civilization' itself."

INSURGENT MEXICO: REDEFINING REVOLUTION AND PROGRESS FOR THE 21ST CENTURY

 *"The political status quo in Mexico died on January 1 [1994]. Every Mexican institution is now in a state of crisis."* — El Financiero *(Mexican business newspaper)*

"If 53 people died in the riots in the Dominican Republic, 53,000 people could die if the Mexicans remember that they are a people with a history of rebellion. If that happens, capitalism in Latin America will go to the devil!" — Venezuelan bank official after anti-austerity riots in the Dominican Republic in the early 1980s

"The comrades say we have been at this for five hundred years. We can wait another five hundred years." — Subcomandante Marcos, of *the Zapatista National Liberation Army (Ejército Zapatista de Liberación Nacional, EZLN), when asked how long his movement would continue to fight*

Subcomandante Marcos' declaration of patience aside, the rebellion in southern Mexico begun on New Year's Day, 1994 promises dramatic social and political upheaval in the enormous "Indian Republic" to our south — events which will not be measured in centuries, but in the next few years.

The mostly poorly-armed insurgents took over five towns, destroyed government buildings and police stations, burned land titles and government records, and liberated prisons and jails, among other feats, before returning to obscure villages and the jungle mist.

Yet, as the charismatic, articulate Marcos, whose writings have made him a national sensation, told the press, "We did not go to war on January 1 to kill or to have them kill us. We went to make ourselves heard." The strategy worked. The dire conditions of the eight million Mexican Indians, and the tenuous condition of the six decade-long social truce in that country since the consolidation of power by the Institutional Revolutionary Party (PRI) in 1929, became common knowledge within days.

Following the revolt came massive military repression involving up to a third of the Mexican army (17,000 troops) with indiscriminate machine-gunning and bombing of villages and vehicles travelling along roads, torture, summary executions, and mass graves. More than five hundred people were killed. Mayan campesinos fleeing from Mexico's southernmost state of Chiapas into Guatemala to escape the violence have been prevented from returning, and Guatemalan refugees in Chiapas have been accused of instigating the revolt, and harassed and intimidated by the Mexican army. *Guardias blancas* ("white guards"), private armies of the rich landowners long responsible for violence in the region, have been mobilizing for further attacks against peasant, labor and human rights workers. (According to human rights groups, some 500 people were disappeared in Chiapas during the 1980s.) Violent clashes over land continue, even since a peace accord was signed between the zapatistas and the government at the beginning of March. Whatever the agreement turns out to be, the war in southern Mexico is far from over.

Undogmatic revolutionaries

In contrast with other guerrilla groups in Latin America, the zapatistas, despite their trappings and tactics, do not present guerrilla war as the only legitimate strategy for social transformation or aim to seize power. Rather, their message is that determination, creativity, daring and flexibility — in their case tactics and a point of view flexible enough to get them labelled "post-modern" revolutionaries by the *New York Times* — can still be effective in resisting oppression and opening new pathways to radical social change.

After a period of defeat and paralysis for workers, native peoples, and popular reform movements suffering under the New World Order, this was an important message for many to hear. And it was heard. In mid-January 150,000 people demonstrating in Mexico City chanted "E-Z-L-N," and striking workers and angry indigenous and peasant organizations rapidly raised the banner of *zapatismo* as their own.

Native peoples throughout the Americas from Argentina to Quebec also took notice and expressed support for the Mayan rebellion. Workers demonstrating in Spain and Italy chanted, "VIVA ZAPATA," and in Northern California, an area already feeling the effects of corporate "free trade" plunder, Anglo and Latino high school students took on a school administration that tried to prevent them from wearing red and black bandannas in solidarity with the Mexican revolutionaries.

The Chiapas revolt emerged not from the handful of leftist intellectuals that apparently helped shape it, but from the most oppressed depths of Mexican society — poor Indians who have been continually and steadily dispossessed of their meager lands by cattle ranchers and big *hacendados* (landowners), while seeing the rainforest, which sustained and sheltered them in myriad ways for countless generations, demolished by big logging interests and small poachers alike. In the last few decades, two-thirds of the Lacandon rainforest (one of the most biologically diverse areas in the country) has been logged. Campesinos who were persuaded by the government to settle in former rainforest areas to grow coffee and bananas for the world market saw their livelihoods decline as the thin rainforest soil became depleted. When world coffee prices plummeted in the 1980s many lost their land altogether to the cattle barons as their money ran out.

Growing coffee and other cash crops, rather than the corn and beans that fed them for millennia, was one of many brilliant ideas dreamed up by the Yale- and Harvard-trained PRI bureaucrats who manage the country from the helm of their decrepit one party "democratic" dictatorship. Mexican President Carlos Salinas de Gortari was instrumental in gutting Article 27 of the Mexican Constitution, which guaranteed land for all Mexicans and protected communal lands from sale. This set in motion the privatization and liquidation of the traditional communally-owned *ejido* farmlands (some with Prehispanic roots and others created after the 1910 Revolution), with wealthy land interests and entrepreneurial pirates practicing "hostile takeovers" on the holdings of Mexico's ten million small farmers.

Of course, the *ejido* system was frequently corrupt and dominated by party hacks and small-time bosses (*caciques*). Such lands can be poor and are increasingly inadequate; as historian John Womack has remarked, "an *ejido* parcel is a ticket to misery."[1] (See page 221 for endnotes.) Nevertheless, before the recent changes, they were at least formally intact in most places; besides being symbolically important to Mexican campesinos, they were often the only thing keeping many, including entire native ethnic groups, from becoming completely landless.

Revolt after revolt

Land reforms achieved by the 1910 Revolution barely affected the south-ernmost state. Chiapas remains a starkly divided, two-tiered society that continues to experience misery and peonage reminiscent of early colonial times. While some communal properties still exist, half of all people own-ing land live on only one percent of it. Huge tracts of land are controlled by rich *hacendados* and cattle ranchers, defended by private armed gangs, the police and army, and the local political apparatus, while the million or so Indians in the state live under horribly abject conditions.

Even though Chiapas produces immense amounts of energy, raw ma-terials and profits for Mexican elites and the international market, its people, especially the Indians, are among the worst off in the country. More than half of the population is malnourished, a figure which approaches eighty percent in the Mayan villages of the highland forests. Some 15,000 people die each year of easily curable diseases — the main killer being malnutrition.[2]

But the people of Chiapas have not passively accepted their misery; the area has been the site of recurrent rebellion. As a political organizer who was previously shot and forced to flee the state told the *Times*, "Now you see guerrillas. But there has never been peace in Chiapas." Nor are the Indians the pawns of leftist agitators, as the government charged. As one anthro-pologist who has worked among them for two decades remarked, "Unlike the guerrillas in Guatemala, [the insurgents] are not seeking out bases for support among the campesinos, but coming up from them." The zapatista revolt comes from a long Mayan tradition — not only the revolts that must have contributed to the demise of what was likely an increasingly authori-tarian, bureaucratic and enfeebled Mayan empire in the ninth century C.E., and against the Toltec conquerors from central Mexico somewhat later, but also against the Spanish *conquistadores* throughout the colonial epoch. The Mayans impeded Spanish domination for several decades after contact. As Michael Coe writes in *The Maya* (1975), their resistance to Spanish coloni-zation was effective for a long period of time precisely because, "unlike the mighty Aztec, there was no over-all native authority which could be toppled, bringing an empire with it. Nor did the Maya fight in the accepted fashion … they were jungle guerrillas in a familiar modern tradition. . . ."

Even after the Spanish established their power, the Mayan peoples continued to fight. "Revolt after revolt continued to plague the Spaniards throughout the sixteenth century," remarks Coe. The Yucatec Mayans rose again in rebellion in 1847 and 1860, and in 1910 the Porfirio Díaz dictator-ship was still suppressing an ongoing uprising in Quintana Roo, at the eastern end of the Yucatan peninsula. There were rebellions among the highland Maya of Chiapas throughout the eighteenth, nineteenth and twentieth centuries, which became the themes of the famous jungle novels of the anarchist novelist B. Traven. The Mayan Tzeltal rose in 1712 and 1868. On January 1, 1994, when the EZLN took San Cristobal de las Casas, named for the sixteenth century defender of the Indians, they burned the municipal archives, financial records and land titles, but on the urging of the archives director, decided to protect the historical archives, with its rich record of the Tzeltal revolts.

Throughout the 1970s and 1980s there were uprisings, land seizures, strikes and protests in Chiapas, with brutal, repressive reactions from the state government and army. (One of the worst perpetrators of violence against campesinos and Indians was General Absalón Castellanos, who later became state governor. Castellanos, now a wealthy landowner, was captured by the guerrillas and released during the New Year's uprising.) In December of 1991, three hundred indigenous people organized a sit-in in the plaza at Palenque (the name of both a small town and the nearby important archeological site) to protest conditions on the 500th anniversary of the European invasion of America, including lack of drinking water, dispossession of their lands, and the encroachment of tourist industries. The demonstration was viciously suppressed, and many people were arrested and tortured. Three months later, three hundred people marched from Palenque to Mexico City to demand redress from the federal government, and were all but ignored.

While the modern Mexican state's official ideology of Mesoamerican *indigenismo*, with its celebration of native roots, left impressive examples in art and architecture, it remained mostly a sentimental, nationalist glorification of ancient Mesoamerican empires. Racism against the Indian endured, and real native communities languished, their lands despoiled in the name of national development and progress, while propertied classes and the political bureaucracy benefited. Thus *indigenismo* has served mostly to conceal the reality of an unending conquest and plunder of native lands and peoples. This war goes back to the European conquest and to the seventeenth century *encomienda* system, which destroyed native towns and villages and allocated their lands to the invaders, parceling out *indio* laborers to mines and *haciendas* (estates).

In fact, the Mexican state carried out the same war of extermination against tribal and indigenous peoples that occurred in the United States, Africa, Argentina, Russia and Australia, a war which has continued into the twentieth century against both large indigenous population centers and smaller groups, settled and nomadic. Though the vast majority of Mexicans are *mestizo* (mixed European and native, with African ancestry in a small number of cases), it did not prevent them from carrying out the military annihilation of nomadic groups like the Apaches and Comanches in the nineteenth century. When in the 1890s the settled, more populous Yaquis rebelled against Mexican incursions into and seizures of their lands in northwest Mexico, their resistance was cruelly suppressed, much of their land confiscated, and at least 8,000 of them were shipped to the Yucatan to be sold as slaves to wealthy planters — a condition of abysmal peonage already experienced by large groups like the Mayans, Zapotecs, and others.

"Now the whites respect the Indians, because they come with guns in hand," Subcomandante Marcos told the press in an interview that has now become famous. Yet political commentators in Mexico have noted that Marcos, the most prominent spokesman of the indigenous movement, is not himself an Indian. For the Mayan people he represents, this may have useful aspects. Fluent in Mexican popular and media cultures, an intellectual with a sophisticated understanding of Mexican politics and history, Marcos is a very effective transmitter of the movement's intentions and point of view, probably in a way that most Indians might not be. He also appears modest about his role.

Nevertheless, such a situation has its dangers, as the media-generated cult around him has demonstrated. The Indians may find it useful to have a spokesman adept at manipulating the signs of post-modern Mexico, who can utilize Mexican historical symbols, contemporary politics, and television humor and soap opera sensibilities simultaneously to get his message across to a population saturated in media discourse. This doesn't prevent mass society's media from manipulating Marcos and his *compañeros* for its own purposes. Newspapers printed surveys on his sex appeal, and the figure of Marcos in his ski-mask quickly became a national pop culture fad printed on tee-shirts and buttons, turned into dolls and even marketed on condom packages. When a reporter presented one of the condoms to another leader of the rebels, Juan, the Indian man said, "We rose up in arms precisely because for many years, since the time of our grandfathers, we have not been respected. What most hurts us — and we want to show it — is that bad people have taken from our dead, from their blood, as though it was merchandise." (*New York Times*, February 2, 1994)

Juan didn't understand that capital functions in exactly such a way, spectacularizing even a revolution that intends to destroy it. By fetishizing Marcos, the media perpetuated the system that has rendered the Indian invisible, and perhaps worked to marginalize the rebellion by trivializing it. Though Marcos told the press the zapatistas didn't revolt merely to get into the newspapers but to fight for their lives, their relationship with the media has been ambivalent. Certainly, much of their impact has been dependent on it. The zapatistas' manipulation of the media may be one desperate measure among many, by a people in a desperate situation. And so far, it has been successful. But one wonders what would happen to their movement, for example — which Marcos has called "not Chiapan, but national" — if the media, under government pressure, say, decided to ignore them? And, as the figure of Marcos looms ever larger, what becomes of the anonymous rebels he represents? How irreplaceable is he — what happens to the movement as a whole if he is captured or killed?[3]

Marcos' eloquence is impressive, but it, too, is partly a function of media presentation, and tends to mask while simultaneously revealing the reality within the native communities he claims to represent. It is clear there is great solidarity among the rebels, and that they have deep roots, but the identity of the EZLN and their actual relationship to the Mayan community as a whole are not so clear. Marcos himself may be an example of the exemplary non-Indian, using his experience in the dominant culture and his political skills to aid native peoples in their autonomous uprising. But his problematic role may result in an indirect kind of colonization as the revolt and its goals are shaped by the non-native consultation this leftist intellectual provides. Support for the basic justness of the revolt should not obscure the recognition, culled from historical experience, that revolutionary goals and their practical unfolding can bring about new forms of unanticipated domination. As mass movements in Latin America have suggested (for example, in the Andean region), indigenism, like other modern political movements, is a two-edged sword.[4]

Land and liberty

Another nationalist slogan and the single most important battle cry of the 1910 Revolution was "Land and Liberty," but these principles, too, were undermined by the failure to transform social relations fundamentally, including abolishing capitalist property relations. From 1910 until 1945 nearly 76 million acres of land were distributed to small farmers and to both traditional and newly established *ejidos*. But not only was much of the land poor, the campesinos still faced class society and the market system.

In his classic study of Mesoamerica, *Sons of the Shaking Earth* (1959), Eric Wolfe writes, "Land reform solved no economic problem; nor did the archives of the Indianist contain a road map to guide the society. . . ." While sectors of the former elites were broken and many of the peons freed by land reform, the new dispensation "created new sources of power in the countryside. For in the very act of distributing land to the landless, the agents of the land reform became the new power-holders in the rural area ... [which] laid the foundations of a new political machine to replace the one overturned by the revolution." This machine was the post-revolutionary, bureaucratic party-state, against which the contemporary zapatistas, wrapping themselves in the mantle of the most profound and liberatory manifestation of the 1910 Revolution, have taken up arms.

Mexico's revolution was the first of the century to overthrow the old order. Like the Soviet Union, the state in Mexico initiated the classic nationalist project of political consolidation, modernization and economic development from a position of relative weakness in a world of powerful, imperial rivals. Unlike the state socialists of the East, the Mexican state chose the path of a mixed economy with massive foreign investment, thus guaranteeing its rapid subservience to the imperialist colossus to its north.

The PRI was not, however, an ideological party like the Eastern varieties that came to power after years of ideological struggle. The Mexican hierarchic pyramid that scrambled to power after a socially devastating civil war was based almost solely on expediency, greed, and the bureaucratic manipulation of a populist base through a patronage system in trade unions, party organizations and the police. The PRI is now loved about as much as the Eastern European parties were before they were toppled at the end of the 1980s, and is apparently even less feared than it once was. It has managed to stay afloat through a combination of petty reforms and repression, by dismantling and privatizing some economic remnants of nationalist party-state monopolies like oil and communications, and by throwing open the gates to deeper penetration by transnational corporations.

Ironically, the PRI now finds itself in a position like that of the Mexican state at the twilight of the regime of dictator Porfirio Diaz — the period of the *"Porfiriato"* before the 1910 Revolution. The late nineteenth and early twentieth centuries saw economic (though not much industrial) development, huge foreign investment and the rise of a small, urban middle class. The political elites — called *científicos* for their ideology of economic liberalism, scientific progress, and technological development — were intent on creating a modern, westernized, industrial-capitalist nation-state and economy. Foreign investment, in the view of these elites trained in European and U.S. universities, would develop Mexico until local capital could stand on its own legs. Economic benefits would eventually trickle down, but until Mexico was fully developed, amenities such as justice, political freedom and social expenditures would have to wait. By the turn of the century, half of the territory of Mexico belonged to a few thousand families and foreigners. According to historian T.H. Fehrenbach, during the sugar boom of the 1890s, some 32 families "came to own virtually all the croplands in Morelos," the state which produced the agrarian revolution later dubbed *zapatismo*. "Villages were deprived of wells and water rights and common fields, and cane was planted in some village squares. Protests, which were often violent, were squelched by the hard-riding *rurales* [rural cops] at the beck and call of the local chief politicos." (*Fire and Blood: A History of Mexico*, 1973)

Approximately a million families were driven from the land "and reduced to vagabondage and peonage" by the new economic developments, writes Fehrenbach. "Only three percent of rural families owned any farmland." The standard week's wage was the same as at the beginning of the century, but purchased about one fourth the amount of corn. The society was immiserated, overworked, hungry, ill, and desperate. The *científicos* and the wealthy investors and landowners they served did not see how the human disaster they were creating on the land was setting the stage for the convulsions to come. By the time Emiliano Zapata and his compatriots rose in Morelos in 1910 and the political system began to unravel, it was too late, and the *científicos* were swept away.

Two Mexicos

This scenario closely resembles the increasing destitution in contemporary Mexico. Today, as then, one finds the same rationale for development, and essentially the same wretched conditions for its victims. Industrialization, modernization and more elaborate communications with the rest of the world, all of which were dreams of *científicos* and many revolutionaries as well, have done little to better the life of the Indian, the campesino, or the poor worker. Instead, poverty has been modernized, petrochemicalized, and mediatized, but people are still as landless, hungry and desperate as they ever were.

Mexico began its industrialization in earnest after the revolutionary wave subsided, and the PRI was firmly entrenched during World War II. The influence of the United States and the emergence of a new capitalist class were key to the shape of modern Mexican society. Industrialization and modernization emulated the "American way of life" to the north in *Gringolandia*. At the end of the 1950s, Wolfe commented that while the Mexican economy had experienced "a phenomenal rate of growth, real wages [had] increased but slightly since 1910." This heavy exploitation of the emerging working class allowed the Mexican state and capitalists to subsidize industrialization. They managed to fend off discontent not so much through revolutionary nationalist rhetoric as through the dissemination of a few consumerist crumbs among those sectors necessary for development.

"The small increase in wages has not gone into a better diet or into better housing," Wolfe explained. "It has gone into the acquisition of the cheap and expendable items of North American culture. Not everyone can participate in their consumption; but their 'demonstration effect' makes 'pie in the sky' seem increasingly available in the here and now, thus masking the hidden exploitation of the industrial labor force." Much of Mexico's industrialization, in fact, went to produce cheap consumer goods for domestic consumption. That, combined with a growing urban society and a narrow but significant middle class with increased buying power, helped to bring about "two Mexicos," a dramatically two-tiered society with a westernized, consumer society resting on the backs of the impoverished, distressed campesinos, Indians, and unemployed and underemployed slum dwellers in the rapidly growing cities.

This, of course, is a picture of much of the so-called "underdeveloped world" (and increasingly of the industrialized North). By the late 1970s more people were landless in Mexico than in 1910. As in the U.S., the decade of the 1980s was a period of massive financial looting and accelerated capital accumulation at the expense of the society as a whole, bringing into being a westernized middle class sold on television, white bread and other imported commodities and habits, and even a handful of billionaires, while simultaneously causing increased penury and desperation for workers and *los agachados*, the have-nots of the lower depths.

In fact, it was partly a recognition of this process that fueled the current zapatista revolt. As the vicar of San Cristobal's Catholic archdiocese, Gonzalo Ituarte, told the *New York Times*, the rage of the poor was not so much that they had grown poorer (though they had), but that roads and radio and television had made it so much easier for them to see how they were being left behind by the more privileged. Correspondingly, point 11 of the EZLN demands brought to the peace negotiations with the government demanded construction of housing in all of Mexico's rural communities, electricity, roads, potable water, and the like, but also insisted on "the advantages of the city like television, stoves, refrigerators, washing machines, etc." Rising expectations, generated by television and consumer society confronting a reality in which conditions are not even adequate to survive, created an explosion whose reverberations continue to be felt. The consumerist ideology that once contributed to social peace for several decades now became a component in the social war.

The political economy of cholera

Mexico is deep in debt, like the rest of Latin America (and much of the rest of the world, for that matter). After a borrowing frenzy in the 1970s for massive industrial development projects, Latin American nation states found themselves heavily in debt to international capital. Throughout the 1980s, they steadily lowered the living conditions of their populations through harsh austerity measures to meet International Monetary Fund demands. A drop in world oil prices and in the prices of other key products, combined with rising interest rates, conspired nevertheless to keep them behind, no matter how much profit they could wring from their people and lands — a scenario evocative of the indebted peon at the company store.

By the end of the 1980s, millions of people were homeless, hungry, and succumbing to disease in a situation one political observer described as the "political economy of cholera." Juan de Dias Parra, of the Latin American Association for Human Rights, recently summarized the consequences at a meeting in Quito, Ecuador, noting that "in Latin America today, there are seventy million more hungry, thirty million more illiterates, ten million more families without homes and forty million more unemployed persons than there were twenty years ago ... There are 240 million human beings who lack the necessities of life, and this when the region is richer and more stable than ever, according to the way the world sees it."

Mexico is no exception. In the last decade, the buying power of the Mexican wage worker has diminished more than 60 percent, and in comparable terms, Mexican factory pay is less than in Haiti. Living conditions consistently and dramatically eroded through the 1980s for all sectors but the upper and middle classes. This situation was underscored by Subcomandante Marcos when he declared, "We have the opportunity to die fighting and not of dysentery, which is how the Indians of Chiapas normally die." Capital, on the other hand, has been very optimistic; in the last year alone foreign investment on the Mexican stock exchange nearly doubled to over $72 billion (a figure which dropped precipitously after the zapatista New Year's party, climbing once more when the army moved in).

But another whirlwind is appearing on the horizon. Two "detonators," as Marcos put it, set off the explosion in January: electoral fraud (a continual, especially brazen phenomenon in Chiapas, but also a notorious national scandal during the 1988 presidential elections), and the North American Free Trade Agreement, which threatens to drive three million more people from the land through consolidation of cash crop agribusiness and the importation of cheap American agricultural products. In both motives, today's zapatistas resemble their *agrarista* precursors.

It is understandable that radicals would take up the figure of Emiliano Zapata, a spontaneous, incorruptible rebel and natural man of the people, a revolutionary deeply rooted in the organic traditions of indigenous community. Zapata's movement had goals parallel to the EZLN's: a struggle against anti-democratic electoral fraud and a demand for electoral reform on the one hand, and for autonomous control of the land on the other. The latest rebellion was also, like the first (in the words of an unfriendly observer in Zapata's state of Morelos just prior to the 1910 revolution), "a real war of the sandal against the shoe, of work pants against trousers. . . ." The movement, according to John Womack's excellent history, was populist and unofficial, enjoying "extraordinary political solidarity." Isolation and poverty had worked to keep Zapata's *agraristas* focused and principled, though provincial. But, as Womack observes, its "insistent provincialism was the movement's strength and its weakness." (*Zapata and the Mexican Revolution*, 1968)

While the Morelos revolution created egalitarian autonomy in that state, its far-reaching and visionary local activities tended to combine with a limited, reformist outlook nationally. Zapata's Plan de Ayala called for "Reform, Liberty, Justice, and Law," demanded electoral reform, but failed to challenge the national capitalist state and class, focusing instead on local problems and narrowly on the hated big landowners. Zapata was not able to make, nor was he interested in making long-term programmatic alliances with other revolutionary armies. After marching into the capital, his army simply withdrew. In 1915, the Manifesto to the Nation, probably written by Zapata's anarchist advisor Antonio Díaz Soto y Gama, called for "War to the death against the *hacendados*, ample guarantees for all the other classes of society." A thoroughgoing revolution in one southern region resulted in half a revolution on the larger landscape. In keeping with Danton's dictum that the makers of half-revolutions only dig their own graves, the *agraristas* ended in martyrdom and defeat, becoming the objects of national devotion once they were safely dead.

Today's zapatistas have qualities that may also be simultaneous strengths and weaknesses. They also have basic demands: land, respect, political freedom, and to be left alone. Much of their revolt is an expression of sheer outrage and protest, a declaration, in their words, that, "Enough Is Enough." Interestingly, they claim they are "not marxists or maoists," and do not want to take state power (though their intention, according to their December 31 "Declaration of War," is to "advance to the capital, overcoming the Mexican federal army"). They desire instead simply "to govern themselves within the borders of their own communities." Though they endorse some kind of socialism, it is distinct from the kind they have labeled "dinosauric."

No room to move

Yet the contemporary zapatistas, too, seem bent on making half a revolution. They state they "only want a democratically elected government and respect for the [indigenous] ethnic groups," and ask "that other powers of the nation advocate to restore the legitimacy and the stability of the nation by overthrowing the dictator [Salinas de Gortari and the PRI], the maximum and illegitimate federal executive that today holds power." They want a "transition government and new elections," and write in conventionally patriotic terms about the Mexican flag and nation.

In the late 1920s, the PRI consolidated power from the vacuum that ensued after the exhaustion of the revolutionary movement and the mutual fratricide of workers and peasants on opposite sides of barricades created by rival *caudillos*. Now that the PRI appears close to the end of its rope, ready to dangle at the end of someone else's, the call for democracy and elections could lead at some point to a new capitalist state formation. This could be dominated by a reformed wing of the PRI (led perhaps by someone like peace negotiator Manuel Camacho Solis, whom Marcos has claimed the EZLN would favor). Another possible competitor for power is the left-liberal loyal opposition, the Revolutionary Democratic Party (led by ex-PRI member Cuauhtémoc Cárdenas, the son of the popular nationalist PRI president of the 1930s, who was robbed of electoral victory in the 1988 elections, and who deplored the uprising while making use of it as a platform to attack the ruling clique).[5]

In any event, the zapatistas may have set off a series of events that, by throwing the PRI into some disarray, could eventually help to usher in a new, "democratic" reform government promising to alter the terms of NAFTA, and to grant some social reforms, while maintaining a variant of the current power structure, the army, and capitalist social relations.[6] Already, in the agreement signed in March between the EZLN and the government, federal negotiators promised to double the pace of rural electrification, increase investment in housing and other basic services, and bolster investment in the moribund coffee economy. The pact promises job training programs, creation of new industries, and other such pork barrel reforms like federal support for Mexican products harmed by foreign competition (which would seem to be a violation of NAFTA). These promises hardly sound like radical social transformation.

But no capitalist state in Latin America has much room to move within the confines of the current world economic situation. They could not turn back a "free trade" agreement with the gringos without dire repercussions; this is not a deal of equals, but of master and vassal. More importantly, they cannot grant profound reforms, providing not only potable water but ambitious infrastructure development, even televisions, washing machines, and the "etcetera" that stands for all the inchoate desires of the poor at the margins of consumer society. They cannot do so because they are in debt up to their ears, because the only way to get money within the international capitalist economy is to do what they are presently doing, selling the country lock, stock and barrel to the transnationals, and most of all because they cannot maintain their privilege, wealth and power and share the "etcetera" with the *pelados* (the "peeled ones," the wretched of the earth), who are too numerous.

The Mexican state is caught between an irresistible force and an immovable object; no one can know what is to come, except widening social conflict. "Is ours the last Central American guerrilla war," asked Mexican political writer Gustavo Esteva in the independent liberal Mexican magazine *Proceso* in February, "or has the new postmodern revolutionary era begun?"[7] There is no way to answer this question before the fact. Mexican novelist Paco Ignacio Taibo II writes, "Are we nearing the end of the oldest dictatorship in the world? ... For now we're walking on shadows, disturbed and filled with hope." A new kind of rising expectation seems to be sealing the fate of official Mexican society. But what is coming?

That depends partly on the zapatistas, the voiceless ones for whom they presently speak, and the rest of society that was stunned and then cheered by the communiqués of Subcomandante Marcos. The desires of the campesinos of Mexico are unclear. Hopefully, they will not be deceived by the same mirage of development that allowed the PRI to create the "postmodern" social and ecological catastrophe that is now Mexico, and in fact the entire industrialized and semi-industrialized world. Avoiding such deception might mean taking seriously poet Octavio Paz's comment in *The Other Mexico: Critique of the Pyramid* (1972), that the paradise promised by progress and development "is not of this world [but] in ... a future that is impalpable, unreachable, perpetual. Progress has peopled history with the marvels and monsters of technology but it has depopulated the life of man. It has given us more things but not more being."[8]

A way out

Determining the character of twenty first century "post-modernity" has now become the central problem of finding our way out of the contemporary nightmare of industrial capitalism. As Ivan Illich has observed, "For the first time, needs have almost exclusively become coterminous with commodities." First World capitalist states, Second World state-socialist dictatorships, and Third World mixed-economy neo-colonies have all been driven by the same motive. As Illich puts it, "the progressive substitution of industrial goods and services for useful but nonmarketable values has been the shared goal of political factions and regimes otherwise violently opposed to one another." But the development of instrumental-economic commodity values exacts its own cost on culture and on human autonomy. "Beyond a certain threshold, the multiplication of commodities induces impotence, the incapacity to grow food, to sing, or to build."

Or to resist. The televisions the zapatistas demand, fixtures of that urban-industrial "etcetera" presently invading not only their psyches but everyone's on the planet, are part of a global process. It is the same international commodification of life, now accelerated by treaties like NAFTA and GATT (General Agreement on Trade and Tariffs), that they already recognized as a death sentence on their bodies and souls. Their culture, and other vernacular cultures like theirs, have managed to survive and endure centuries of exploitation and oppression precisely because of their native traditions and their direct relationship to the reproduction of their culture and their subsistence. It is such self-reliance that urban-industrial values explode, so that ultimately it may not be helicopter gunships that subdue them, but their own victory, and the Mexico City soap operas, news and commercials that will consequently be delivered to them.

For the poorest people on earth who to some degree still live in vernacular societies — societies which, despite conflicts and injustices, continue to sustain themselves physically and psychically at least in relative independence from the energy, commodities and information delivered by a destructive global grid — the modernization of poverty can only occur on two levels. Naturally, it will first of all mean an increasing dependence on machines and market-produced values for what people previously could provide for themselves. Secondly, it will be dependence at the very lowest rungs of a world economic empire based on capital accumulation, industrial production, resource extraction, and the structural need for cheap labor and geographic sacrifice zones.

This process is already in motion all over the globe, of course, where the poorest people already find themselves at that lowest rung, losing what remains of local, bioregional, ancient subsistence and culture patterns for an inadequate and increasingly precarious position within the global work machine. They are coming to resemble one another in their absolute poverty just as the international middle and upper classes look more and more the same in their restless consumerism and banality. If in the next few decades revolutionaries only succeeded in "democratizing" a spectacular-commodity society, then for all the blood and sacrifice, the revolutionaries of the '90s will be shot down and the new political technocrats of the twenty-first century will reconstitute the industrial pyramid with themselves at the pinnacle. Worst of all, the entire human legacy of traditional, vernacular and native modes of being will be extinguished in the process — among them the very forms of social solidarity that have animated the Mayans to continue resisting conquest for centuries.

This is not to deny that cultures have changed, will change. But will the oppressed fight a revolution for washing machines, televisions, etc.? Free elections to appoint and anoint a new set of bureaucrats to manage the consumer spectacle and the police? What should any of us be fighting for? Illich writes, "Modern societies, rich or poor, can move in either of two opposite directions. They can produce a new bill of goods albeit safer, less wasteful, more easily shared — and thereby further intensify their dependence on consumer staples. Or, they can take a totally new approach to the interrelationship between needs and satisfactions. In other words, societies can either retain their market-intensive economies, changing only the design or the output, or they can reduce their dependence on commodities … One sees the necessity of going beyond the expert redistribution of wasteful, irrational, and paralyzing commodities, the hallmark of Radical Professionalism [or professional radicalism], the conventional wisdom of today's good guys." (*Toward A History of Needs*, 1978)

One is reminded of Rigoberta Menchu's description of a ceremony in which the Quiché Mayan Indians of her village would gather store-bought and machine-manufactured commodities like Coca Cola and other products to contrast them unfavorably with their own home-made, traditional objects as a reminder to follow their Indian ways. (*I Rigoberta: An Indian Woman in Guatemala*, 1984.) All traditional, vernacular and subsistence societies face this struggle. We in the industrialized north must also find our way beyond the false dichotomy of capitalist plenitude — impossible to achieve for everyone on the planet, in any case — and capitalist poverty.

Instead, societies now rich and poor (and the deeply divided classes within them), if they are to make the transition toward human community and ecological sanity, must explore a different kind of "convivial austerity," as Illich puts it. Such a postmodern austerity would "inspire … a society to protect personal use-value against disabling enrichment" — the kind of enrichment, to give one small example, which has convinced perhaps millions of Mexicans that gringo Wonder Bread (called *Pan Bimbo* in Mexico) is preferable to the nutritious tortilla. The kind of pseudo-enrichment which has convinced North Americans that television is preferable to conversation and to silence, and high-powered cars preferable to stable communities, clean air and clean water.

Fight for more being

Hopefully, the Mexican campesinos will not fight a revolution for more things — they would have second thoughts if they could see the erosion of the spirit the availability of more things has brought here to *el Norte*. Hopefully they are fighting for more being. Then revolution won't be a matter of electoral reform, formal "respect" for indigenous people, post-modern patriotism, electrification or attaining the rewards of consumer society, but a social transformation that goes beyond all such categories, redefining freedom and the idea of what the good life should be.

No matter how important such questions are, one way or another, the Mayan people have no alternative but to fight. For them it's not a question of dying on their feet rather than living on their knees; they are dying on their knees. Ultimately, we have no alternative either, but to challenge all the dictators, north and south, east and west, and all their agreements — even if some of us have more margin than the Indians of Chiapas.

Contrary to the imaginary lines called borders and the fantasies of racist patriots who would wish somehow to close them to halt the countless refugees from misery and despotism, our destiny in the North is intimately linked to the destiny of the people to the South. If they lose their struggle, we will also lose. Our capacity to challenge the terms of wealth and poverty, to deconstruct the consumerist pseudo-paradise that now more and more resembles the two-tiered hell they are fleeing, will have repercussions throughout the southern provinces of the empire, from the Brazilian *favelas* to the poor *pueblos* of Mesoamerica.

Meanwhile, the U.S. government is watching events closely, and CIA agents are already advising the Mexican state, developing dossiers on the insurgents even as they negotiate. President Clinton very quietly sent military advisers to Guatemala and State Department operatives to Chiapas during the early stages of the revolt — for "humanitarian reasons," to be sure. U.S. helicopters and arms, and massive amounts of money provided for the "drug war," are also already playing a role in Mexican events. We need to find ways to undermine their plans, to create more vibrant, imaginative situations and movements to stop the ongoing massacre.

Finally, despite reservations, one can only be cheered by the monkey wrench the zapatistas have thrown into the gears of the New World Order, and inspired by the creative spirit and even the humor they have shown in the face of real hardship and suffering. We are all "walking on shadows," and those who are attentive to the shaking earth may discern the vague outlines of a crumbling empire. Almost any resistance to it should be welcome. We may even be able to do something about what is to come.

The tendrils of oppression and revolt extend throughout the Americas all the way to the belly of the monster. We are all connected.

The Mayans' fight is our fight. Let's fight for more being.

VIVA ZAPATA!

(1994)

Postscript: After this essay was printed in the Summer 1994 *Fifth Estate*, we received a letter (printed in the Summer 1995 issue) from the Yucatan, from a "Cualquiera," which, like the pseudonym I used on the article ("Fulano"), means "So-and-So," or "anyone." Denying that the zapatistas had signed any agreement with the government, the writer explained that "after a thorough process of consultation with the indigenous communities that make up their base of support, they rejected the government's offer as an attempt to buy them off and to reduce a national revolutionary struggle to the local level."

Cualquiera had a far greater objection to the anti-development politics of the essay, writing,

> I share your disgust at the consumer society and also recognize that it's probably economically and ecologically impossible for the entire world to make commodities the center of life as the First World does. But I think it is an error to say that the zapatistas suffer from the influence of consumerist ideology. In your article, you do justice to the more profound causes of the struggle, but to then characterize the EZLN as "fighting for television sets" is really a distortion of everything they have said in their communiqués, interviews, and speeches. If they did mention television, stoves, refrigerators, and washing machines in their demands (which they alone have the right to determine), I don't think this means they have fallen into the consumer trap.
>
> T. Fulano, I assume you have gotten rid of your own stove and refrigerator and you don't wash your clothes in a washing machine if you are going to say that an indigenous woman should not have a machine that could save hours of drudgery. I don't imagine you've ever spent several hours a day scrubbing clothes on a rock by a river. Not just one day, but every day for the rest of your life. Not just your own clothes, but clothes for an entire family. Not just clothes that smell a little funky under the armpits, but clothes soiled with dirt from the fields. I think the appropriate place to start reducing dependence on commodities is right up there in the land of the blind and the home of the KKK. . . .

Part of my reply follows:

Cualquiera has missed the point. The essay did not merely express disgust at consumer society, but was an attempt to critique epochal social developments. Consumerist ideology, as my article indicated, was an important component in the consolidation of power by the bureaucratic party state in Mexico (which was also true in state socialist societies). Conversely, one of the reasons for the continuing relative cohesion of indigenous resistance to empire has been a certain fidelity to old ways and a refusal of (or lack of access to) industrialized development. Clearly, revolutionary movements like the zapatistas have also been motivated by the spectacle of consumer plenitude as the messages of mass communications have seeped into the rural fringes of industrial civilization. Thus, rising expectations of the society at large have fueled resentments and radical agitation among specific marginalized sectors. All this was laid out in my essay.

Development spurs revolt, yet it simultaneously tends to undermine the wellsprings of community and solidarity that underlie an ability to resist.

How can this crisis be understood and perhaps resolved? I don't pretend to have any unambiguous answer; I ended my exploration of this problem with a call for solidarity with the people of southern Mexico, whatever the outcome. But I felt compelled to ask (and I believe it imperative for radical critique to ask), whether this troubling dialectical development would lead the oppressed to limit their horizons to a fight for a "reformed" industrialism and a correspondingly precarious niche at the bottom of the hierarchy. It's easy to declare that these are not at all the intentions of the Mayan campesinos (or the possible unforeseen outcome of their actions), but if their demands include the accoutrements and appliances of industrial civilization, in addition to land and clean water, don't they indicate the influence of consumer ideology?

True, I live in the industrialized world, enjoying its cornucopia of freeways, television, packaging and allegedly labor-saving devices. Nevertheless, one of the most important contributions of anti-authoritarian politics and radical ecology has been to demystify the illusory nature of this alienated existence (thus converging in many ways with the outlook of traditional indigenous peoples). If revolutionaries in the South are demanding televisions (and with them "everything necessary to make housework easier," as the zapatista document phrases it) and in the industrialized North radicals are smashing the same machines in demonstrations, the issue of development is clearly one which needs to be addressed from both ends of the spectrum.

Unfortunately, Cualquiera reduces the question to whether or not I wash clothes by hand. As a matter of fact, I *have* washed my clothes by hand, with water drawn from a village well. In Portugal, where I lived for a time in a small village, I didn't reap the rich experience of local women, who did it as a group one festive day every week or so. But I know what hard work washing is, and I rather think there is something to be said for it. (In fact, the introduction of washing machines by a few households while I was there aggravated muffled class antagonisms in the village, isolated certain women in their houses, and wasted large amounts of water from the village commons.) My companion and I also lived quite well without a refrigerator, by the way (and still do without a television and several other almost ubiquitous gadgets), but we did use a simple stove. I believe it necessary to be pragmatic, which was precisely why I raised these issues as explorations, not as absolute judgments.

Survival being what it is here, my life in Detroit is decidedly different than it was in the village. I use a washing machine, a car, and many other industrial processes and machines. I try to make careful decisions about how and what I use, and I don't always make good ones. I doubt that my correspondent, most likely a self-styled enemy of capitalism and the state, has decided in the name of principle to throw away money and passport. But is this really the point?

Does questioning industrialization and the ideology of development automatically render one a defender of human misery? Cualquiera seems unaware that working to overcome one kind of drudgery can bring about another. Washing machine factories (and tv factories, too) have to be built, maintained and supplied with energy. Perhaps Mayan women can get jobs in them and take on the notorious "double duty" so common everywhere in the developed and developing worlds, working ten hours a day for Whirlpool or Westinghouse and then a few more in the evening watching tv while folding clothes at the laundromat. (I won't accuse C. of never having experienced this form of drudgery.)

Cualquiera's concern for poor women is touching; industrial planners, state bureaucrats and developers everywhere share it. Yet it lacks a critical understanding of the problems modernization brings; even an awareness of gender politics is missing. Indeed, if the problem is women's work, why must the solution be found in factory construction and the concomitant nightmare of power plants, steel mills, distribution bureaucracies, ecological devastation, and the rest, rather than in a relatively low tech focus on the age-old division going back to the origins of patriarchy and class society, namely, having men share such tasks? That might make laundry day a rather festive affair.

Despite the perfunctory qualifications, Cualquiera seems to fancy the industrial option, what Ivan Illich called the "conventional wisdom of today's good guys." And since the zapatistas "alone have the right to determine" their needs, we outsiders should only engage in an entirely unreflective solidarity. Yet that is precisely where we should be cautious.

I detect a similar lack of caution in Cualquiera's description of zapatista decision making. Perhaps I was inaccurate in describing a cease-fire as a peace accord and stand corrected. How the proposed agreement was later rejected is another issue. We don't know exactly how 98 percent of the population rejected the peace acccord, and most written material produced so far on the zapatistas is vague on the matter of their internal politics. Either we have to accept uncritically the words of the zapatista representatives or we keep a critical distance. I'm for maintaining criticality, while trying to find ways to show solidarity with social struggles there.

Endnotes

1. See "Chiapas Is Mexico," by Dick J. Reavis *(The Progressive*, May 1994).
2. Much useful information can be found in a document published by the zapatistas, "A Deconstructed Tour of Chiapas." In an ironic and subtly enraged voice, the text, purporting to address a hypothetical tourist, presents a political economy of

the region. The description of Ocosingo, called the "gateway to the Lacandon Forest" in tourist promotions, and one of the highland towns captured by the zapatistas, gives a vivid picture of the state: "Take a quick tour around the city. Principal points of interest? The two large buildings at the entrance are brothels, next door is a jail, the building further beyond, a church, this other one is a beef-processing plant, that other one, army barracks, over there is the court, the Municipal building, and way over there is Pemex [the oil company]. The rest are small piled-up houses which crumble when the huge Pemex trucks and ranch pick-up trucks pass by." (See *Voice of Fire: Communiqués and Interviews from the Zapatista National Liberation Army,* edited by Ben Clarke and Clifton Ross [Berkeley: New Earth Publications, 1994], p. 23. See also pp. 39-42 for a listing of the "revolutionary laws" of EZLN "liberated territories.")

As Jose Luis Morin writes, "NAFTA's effects — acceleration of foreign investment and intervention leading inevitably to greater displacement and exploitation of the region and its peoples — are already evident in the Chiapas region. Major oil companies are planning to exploit the rich oil deposits [actually extensive oil extraction is already going on, with significant ecological destruction]; transnational corporations such as Nestlé are seeking to convert land to coffee production; investors are eyeing major expansions of the tourist industry centering on the great Mayan ruins, despite native people's protest that these are the homes and temples of their ancestors. The treaty, in the words of rebel leader Subcomandante Marcos, is the 'death sentence' for Mexico's indigenous peoples." ("An Indigenous Peoples' Struggle for Justice," *Covert Action Quarterly,* Spring 1994. This issue also contains the now famous interview with Subcomandante Marcos from the Italian paper *L'Unità* and other valuable material on the uprising.)

In another interesting piece, Mexican novelist and political commentator Paco Ignacio Taibo II writes that the famous, historic Chiapas town, San Cristobal de las Casas, "a gathering place for hippie tourists, has three Zen centers and hundreds of satellite dishes, and barefoot Indians walk through its streets unable to find work as bricklayers." (See his article, "The Phoenix Rises," in the March 28, 1994 issue of *The Nation.*)

3. So far Marcos has handled this situation with cunning and verve. When the inevitable controversy over his identity ensued after the January revolt, he compared the masks of the guerrillas to the false facade of modern Mexican society, writing in a communiqué, "We could show our faces, but the big difference is that Marcos has always known his real face, and the civil society is just awakening from the long and lazy dream of 'modernity' imposed at all cost to all. Subcomandante Marcos is ready to take off his mask. Is Mexican civil society ready to lift its mask?" (*Christian Science Monitor,* February 16, 1994)

4. See my "Indigenism and its Enemies" (written under the pseudonym Primitivo Solis), in the July 1981 *Fifth Estate.*

5. Of course, the PRI remained in power with the defeat of Cárdenas and the election of Ernesto Zedillo, a regime which continues to deepen the political vacuum.

6. This situation of instability and uncertainty was aggravated by the assassination of Salinas' heir apparent, Luis Donaldo Colosio, by a self-proclaimed pacifist, no less, with probable inner-party involvement as well.

7. Quoted by Alexander Cockburn in his "Beat the Devil" column in the March 28, 1994 issue of *The Nation*.

8. One hesitates nowadays to even mention the name of Octavio Paz, once a great writer and poet, a profound thinker who turned reactionary and brittle in his old age, defending Reaganism, the Cold War, U S. intervention in Central America, and even recently reaching new depths of dishonor by denouncing the zapatistas as murderous, leftist totalitarians, while the army was summarily executing peasant rebels. What Paz has become does not invalidate what he once said.

DEEP ECOLOGY & ENVIRONMENTAL PHILOSOPHY: ON THE ETHICS OF CRISIS AND THE CRISIS IN ETHICS

A deep social ecology?

The implications of a deep ecological vision as a broad, intuitive sensibility — a refusal of instrumental, commoditized relations with the Earth; the notion of kinship with the land and a land ethic; the understanding that the full realization of the personhood of the human subject and of the planet do not compete with one another but correspond; an affirmation of the primal, animist wisdom that places humanity within the web of life and not at the top of some hierarchy — the rediscovery of this constellation of insights is in my view a fundamental precondition for breaking out of the prison-house of urban-industrial civilization and creating a family of free cultures in harmony with one another and with the earth.

The same goes for the idea of social ecology, which implies an investigation into the social roots of our permanent crisis in culture and character, an articulation of the manifold forms of freedom and revolt expressed in and against history, and a radical refusal to be reduced to commodities, resources and machines ourselves. The adjectives accompanying the term "ecology" say enough to be suggestive of a new synthesis of primitive and modern, but they do not say enough to be exact. Turning them into "platforms" undermines their energies and broad promise.

This essay shares with the perspective of social ecology the idea that our species' deadly conflict with the natural world is rooted in social conflict, though it distinguishes itself from the "platform" elements that came to be expressed by Murray Bookchin during the course of his debates with deep ecologists — in particular, the suggestion in some of his work that technological relations are merely the consequence of underlying social relations, and his essentially irrational rejection of irrational and intuitive aspects of our reconciliation with nature, aspects which have been admirably explored by some deep ecology writers.[1] (See page 240 for endnotes.)

It is the purpose here to investigate deep ecology's failure to place the "nature question" into the broader social context, to see ecological and philosophical questions as rooted in social and historical ones, and to expand the discussion to show how these same problems occur throughout much of current environmental philosophy.[2] Deep ecology and environmental ethics cannot avoid confronting the social question if they hope to realize their promise of laying the groundwork for a culture based on harmonious, rather than sociopathic and suicidal relations with the rest of nature.

What, specifically, is deep ecology's promise and project? George Sessions and Bill Devall state in their book *Deep Ecology* that it "goes beyond a limited piecemeal shallow approach to environmental problems and attempts to articulate a comprehensive religious and philosophical world view."[3] Sessions has characterized it as one of "the two main post-modern philosophies of the future" (along with, the reader may be surprised to learn, New Age philosophy).[4] Bill Devall argues that deep ecology is "heir to the three great intellectual, perceptual revolutions in the west — Copernicus, Darwin, and ecological (Thoreau, Leopold),"[5] thus locating the perspective within a notion of scientific progress.

Such claims are bound to invite criticism, and they have. When progress and scientific progress are unquestioningly included in a perspective (rather than being seen as historically-generated constructs and epistemologies, as they would be by a cautious social ecology), one cannot take entirely seriously the claim of deep ecologists to ask "why" more insistently and consistently than others and to take nothing for granted, as Arne Naess, the founder of deep ecology, urges.[6] Nor can one accept deep ecology's implicit, and, at times even explicit, claim to establish a neutral ground to analyze humanity's relationship to nature (the biocentric or ecocentric starting point). The claim is made, for example, in Alan Drengson's observation that it "applies ecological paradigms not only to plants and animals but also to human culture and its internal and external relationships."[7] It allegedly thinks primarily "in biotic rather than social terms," writes journalist Kirkpatrick Sale in attempting to clarify the differences between deep ecology and its critics.[8]

But, of course, all our terms are social before they are biotic or anything else. Indeed, while deep ecologists claim to take nothing for granted, the terms by which they define their process of inquiry go unquestioned. Assuming — rather than critically examining — the premise that human activities can be explained according to the tenets of ecological science, deep ecologists apply ecological models to everything, from the yearly migrations of birds to the forced migrations of war refugees. Any reference to social causes is met by accusations of "shallowness," since at some level at least, ecological relations do underlie human society. But the real question concerning society isn't whether ecological relations underlie "human culture and its internal and external relationships," the question is whether ecological analysis is sufficient to explain human culture's history and conflicts. And in answering this question at least, deep ecologists have proven to be far shallower than their critics.

Deep ecology has suffered not only from ecological reductionism but from a tendency to graft unexamined, gratuitous political positions onto it as well. Such slipshod analysis has led to some monstrous conclusions among some deep ecology adherents. This includes, on the one hand, the aberrations of a survivalist catastrophism and misanthropy, and, on the other hand, an eclectic green liberalism (a variant of the shallow ecology that deep ecologists claim to supersede). While deep ecology philosophers may not be directly responsible for these aberrations, their failure to address them undermines their perspective's radical potentiality. When Kirkpatrick Sale comments in the article cited above that deep ecologists "regard the fundamental issue to be the destruction of nature and the suffering of the rapidly dying species and ecosystems, as distinct from those who regard the basic issue as the absence of justice and the suffering of the human population," he is imposing a contrived dualism on what is in reality a cluster of interlocking crises. The "biotic terms" of ecology are in some ways as patently inadequate as they are in other ways indispensable. Deep ecology's lack of social critique renders invisible those very forces of domination and alienation that are reducing the planet to a petrochemical gulag.

The discipline of environmental ethics suffers from the lack of social critique that limits deep ecology, along with other critical problems. The discourse on the idea of an environmental ethic has become a veritable industry. It may be ironic, but it is certainly no accident, that much of the discussion around establishing a grounding for intrinsic value in nature and a nonanthropocentric ethics is to be found in books and journals outlining the catastrophic mass extinction of species and ecosystems being carried out by the day-to-day operations of the industrial megamachine. Minerva's owl flies, it appears, only at dusk.

Thus, the legal debate around giving "rights" to wilderness and to other species tends to signal their disappearance. Similarly, the elaboration of highly articulated ethical systems has only accompanied a widening swath of violence and destruction and the armoring of the human personality — such systems are mere pieties as far as capital accumulation is concerned. Reading the literature of deep ecology, animal liberation and environmental ethics, one might think that the rights of human beings have been firmly established, and must now be widened to accommodate a deeper land ethic — this in the age of mass exterminations of people in gas chambers, carpet bombings of whole populations, chemical-biological warfare and the threat of nuclear incineration in increasingly volatile gambles to defend the markets and resources of rival empires.

This has to be a central element in any radical critique of deep ecology: not the perspective's poetic identification with the natural world, but its naiveté (and the cynicism of some of its adherents) about power relations — a naiveté (and perhaps a cynicism as well) it inherited from the liberal environmental and conservation movements from which it emerged. One can only shake one's head upon reading how encouraged Arne Naess was after writing numerous "experts" about his deep ecology platform, including "top people in ministries of oil and energy," when "many answered positively in relation to most or all points." According to Naess, we are to be encouraged that "there is a philosophy of the man/nature relationship widely accepted among established experts responsible for environmental decision" which will bring about "substantial change of present politics" to protect the Earth from "shortsighted human interests."[9] This simplistic contrast of nature and human interest, shortsighted or otherwise, leaves Naess blind to the actual organization of power, as well as to the operational characteristics of what is fundamentally an *exterminist,* global megamachine.

Deep ecology and dualism

Another, mostly implicit assumption of deep ecology is its simplistic dualism, which is reflected in its generally unidimensional contrast between nature and an undifferentiated humanity. The dualism occurs simultaneously on two mutually contradictory levels. On the first level, humanity is seen as simply "one" with nature. Any discussion of humanity's specific problems is seen as "anthropocentric" and an affront to a biospheric egalitarianism — a view that does not investigate history or distinguish between differing levels of complexity. Yet on the second level, humanity is seen at least implicitly as a uniquely negative force and as involved in a polarity with nature.

Starting from a legitimate revulsion against the destructiveness of urban-industrial civilization, deep ecology takes for granted an economistic, "zero-sum" picture of the world and nature, in which humanity can thrive only by causing nature to lose. This is essentially the world view of bourgeois civilization, of Adam Smith, Parson Malthus and Thomas Hobbes: "man" struggles against nature, carving progress out of rough, resistant stone. In the deep ecology view, the values or poles are simply reversed; the undifferentiated mass of humanity is compelled to don sackcloth and ashes and make sacrifices in its standard of living to preserve nature. The values themselves are not treated critically as socially and historically generated, as consequences of conditioning within the capitalist commodity system. They are the comforts to which progress itself has mysteriously led, and must be piously given up for the good of a nature that is wholly other. The same dualism is played out in several overlapping polarities. From this ambiguous contrast of biocentrism and anthropocentrism come various other polarities: of intrinsic or inherent value in nature vs. utilitarian or instrumental value (value for human beings); of biospheric egalitarianism and non-interference ("let nature be") vs. "resourcism" or "stewardship" (which is taken to imply a totally administered nature cultivated for the good of some undifferentiated human species "need"); of "humanism" (seen as a kind of human chauvinism) vs. an ostensibly neutral ecocentrism, along with wilderness.

Yet in his environmental history, *Changes in the Land: Indians, Colonists, and the Ecology of New England*, William Cronon reveals the problems with the kind of dualism characteristic of deep ecology. In social and ecological discourse, he points out, the question is not one of an untouched, "virgin" landscape contrasted with a human one, but between distinct "ways of belonging to an ecosystem." Such a perspective, he argues, "would therefore describe precolonial New England not as a virgin landscape of natural harmony but as a landscape whose essential characteristics were kept in equilibrium by the cultural practices of its human community." Cronon quotes Thoreau, who writes in *Walden* that he would like to know "the entire poem" of nature. But this is not possible, Cronon argues. "Human and natural worlds are too entangled for us, and our historical landscape does not allow us to guess what the 'entire poem' of which he spoke might look like. To search for that poem would in fact be a mistake. Our project must be to locate a nature which is within rather than without history, for only by doing so can we find human communities which are inside rather than outside nature." [10] Cronon is speaking to environmental historians, but his advice makes sense for those who would begin to discuss our relationship with the natural world and the present crisis in it.

We must therefore show restraint and some humility in judgments about nature and society. Simply stated, it is one thing to argue that "nature knows best." It is quite another to assume that one philosophical current knows what is best for nature. Such reasoning constitutes a kind of teleology based on assumed omniscience. The resonant remark by Aldo Leopold, "A thing is right when it tends to preserve the integrity, stability and beauty of the biotic community," provides no answers; it only poses a series of questions.[11]

Such a view, as Peter A. Fritzell writes in a very thoughtful essay on the subject, "explains human actions as functions in and of evolving ecosystems only when those actions are consonant with the needs of other elements in such systems, where *consonant* means conducive to the continued, healthy existence of all present species — *as defined and determined by humans and human science.*" [emphasis added in latter phrase]. Commenting on Leopold's celebrated passage cited above, Fritzell observes, "Is man to determine when the biotic comunity is stable and beautiful? Or must man take counsel from other citizens of the community — not only pines, deer, and wolves but cheat grass, gypsy moths and rats? Can man take anything other than human counsel with the other members of the land community? Can such counsel ever express more than the ecological interests of humans and the species they most closely identify with?" Further on he remarks, "The paradoxes of wilderness preservation are less logical problems than they are communal concerns."[12] And, we might add, concerns which are rooted in a matrix of social conflict and domination.

Of course there is much to be affirmed in an environmental ethic. Nevertheless, it is important to recognize the limitations of ecological thinking and the anthropocentrism/biocentrism contrast as a tool of radical critique or as an alternative, new paradigm for thinking. The scientific rationalism on which it rests is extremely contradictory and problematic, a knife with no handle. The permanent revolution of the methodological categories and language of science is a reflection of the constant transformations in technological apparatus and the commodity system by which capital itself expands. Science's description of the world is a description of *its* world; as Goethe knew, "everything factual is already theory."

Regarding this statement by Goethe, Theodore Roszak quotes twentieth century physicist Werner Heisenberg's comment, "In natural science the object of investigation is not nature as such, but nature exposed to man's mode of inquiry."[13] The violence that the empirical method implies cannot be discerned by Heisenberg's bland statement; one must look to its origins in the scientific revolution and the experimental method, as expressed by Francis Bacon, that "nature exhibits herself more clearly under the trials and vexations of art than when left to herself" — which was to say, when confined and tortured by mechanical devices. For Bacon it was necessary to "hound nature in her wanderings," without scruple "of entering and penetrating into these holes and corners, when the inquisition of truth is man's whole object."[14]

As Carolyn Merchant, quoting from Bacon, explains, nature had to "be bound into 'service' and made a 'slave,' put 'in constraint' and 'molded' by the mechanical arts ... The interrogation of witches as symbol for the interrogation of nature, the courtroom as model for its inquisition, and torture through mechanical devices as tool for the subjugation of disorder were fundamental to the scientific method as power."[15] Of course, the actual suppression of women and others as witches, through torture and murder, was contemporaneous with the rise of the modern scientific method, and both were in fact carried out by the same social class of men — indeed, by many of the same men.

For these men, who not only "vexed nature" but slaughtered midwives and healers with their mechanical arts, "sexual politics helped to structure the nature of the empirical method that would produce a new form of knowledge and a new ideology of objectivity seemingly devoid of cultural and political assumptions," Merchant writes.[16] Behind this new ideology of science lay the horrors of gynocide — a holocaust against hundreds of thousands, possibly millions of women, from the 14th to the 18th century. The emerging mechanical and industrial technology developed by the rising scientific and economic elites to carry out their "vexations" of nature's body and the bodies of women helped to rapidly extend and consolidate this ideology's power. As Mary Daly has written in her powerful description of the witch burnings, "The escalation of technology and of persecution goosestepped together in the 'march of progress.'"[17] To return to Goethe's remark, the facts which generate this torturous theory were themselves derived from a theory of tortures.

The problem of scientific naturalism

The emergence of a new recognition of kinship with nature also has its source in part in that scientific naturalism — in fact one of the traditions of humanism itself — which tore human beings from their traditional metaphysical milieu and redefined them as natural objects. But this "objective" decentering of humanity doesn't stop there; it tends to erode the essentially spiritual intuition of inherent value as soon as it starts to suggest it. Scientific naturalism provides no easy answers to the question raised by Leopold and plagues the contrast between what is anthropocentric and what is biocentric with the same epistemological problem that deep ecology would like to forget: how to establish an ethical ground. Given the corrosiveness of scientific naturalism and the limitations of knowledge, on what ground could deep ecology base its ethical (and consequently, social and political) judgments?

After all, despite the intuition of ecological egalitarianism, from the point of view of scientific naturalism on which ecology rests, there is no egalitarianism. Not only that, organisms — be they viruses decimating seal populations in the North Sea, crown-of-thorns starfish scouring the Great Barrier Reef, zebra mussels colonizing the Great Lakes, or the Purple Martins that chase the bluebirds away from the house we built for them — do not recognize ethics, equality or intrinsic worth. Neither, for that matter, do hurricanes or volcanoes. As Hegel put it, animals "do not stand stock still before things of sense as if these were things *per se*, with being in themselves: they despair of this reality altogether, and in complete assurance of the nothingness of things they fall-to without more ado and eat them up."[18]

Exploring the problem of intrinsic value and scientific naturalism (which he calls "holistic rationalism"), J. Baird Callicott argues that "if one defends one's intuition that biological impoverishment is objectively wrong by positing organic richness as objectively good, one might well be accused of temporal parochialism and a very subtle form of human arrogance." Callicott cites the periodic mass extinctions of species on earth to support his argument. "Considering our time as but an infinitesimal moment in the three and one-half billion year tenure of life on planet earth (let alone the possibility that earth may be but one of many planets to possess a biota), man's tendency to destroy other species might be viewed quite disinterestedly as a transitional stage in the earth's evolutionary odyssey."[19] Minimally, his observations suggest the tenuousness and inadequacy of ecological science as the sole basis for social critique or ethical action.

Elliot Sober has argued (in an essay in part replying to Callicott) that "to the degree that 'natural' means anything biologically, it means very little ethically. And conversely, to the degree that 'natural' is understood as a normative concept, it has very little to do with biology." From the point of view of science, what is "natural" is ambiguous. Our intuition, Sober writes, tells us there is a fundamental difference between a mountain and a highway system, "but once we realize that organisms construct their environments in nature, this contrast begins to cloud. Organisms do not passively reside in an environment whose properties are independently determined. Organisms transform their environments by physically interacting with them. An anthill is an artifact just as a highway is."[20]

By such an implacable logic, Sober infers the ultimate indifference to which scientific naturalism can lead. His essay also suggests the problems with an ostensibly omniscient biological egalitarianism like deep ecology, that simultaneously sees humanity as "one with nature," "one more species among many," and yet also as a unique source of evil in the biosphere. Any species, after all — from humpback whales to the ecoli bacteria in human feces — is only "one among many," whatever that means. In the case mentioned, do we assign them equal value, meaning, grandeur? If so, why then do deep ecologists complain? As Callicott has suggested, nothing civilization does, not even nuclear war, will destroy life itself, only complex life; what remains would probably follow the tendency to diversify and evolve, as the biota did after other mass extinctions, such as the Permian, when over 90 percent of species disappeared — long before dinosaurs or mammals.[21]

If we are entirely one with nature then we are no different from red tide or viruses or a destructive meteor from space, and nature is doing this strange dance with itself, or is chaos. Even the Earth is "one mere planet among many," a speck in the cosmos. In the big picture, extinction is inevitable, since the Earth eventually will be destroyed as the sun expands to a supernova (again, according to the best available scientific theory). In 65 million years (long before that remote end), will we be much more than a layer in the sediment? It is impossible to tell, but I am both fascinated with and repelled by scientific naturalism. Its insights compel me to withhold final judgment on such matters and to begin where I am: a human being in a world layered with natural, historical, and social interrelationships, conflicts, affinities and obligations. I don't reject my humanity by identifying with the planet; I am *responding* to it.

Beyond intrinsic value

Environmental philosophers have been unable to reach a conclusive view of the problem of intrinsic worth. Some have argued that human-centered values should not be discarded and can provide a powerful set of motivations for preserving wilderness and protecting the natural world. Even if one avoids the more instrumental character of some arguments of this type (that rainforests contain a wealth of future medicines or food crops, for example), the defense of wilderness as an expression of our own innate biophilia or love of and identification with life, is extremely strong, as when naturalist Edward 0. Wilson argues, "We are in the fullest sense a biological species and will find little ultimate meaning apart from the remainder of life."[22] To follow Theodore Roszak's insight, the personhood of the human being is interrelated with and contingent upon the personhood of the planet.[23]

Sober argues that the value of nature and wilderness is ultimately aesthetic, which is not to say frivolous, and he compares the preservation of a majestic cliff to that of the ancient temple which stands on it, seeing them both as important. Indeed, the comparison of natural objects to aesthetic masterpieces is a common motif in all environmental literature, from John Muir's comment during the campaign to save Hetch Hetchy from developers that "everybody needs beauty as well as bread," to Edward

Abbey's comparison of the damming of Glen Canyon to the destruction of the Taj Mahal or the cathedral at Chartres, with the distinction that the natural object is alive "and can never be recovered." Another writer argues that "our duties toward species arise not out of the interests of the species, but are rooted in the general obligation to preserve things of value."[24]

Even David Ehrenfeld, who attempts in his provocative if flawed book, *The Arrogance of Humanism*, to explode all the "humanist" shibboleths and along with them this anthropocentric aesthetic criterion, falls into the same reasoning. Ehrenfeld even criticizes the humanism in the land ethic and in related aesthetic criteria as a form of "condescension" that is "not in harmony with the humility inspiring discoveries of ecology." Instead, he argues for a "Noah principle," stating that natural objects and species "should be conserved because they exist" (a very problematic and ambiguous formulation — *everything* exists), and because this existence "is itself but the present expression of a continuing historical process of immense antiquity and majesty." Yet concern for antiquity and majesty represents an obviously aesthetic, even classical humanist motivation.[25]

Holmes Rolston considers a distinct intrinsic value impossible, finding "both instrumental and intrinsic values ... objectively present in ecosystems. The system is a web where loci of intrinsic value are meshed in a network of instrumental value," since organisms value the rest of nature instrumentally, while valuing themselves intrinsically, in his view. But because neither term is satisfactory "at the level of the holistic ecosystem," he continues, "we need a third term: systemic value." In this way ethics will not be complete "until extended to the land."[26] Rolston's argument confirms the insight of what we might call a "deep social ecology" which gathers the contributions of both sensibilities: the need to move beyond dualism and even beyond the limitations of science towards an animist mode of kinship, mythopoetic and future-primitive, at the level of the gift, which stands in utter opposition to an economic civilization that reduces the world — including human beings — to resources, to dead units of production and consumption. The presence of agonistic philosophical questioning of humanity's relation to nature — while the very fabric of life appears to be coming apart — seems another bitter irony. But it, too, suggests that the emerging ecological ethic may signal more a mythic return, the coming around of a cycle, than a model of advancing progress as one sometimes finds in environmental ethics, in notions of "paradigm change" culled from the concept of scientific revolution, or in Bookchin's social ecology dialectic.

This idea may seem more valid when we consider the notion of a land community that was already present in the world view of primal peoples. As Callicott has written, not only did Native Americans "regard all features of the environment as enspirited," the social circle and community included nature and other beings (including winds, rivers, stones, and so on) along with human kin.[27]

The original inhabitants of this land knew what Hans Peter Duerr reports in his remarkable book *Dreamtime: Concerning the Boundary Between Wilderness and Civilization*: "To get to the point of origin, to be able, for instance, to 'speak' with plants, a person needs what the Indians call 'reverence.' Humans must become unimportant before the other beings of nature: 'When I was still a child, my parents and the old people taught me to treat everything with reverence, even the rocks, the stones and the small crawling insects, for they are all *manitus*,'" Duerr quotes a Native American, and he adds: "To 'become a part' of the *manitu* of all things means to 'speak the common language of all things.'"[28]

A sense of reverence — isn't this fundamental to a reawakening of our proper relationship to the planet and to ourselves? And isn't it clear that this implies neither a mechanistic imitation of primal society nor the grafting of its insights onto an instrumental science or dualistic model based on competing interest? Where does this reverence come from and how can it be expressed? The current discourse in which deep ecology participates constrains meaning in a language that is already instrumentalized. It not only mechanistically isolates and fragments so-called inherent value from instrumental value, but bases itself on a model of necessity and need that reflects the alienated discourse of bourgeois materialism and the capitalist market themselves.

When Arne Naess writes that the "vital needs" of human beings must be met, he tries to evade the problems such a formulation suggests by leaving this notion "deliberately vague."[29] But he resolves nothing and leaves the entire notion itself unexamined. The dualism of human "need" struggling against natural law — isn't this distorted construct, assuming as it does a polarity between an undifferentiated nature and an equally undifferentiated, simplified "human" need, only an image of this society? Starting from the ideology of natural and historical necessity, the reigning ideology assumes the inevitability of scarcity and its consequent generation of needs. For liberal and marxist alike, increasing needs are a factor of progress; for the deep ecologist, they are the result of increasing numbers — the progress of factors. In these complementary ways, views that are ostensibly diametrically opposed actually share in the mystique produced by the bourgeois civilization that spawned Malthusian scientism, a mechanico-materialist marxism and technocratic liberalism: the ideology of instrumentalism.

But is it possible in nature, as in primal societies, that there is no instrumental value at all, no need, just as there is no economy, no production? Writing about the fundamental differences between objects in western and indigenous contexts, Jamake Highwater observes, "The objects of Indians are expressive and not decorative because they are alive, living in our experience of them. When the Indian potter collects clay, she asks the consent of the river-bed and sings its praises for having made something as beautiful as clay. When she fires her pottery, to this day, she still offers songs to the fire so it will not discolor or burst her wares. And, finally, when she paints her pottery, she imprints it with the images that give it life and power — because for an Indian, pottery is something significant, not just a utility but a 'being' for which there is as much of a natural order as there is for persons or foxes or trees. So reverent is the Indian conception of the 'power' within things, and especially the objects created by traditional craftspeople, that among many Indians, the pottery interred with the dead has a small perforation, a 'kill-hole,' made in the center in order to release the orenda — 'the spiritual power' — before it is buried."[30]

Again the idea of reverence is raised, and we can see that it is not even a question of refusing to allow what we consider alive by scientific standards to be turned into "dead things," but rather two opposed visions: an ecstatic vision in which everything is alive, and that of capital, within which everything becomes lifeless, dead matter. Intrinsic value has its place on the altar in such a scheme, but instrumental value is the iron hand that rules the world, the iron hand of necessity.

As Jean Baudrillard writes in *The Mirror of Production*, his devastating attack not only on marxism but on all of productivist civilization, necessity is "a Law that takes effect only with the objectification of Nature. The Law takes its definitive form in capitalist political economy; moreover, it is only the philosophical expression of Scarcity." But what is scarcity, this centerpiece of Malthusian ideology? "Scarcity, which itself arises in the market economy, is not a given dimension of the economy. Rather, it is what produces and reproduces economic exchange." Scarcity, produced by the emergence of economic exchange, becomes the justification for the forces that generated it, and ends in a pre-capitalist mystique of the "tragedy of the commons" and a "life-boat ethic," "the survival of the fittest," "us against them."

Yet neither nature nor primal societies are determined by need, which arises out of this phantasm of scarcity that both fuels and results from capital accumulation; none of this exists, Baudrillard argues, "at the level of reciprocity and symbolic exchange [as in primal society], where the break with nature that leads to ... the entire becoming of history (the operational violence of man against nature) ... has not occurred." Hence need and social interest are the products of such an economic order, not natural phenomena — and with them, the cleft between intrinsic and intrumental value, between human well-being and the integrity of nature." "The idea of 'natural necessity,'" writes Baudrillard, "is only a moral idea dictated by political economy."[31]

Anthropologist Dorothy Lee puts it another way. She does not claim "that there are no needs; rather, that if there are needs, they are derivative not basic. If, for example, physical survival was held as the ultimate goal in some society, it would probably be found to give rise to those needs which have been stated to be basic to human survival; but I know of no culture where human physical survival has been shown, rather than unquestioningly assumed by social scientists, to be the ultimate goal." To follow the model of deep ecologists, for example, one would assume that "humans" are devouring nature by following a basic species "need" to maximize food. This ideological image teaches us nothing about the natural history of human beings and even less about the kind of society that maximizes the production of crops even by mining and destroying the very soil on which they depend.

"To the Hopi," on the other hand, writes Lee, "corn is not nutrition; it is a totality, a way of life. Something of this sort is exemplified in the story which Talayesva tells of the Mexican trader who offered to sell salt to the Hopi group who were starting out on a highly ceremonial Salt Expedition. Within its context this offer to relieve the group of the hardships and dangers of the religious journey sounds ridiculous. The Hopi were not just getting salt to season their dishes. To them, the journey was part of the process of growing corn and of maintaining harmonious interrelations with nature and what we call the divine. It was the Hopi Way, containing Hopi value. Yet even an ethnographer, dealing with Hopi culture in terms of basic needs, views the Salt Expedition as the trader did and classifies it under Secondary Economic Activities."[32] The Hopi Way and the mode of life of many primal cultures indicate very clearly to us what the foundations are for the kind of reverence that will bring us back into contact with the planet, but only if we have eyes to see, and enough vision to break through the categories that have been imposed by capital and its thorough instrumentalization and commodification of the world.

"All my relations"

The sciences have confirmed the animist intuition that we are physically and psychologically continuous with the rest of nature. Geology, astronomy, biology, evolutionary science and genetics all demonstrate that our very bodies are made up of the same elements that existed during the formative period of the Earth and have made their way down to us through time and all the evolutionary changes of the last several billion years. The salt of the oceans whence we emerged flows in our veins, and the slow development of our backbones and brains have laid the foundations for our very consciousness. Our first dances and songs moved with the rhythms of the earth. We are also biological kin to other organisms.[33]

But as I have already noted, none of this scientific reasoning can guarantee that we will develop ethical concern or a proper relation to the biosphere, any more than the knowledge that other human beings are our genetic kin will prevent us from annihilating them in war. Indeed, such generalizations can lead to a sociobiological reductionism, suppressing the complex relationship between natural and social evolution that provides insight into the problematic uniqueness of our troublesome species. Just as Einstein's theory had multiple implications, not the least of which turned out to be nuclear energy's somatic and genetic assault on complex forms of life, so modern ecological theory and its systemic paradigm may well usher in a bioengineering age that will culminate in the final conquest of nature as we know it (soon to be followed, obviously, by our extinction). Much of this could flow directly from an ecological impulse to save the planet from an otherwise inevitable degradation of its biodiversity, through the adoption of genetic banks and bioengineering. I am reminded of Marcuse's parallel comment on nuclearism. "Does not the threat of an atomic catastrophe which could wipe out the human race also serve to protect the very forces which perpetuate this danger?" he asked. "The efforts to prevent such a catastrophe overshadow the search for potential causes in contemporary industrial society."[34]

Yet to point to the ambiguities in the ecological vision is not to deny aspects capable of affirming kinship with and respect and reverence for the land — those elements in evolutionary science capable of confirming the world view of animist native peoples now standing in such stark contrast to and in condemnation of this instrumental civilization. An ethical element can be derived, in part at least, from evolutionary science. Callicott proposes a "bioempathy" similar to Wilson's notion of biophilia (or perhaps a social aspect of bioempathy standing on the shoulders of biological kinship), rooted in our mammalian evolutionary development. If nature is an "objective, axiologically neutral domain," he asks, "how is it possible to account for the existence of something like morality or ethics among human beings and their prehuman ancestors in a manner consistent with evolutionary theory?"

Drawing on Darwin, he points out that the prolonged parental nurturing of offspring, and the strong emotional bond that accompanies it, would explain such a phenomenon, even suggesting why such groups in which this trait was more pronounced would have increased chances of survivability. Of course the thread that led Kropotkin to write *Mutual Aid* is recognizable here — a work that despite its illusions about progress and technology and its romantic whimsy (this latter is actually part of its appeal), drew a portrait of evolution stressing cooperation that is now being vindicated by evolutionary theory's deepening understanding of symbiosis and mutualism in nature.[35]

It's possible that there may be a bit too much sociobiology in Callicott's description as well, but it does suggest that an environmental ethic can be rooted in an explicitly human context and need not (and probably cannot) be based on a perspective of neutrality or one-dimensional identification with the otherness of nature. When we anthropomorphize by calling the earth our Mother, we are reiterating our biological link to the planet and also to our real mothers (and by extension, to our families and communities), just as when Native Americans refer to other species as "all my relations" they are not denying kinship with their human relatives but integrating kinship on both levels.

Such forms of kinship and community are interlocked but not entirely identical. As Rolston notes, "Cultures are a radically different mode" from the ecosystem and thus demand different criteria for judgment and action. "Relations between individual and community have to be analyzed separately in the two communities," he writes. "To know what a bee is in a beehive is to know what a good (functional) bee is in a bee society, but ... nothing follows about how citizens function in nation-states or how they ought to."

Accordingly, "It may be proper to let Montana deer starve during a rough winter, following a bonanza summer when the population has edged over the carrying capacity. It would be monstrous to be so callous about African peoples caught in a drought. Even if their problems are ecologically aggravated there are cultural dimensions and duties in any solution that are not considerations in deer management."[36] Ethical considerations aside, the differences in the sources of the two events cannot be forgotten. No one has demonstrated that famine in Africa is any more than the result of social conflicts and capitalist looting. Those sources must be attended to before we can begin to judge the related environmental factors.

Biocentrism cannot therefore replace a social critique or social solidarity. Our recognition of our kinship and community with nature is intertwined with our understanding of the global "planetariat" that we have become since the original rupture in primitive society and the origin of the state megamachines. To turn away from the long, rich traditions of communal revolt and from solidarity with other human communities in their ongoing struggle for freedom would be as violent an error as to deny the biosocial roots of our connections to the land.

Saving ourselves

To save ourselves: to restore the land, to restore ourselves to the land. None of us is absolutely certain how to bring this vision about. And so a sense of humility, in the face of the urgent constellation of challenges that lie before us, is called for. An ethic of respect for the land is emerging as the shadows lengthen over civilization. As Theodore Roszak writes in *Person/Planet*, "We are finally coming to recognize that the natural environment is the exploited proletariat, the downtrodden nigger of everybody's industrial system." But we are the land and must renew our connection with it. "For the Earth is not merely a factor of production; she is a living thing that makes an ethical claim upon our loyalty. Our identity is organically woven into her history; she has generated us out of herself, nurtured, shaped and sustained us ... And she will be heard."[37]

Every scar on the earth's body, every broken thread in its tapestry, diminishes us, undermines our own evolutionary destiny. To save ourselves we must save the earth. To save the earth, we must find a way to create a humane, egalitarian and ecologically sustainable society. If we cannot, we will continue around this vortex created by urban-industrial capitalism down to extinction. It may even be already too late, but there is still life in us, so we keep on. An environmental philosophy that fails to recognize the interrelatedness of the social and natural crises, and the roots of ecological crisis in class, race, gender and historical conflicts within historically generated societies, will fail to uncover and confront the real sources of the ecological meltdown occurring today. The anthropocentrism that many deep ecologists decry as the source of the ecological crisis is little more than window dressing on this civilization's bloody history of plunder, massacre and devastation.

No development scheme, no poisoning of water, no squandering of the soil, no levelling of forests and no mass exodus or slaughter of human populations occurs as a response to "human need" or "human-centeredness" or as the direct consequence of the explosion of human numbers. These phenomena exist, rather, to continue the accumulation of capital and the smooth functioning of a global, imperial work pyramid. To pretend otherwise in the name of ecology is to affirm the very social model that deep ecology wishes to replace. Such a perspective, once it reaches the terrain of social practice, will lead, as it has led, either to a "shallow ecology" form of liberal politics that uses revolutionary rhetoric to lobby for fragile, tenuous environmental reforms that leave the megamachine structurally intact, or to a kind of survivalist catastrophism which is little more than a dangerous pose.

The collapse of the global ecosystem as we know it is not a far-fetched prospect. The Earth's vital signs are showing increased, profound stress, and we have no idea at what point what thresholds will be crossed. We will only inherit the consequences. The possibility that human societies can be transformed in time seems remote, not because we are too many, but because of the social chaos, the entropy that goes in capital's wake. On the other hand, there is a possibility that we can bring about a revolutionary social ecological transformation, that our grandchildren or great-great-grandchildren may inherit an Earth which is slowly mending itself, renewing itself. We have a chance, but we must find a way to articulate a dramatic appeal to the people who presently languish under the spiked wheels of the megamachine, who make it go and yet have no stake in it, who have nothing to lose and a world to gain: the oppressed, landless, contaminated, irradiated, and alienated planetariat, the people who will recover the planet and rediscover their own planethood. And if we cannot, the catastrophe will already have occurred, and nature will surely do the rest.

(1989)

Endnotes

1. See, for example, Gary Snyder's lucid and generous book, *The Practice of the Wild* (San Francisco: North Point Press, 1990).
2. For a previous critique and overview of deep ecology, particularly as practiced by some Earth First! activists, see my *How Deep Is Deep Ecology? With an Essay-Review on Woman's Freedom* (Ojai, CA: Times Change Press, 1989); also "Was Malthus Right? An Exchange on Deep Ecology and Population" (with William Catton and others), *Fifth Estate,* Spring 1988; and "Return of the Son of Deep Ecology: The Ethics of Permanent Crisis and the Permanent Crisis in Ethics," *Fifth Estate*, Spring 1989. This essay is a revised and considerably abridged version of the last article, which also deals extensively with the question of wilderness and other debates among the radical ecology milieu.
3. Bill Devall and George Sessions, *Deep Ecology: Living as if Nature Mattered* (Salt Lake City: Peregrine Smith Books, 1985), p. 65.
4. George Sessions, "Deep Ecology and the New Age," *Earth First! Journal*, Mabon edition, 1987.
5. Bill Devall, personal correspondence, December 7, 1987, unpublished.
6. "Interview with Arne Naess," in Devall and Sessions, *Deep Ecology*, pp. 74-77.
7. Alan Drengson, "Developing Concepts of Environmental Relationships," *Philosophical Enquiry*, Vol. VIII, 1-2 (Winter-Spring 1986).
8. Kirkpatrick Sale, "Deep Ecology and Its Critics," *The Nation*, May 14, 1989.
9. Arne Naess, "The Deep Ecology Movement: Some Philosophical Aspects," *Philosophical Enquiry*, Vol VIII, 1-2 (Winter-Spring 1986). For another example of this naiveté, see Fritjof Capra, "Deep Ecology: A New Paradigm," *Earth Island Journal*, Fall 1987.
10. William Cronon, *Changes in the Land: Indians, Colonists, and the Ecology of New England* (New York: Hill and Wang, 1983), pp. 12-15.
11. Aldo Leopold, *A Sand County Almanac* (New York: Ballantine Books, 1970), p. 262.
12. Peter A. Fritzell, "The Conflicts of Ecological Conscience," in *Companion to A Sand County Almanac*, J. Baird Callicott, ed. (Madison: University of Wisconsin Press, 1987), pp. 141-151.

13. Goethe and Heisenberg, quoted and discussed in Theodore Roszak, *Where the Wasteland Ends: Politics and Transcendence in Postindustrial Society* (New York: Doubleday and Co., 1972), pp. 329-334.

14. Carolyn Merchant, *The Death of Nature: Women, Ecology and the Scientific Revolution* (New York: Harper & Row, 1980), p. 169.

15. Merchant, ibid., p. 168.

16. Merchant, ibid., pp. 168-172.

17. Mary Daly, *Gyn/Ecology: The Metaethics of Radical Feminism* (Boston: Beacon Press, 1978), p. 190.

18. G. W. F. Hegel, *The Phenomenology of Mind* (New York: Harper Torchbooks, 1967), p. 159.

19. J. Baird Callicott, "On the Intrinsic Value of Nonhuman Species," in *The Preservation of Species: The Value of Biological Diversity*, Bryan G. Norton, ed. (Princeton: Princeton University Press, 1986), p. 151.

20. Elliot Sober, "Philosophical Problems for Environmentalism," in *The Preservation of Species*, pp. 180–188. Many of the categories within biological science are highly problematic. In his essay on the current extinction spasm, "Why the Ark is Sinking" (in *The Last Extinction*, Les Kaufman and Kenneth Mallory, eds. [Cambridge: MIT Press, 1986]), Les Kaufman demonstrates how different communities of rock hopper penguins, ostensibly members of the same species, cause great problems for taxonomists. There are anywhere from eleven to eighteen different species, depending on which taxonomist is judging; hence, "our notion of what a species is, or isn't, is largely an artifact of human bias." (p. 9) One can only imagine how such problems are magnified when biology, as current scientific discourse may posit it, invades political discourse. This is why one feminist critic of science, Sandra Harding, suggests that rather than imposing biology on politics, "much of biology should already be conceptualized as social science." In fact, she observes, "'paradigmatic theories in particular areas of inquiry eventually wear out as fruitful guides to research,' as Kuhn's theory of scientific revolutions suggests. "Shouldn't this also be true for science as a whole?" See *The Science Question in Feminism* (Ithaca: Cornell University Press, 1986), pp. 43-44.

21. J. Baird Callicott, "On the Intrinsic Vaue of Non-human Species," p. 151.

22. Edward O. Wilson, *Biophilia* (Cambridge: Harvard University Press, 1984), p. 81.

23. Theodore Roszak, *Person/Planet: The Creative Disintegration of Industrial Society* (New York: Anchor Books, 1978).

24. See Roderick Nash, *Wilderness and the American Mind* (New Haven: Yale University Press, 1982), p. 165; Edward Abbey, *Desert Solitaire* (New York: Ballantine Books, 1968), p. 174; Lily Marlene Russow, "Why Do Species Matter?" in *People, Penguins, and Plastic Trees: Basic Issues in Environmental Ethics*, Donald VanDeVeer and Christine Pierce, eds. (Belmont: Wadsworth Publishing Company, 1986), p. 120.

25. David Ehrenfeld, *The Arrogance of Humanism* (Oxford and New York: Oxford University Press, 1981), pp. 207-208. In this same passage Ehrenfeld attacks the humanism or anthropocentric arrogance even in those attempts to find aesthetic, non-utilitarian motives for preservation. These are "purely selfish reasons," he argues. Yet not only do we survive at least partially for "purely selfish reasons" (an observation he himself makes a few pages later), the sense of awe and humility before the immense beauty of nature is precisely what inspires an ecological ethic, the result of sensitive identification with nature that refuses, out of a partially "humanist" sensibility, to be reduced to a utilitarian science of energy bits and caloric counts.

26. Homes Rolston III, "Duties to Ecosystems," in *A Companion to A Sand County Almanac*, pp. 268-70.

27. J. Baird Callicott, "Traditional American Indian and Western European Attitudes Toward Nature: An Overview," in *In Defense of the Land Ethic: Essays in Environmental Philosophy* (Albany: State University of New York Press, 1989), p. 189. Here Callicott seems to be answering his own question, posed in his essay, "On the Intrinsic Value of Nonhuman Species" (printed in both the Ryan Norton anthology and *In Defense of the Land Ethic*): "What are the ethical systems, and more generally, the world views in which claims of the intrinsic value of nonhuman species are embedded?"

28. Hans Peter Duerr, *Dreamtime: Concerning the Boundary Between Wilderness and Civilization* (Oxford and New York: Basil Blackwell, 1985), pp. 110-111.

29. Arne Naess, ibid.; also Naess and George Sessions, "Basic Principles of Deep Ecology," in Devall and Sessions, *Deep Ecology*, pp. 69-77.

30. Jamake Highwater, *The Primal Mind: Vision and Reality in Indian America* (New York: Meridian, 1981), pp. 77-78.

31. Jean Baudrillard, *The Mirror of Production* (St. Louis: Telos Press, 1975), pp. 58-61.

32. Dorothy Lee, *Freedom and Culture* (New York: Prentice Hall/Spectrum, 1959), p. 73. It may be impossible to get entirely beyond this tension between need and necessity and the universe described by Baudrillard and suggested by Lee, Marshall Sahlins (*Stone Age Economics*) and others. On some level, "need" may be said to exist if people go hungry, and people went hungry during certain periods of the seasonal cycle in primal society. For the way in which such periods were integrated into the mythic and gift cycles by one group of native peoples, see the beautiful tales collected and translated by Howard Norman, *Where the Chill Came From: Cree Windigo Tales and Journeys* (San Francisco: North Point Press, 1982). Windigos, usually shown in the form of "a wandering giant with a heart of ice," are the cause of chaos and starvation during lean times. The Windigo is often thought of as the spirit of all those who have ever starved to death. Yet it is also a reflection of a disruption of the gift

cycle in the community rather than a simple biological fact. Scarcity — a "law" imposed by bourgeois economic modes of thinking — does not determine the activities of the Cree, though it may certainly be argued that scarcity, and hence need, determine human action where the economic reigns. Thus it may be impossible to escape entirely the notion of defending our "interest" or acting to satisfy "need" even as we recognize the problematic, imposed character of these categories.

Cronon's book *Changes in the Land* contains an extremely interesting discussion of scarcity that may be helpful here. Reporting that the northern New England natives "accepted as a matter of course that the months of February and March, when the animals they hunted were lean and relatively scarce, would be times of little food," he writes that the Europeans "had trouble comprehending this Indian willingness to go hungry in the late winter months" and their "apparent refusal to store more than a small amount of the summer's plenty for winter use." The colonists could not understand such an attitude when it would have been patently easy for the natives to gather and store more. The natives were nonplussed, replying, "It is all the same to us, we shall stand it well enough; we spend seven and eight days, even ten sometimes, without eating anything, yet we do not die." What was more ironic, Cronon observes, was that native people "died from starvation much less frequently than did early colonists. . . ." Here we see the refusal of surplus, which is another way of saying, the refusal of scarcity. (pp. 40-41)

33. See J. Baird Callicott, "The Search for an Environmental Ethic," in *Matters of Life and Death: New Introductory Essays in Moral Philosophy* (New York: Random House, 1986).

34. Herbert Marcuse, *One Dimensional Man* (Boston: Beacon Press, 1966), p. ix.

35. Callicott, "On the Intrinsic Value of Nonhuman Species," pp. 156–158. For Kropotkin, see Graham Purchase, "Kropotkin's Metaphysics of Nature," *Fifth Estate*, Late Summer 1991.

36. Rolston, in Callicot, *A Companion to A Sand County Almanac*, pp. 264-265. Here the political terminology, even more than the natural resources terminology, reveals once more the limitations so far of environmental philosophy as radical critique.

37. Roszak, *Person/Planet*, pp. 32 and 273.

HOMAGE TO FREDY PERLMAN
(1934–1985)

I. The death of
Fredy Perlman

Fredy Perlman escaped Czechoslovakia as a young child just before the Nazi invasion, thus barely avoiding, in his words, that "rationally planned extermination of human beings, the central experience of so many people in an age of highly developed science and productive forces. . . ." His life experiences and his ideas were framed within that context — the life-crushing machinery and the varieties of human response. In his view, the problem of freedom is always present: one might learn from the pogroms to resist or flee, or be brutalized enough to become a pogromist oneself — a possibility which he poignantly explored in the essay, *Anti-Semitism and the Beirut Pogrom* (1982). Since human decisions are never pre-determined, a life-affirming response is always at hand.

A great part of Fredy's theoretical and practical struggle was an investigation of the process of alienation and fragmentation by which human beings surrender their autonomy and participate in their own suppression. He wrestled with this problem in essays such as *The Reproduction of Daily Life* and his book on C. Wright Mills, *The Incoherence of the Intellectual.* In his own life as well he resisted fragmentation and "rationalized incoherence" writing emphatically in the book on Mills, "What is involved is a location of oneself and a definition of reality which makes coherent action possible." Just as much for factory workers, clerks and students as for intellectuals, it was necessary "to get to the root of what is happening and what might be done about it."

Radical means "at the root," and such was the radical perspective of Fredy Perlman. As in theory, so in practical activity, in life. The problem was to exercise freedom appropriately to become a "masterless" human being, to overcome the split between thought and action. "The first step away from social schizophrenia,"he wrote, "is to unite one's split self, or at least to define the conditions for one's own coherence."

The seriousness with which he confronted this problem led Fredy to many important decisions, notably the decision to leave the United States in the wake of the Cuban missile crisis, the decision to abandon his university teaching job at the end of the 1960s, and to create, with his wife Lorraine and others, the Black & Red publishing project and the Detroit Print Co-op.

Fredy was often an animating influence in our Detroit circle because he was courageous enough, masterless enough, to follow his instincts. He was not afraid to recognize the consequences of his discoveries. In the 1970s he moved beyond marxist theory and anarchist historiography, beyond technology, beyond modernity, to a rediscovery of the primitive and of primal human community, and to the understanding that capital is not the inevitable outcome of some "material" historical development, but a monstrous aberration. Nevertheless, still central to his concerns was the problem of freedom — why people choose to remain passive participants in their own alienation, why they continue to reproduce the conditions of their own misery. In 1969 he described the power of capital as residing in the daily activities of living people, and the result of this power: "Men who were much but had little," he wrote in *The Reproduction of Daily Life*, "now have much but are little."

Against History

By the early 1980s he had taken up the question of just how much people once were and how much they had lost in his *Against His-story, Against Leviathan!* In this feverishly written book, he portrayed the original dissolution of ecstatic human communities and the emergence of a repressive leviathan — "a cadaverous beast excreted by a human community," "an Earthwrecker," "a carcass of a worm ... its body consisting of numerous segments, its skin pimpled with spears and wheels and other technological implements." The complicity of people in the theft of their living energies is described not so much theoretically but in vivid, concrete images: "the entire carcass ... brought to artificial life by the motions of the human beings trapped inside."

For Fredy, this was not some historical puzzle, but our own dilemma. Leviathan, he emphasized, "is not exotic. It is our world." And the question remained: "Why do people do it? This is the great mystery of civilized life." What had begun as a burden, he offered, has become "like a heavy armor or an ugly mask," more and more difficult to remove, fused to the individual, "emptying its victim of life, of ecstasy. The empty space is filled with springs and wheels, with dead things, with Leviathan's substance."

But the same energy which helped Fredy to describe the horrors of civilization made it possible for him to summon up the forces of life and expectations of hope. It became clearer that the "harsh material conditions" before civilization had not been as harsh as we are told; the phrase "men who were much but had little" described a life in which "material conditions" were secondary or irrelevant to a kind of possession, "not Possession of things but possession of Being," as he wrote in *Against History*. Fredy's ideas were becoming more subtle, just as his voice was becoming more poetic, visionary.

The rediscovery of the primitive signaled a return to nature — to our own nature — and a new direction for freedom. He wrote, "The state of nature is a community of freedoms" — a garden of earthly delights "filled with dances, games and feasts." This was no less than the affirmation of paradise on earth — both in the remote (and suppressed) past and as a dormant, yet imminent, promise. It is obvious that such provocative declarations would elicit some negative response — the same kind of arrogance and contempt, we should remember, that was shown towards witches, pagan dancers, and native communities as they were put to the torch. Rationalism, the brutalized metaphysic of slaves whose insides are filled with springs and wheels, cannot bear the possibility of paradise. "They apply the word 'wild' to the free," Fredy wrote. "But it is another public secret that the tame, the domesticated, occasionally become wild but are never free so long as they remain in their pens."

The imminent capacity to become wild, to transgress the limitations of our pens, allows for hope. "I take it for granted that resistance is the natural response to dehumanization," he observed, "and, therefore, does not have to be explained or justified." And the potential is immediate, a presence within all of us, since people "never become altogether empty shells. A glimmer of life remains. . . ."

From theoretician to singer

Fredy went from brilliant theoretician to singer, from political activist to intuitive rebel. His desire was what it had always been, but he was approaching those now forgotten archaic rhythms which beat deeply in us all. Something was coming to fruition, like the craftsmanship that went into his creations, but it had grown in him for many years. His 1962 play, *Plunder*, makes this clear. In that morality play on imperialism, a young Indian, Nathuram, approaches his artisan friend Krishna, who is making bowls, and asks scornfully, "Still making bowls and dreaming of *Bhagavad Gita!* When will you get married, Krishna?"

"I am married," replies Krishna, "and you are a beggar. I am married to Earth. Each bowl is made of earth-substance. I take the substance in my hands, give it roundness, my imagination peoples it, and I have a world — a roomful of worlds. How can you say I am not married? Earth is my bride; with her I conceive worlds, ages of men, of animals, of loves, adventures and deaths. Here, look into this bowl, Nathuram: do you see the fierce armies facing each other, and in the center Arjuna, struggling with his soul — should he fight, or shouldn't he? And on this one, Nathuram, is India herself, rising like a sick man, shaking the plague from her body."

"Can you cure my brother's sickness by telling him to shake it off?" asks Nathuram. "Teach me, Krishna, teach me to feed my brother's family by showing them there is food on it. If the soul of India is sick, can the sickness be shaken off on bowls?"

"Nowhere else, Nathuram. I cure India's sickness with bowls. You could cure India with cloth."

India is the world, and Fredy fulfilled his curative role with stories, essays, plays, music, and by his participation in many anticratic and communitarian projects. Our community in Detroit, being far greater than the sum of the individuals who make it up, was much diminished by his untimely passing. But cloth remains to be spun. Just two days before his death he was working on a Black & Red project, mailing out a new book of poetry, Christina Pacosz's *Some Winded, Wild Beast*. He would, and we should, expect no less of those of us who survive him.

This appreciation of Fredy's work so far has said next to nothing about our friend's physical presence, his preposterous jokes and pointed stories, the sound of his voice, his handshake and his unique way of greeting people, and so many other aspects of his life. At his memorial, someone recalled that whenever Fredy and Lorraine visited him and his companion in the distant city where they lived, there was always a feeling at the conclusion of the visit that not enough had been packed in, that there was still so much more to say. He had that same feeling after Fredy's death. Someone else added that he had resisted the urge to embrace Fredy and tell him he loved him the day before the surgery, since it would have sounded too pessimistic, like a farewell. Now he said it for all of us.

"There is no death," an old Indian once said. "only a change of worlds." On his last trip to the shores of Lake Huron, Marilynn and Lorraine brought

him a stone with mysterious markings. Were they the bodies of the ancestors, a message meant for him? Later, we passed the stone from hand to
hand there in their dining room, feeling its strange and friendly power.
Fredy hadn't crossed the dunes to the lakeshore; his heart was already
failing him. So the message stone made its crossing to him: a gift, a small
mirror of paradise, a shard of dreamtime. His friends think long and hard
upon this stone and we can feel him. Now he has crossed over, and rests in
a garden conversing with stone spirits.

And we carry him with us through our days, like a small and lustrous
stone.

(1985)

2. An exemplary life:
A memoir of Fredy Perlman

A review of *Having Little, Being Much: A Chronicle of Fredy
Perlman's Fifty Years*, by Lorraine Perlman, Black & Red (Detroit:
Black & Red, 1989)

I cannot say with any certainty what kind of response this perceptive,
if rather abbreviated memoir would elicit from a person who did not know
Fredy Perlman or his writings. It was written for those at least familiar
with his work, and they, without a doubt, will enjoy this glimpse of the man
whose voice played such a large role in reviving libertarian traditions and
articulating the critical primitivism that has so profoundly transformed anti-
authoritarian ideas during the last decade.

This book makes no claim to be a comprehensive intellectual biography. That would take far more than its 150 or so pages. But it nevertheless
succeeds not only in giving a thoughtful survey of Fredy's "intellectual trajectory" (as the author, his companion of a quarter century, Lorraine Perlman,
puts it in her introductory note); it also manages to capture, sometimes strikingly through characteristic moments and statements, the whole man.

One is struck alternately by the universal and unique aspects of Fredy's
life. A refugee in a century of refugees, he narrowly escaped disappearing
down the same abyss of the Nazi Final Solution in which he lost many of
his relatives. An immigrant in the Americas, he spent his childhood in
Bolivia, speaking Czech, German and Spanish. (One of his most vivid childhood memories was that of being chased and frightened by a llama.) Later,
he came with his parents to the United States, where he grew up in New
York and Kentucky, a student of merit who once won a television set in an
essay competition on the theme of freedom, and who as a youth found

refuge in one of those representative circles that sought to resist the stultifying effects of the conformist culture of the 1950s in jazz, classical music, and intellectual conversation.

How an individual becomes a rebel and a dissident is a question that is indirectly raised but left unanswered by the book; those who have themselves been radicalized will see traces of their own lives in the relationship between Fredy and his brother, a talented and intelligent person who wholeheartedly embraced U.S. culture and followed the path of middle class life. One may get the impression from the book that there never was any choice for Fredy, but that is not true. He struggled with his desires and his conscience, both as a young person and later, for example, during his brief academic career. But Fredy yearned for something other than what his brother and so many others have chosen, carrying within him a voracious hunger for authentic experience and understanding, and little ambition in the terms of this world.

From rebel to revolutionary

The nothingness of life in the 1950s seems to have done to Fredy what it did to so many others, and as a youth he set out from Kentucky in his car and drove straight to Los Angeles, where, archetypically, he went to sleep on the beach by the Pacific after spending his last few cents on coffee and cigarettes. In LA, he enrolled at UCLA and became involved in the *Daily Bruin*, the student paper, participating in a high-spirited struggle against the anti-communist witch-hunts on the campus McCarthyites dubbed "the little red school house." When that fight was essentially lost, he found his way to New York City, to Columbia University and engagement with radical sociologist C. Wright Mills (who strongly influenced him), and to the young music student from Iowa, Lorraine Nybakken, who became his lifelong companion. After a period of vigorous intellectual activity and political involvement, they decided to abandon the U.S. with its growing war hysteria for life in Europe, where they spent nearly four years.

Many of Fredy's pivotal intellectual and political concerns were formed in this period, both in New York and in Yugoslavia: the desire to understand civilization systematically, to find a critical coherence; particularly, the analysis of empire that informed so much of his work, allowing him to radicalize marxian thinking and to move beyond its assumptions of technological progress. His experiences and studies in Yugoslavia helped him later to describe the emergence of capitalist relations (no matter what their labels) and to appreciate and defend the values of those vernacular societies bulldozed by so-called progress and development. But it was Paris '68 that truly galvanized Fredy. Whatever he was and thought before passing through that crucible, he would be forever changed. The revolutionary upheaval in France brought him into contact with dangerous new ideas and radical traditions he had not previously known. The watershed of 1968 led him eventually back to the U.S., to revolutionary publishing and to Detroit.

If 1968 and its aftermath led Fredy to investigate the mysterious process of alienation by which human beings reproduce their own misery, as well as the process by which they resist and thus renew what is human in themselves, the experience of organizing and working on the Detroit Print Co-op showed him in practical terms that people could cooperate and create communities, even under the countless pressures of capitalist society. During that time, as Lorraine observes in retrospect, their motor trip to Alaska opened his eyes more than ever to the terrible cleft between humanity and the natural world, and then inevitably to deeper, sometimes obscure, but always fruitful questions about the process of domestication of nature and human beings. One detects his later "primitivism" taking seed in this period, only to become manifest afterward, during the late 1970s and early 1980s, as our intense discussions and arguments — often around the kitchen table at Fredy and Lorraine's house on Detroit's southwest side — led us to a deeper conception of politics: a critique of civilization itself.

An exemplary life

Always skeptical of programs and ideologies, of all "isms," Fredy shied away from party politics in the 1950s and 1960s and wisely declined to become a pro-situ ideologue in the 1970s. He reassessed politics, even revolutionary politics, in his search for new paths to social transformation and human self realization. Eventually, he immersed himself in the study of native peoples, looking for ways to subvert and retell History's official, falsified story. This was the project in which he was so intensely engaged when his life was cut short by a body that could not match his spirit. His last book, a novel about the original people of this area and those who came later, was published posthumously as *The Strait*.

Lorraine Perlman's memoir gives a good sense of Fredy and his ideas. She has also accurately (even perhaps too generously) captured the community life here in which Fredy and Lorraine participated so actively. Her direct and unadorned style lets Fredy's life speak for itself; one cannot help but see it as exemplary. I mean exemplary not in the sense of being entirely and consistently correct or somehow saintly. Claims of sainthood and larger-than-life heroism are for the kinds of racketeers that Fredy and Lorraine critiqued in many of their Black & Red publications. Fredy was completely

PART IV: CIVILIZATION IN BULK

human: generous, supportive, loyal, sometimes zany, but also unyielding in disagreements, occasionally suspicious of other people's motives, even petty.

Fredy was exemplary, nevertheless, because his personal trajectory was representative of a time when rebels had to reexamine their forms of revolt and their lives as they found them being conquered and colonized by the very forces they had originally set out to oppose. His politics matured into a deepening refusal that overlapped with a corresponding affirmation of things that modern politics forgets: the toughness, self-reliance and creative resilience of traditional cultures, the manifold ways in which individuals manage to grow by breaking through the cracks in civilization's concrete, the need to remember and the need to sing. As Gary Snyder has written in *The Old Ways*, "At very bottom is the question 'how do you prepare your mind to become a singer.'" Fredy grappled with this question even as his physical heart was giving out.

My main criticism of the book is that there is too little of Lorraine in it. She argues that this is not full-fledged biography but a memoir; and, one must concede, she has done the writing and thus is not obliged to tell more than she has. Fair enough; the story still overflows its subject, as it should, to his milieu, his time, and to the large questions with which he struggled — the possibility of freedom, of reconstituting human community, of reconnecting with the rhythms of the natural world, of simply maintaining one's integrity under capitalism. The book affirms the possibility that people can survive, change, even thrive.

We live in grim times. The book did not let me forget this reality either. I was somehow reminded, particularly in the final chapters, of how far things have gone since the appearance of the mechanized dead thing he called Leviathan. I think that Fredy chose to explore the possibility of singing in fact because so many forms of resistance appeared exhausted and problematic. But his singing reminds us that anything, and perhaps everything, is still possible — that the Golden Age, as Rousseau once remarked, lies neither behind us nor in the distant future but within us. I, too, must confess, along with Lorraine, that I feel privileged to have known him and to have shared a part of his journey.

(1990)

THE UNABOMBER & THE FUTURE OF INDUSTRIAL SOCIETY

" ... *If one has courage and daring without benevolence, one is like a madman wielding a sharp sword; if one is smart and swift without wisdom, one is as though riding on a fast mount but not knowing which way to go.*

"Even if one has talent and ability, if one uses them improperly and handles them inappropriately, they can only assist falsehood and dress up error. In that case it is better to have few technical skills than many.

"So, the ambitious should not be lent convenient power; the foolish should not be given sharp instruments."
— *taoist adept, 2nd century B.C.E.*[1] (See page 265 for endnotes.)

"We aren't the first to mention that the world today seems to be going crazy. . . ." — "Industrial Society and Its Future" (the "Unabomber manifesto")[2]

I: Go, Unabomber

Is the taoist master's advice more relevant to a serial bomber or to the society that engendered him? Now that the Unabomber's fifteen minutes of fame may be nearly ended, perhaps we can begin to discern his ambiguous significance to the megatechnic system he wants to overthrow.[3]

Clearly, the Unabomber struck a chord in the culture, rapidly becoming a perverse folk hero. If most considered his means mad, some of his stated motives received a good measure of sympathy. This must have been particularly true among people physically damaged by industrial processes, or who have seen their livelihoods erased by automation, or been coerced into progressively constricted and surveilled routines by computerization, or witnessed some beloved place bulldozed in the name of progress, or simply felt the crushing burden of a world of machines, noise and dreary offices.

Suppressing a natural compassion for his victims — in the larger scheme of things, most of them little more than bystanders — some people secretly rooted for the Unabomber. Perhaps they did so hoping he would improve his aim while sharpening his arguments (though few people actually read more than excerpts in the print media, and those who did, ironically, probably got the document off the Internet). In fact, his aim was decidedly scattershot, if he intended to strike effectively and clearly at major policy-makers within the megamachine. But in post-modern, pop culture North America, the Unabomber seemed to be all we technophobes had; he stood in for a mass movement that few of his secret admirers even noticed was lacking. He was, instead, a slice of mediatized saturnalia, a murky Robin Hood who put a scare into the normally smug "techno-nerds" while thumbing his nose at the police.

While humor can often be subversive, there was also an unmistakable element of cynicism (and thus resignation) in the comedic response to the Unabomber. Not only is life cheap (as soon as an airplane crashes the jokes start), when the media picks up a message, the meaning implodes. In the Unabomber's case, his own argument — an astute one, though hardly new, that revolutionary action has unforeseeable consequences — took an ironic turn: his image was emblazoned on bumperstickers (as in, "Don't Blame Me, I Voted for the Unabomber"), and sweatshirts (one marketed in California showed the famous suspect sketch with the words, "There's a package for you...."), and became the raw material for tv and radio comedy.

The Unabomber even became an attraction on the Internet. Several web pages were devoted to him, including an area of multimedia giant Time Warner's Pathfinder site containing a game called "Find the Unabomber," which asked visitors, "Is there a little of the Unabomber in all of us?" Metroactive, a site formed by three Northern California newsweeklies, commented on the FBI suspect sketch, offering an updated, more fashionable sketch with the explanation, "This anarcho-terrorist is looking dynamite in wraparound sunglasses, $140 by Giorgio Armani; black pin-striped suit, $1,550; white corduroy shirt, $395; and black silk tie, $125, by Hugo Boss. Styled by André." A student involved in Internet discussions of the Unabomber commented, "People aren't really fans, they're just impressed."[4]

Another typical occurrence was the "Name the Unabomber" phenomenon. I suffered this common experience of being chided by co-workers for being the Unabomber because of my openly luddite attitudes. I'll probably never know if anyone seriously considered me a suspect, but it's sobering to know that at least 20,000 tips were received by the FBI Unabom Task Force hotline before Kaczynski was arrested. If enough technophobia was in the air to elicit at least a muted, comic sympathy for the Unabomber, a widespread atmosphere of mutual suspicion and identification with the nation's secret police reflected quite a different aspect of the populace's character.

2: Enter Ted Kaczynski

Through Ted Kaczynski's countenance, the media inundated the public with images of the "twisted genius," disheveled and dirty, eyes unfocused, an inaccessible and furious enigma. But it behooves us to contrast that image with another gracing the magazine and book racks — clear-eyed, stolid, spit-and-polish, a presence both comforting and commanding to the citizens. A retired military leader and former head of the Joint Chiefs of Staff, this person is widely admired and thought to be an appropriate alternative to the national political morass.

Whereas the brilliant "misfit" Theodore Kaczynski, if he is the Unabomber, only managed over a period of several years to kill three and injure 23 people, Colin Powell, hardly brilliant but undeniably competent and well-adjusted, oversaw in just a few weeks the deaths and injuries of perhaps several hundred thousand Iraqi soldiers and civilians. And Powell's war — against the technological and social infrastructure of the enemy nation — continues to prove effective, consigning its victims to death by malnutrition and disease.[5] While Kaczynski was reviled in the press and thrown into a cell (and may ultimately be executed by the state), Powell's deadly project is praised as the reasonable actions of enlightened, civilized polity. For his illustrious career in the service of death and destruction, Powell has been rewarded with parades, medals, a handsome pension, book tours and offers to run for public office.

The question "Who is sane? Who is mad?" immediately presents itself to anyone who doesn't take for granted the dystopian nightmares cooked up daily in industrial capitalism's laboratories, think tanks and board rooms. Compared to Bush, Schwartzkopf and Powell, with their arsenal of "dumb" and "smart" bombs, the Unabomber's damage was pitiably small.[6] Compare, as well, the "irrationality" of the lone bomber and the "rationality" of the presumably respected mathematician Claude Shannon, cited in the Unabomber manifesto: "I visualize a time when we will be to robots what dogs are to humans, and I'm rooting for the machines." Such celebrations of humanity's reduction to "servoprotein" and nature to laboratory dross are a familiar enough banality; that this banality reflects the potential extinction of human beings as an integral organism, and the actual, unprecedented physical extirpation of much that is recognizable in the natural world in which humanity evolved, might seem grounds enough to take desperate measures.

But while apt, the "who is sane" idea remains inadequate. Even perceptive technocrats have noticed the radical ambivalence of the Unabomber. Venture capitalist and cyber-maven Esther Dyson commented, for example, that she is "fascinated by the Unabomber ... No. 1, he's a maniac. No. 2, he's asking valid questions. . . ."[7] Indeed, elaborate evidence should be unnecessary to demonstrate that someone who has spent almost two decades sending fastidiously crafted bombs through the mail is one variety of maniac. The text, too, which took the counter-culture concept of "self-publishing" to unprecedented extremes, is a curious admixture of insight, ponderous scholasticism and delusion. Its description of the abundant maladies resulting from humanity's inability to adapt to the modern artificial environment — among them depression, anxiety, suicide, and "pathological, even murderous alienation ... [a] hallmark of our time," Robert Wright observes — brings to mind the Unabomber himself. As Wright comments, "The Unabomber is Exhibit A in his own argument."[8]

There may indeed be a little of the Unabomber in us all, as numerous mass market publications have so cleverly noted. But judging from the pattern of bombings and the text, it's also apparent that the bomber shared not only his understandable luddite frustrations with modern society but that inchoate rage pervasive in today's mass psychology, expressed in every possible response from passive withdrawal to shooting up schoolyards. Despite the fatuous idea voiced in one anarchist flyer lauding the Unabomber, that "it's just a matter of listening to yer own rage," most people understand that such rage frequently turns out to be a large part of the problem.[9]

There are countless men exhibiting a combination of smoldering rage and technical dexterity nowadays; they have generally been more likely to blow up their coworkers with the boss — or their ex-wives. Generally blind to ambivalence and nuance, rage by itself can engender a Unabomber, perhaps, but rarely an authentic revolutionary, who — if I may, at the risk of seeming ridiculous, quote one of my boyhood heroes — is "guided by great feelings of love." Leaving aside his rightful sense of urgency, the Unabomber's terrorist enterprise was less a reasoned response to a world gone mad than simply one more of the myriad dangers we who live in mass society must negotiate daily — hostages not only to the murder, mayhem and dysfunction issuing from the powerful institutions that rule this pathological civilization, but also to the acts of revenge and grievance carried out by its anonymous, disaffected victims.

The Unabomber does, in fact, have his enthusiasts — including a not entirely tongue-in-cheek "fan club" on the West Coast (though in post-modern radicalism, irony and gravity inevitably commingle), Green Anarchists in England (not much irony there), and an anonymous flyer showing a color reproduction of Kaczynski with the cut-out, ransom-letter style legend, "Be like Ted." In Berkeley, California, a punkish anarchist told a *San Francisco Chronicle* writer, "We all think he's pretty great ... I totally know where the guy's coming from. Everybody's just kind of laughing. They're hoping he blows something up in Berkeley so they can see it. I wish they'd start selling T-shirts that said, 'I ♡ the Unabomber,' because that would be kind of funny."[10]

In a *New York Times* interview depicting him as a "prominent anarchist" and "guru of sorts for anti-technology leftists," John Zerzan judged the FC text to be a "pretty thoroughgoing critique." In the flyer cited above, he extols the Unabomber's "profoundly radical vision" of "a return to 'wild nature' via the 'complete and permanent destruction of modern industrial society,'" and in another he praises the Unabomber's "critique, in acts as well as words." "I see in the eyes of Ted Kaczynski a sorrow reflecting what we have lost," Zerzan writes. "But the Megamachine has not eradicated all resistance ... And at the very least we have seen the courage and honor of one who would not buy into this fraudulent society, who fought the Brave New World with pen and sword." But the eyes of another sometimes reveal to us what we are most predisposed to find. Reading Zerzan, one almost forgets how obscure most of the Unabomber's victims were.[11]

True, Zerzan did not wholeheartedly endorse either the method or the manifesto. He argued that more than industrialism would have to be eliminated to achieve freedom, and judged mail bombs "too random," their potential "collateral harm [a military term that came into use during the Persian Gulf War] not justifiable."[12] According to Zerzan, Kaczynski's "betrayal ... at the hands of his brother reminds us that pacifism, in its smug cowardice, is always, at base, the defender of what is." But life is more complex than the pithy utterances on flyers. There is more than one kind of cowardice, just as there is more than one variety of courage and honor. If we can approve of some of the Unabomber's motives without supporting all his means, it seems fair to grant the same consideration to David Kaczynski, who simply acted on the belief that "collateral harm is not justifiable."[13]

David Kaczynski, who likely knows him better than anyone, came to believe that his older brother was the Unabomber (and thus that he himself had, by giving his brother money, unknowingly subsidized some of the bombing campaign). Judging by what the younger Kaczynski had to say, if his brother was responsible, he was motivated by more than high principles and heroism. "The truth from my point of view," David told the *Times,* "is that Ted has been a disturbed person for a long time and he's gotten more disturbed."[14]

Actually, if his brother were responsible for the bombings, the desire to publish his manifesto and to stop killing people could have meant Ted was becoming less and not more disturbed. (Curiously, the plaint in one communiqué against the tedium of making and testing bombs suggests that even criminal intransigence in the name of revolution can become an oppressive routine.)[15] That the Unabomber could examine his own actions and try to articulate a more coherent perspective on modern society's discontents offers some hope that others, seemingly incapable, may also be able to change.

3: Enter the neo-luddites

A form of "Name the Unabomber" inevitably occurred in the media, too. When he was shown the manifesto, Kevin Kelly, executive editor of the fashionable digerati magazine *Wired,* snorted, "If I didn't know better, I'd say he sounds a lot like Kirkpatrick Sale."[16] Sale's book *Rebels Against the Future: The Luddites and Their War on the Industrial Revolution,* and his recent performances smashing computers (an instructive stunt which anarchists have practiced for several years), have earned Sale the media role of an official neo-luddite spokesman, in another serviceable media scenario of "techno-nerds vs. neo-luddites."[17]

For his part, Sale argued in the pages of *The Nation* that the newspapers should agree to the Unabomber's offer to stop killing people and publish the manifesto. Publishing it would likely prevent more deaths, and newspaper editors "needn't worry about the propaganda effect" of the text, he pointed out, "since it is a woodenly written term paper, full of academic jargon and pop psychology, repetitive and ill-argued, that will keep only the most dedicated readers awake beyond its opening paragraphs."

"Which," Sale continued, "is a shame," since the Unabomber's main point, that industrialism has been a "disaster for the human race," is "absolutely crucial." The greatest flaws in the document, Sale averred, were its manipulative idea of political change, its lack of a genuine ecological perspective, and its failure to cite or trace its origins to "the long Luddistic strain in Western thought" or "the great modern critics of technology such as Lewis Mumford, Jacques Ellul," and others.[18]

Sale's exposition on the Unabomber text, while one of the better discussions I saw in the press, is alternately insightful and pedantic, his reading peevish and occasionally inaccurate. His criticism of the text's "appeal to nature [as] entirely utilitarian," and of the Unabomber's "faintest grasp of the principles of ecology," lacks nuance and attention to the text. For example, according to Sale, the Unabomber "gives only a passing glance to the multiple environmental disasters the system is producing for itself and never mentions the likelihood ... that the complex industrial house of cards will not hold." In fact, after writing in paragraph 5 that his text does not go into the question of "environmental degradation or the destruction of wild nature, even though we consider these to be highly important," the Unabomber nevertheless returns to technologically-caused ecological catastrophes several times, and clearly argues the possibility that industrialism may collapse on its own. Sale seems mostly annoyed that the Unabomber doesn't properly acknowledge deep ecology ideas, but, if anything, the Unabomber's implied approval of "the idea that wild nature is more important than human economic welfare" places him close to deep ecology, if only to a misanthropic, catastrophist variety of it.[19]

According to Sale, the text's reference to "anarchist and radical environmental journals" reveals that the Unabomber knows "something about the current [technology] critics," and he adds parenthetically, "If I had to guess which has been most influential on him, I'd say the *Fifth Estate*, a feisty antitechnology paper published out of Detroit for the past thirty years. ..." To describe the Unabomber as somehow both "prescient" and an "incoherent" fanatic of mediocre intellect, and to censure his lack of identification with the "long Luddistic strain" in the Western tradition and his failure to quote from this tradition, and then to name the *Fifth Estate* (which is clearly in this tradition and which quotes extensively from it) as the Unabomber's most probable influence, seems a rather studied, if indirect, potshot. As a long-time FE reader, Sale had to know that neither the Unabomber's language nor his strategy resembled the FE's work, that at best we share with him what Sale shares with him — a sense of urgency about technological catastrophe and a jaundiced view of industrialism's false promises.

Contrary to Sale's volunteer detective work, we found no evidence that the Unabomber was on our subscription list. Nor did anything like the Unabomber text turn up in our files of rejected manuscripts, though if it had, it was too long, too badly written and too confused for us to have accepted it. Sadly, if the Unabomber couldn't expect his text, despite its urgency, to be published in an anarchist antitech journal like the *Fifth Estate*, one can understand his sense of desperation. After all, the issues he raises — the destruction of wild nature, technological domination, genetic manipulation and ecological apocalypse — however confused their elaboration and whatever his shortcomings as a writer, are pressing. And if it takes a madman to tell us in his own mad way that our world is mad, then so be it. Truth be told, industrial capitalism is tattering the complex web of life to the point of global collapse, and legions of functionaries like the last two corporate bureaucrats the unabombs killed are reaping lavish benefits for helping the process along. Unfortunately, apart from pinprick attacks on a few of capital's relatively lower-level minions — switchmen along the tracks to capital's ecospheric Buchenwald, we might say — and random violence against secretaries and others, the Unabomber ended by playing into the hands of the very forces of media and mass culture he opposed.

"To make an impression on society with words is … almost impossible for most individuals and small groups," he writes. "Take us (FC) for example. If we had never done anything violent and had submitted the present writings to a publisher, they probably would not have been accepted. If they had been accepted and published, they probably would not have attracted many readers, because it's more fun to watch the entertainment put out by the media than to read a sober essay. Even if these writings had had many readers, most of these readers would soon have forgotten what they had read as their minds were flooded by the mass of material to which the media expose them. In order to get our message before the public with some chance of making a lasting impression, we've had to kill people."

Not only does this statement sound strikingly like rationalization long after the fact for some wayward grudge killings; by its self-immolating logic, the propaganda of the deed is completely supplanted by the brute fact of the deed itself. According to the argument, only violence would have gotten the text published; without it the text would not have attracted readers. But even if it had found a large audience without the author having to resort to violence, its readers, overwhelmed by the flood of media-generated information, would have forgotten it anyway. Thus, the Unabomber believed, as technology critic Jacques Ellul has put it, "In a battle between propagandas, only propaganda can respond effectively." But it did not occur to him, as it did to Ellul, that "the effects of one's propaganda on the personality are exactly the same as those of enemy propaganda. . . ."[20]

Naively hoping to "make a lasting impression," even to destabilize industrialism, the Unabomber only managed to provide titillation (and further official pretext for harassment and surveillance of activists). His deadly "lasting impression" has faded with yesterday's newspapers, and his bombs — weapons which a century or so ago anarchist revolutionaries praised as "great equalizers" against authority — are now almost imperceptible in a landscape where bombs of every magnitude and variety, in the service of every ideology and grievance, have become ubiquitous.[21] (And bombings, of course, are only one manifestation of an endless array of modern disasters. It no longer matters whether an airplane crashes because of terrorism, corporate cost cutting or the inevitable systems-errors of complex technology. In the mass society we inhabit, the first two causes are categories of the last.)

4. Two, three, many Unabombers?

We may never know if Ted Kaczynski is the Unabomber, but he clearly shares an enduring hatred for technology and love for nature with the author of the text. And though there is little evidence that high tech genocide in Vietnam directly influenced his decision to drop out (as some have suggested), there would only have been honor in his decision if it did.[22] On January 20, 1969 — the day of Richard Nixon's presidential inauguration — he resigned from the University of California-Berkeley math department and, emulating Thoreau, left to live his life deliberately at society's margin.

At the time Kaczynski dropped out of the university, Lewis Mumford was finishing his landmark work, *The Pentagon of Power*, a book that could easily have been titled *Industrial Society and Its Future*. In that great, dark jeremiad, Mumford described two contrasting characterological types in megatechnic society. In one we find a Colin Powell: what Mumford called the "Automated, or Organization Man: he who takes all his orders from the system, and who, as a scientist, engineer, expert, administrator, or, finally, consumer and subject, cannot conceive of any departure from the system, even in the interest of efficiency, still less for the sake of creating a more intelligent, vivid, purposeful, humanly rewarding life."

This automaton — perhaps a timber lobbyist or genetics researcher — this "limited, docile, scientifically conditioned human animal, completely adjusted to a purely technological environment," was nevertheless "not born alone." Rather, this personage has come with "a twin, a dark shadow-self: defiant, not docile: disorderly, not organized or controlled: above all, aggressively destructive, even homicidal, reasserting the dammed-up forces of life in crazy or criminal acts." Though Mumford considered the aim of this "subversive" type to be the destruction of "higher attributes ... whose gifts of love, mutuality, rationality, imagination, and constructive aptitude have enlarged all the possibilities of life," he was not posing an argument for more control, more damming up, more technology, more adjustment and passivity. "It is in the light of [the megamachine's] impending negations and destructions," he emphasized, "that the whole concept of subjugating nature and replacing man's own functions with collectively fabricated, automatically operated, completely depersonalized equivalents must at last be appraised."[23]

Mumford would certainly have been surprised to find the nihilist "shadow twin" carrying out "crazy, criminal acts" in an explicit, calculated war against the automaton "techno-nerds" (as the Unabomber characterized them). It is as if instead of hanging himself, the Savage of Huxley's *Brave New World* had decided to start killing the Alphas and Betas. But the bomber is more a symptom of crisis than any model for response. Indeed, rather than the "glint of hope" Zerzan found in the Unabomber's campaign and manifesto — that, "In distinction to the widespread feeling that everything outside the self is beyond our control, the monopoly of lies has been broken" — the Unabomber's pathetic one-man war both embodied and reinforced the bleak suspicion that the isolated self is all we have, undermining the contrasting sense that people working openly together may succeed in bringing about substantive change. (Oddly, the bombmaker's lonely operations at his work table parallel the solitary hacker in a cubicle, sending a different variety of poisoned gift into the technocratic void — a virus, perhaps, to "promote social stress and instability in the industrial system," as "FC" urged, or simply to engage in some monad's notion of dangerous play.) In the end, the bombings mostly left the "monopoly of lies" intact — a monopoly, in any case, that a small but growing number of people are starting to see through without the help of bombs.

No doubt, given the willingness of well-adjusted, well-rewarded automatons to experiment secretly with nuclear materials on human beings for decades, and their recent success in roughly mapping the human gene code, among other accomplishments (and under the rubric of the highest humanitarian ideals, of course), one is tempted to welcome any response, even, if I may paraphrase my boyhood revolutionary hero, to invite "two, three, many Unabombers." As Mumford might have put it, the Unabomber represents, in however distorted a form, the "dammed-up forces of life." We should not be lulled into forgetting the real terrorist system, with its doomsday apparatus, its investment portfolios in mass extinction. As the anarchist revolutionary Voltairine de Cleyre wrote after a bomb incident in New York's Union Square in 1908, "For truly, Anarchism has nothing in common with violence, and can never come about save through the conquest of men's minds. But when some desperate and life-denied victim of the present system does strike back at it, by violence, it is not our business to heap infamies upon his name, but to explain him as we explain others, whether our enemies or our friends, as the fated fruit of the existing 'order.'"[24]

It could be argued that there are no innocent "bystanders." To one degree or another, the rest of "us" participate in the apparatus, earning our daily bread, our own short-term dividends from apocalypse, as workers, functionaries, secretaries and the like, all dependent on the industrial bribe.[25] But there is no revolutionary short-cut to social transformation, no simple lever to apply the brakes, no fast track to the future. As much as the Unabomber may believe that "active, determined minorities" are the sole makers of history, only majorities can ultimately bring about the social change needed to turn back from extermination. A frightening prospect, surely, given both how "functional" and "dysfunctional" people have been and are becoming in this society, but however different we might wish things to be, a campaign of destabilization to spark industrial collapse (which industrialism seems to be bringing about quite well on its own, thank you very much), will probably only succeed in driving the inmates of industrial society further into the protective embrace of the megatechnic state.

Active, determined minorities and individuals *can* make a difference and have done so, of course. After all, Thoreau was a relative loner and outsider, yet his influence eventually became immense. And to provide only one contemporary example, anyone who reads radical environmental journals, as the Unabomber recommends, can find evidence of active minorities and individuals who are making a large difference. As planetary life conditions inevitably deteriorate further under industrial capitalism, more isolated acts of hope and despair like the Unabomber's are to be expected. Nevertheless, we are not likely to find our way through the examples of either lone assassins or terrorist cells. Rather, we must look to communities of people working both within and against this society to transform it for pathways to a new mode of life. The transformation is in fact already occurring in many seemingly unrelated social movements and cooperative endeavors around the world. Whether they are creating alternative institutions, resisting domination, or defending their neighborhoods, people acting as the subjects of their history participate in a kind of Eternal Return, moving beyond history's limits. Resisting and working together creatively, they fulfill the same necessary role whatever the context or the outcome, recreating and rearticulating not only their faith in the continuity of life *but life's continuity itself.* That is what the luddites did in smashing machines and engaging in other insurgent activities, a far more powerful act both politically and existentially than smashing a computer on stage (however dramatic or worthwhile the gesture), or sending a bomb through the mail (whoever does it).

The Unabomber text is a tormented scream against an empire whose claims to human improvement cannot conceal deepening domination and the ruination of the natural world. While it contains worthwhile insights, its abstract, mechanistic sociologism informs a survivalist, individualistic notion of freedom and a utilitarian outlook that considers any undertaking other than the most meager grubbing of food, clothing and shelter (but also, tellingly, the pursuit of status or revenge) to be an alienated, "surrogate" activity. This Crusoe's text, with its pioneer flavor and autarchic notion of autonomy, does not stray far from the classic bourgeois political economy whence it came. In some sense it is a protest against the idea of *any* society. While it astutely sees through the rationalization and repression of modern civilization's claim to universality, the text's rejection of any human universality is an obscurantist idyll. Correspondingly, it rejects what it calls the "most basic values" of this society as "industrial values." Among the values it rejects — the "official values of our society [because] they are useful to the industrial system," — it names racial and sexual equality, helping the poor, "peace as opposed to war," kindness to animals, and the idea that individuals have obligations to society and society to individuals. In fact, these represent a mix of modern and far more archaic values, some of them the very intuitions we most need in order to resist and overcome the forces of technological domination.[26]

The Unabomber's harsh, if naive, politics of catastrophism fails to recognize that the horrific future he predicts if industrialism doesn't collapse dramatically, rapidly and soon, *is already upon us.* People of the future, he warns, "won't be able to just turn the machines off, because they will be so dependent on them that turning them off would amount to suicide." But people are already dependent; it is precisely this suicide that the Unabomber advocates. As for the potential negative consequences to human beings and even, one must surmise, to ecosystems, he shrugs, "Well, you can't eat your cake and have it too. . . ." And he proposes that revolutionaries do everything possible to bring about this collapse to avoid technology's far more destructive triumph. There is something evocative in this of an International Monetary Fund consultant's recommendation of economic "shock therapy" and starvation of some populations to improve their countries' laggard economies over the long run. It is the logic of someone who, either because they are sitting in an air-conditioned high rise or hiding in a cave, is somehow not connected to life. A situationist once remarked that the bloodiest revolution would be far less painful than any weekend under capitalism, but the social-ecological disaster into which we are presently sliding, whether it be helped along by "determined minorities" or not, may prove far worse than we can imagine.

5. Things fall apart

Toward the end of his life, Mumford confided to Roderick Seidenberg, "I think, in view of all that has happened the last half century, that it is likely the ship will sink." In another letter, to his friend Bruno Levi, he wrote, "I have not the heart to tell [people] ... what I actually think about our human prospects unless something approaching a miracle takes place."[27]

But Mumford still left open the possibility of such a miracle. He believed that if there was to be a successful revolutionary transformation, it would begin at society's margins in "gestures of non-conformity" and withdrawal. He defended "every act of rebellion, every exhibition of group defiance, every assertion of the will-to-live, every display of autonomy and self-direction, at however primitive a level," as attempts to stay the leviathan, prevent a cataclysm that a life worth living might not survive. To Mumford it was the anarchist Thoreau, not Marx, who represented the genuine "arch-enemy" of this complex pentagon of power, for his emphasis on disobedience and a life lived deliberately at the margins of society.[28]

But if Thoreau, writing during a time of this civilization's youthful exuberance, was able to bequeath us some of our wisest and most vivid insights into it, the Unabomber, writing in an era of disillusion, resignation, rage and social decomposition, could only produce a choleric, aridly rationalistic, nihilistic epistle and a scatter of explosions. We need neither condemn nor condone him; his text and his haphazard, deliberate campaign of terror are mostly ominous reflections of how thoroughly we are now pinioned in the gears.

It has not been my intention to reduce to objects of discourse, rather than confronting as subjects, the author of the Unabomber text, or the suspect Theodore Kaczynski, or outsiders known or unknown who might now be expressing our age's deepest truths, or anyone else. That what I know about the Unabomber has come from the media makes this tendency inevitable. In any case, whoever the Unabomber turns out to be, he deserves pardon on the basis of insanity — an insanity that is more collectively ours than his alone. For how can it be that men continue to make their fortunes by unraveling the very foundations of complex life, reducing millions of years of evolution to rubble? Are they not the ambitious, exercising their convenient power, and the arrogant fools with their sharp instruments, as the wise one in this essay's epigraph described them — are they not also the prosecutors and police, the judges and good citizens who may condemn to death the one they take to be this bitter doomsayer, this avenging angel?

And so this is also a plea for Ted Kaczynski, now set to take the rap. It is a plea for the Unabomber, whoever he may be. I do not know what should be done to such people or for them, only that this society, with its faceless machinery of murder, should not be allowed to carry out its sanctimonious determination to take his life as punishment for taking life, while continuing its far more grisly business. Surely this society faces far more imperative matters. If there is poignancy in the Unabomber's final note that his arguments are likely imprecise and even "flatly false," only "a crude approximation of the truth," his ominous and ambiguous significance recommends similar humility on our part. Perhaps we can expect no miracles, only catastrophe after all. But we focus on this small parcel of armageddon at our tragic peril.

The Unabomber phenomenon, a comet briefly throwing its harsh, weird light across deepening shadows, is a sign that neither business-as-usual nor absolute intransigence, neither this society's coherence nor any variety of its incoherence, will have predictable results on a vortex that absorbs and neutralizes every opposition. Yet in his fury, isolation and ultimate failure he also reminds us that it is, paradoxically, only those everyday acts — of mutual aid, trust, empathy, and attentiveness to life through which we nurture what is worthwhile in this society or any other — that hold the transformative energies we need to carry us through this storm.

If things do fall apart, they won't need puny bombs and manifestos. Industrialism cannot continue without smashing on reality's rocks. Ultimately, if we love the living earth, our hope lies beyond even the prospects of our species' survival. Life itself is more intelligent than either the megamachine or its enemies, and will survive and thrive with or without us. Yet when all is said and done, most of us fight for what we cherish of the world we know. Connected to people and place, we have our feet planted in this world, even if our dreams open thresholds to another. Unlike the Unabomber, who argues that the destruction of technology "must be ... the single, overriding goal," we have many complex, interrelated aims that cannot be resolved by this mechanistic, monomaniacal determination alone. We do battle, as the taoist sage recommends, "not ... to destroy what exists but to preserve what is perishing."[29] That will mean carefully backing our way out of the labyrinth we have helped construct, like the hero following his lover's thread to sunlight.

(1996)

Endnotes

1. Quoted in *The Tao of Politics: Lessons of the Masters of Huainan,* translated and edited by Thomas Cleary (Boston and London: Shambhala, 1990), pp. 60-1.
2. Printed in a special section of the September 19, 1995 *Washington Post* under the signature "FC."
3. This essay does not presume that Theodore Kaczynski is the Unabomber. Though it may be a reasonable premise, given what we can know about the case, Kaczynski faces the possibility of being executed if convicted, based on evidence gathered by the FBI — an agency known to be one of the biggest lie machines in memory. He is a fascinating figure, from what we know of him; but given the charges and the possible repercussions, simple decency compels us to let the bombings, the manifesto and society's response speak as much as possible for themselves.
4. "On the Internet, the Unabomber Is a Star," the *New York Times,* April 6, 1996. Most likely Time Warner shared its information with the FBI, using its

site to draw "potential terrorists" and sympathizers into the police "web." The website could have been created in part with that goal in mind.

5. According to United Nations reports, more than a half million children have died in Iraq since the end of the Persian Gulf War as a result of continuing sanctions.

6. In some ways the Unabomber is reminiscent of Norman Mayer, who was killed in December, 1982 by a police SWAT team in Washington, D.C. after occupying the Washington Monument and threatening to blow it up if the nuclear superpowers did not move toward rapid disarmament. Mayer, who protested the deadliest arsenal in history, only threatened property, but he was killed anyway (it turned out he had no bomb). See my essay, written under the pseudonym George Bradford, "Who Is Sane? Who Is Mad? Norman Mayer and the Missile X," in the Winter 1982-83 *Fifth Estate*.

7. The *New York Times Magazine*, July 7, 1996.

8. Robert Wright, "The Evolution of Despair," *Time*, August 28, 1995. Of course, we should not forget that the definition of sanity and insanity is a complex question of power, representation and consent. Modern civilization's medicalization and sordid treatment of psychic difference is one more measure of our alienation. Many expressions of what we now tend to consider madness should have a place, as there seems to be in some cultures, to play a legitimate role in the spectrum of human expression and experience.

9. See John Zerzan, "Whose Unabomber?," from AAA, PO Box 11331, Eugene OR 97440.

10. "Are You the Unabomber? Or You? Or You? Or You?," *San Francisco Chronicle*, July 31, 1995.

11. This flyer is probably also available from AAA, PO Box 11331, Eugene OR 97440. See also "Prominent Anarchist Finds Unsought Ally in Serial Bomber," the *New York Times*, 5/1/96. While no one at the *Fifth Estate* was willing to speak to the media, that doesn't automatically invalidate Zerzan's decision to speak to the *Times* and several radio stations — despite his well-known explicit rejection of all compromise and his notion of "the drastic as the minimum response toward health." (*Future Primitive and Other Essays* [New York and Columbia: Autonomedia/Anarchy, 1994], p. 137) In an open letter distributed to anarchists, he answered those who criticized him for speaking to the press by questioning "deliberate self-marginalization [that tries] to put forth ideas to change an insane world while at the same time disdaining all contact with that world." He adds, "Is it manipulative to want to break out of our tiny ghetto and connect with universally suffering human beings?" (The letter is probably available from the above PO Box.) Actually, in the interview with the *Times*, Zerzan comes off as honest, thoughtful and unpretentious. His reasoning for speaking to the media suggests that however complex and ambiguous the problem of addressing others through mass society's means, the spectacle is never

absolutely hegemonic, and, given how terrible the times are, it might make sense to try. That our situation is dire does not automatically tell us *which* desperate measures might therefore be appropriate. Apparently, even intransigence may sometimes require compromise. The relationship between principles and strategies is not clear cut.

12. Zerzan criticizes the Unabomber text for its excessive emphasis on industrialism; actually, he argues, *agriculture* is a deeper, far more serious impediment to freedom. Will someone now start bombing soybean farmers? No more tofu?

13. According to his interview in the April 26, 1996 *Times*, he tried to communicate with his brother when he began to develop suspicions, but was rebuffed.

14. See the extensive coverage in the May 26, 1996 *Times*.

15. The letter was printed in the *New York Times,* April 26, 1995.

16. See the particularly smug and stupid article by Bob Ickes, "Die, Computer, Die!" in the July 24, 1995 issue of *New York*. For an inane argument between Sale and Kelly, packaged in Kelly's favor, of course, see "Return of the Luddites," in the June 1995 *Wired.*

17. *Rebels Against the Future* (New York: Addison-Wesley Publishing Company, 1995) provides a vivid account of the luddite revolt, and a sloppy, theoretically deficient discussion of the history of technological discourse and the recent emergence of revolt against mass technics.

18. Kirkpatrick Sale, "Unabomber's Secret Treatise: Is There Method In His Madness?" *The Nation*, September 25, 1995.

19. A certain primitivist catastrophism can be found among some deep ecologists, anarchists and others, expressed for example by Christopher Manes' idea, in his *Green Rage: Radical Environmentalism and the Unmaking of Civilization* (Boston: Little, Brown and Company, 1990), that "the time to make the choice between the natural and cultural world has come" (p. 248), whatever that conundrum is supposed to mean. For a discussion and critique of ecological catastrophism, see my "Return of the Son of Deep Ecology," and related essays, in the Spring 1989 *Fifth Estate.*

20. Jacques Ellul, *Propaganda: The Formation of Men's Attitudes* (1962, 1965; New York: Vintage Books, 1973), p. 137.

21. The *New York Times* reports that the country is currently witnessing "a proliferation of a sort of garden variety bomber," leading to arrests of mostly white suburbanites, for example, in Georgia, Arizona and Washington State. Bombings and attempted bombings increased by more than fifty percent in the last five years, and have nearly tripled over the last decade. "The number of criminal explosions and attempts went from 1,103 in 1985 to 3,163 in 1994," according to the article. See "Terrorism Now Going Homespun As Bombings in the U.S. Spread," August 25, 1996.

22. See "The Unabomb Case Is Linked to Antiwar Tumult on U.S. Campuses in 1960s," in the June 1, 1996 *New York Times*.

23. Lewis Mumford, *The Pentagon of Power: The Myth of the Machine Volume II* (New York and London: Harcourt Brace Jovanovich, 1970), pp. 192-3, 284.

24. Quoted in *An American Anarchist: The Life of Voltairine de Cleyre,* by Paul Avrich (Princeton: Princeton University Press, 1978), p. 140.

25. What, indeed, is sanity and what is insanity in this late day? In his post-apocalyptic satire *Galápagos* (1985), Kurt Vonnegut writes of the late twentieth century that "human brains back then had such copious and irresponsible generators of suggestions as to what might be done with life, that they made acting for the benefit of future generations seem one of many arbitrary games which might be played by narrow enthusiasts — like poker or polo or the bond market, or the writing of science-fiction novels.

"More and more people back then ... had found ensuring the survival of the human race a total bore.

"It was a lot more fun, so to speak, to hit and hit a tennis ball."

26. The text's tedious, simplistically psychologistic critique of "leftism" — by which is meant any reform or humanist impulse, or notion of universalism, or altruistic act of solidarity with the suffering or oppression of those other than oneself or one's closest cohort — is an example of the dubious monadic individualism of the Unabomber. Leftism, he warns, with its identification with victims, its "moralistic tone," its willingness to work in the interests of others, and its tendency to oppose violence and competition, is "inconsistent with wild nature," which must therefore be competitive, violent, selfish and without moral significance. Strangely, the terrorist cell "FC" that the text identifies as its authors evokes the worst kind of clandestine, authoritarian, leftist group.

27. Quoted in *Lewis Mumford: A Life,* by Donald Miller (New York: Weidenfeld and Nicolson, 1989), pp. 541, 422.

28. Mumford, *The Pentagon of Power,* pp. 433, 377, 330.

29. *The Tao of Politics,* ibid., p. 50.

V.
THESE ARE NOT
OUR TROOPS

Illustration by Johann Humyn Being

Illustration by Freddie Baer

1492 – 1992: THE FALL
OF THE 500-YEAR REICH

"How can the spirit of the earth like the White man? ... Everywhere the White man has touched it, it is sore." — a woman of the Wintu tribe (California)

Among the many places too numerous to name that have been defiled and destroyed by western civilization, there is a mountain in a place called Arizona, a mountain called *Dzil nchaa si an* (Big Seated Mountain) in the language of the earliest known human inhabitants, Mount Graham on modern maps. This is the abode of the Spirit Dancers (*Ga'an*), who taught the Apaches their sacred songs and dances. It is the highest peak in the Pinaleno Mountains, situated at the meeting place of four biotic zones — the Chihuahuan and Sonoran deserts and the Rocky Mountain and Sierra Madre forests.

Dzil nchaa si an rises out of the desert to more than ten thousand feet and contains a wider range of life zones — from boreal forest to Sonoran desert — than any other mountain in the United States (another modern map name, of the empire laying claim to that region and to a good part of the planet). The mountain is the last remnant of Pleistocene forests in the American southwest, home to many unique and rare species, among them the red squirrel and the northern goshawk. At least eighteen species of plant and animal are entirely unique to the mountain. The Apaches collect healing herbs and waters and practice ceremonies there. It is an entire cosmos — biogeological, spiritual, phenomenological. There is no other place like it anywhere. It could never be replaced or reconstructed.

Now a familiar array of political, scientific and economic powers are colluding to seize and destroy this place. Through lies, corruption and circumvention of even their own laws, these powers have built roads onto the mountain, locked the herb gatherers out, arrested dozens who have tried to stop the destruction, and clearcut some two thousand acres of irreplaceable forest. They are murdering the mountain because it is prime real estate, shredding a complex life web for an abstraction they worship called property. Property is money, and there is money to be made, power to be consolidated, more imperial adventures to commence.

A consortium of capitalist institutions, from the University of Arizona to other U.S. and European academic institutions, and even the Vatican, plans to build an astronomical observatory — a chain of them, in fact. This could be done elsewhere, surely, but that does not matter. They want this land, this forest. Having ruined so much of the planet they stand on, they are uninterested in what little so tenuously remains; they prefer instead to gaze into space, perhaps in search of new territories to exploit, or perhaps to see their sky god, harsh father who sends them ever onward to level everything in their path. Even though some of the universities have dropped out due to expense and public pressure (certainly not because of any change of heart), the University of Arizona, the European institutes and the Vatican persist — with the Vatican assuring all that the mountain is not sacred to the Apaches, or at least that there is *no evidence* to support the Apache claim.

History symbolic

"The more we come to know of history," writes Frederick W. Turner in his *Beyond Geography: The Western Spirit Against the Wilderness* (1980), "the more it reveals itself to be symbolic, as the discrete events, artifacts, and personages tend to lose something of their individualities and become increasingly representative." How appropriate, then, that this cosmological expedition that will kill a mountain is called — not by its opponents but by its authors — the Columbus Project. And that it is all coming to a head during the year of celebrations by western capital of its initiation, what has been aptly called "the 500 year Reich."

All of the original elements are present: the greed for gold and glory, justified by a punitive, shrivelled, otherworldly religion; the maniacal disregard for the profound interrelationships in time and space that make up the myriad mystery we call life; the attitude that land is nothing but dead resources to be mined, poisoned, reduced to waste; the idea that such waste is plenitude and the highest sign of human health and happiness. That is the story of the whole western world, of course — the story of modern capitalism. It is the story of the United States. It is the story of the University of Arizona, of the Vatican, of all the Columbus Projects and Columbus conspiracies, starting with the first.

Indeed, as soon as Columbus arrived on the island shores around these turtle continents, he looked upon their beauty with the same dead eyes the astronomers now cast on the place of the Spirit Dancers. (And all places have had their Spirit Dancers. Capitalism isn't simply an "economic system" — though that is how it names itself. It is a disorder of the Spirit.)

"They traded and gave everything they had, with good will ... and took delight in pleasing us," wrote the Admiral to his sovereigns of the people he had encountered. "They are very gentle and without knowledge of what is evil; nor do they murder or steal ... I believe that in all the world there is no better country. They love their neighbors as themselves, and they have the sweetest talk in the world, and are gentle and always laughing."

The Europeans would quickly demonstrate the differences between good, evil and value. Of the land the Admiral reported that it was "very green and fertile and the air very sweet," bearing "trees ... more beautiful to see than any other thing that has ever been seen." He told the crew to earn the natives' trust, "that something profitable might be had, since it didn't seem the land could be anything but profitable, by its beauty."

Of these people without knowledge of evil Columbus wrote that they were "fit to be ordered about and made to work, to sow and do everything else that may be needed," and he ordered his sailors to kidnap a number of them to carry them back to Europe. Soon followed a series of incursions into what the Europeans suspected might even be the terrestrial paradise itself, the explorers "looting and destroying all they found," as the Admiral's son would write of an expedition onto the island of Guadeloupe, where the Europeans slaughtered humans and animals alike.

Bartolomé de las Casas, one of the authentic voices of conscience during the period, would later write that it was "cruelty never before seen, nor heard, nor read of...." Wrote another Spaniard, Alonso de Zuaso, to a friend in Spain, "If I were to tell you all the damage that has been done, I should never make an end ... Although these islands had been, since God made the earth, prosperous and full of people lacking nothing they needed; yet ... they were laid waste...."

The legacy of progress

That letter was written in 1518. How much damage has been done since that time! True, the native people were not necessarily inclined to be ordered about or to work, and they fought back. But they were pushed back and overwhelmed by more and more waves of invaders. Far from being remarkable, the first Columbus Project was only the first in a long line of outrages. Every single day is the anniversary of some awful calamity.

But capital is commemorating the first encounter both to celebrate and to veil the real meaning of its origins. Those who administer the capitalist power complex understand, if only inchoately, that the conquest of the so-called new world, the enslavement of and genocide against its peoples, the rapid despoliation of its sacred places, and the kidnapping and enslavement of African peoples — the "imported indigens" who would work the land under the lash of the whip — all subsidized the emergence and consolidation of power of the capitalist traders as an international ruling class.

Correspondingly, the conquered villages, peasants and artisans of Europe whose commons were stolen and ransacked by that class would be channeled into the armies of conquest in the expanding empire that now rules, in one form or another, the entire planet. Thus, like many mythologies of origin, the Columbus mystique conceals a crime, an original violence. The Columbus hoopla is becoming a deafening din because of the enormity of the crimes it conceals.

That is why they are celebrating in Seville, and in Barcelona (which Spanish dissidents have renamed Carcelona, containing the Spanish word carcel, meaning jail, and a suggestion of carcinoma, the same word in English and Spanish, meaning cancer). That is why they are celebrating in all the Colombias, Columbias and Columbuses named for the Admiral, and in Washington D.C., on Wall Street, at the presidential palaces of death squad dictatorships, at the University of Arizona and the Vatican. That is why, in a gesture evocative of an absurd scene from some magic-realist novel, a tin-pot strongman has cleared away poor barrios of Santo Domingo to build a preposterously huge lighthouse, far from the sea itself, in honor of the "discoverer" of America.

In just a few centuries of plunder, more damage has been done to the living fabric of the land than in all previous ages combined. That is the legacy of five hundred years of capitalist civilization, of progress. It started with a place mis-named America, a place described by the Admiral as a virgin whose white knight he was fated to be. And its exemplar became, at least until very recently, a powerful cabal called the United States of America. But now there are other rivals; the plague is everywhere. Its progress in methods of ruination has steadily accelerated to a point at which the whole global organism is being unhinged by continued looting and destruction.

Every day is the anniversary of a theft, kidnapping, slaughter, desolation, fraud, immolation, betrayal, abuse. Every day the anniversary of a people's disappearance, the poisoning of a waterway, the razing of a forest, the extinction of a species, the demise of still another subtle facet of being. Every day the anniversary of the origin of a lie and every day the perpetuation of the lie. Every day the extension and acceleration of conquest, the cut-and-run pillage of a refuge, the declarations of war, the stupefaction of the spirit. Every day its business deals, every day its clear-cuts, every day its oil spills, every day its bombing runs, every day its "collateral damage." Today's expedition setting sail toward the mountain where the spirits dance is not remarkable, either, only exemplary and emblematic. The conquerors will dis-cover, strip the mountain, grind its bones to erect their telescopes. They will commence their reconnaissance of the heavens. Even the stars will tremble with dread.

A drop of vengeance

In a powerful essay on the nuclear threat, Alice Walker discusses a very old "curseprayer" collected by Zora Neale Hurston in the 1920s, a violent, potent curse "by a person who would readily, almost happily, commit suicide, if it meant her enemies would also die. Horribly." (See "Only Justice Can Stop A Curse," in *In Search of Our Mothers Gardens* [1983].) Walker wonders if the revenge in that curse, which she surmises must have been uttered first by a conquered woman of color, is now coming to pass in the current, global mass extermination crisis.

Might human extinction be preferable to this civilization's further conquest of the universe? she asks. "If we have any true love for the stars, planets, and the rest of Creation, we must do everything we can to keep white men away from them. They who have appointed themselves our representatives to the rest of the universe. They who have never met any new creature without exploiting, abusing, or destroying it. They who say we poor (white included) and colored and female and elderly blight neighborhoods, while they blight worlds ... Under the white man every star would become a South Africa, every planet a Vietnam."

Walker's essay illuminates that radical despair that induced captives to jump from slave ships into the open sea, slave women to kill their own children to keep them from the master's grasp, Vietnamese peasants to live in tunnels for years under the carpetbombing of U.S. B-52s and to continue fighting against enormous odds. It is the desperation beyond despair that prompted the people of Boipatong, South Africa, to taunt the cops to shoot as they raised their guns against the community, after some forty had already been butchered (and the cops did shoot, killing more). It is the desperation beyond all despair that leads enraged human beings to burn down "their own neighborhoods." It is the poisonous vengeance fermenting just below the surface of capitalism's anniversary celebrations.

A drop of this poison, a drop of this vengeance, then, to steel us, to fortify us. But Walker is not arguing for a suicidal conflagration, concluding instead that the earth is her home and that she intends to protect it. This earth is our home, too, this abused continent, this wounded place of the strait between the lakes. We, too, intend to fight for it. For all the places where the spirits dance, or where they might dance again.

In some of the old native prophecies the coming of the Europeans set in motion the end of one world, one whole cosmos, and the birth of another. This New World Order was not itself everlasting; it was also limited in time and would eventually end. Just as the catastrophe then had its signs and its omens, there are enough signs now that this elaborate, grisly illusion, this 500-year Trail of Tears, is unravelling. Where they have ravaged the land they gaze at the sky. But the sky will not save them.

"I wonder if the ground has anything to say?" declared Young Chief, of the Cayuses, at the signing of a treaty that would confine his people to a reservation. But he knew what the ground was saying, that they "should take good care of the ground and do each other no harm." (Cited in *Touch the Earth: A Self-Portrait of Indian Existence,* compiled by T.C. McLuhan [1971]) Listen now what the land is telling us — all of us, the remnants and orphans of pillaged and scattered tribes. It is telling us that the time has come, that the empire's days are running out, that it is time to begin a dance, a variegated, brilliant Ghost Dance for the end of the millennium, that will bring together all the broken villages, the runaway slaves, the rebels who have regained their humanity by deserting the machine, all those who are seeing the signs and beginning to understand that it was always a lie, and that one way or another it will come to its end.

The forest beckoning

A multicultural Ghost Dance, then. We are all in need of it. Shango and the Delaware prophet and Lao-tse. Shaman dreamers and the general strike. Mad love and the beach beneath the pavement. The forest beckoning. "A lawless people, but ... on good terms with the Great Spirit," as Tatanga Mani (Talking Buffalo) of the Stoney tribe described his people in the last century. Hearing what the ground has to say. Hearing the heart. According to the Lakota philosopher Luther Standing Bear, the roots of the tree of our lives had to grasp rock and soil, the formative processes of this continent, before we newcomers could ever understand it — or ourselves. And with the passing of time, some have come to a loyalty to the land. Now, out of necessity, because we are squeezed against the edge of a precipice — or perhaps because it was already long ago understood and dreamed — we are beginning to understand. We are beginning to listen to the land, to let it speak through us. It's an appropriate time to put an end to the geographical, now astronomical mystique, the empire fever, the mechanical somnambulance, and to pay attention to the spirit dancers. The spirit dancers at *Dzil nchaa si an*, where the conspirators must be stopped; but also the spirits at Big Mountain, at Sand Creek, at Pine Ridge, at James Bay and Wao Kele O Puna and Sarawak, and the Loire, the Amazon, everywhere the spirits might rise and dance. Even here, in this neighborhood, by the Strait, they are struggling to open their battered wings, and we with them.

Let the curse-prayer fall on the conquerors, on the University of Arizona and the Vatican, on the Columbus Project, on the whole imperial procession. Their half-millennium is over. The rest is ours!

(September-October 1992)

LOOKING BACK ON THE VIETNAM WAR

Introduction: 20 years after the war

When this essay first appeared in the *Fifth Estate* in the spring of 1985 ten years after the war, the American invasion of Vietnam already seemed to be receding into ancient history. Central America was at that time being battered by the latest incarnation of "the best and the brightest," and it was being done more conveniently with money and proxies, rather than with "American boys," who tend to get themselves unceremoniously killed while smashing up other people's neighborhoods. A few hundred thousand deaths and mutilations later, we still await the tearful retrospectives with their admixture of regret and denial.

American society was left little wiser by its experience in southeast Asia; the United States has a handful of interventions and wars under its belt since 1975, and even some failures to intervene where it might, as in Bosnia, have prevented a massacre. (Yes, I know, on some other planet with an entirely different history. The Vietnam War taught my generation that any empire intervening anywhere was bound to be disastrous. Yet who can deny that the issues have become more clouded and not less so? Even marxist pundit Alexander Cockburn admitted in a Detroit speech in the fall of 1994 that he had mixed feelings about the U.S. invasion of Haiti. That Haiti and the former Yugoslavia further fragmented what remained of the left reflects shifting ground and the collapse of old categories.)

Ten years later, the essay seems completely contemporary. Reality continues to be manufactured, perhaps more efficiently than ever, by the ideology industry. Real Vietnamese remain largely invisible to Americans. The war criminals continue to expire peacefully in their beds (Nixon), pontificate in televised policy debates (Kissinger), and cash in on their memoirs (McNamara). The "Vietnam syndrome," declared defunct by a triumphant George Bush after his "turkey shoot" in the Persian Gulf, guarantees continued slaughter so long as it is not too costly to North Americans. The thoroughly nazified society, complacent amid its bloodbaths, as described by Noam Chomsky in essays on the war in the mid–1960s, remains intact.

The differences are also worth noting. The response to the war twenty years later, if a *Time* retrospective is any indication, had a more muted, almost postmodern uncertainty to it. The editors assure the reader psalmodically that "Vietnam may be the war that passeth all understanding," and one *Time* essayist, declaring all conflicts unique, concludes that the war offers no lessons, "no guide to the future."

Essentially a new spin on an old canard, this uncritical line recycles the persistent myth, common both inside and outside the antiwar movement of the day, that the war was a terrible mistake, a tragedy. Certainly the war was a tragedy of unforeseen consequences; U.S. objectives were murky even to the generals. But this now dominant interpretation serves in its vagueness to dissipate responsibility and the possibility of a coherent historical critique. McNamara's argument that the war did not originate in evil intentions, but in a failure "of judgment and capability," is only the latest reiteration of the official story. It conceals the fact that the U.S. *created* a war where one had just been concluded, and concocted a regime out of a quisling apparatus, property of the Japanese and then the French, that had justly collapsed. The "Murder, Inc." the CIA and Pentagon ran in that unhappy region for more than two decades was, in reality, only one arm of a vast operation constructed to overthrow and reconstitute states and decimate human beings at will all over the globe, not only in Indochina but in Iran, Guatemala, Indonesia, the Dominican Republic, and Chile, to name some of the more infamous examples.

Thus Chomsky's argument — that the Vietnam War was not an unambiguous defeat for American imperialism — is compelling. As he has argued in a number of places, central U.S. aims and a partial victory were achieved. Incapable of defeating the Vietnamese on the battlefield, the U.S. could at least destroy the society enough to impoverish horribly and make a bitter example of it. This "demonstration effect" sent a grim message to other nationalist rebels attempting to stray from the neocolonial orbit, a strategy used effectively in the 1980s to discipline Central America and beat Nicaragua into submission.

In fact, the *Time* twenty-year retrospective affirmed Chomsky's analysis in one significant way. Following a typical televisionesque reduction of history covering the last ten days of the war (next time the last ten *minutes* will be the theme), comes an article, "Vietnam: Back in Business," attesting to the new climate in which former enemies can work together to plunder the country. Now that the Saigon landlords and military mandarins have been swept away, not into the dustbin of history, mind you, but to comfortable neighborhoods in San Diego and Virginia Beach, Vietnamese commissars will deliver up resources and cheap labor to international corporate capital, sometimes to the very same exploiters they spent thirty years fighting. It should be no surprise that Vietnamese army veterans are beginning to ask what exactly it was they fought for.

Understandable doubts among the Vietnamese in no way excuse the continuing arrogance of Americans. Novelist Tobias Wolff, for example, who has written admirably about his experiences in Vietnam (see his memoir, *In Pharaoh's Army,* for example), repeats the myth — obviously true in some individual cases but a mystification generally — that the U.S. soldiers went there "to be of help." Noting in his *Time* essay the harshness of the victors, who impelled some 800,000 people to flee the country, Wolff doesn't bother to consider that the horrific war waged by the Americans and the ruinous conditions left in their wake might explain, at least in part, the vengeful nature of the new regime.

Wolff illustrates the deep gulf dividing Americans on Vietnam by describing a discussion group of vets, former antiwar activists and other Vietnam generation men which eventually disbanded because of an inability to find common ground. I, too, was keenly reminded of how deep the divisions are, upon reading, "Only the most self-satisfied ideologues on either side of the problem could avoid questioning their own motives" for fighting the war or resisting it. Those who protested, he explains, might reasonably worry that, "however unintentionally ... [they] were encouraging a hard, often murderous enemy who was doing his best to kill boys you'd grown up with."

Perhaps Wolff doesn't realize his attempted middle ground is itself an ideologue's argument. He doesn't seem to appreciate the impact our witness of the war had on many young people here — the images of torture and massive bombing raids, of a mother holding her burned infant and a swaggering soldier setting aflame the thatched roof of her household with his cigarette lighter.

What *were* those American boys I'd grown up with doing there, after all, collaborating with the death machine? I knew they were in most cases victims themselves — of propaganda, of poverty, of the draft. In fact, I actively participated in campaigns to support the Vietnam Veterans Against the War and to defend GI rights and resisters in the military, sending antiwar information to soldiers and sailors, including to my own brother. That didn't stop me from desiring the defeat of U.S. forces as fervently as I would have worked for a German defeat had I been an anti-nazi German during the Second World War.

I don't consider such a comparison at all exaggerated. Both conflicts have stark, parallel examples of conscience and cowardice, of unspeakable brutality, both personal and bloodthirsty on the one hand, and remote and numbly bureaucratic on the other. At the first antiwar teach-in I attended in the fall of 1966, I saw M.S. Arnoni, the editor of a left liberal magazine, *The Minority Of One*, make the nazi analogy in a powerful gesture. A Polish Jew who had survived the death camps, Arnoni delivered his speech wearing a striped concentration camp smock. "I have donned this uniform," he began, "to remind you and myself of an era that is not over, of human suffering that continues, of gas used in Auschwitz and in the villages of Vietnam, of consciences that still stop at the national boundary, of Lidice and Cam Ne."

The Vietnam War was possibly as much a watershed and formative event in my life as it was for those Americans who fought there. (Forgive me if I cannot bring myself to write, "who *served* there.") I can trace much of my response to the impression Arnoni's speech made on me. Despite *Time* magazine's uncertainty, Vietnam provided the same stark lesson Arnoni derived from his camp experience in his decision never to become an oppressor. "I have no preference for an oppressor who is American or any other nationality," he declared. "I do not prefer him over the Nazi oppressor."

American aggression in Vietnam was "as reprehensible as … the Nazi crimes," he continued, and he called on Americans to engage in massive resistance, and especially on American youth — soldiers and civilians — "to join the resistance of those who only yesterday were their prospective victims." Arnoni was encouraging the boys I'd grown up with to turn the guns around, and young people in general to "go to Vietnam and volunteer their services to help ameliorate the suffering inflicted by their fellow countrymen on the Vietnamese."

It became my intention to find a way to Vietnam to fight against the U.S. forces. At fourteen, I might have been fighting already had I been Vietnamese. I later realized that it wasn't a realistic plan, but I did what I could to stop the war, and not always as consistently as I later thought I should have. I don't know if Arnoni kept his promise; I don't know what happened to him after he folded the magazine and emigrated to Israel in late 1968. But I took his lesson seriously, not to be an oppressor or to tolerate oppressors.

Enough people came to this conclusion in that period for there to be widespread, organized resistance during the late 1970s and 1980s to the U.S.-administered holocaust throughout Central America. True, the resistance wasn't enough to halt the war machine there or in Iraq, but it at least obstructed the murderers in their work and preserved fragile memory in the face of official lies.

That was what the essay below was about: remembering what is in the interest of the empire to suppress. The country as a whole continues to sleepwalk through one imperial fiasco to the next, smashing people and places at every turn. But some people are capable of hearing what the essay tries to say: that conscience, even if reduced to a single voice, to a "minority of one," perhaps, can at least bear witness to lies and speak the truth. As Frances Fitzgerald observed a decade after the war, "The past is not just a matter for historians. It is what we are."

And so, who are we going to be? Those who follow orders, and those who give them, have decided who *they* are. McNamara decided. When the war failed to go according to plan, he jumped ship to a comfortable position at the head of the World Bank. (And if and when the real toll is added up, it may turn out that he caused as much mayhem and destruction managing the daily affairs of that institution as when he and his cohorts were in the daily business of mechanized genocide.)

McNamara's memoirs reminded me of another protagonist in the war, an obscure hero of my youth whose image on a poster remained taped to my wall for a number of years. Nguyen Van Troi won't have the opportunity of writing his memoirs; the young Vietnamese worker was executed by firing squad on October 15, 1964 for attempting to assassinate U.S. Secretary of Defense McNamara. Of course, if he had succeeded, another Secretary, and another would have followed, just as others would have replaced Eichman had partisans managed to assassinate the nazi technocrat. That is not the point, but rather, who and what we remember, and who and what we are and are going to be.

Thus, in the spirit of "giving aid and comfort" to the enemies of all imperial states, I dedicate this essay to the memory of a defiant young patriot who refused a blindfold at the execution post so he could look one last time on his "beloved land," who risked his life "to be of help," who was a naive nationalist, surely, perhaps a poet, and who did not live to look back with regrets, contrived or otherwise, on "an era that is not over." I dedicate it to the idealists and against the conspirators and functionaries of genocide, to conscience and against collaboration, to memory and against forgetting. For history isn't just a matter for the rationalizations of mass murderers, history is what we are and must be. It is our history, too. We are Nguyen Van Troi.

— June 1995

Looking Back on the Vietnam War: History & Forgetting

"Without the exposure of these Vietnam policies as criminal, there is every likelihood of their repetition in subsequent conflicts." — Richard Falk, speaking at the Congressional Conference on War and National Responsibility, convened in Washington, D.C. in early 1970

"Historical memory was never the forte of Americans in Vietnam." — *Frances Fitzgerald,* Fire in the Lake, *1972*

I. An Orwellian war

"When I use a word,' Humpty Dumpty said in a rather scornful tone, 'it means just what I choose it to mean, neither more nor less.'

'The question is,' said Alice, 'whether you can make words mean so many different things.'

'The question is,' said Humpty Dumpty, 'who is to be master, that's all.'"

— Alice in Wonderland

It is Spring, and as in the song, the graveyards are in flower. Old wars are being commemorated, new wars coordinated. In Germany, the American president makes his pilgrimage to lay a wreathe at the nazi military cemetery at Bitburg, while in Central America (and elsewhere), stormtroopers in his pay add still more atrocities to a seemingly never-ending list.

Spring, 1985: ten years after the fall of Saigon to the Vietnamese. The media barrage has been deafening — a retrospective which, like the warmaking itself, mostly ignores the realities of Vietnam. Self-absorbed, solipsistic, blind to the world, America is reassessing its experience in Vietnam.

One could only anticipate this anniversary with dread, not so much because America still does not understand Vietnam or the role it played there; after all, America has never come to terms with its history on this continent stolen from its original inhabitants. The dread comes deepest from what is concretely being manufactured out of the anniversary. That defeat of imperial power is now being employed to mobilize for new imperial adventures, for a new wave of war and destruction. The lessons are being turned on their heads so that the bloody crusade may continue.

So, the war remains what it always was: an Orwellian charade. Now, as then, reality is being manufactured by an apparatus in the service of unbridled power. The victims are dressed in the clothing of the perpetrators; the murderers, free and unrepentant, live well, comfortably writing their memoirs and explicating the war which they managed for so many years. Now more sure of themselves that history has receded and the blood stains have faded, they speak more loudly, in self-righteous tones, claiming that their carnage was just, that it didn't go far enough, claiming that the aftermath of the war vindicates them.

There was no Nuremburg trial after the U.S. defeat in Indochina; no court ever punished the administrators of the American war — Nixon, Kissinger, Johnson, McNamara, Rusk, and the rest — for their crimes. They either died peacefully in their beds or went on to more lucrative jobs in the same line of work. Now they extol their "noble cause" and hint of treachery and betrayal. Now they say they could have, indeed should have, won. Perhaps they didn't unleash enough bombs, declare enough "free fire zones," defoliate enough lands. Perhaps not enough people were rounded up into concentration camps, their thatch villages burned and bulldozed. Perhaps not enough were incinerated by napalm and phosphorous (mobile Dachau's), not enough machine-gunned and bulldozed into open ditches, not enough of their defeated converted into prostitutes, lackeys, mercenaries. If America had spent more money, sent more troops, embraced a more ferocious national spirit, and ignored its own wounds, if it had been ready to risk everything in a deadly gamble to destroy all of Asia "in order to save it," then perhaps America could have "won" its war. A few million more would have been sacrificed. And countless more did die in the aftermath: see how evil, how savage they are, America says through its propagandists; after our bloodbath ended, they undertook their own. Surely, ours was inadequate — we could have pacified more, neutralized more, killed more. We learned our lesson, say the loudspeakers: next time we must not lack the will to kill them all. And the blueprints are out on the tables.

America has not yet confronted its role in Vietnam. It has licked its wounds, engaged in recriminations without taking either its own history or the Indochinese people into account. They were simply "natives," a hostile landscape before which the American crusaders fought their war against the Wilderness. This war has gone on since the origins of America, and so it has never envisioned that enigmatic "other" on any terms but those of its own distorted projections.

One veteran officer, William Broyles, Jr., in *The Atlantic Monthly*, writes, "For us the war never really ended, not for the men who fought it, not for America." A symposium in *Harper's* magazine makes one of its central inquiries, "Vietnam stands for America's loss of innocence. How have Americans endured this loss?" *Newsweek* asks, "What did Vietnam do to us?" before asking, "What did America's involvement in the war do to Vietnam?" And a wounded vet tells a *New York Times Magazine* writer that "whatever happened to us there is inexplicable, but what it did for us as men is worth the price."

It is partly my purpose to assess the "price" of the war but not so much to the American soldiers, who were both victims and perpetrators, but to the real victims and heroes of that war — the Indochinese people who resisted American aggression. But to do so, it is imperative to demolish the Big Lie which begins from the lie of American "innocence" and proceeds to such dishonest formulations as "America's involvement in" a war which was America's creation. The truth is harder to face for America, but it is there. "Just about every Vietnam vet hated the Vietnamese," one told Joseph Lelyveld of the *New York Times Magazine*. And a young U.S. embassy officer in Saigon, during the war, exploded at Frances Fitzgerald, "Don't you realize that everything the Americans do in Vietnam is founded on hatred of the Vietnamese?"

The suffering of the American soldiers should not and cannot be ignored. They, too, were victims, pawns of the policy-makers who blithely sent them to their brutalization and death while themselves living comfortably in suburban luxury, spending their time analyzing "body counts" and writing policy statements. But decency requires that a sense of proportion to the suffering be maintained. The soldiers were an occupation army engaged in a vicious war against a whole population. The enemy was, quite simply, the Vietnamese people, indeed, it was the land itself, a "godforsaken mudhole," as I heard many people, both for and against the war, describe it. So what did it mean to burn villages, run down peasants in tanks and trucks, shoot anything that moved?

2. A shooting gallery

The U.S. war against Vietnam was no loss of innocence, no aberration, any more than the massacre at My Lai was exceptional. My Lai will be remembered as the subhamlet in the Quang Ngai province in which a company from the 11th Brigade of the Americal Division murdered 347 old men, women, children and infants, then systematically burned the homes and huts. This happened in early 1968, but was covered up until late 1969. As the My Lai events were the logical outcome (and in fact only the most notorious of such massacres) of U.S. policy, the war itself was the inevitable outcome of America's history. Could this outcome have been anything but a series of brutal pogroms such as My Lai?

Even the official Pentagon report revealed that My Lai was not extraordinary. In his study of the continuity of massacre and conquest in American history, *Facing West: The Metaphysics of Indian-Hating and Empire-Building*, Richard Drinnon writes, "On the very same day of the butchery there, another company from the same task force entered the sister subhamlet My Khe 4 with one of its machine-gunners 'firing his weapon from the hip, cowboy-movie style.' In this 'other massacre,' members of this separate company piled up a body count of perhaps a hundred peasants — My Khe was smaller than My Lai — 'just flattened that village' by dynamite and fire, and then threw a few handfuls of straw on the corpses. The next morning this company moved on down the Batangan peninsula by the South China Sea, burning every hamlet they came to, killing water buffalo, pigs, chickens, and ducks, and destroying crops. As one of the My Khe veterans said later, 'what we were doing was being done all over.' Said another: 'We were out there having a good time. It was sort of like being in a shooting gallery.'" None of this came out until writer Seymour Hersch obtained the forty or so volumes of the Pentagon report and summarized them in *Cover-Up* (1972), the source of Drinnon's quotations. No one was tried for murder at My Khe.

Yet even these massacres do not convey the reality of the war. In war crimes hearings held by anti-war Congressmen in Washington, D.C. in 1970, journalist Jonathan Schell testified that in 1967 he had spent a month in that same province of Quang Ngai, surveying the damage of the war from the air and on the ground. "When I first looked down from the plane over Quang Ngai province," he reported, "I saw that the land below me had been completely devastated ... What I discovered was that by the end of 1967, the destruction of society in Quang Ngai province was not something we were in danger of doing; it was a process we had almost completed. About 70 percent of the villages in the province had been destroyed."

Schell decided to see an operation from its beginning to end in a forward air control plane. The operation was near Chu Lai, and was one of thirty or so such operations proceeding against the Viet Cong at the time. The area he studied had a population of about 17,000, and had not yet been destroyed. Flying for two weeks with the forward air control planes, he saw the daily bombing of villages and their burning by U.S. ground troops.

He had been told by the psychological warfare office that villages were never bombed unless already given warnings. Checking at the base at Chu Lai after the operation, he asked for a full catalogue of warning leaflets. "I hardly needed to do this," he said, "because I had seen the people running from their burning homes, and I had seen no leaflets dropped prior to the bombings. Indeed, five or six leaflets had been dropped, and not one of them had been a warning." They were simply anti-Viet Cong tracts. When he asked if civilians had been evacuated, he learned that "initially the colonel in charge of the operation had given an order that no refugees, as they call them, would be taken out of the area. Late in the operation that decision was reversed, and 100 of the 17,000 were taken out. But even those 100 were taken out after most of the area had been destroyed. In other words, an area inhabited by 17,000 people was about 70 percent destroyed with no warning to the residents ... and with only 100 people evacuated from the area."

In the same hearings, international law specialist Richard Falk discussed the My Lai massacre, observing that "long before these disclosures there was abundant evidence that the United States was committing war crimes in Vietnam on a widespread and continuing basis." But far more serious than these atrocities alone, he added, was "the official reliance by the United States Government on a set of battlefield policies that openly deny the significance of any distinction between civilians and combatants, between military and nonmilitary targets. The most spectacular of these practices are the B-52 pattern raids against undefended villages and populated areas, 'free-fire zones,' 'harassment and interdiction fire,' 'Operation Phoenix,' 'search and destroy' missions, massive crop destruction and defoliation, and forcible transfer of the civilian population in Vietnam from one place to another against their will ... In fact, the wrongdoers at My Lai, whether or not they were carrying out specific command decisions, were indeed fulfilling the basic and persistent United States war policies in South Vietnam."

American policy was one of wanton, utter annihilation of the defiant land it faced. As U.S. Secretary of the Navy (later an arms control negotiator for Reagan) Paul Nitze said in 1965, "Where neither United States nor [South] Vietnamese forces can maintain continuous occupancy, it is necessary to destroy those facilities." And, surveying the destruction of Ben Tre during the Tet Offensive in 1968, an army officer told an AP reporter, "We had to destroy it to save it."

3. Indian fighters

Such a statement reflects what salvation has always meant for these grim crusaders: a desolation. William Appleman Williams has written that for U.S. policymakers, "America was the locomotive puffing away to pull the rest of the world into civilization. Truman talked about the hordes of Asians — the wilderness — threatening to overwhelm civilization ... Those images and metaphors ... tell us most of what we need to know about why we went to kill people in Vietnam. We were transforming the Wilderness in order to save the City on a Hill."

"I felt superior there," said Lieutenant William Calley. "I thought, I'm the big American from across the sea. I'll sock it to these people here ... We weren't in My Lai to kill human beings, really. We were there to kill ideology that is carried by — I don't know. Pawns. Blobs. Pieces of flesh, and I wasn't in My Lai to destroy intelligent men. I was there to destroy an intangible idea." Drinnon quotes another My Lai veteran who "equated 'wiping the whole place out' with what he called 'the Indian idea ... the only good gook is a dead gook.' The Indian idea was in the air in Vietnam."

This was only the latest unfolding in that westward movement, the empire's relentless drive to destroy and subdue wilderness, the "savages" who inhabited it, and all of nature. The situation was essentially the same when the U.S. began to intervene in Vietnam as it was for Frederick Jackson Turner in 1893 when he wrote his famous declaration that the dominant fact in American life had been expansion of its frontier. Though expansion had reached the Pacific coast, the rising imperial star of the U.S. indicated clearly to him that the movement would continue. This national mystique of Manifest Destiny had plunged the Anglo-Americans into wars in Mexico, Central America and the Caribbean, the Philippines, and beyond.

In the mid-nineteenth century, William Gilpin had written of the American destiny "to subdue the continent — to rush over this vast field to the Pacific Ocean ... to stir up the sleep of a hundred centuries — to teach old nations a new civilization — to confirm the destiny of the human race ... to cause a stagnant people to be reborn — to perfect science ... to shed a new and resplendent glory upon mankind. . . ." This "perfected science" was the locomotive of modernity crystallized in the American empire and its dream of conquest. The destruction of Vietnamese society by the bureaucrats and the Calleys was only the most modern incarnation of that "glory." By the time these conquerors and Indian fighters reached Indochina the frontier had become Kennedy's "New Frontier," his "relentless struggle in every corner of the globe." As Drinnon writes, the troops were now being sent "into action against disorder on a frontier that had become planetary."

In 1966, General Maxwell Taylor, leaving the ambassadorship in Saigon, revealed how deeply imbedded was the "Indian idea," describing the "pacification" program: "We have always been able to move in the areas where the security was good enough. But I have often said, it is very hard to plant the corn outside the stockade when the Indians are around. We have to get the Indians farther away in many of the provinces to make good progress."

Fitzgerald comments that "American officers liked to call the area outside GVN [Government of Vietnam] control 'Indian country.' It was a joke, of course, no more than a figure of speech, but it put the Vietnam War into a definite historical and mythological perspective: the Americans were once again embarked upon a heroic and (for themselves) almost painless conquest of an inferior race. To the American settlers the defeat of the Indians had seemed not just a nationalist victory, but an achievement made in the name of humanity — the triumph of light over darkness, of good over evil, and of civilization over brutish nature. Quite unconsciously, the American officers and officials used a similar language to describe their war against the National Liberation Front (NLF). According to the official rhetoric, the Viet Cong did not live in places, they 'infested areas'; to 'clean them out' the American forces went on 'sweep and clear' operations or moved all the villagers into refugee camps in order to 'sanitize the area.'"

The Vietnamese, whether they were the enemy or the vassals of the U.S., were considered stupid savages, "Orientals," in General William Westmoreland's words, who placed a lower value on life than westerners. The NLF were nothing but "termites" in the General's eyes, who showed his humanitarian concern for the country by advising, "We have to get the right balance of termite killers to get rid of the termites without wrecking the house." And an adviser in Pleiku told the head of the International Voluntary Service that the Montagnards (tribal highlanders) "have to realize that they are expendable," adding that the "Montagnard problem" could be solved "like we solved the Indian problem."

"Is it an exaggeration to suggest," wrote Noam Chomsky in 1970, "that our history of extermination and racism is reaching its climax in Vietnam today? It is not a question that Americans can easily put aside." Indeed, this is Drinnon's theme: since there was no end to this frontier being vanquished by the Empire, "Winning the West amounted to no less than winning the world. It could be finally and decisively 'won' only by rationalizing (Americanizing, westernizing, modernizing) the world, and that meant conquering the land beyond, banishing mystery, and negating or extirpating other peoples, so the whole would be subject to the regimented reason of one settlement culture with its professedly self-evident middle-class values."

But the "stagnant peoples" had their own vision of destiny. A veteran told the *Times*' Lelyveld, "I don't think the people wanted to be saved. . . ." When the conquerors saw the people wouldn't, and couldn't, be "saved," they set out, within the terms of their mad equation, to destroy them, using all the perfected science at their disposal to accomplish the destruction.

4. The "Lunarization Program"

The monstrous absurdity of pioneer arrogance saw its culmination in a war Vice-President Hubert Humphrey dubbed "America's finest hour." The entire might of the technological megamachine was pitted against a small, poor, archaic peasant region. The proportions — in comparative wealth, in technology, in firepower — were obscene. At any given time, the difference in firepower ranged anywhere from 50 to 1, to 500 to 1. The war represented "the triumph of the principles and values of the industrial bureaucracy," a "General Motors of Death," as Gordon Livingston, a regimental surgeon who served there, put it later. At the 1970 Congressional war crimes hearings, he testified, "The magnitude of the effort, the paperwork, and the middle-management attitude of many of the participants, as well as the predilection for charts and statistics — including that most dehumanizing and absurd figure of all, the body count — all these represent the triumph of technocracy over reason."

This technobureaucratic campaign against Vietnam flowed from the same hatred and poverty of spirit that fueled the wars against the indigenous peoples of this continent. It was a deep-seated hatred, founded upon guilt and a sense of separation, so it had to be manifested in a war against the earth itself. But this time, all the demonic instruments of technology were available to the crusade.

The aerial bombardment was unrivaled in the history of warfare. Already, by 1969, South Vietnam, North Vietnam and Laos were the three most heavily bombed countries in history. "The unparalleled, lavish use of firepower," a U.S. military analyst wrote laconically, "is an outstanding characteristic of U.S. military tactics in the Vietnam war."

"Translated into human terms," commented Gabriel Kolko, "the United States has made South Vietnam a sea of fire as a matter of policy, turning an entire nation into a target." "On some days in 1969," reported ecologist John Lewallen in his book *Ecology of Devastation* (1971), "eight hundred sorties were flown [in northern Laos], dropping napalm, phosphorous, and antipersonnel bombs. One old man described the effects: 'First the houses and fruit trees were burned, then the fields and the hillside and even the stream was on fire.'" Bombing became so intense by that year that at times it went on for twenty-four hours a day, and farming, if it could be done at all, could only take place at night.

The use of herbicides was equally devastating. "To a counterinsurgent," wrote Lewallen, "plants are the allies of the insurgent." E. W. Pfeiffer, a zoologist sent to Indochina by the American Association for the Advancement of Science to study ecological consequences of the war, compared the U.S. policy of bombing, defoliation, and mass plowing with giant bulldozers with the extermination of the buffalo herds in the American west. "This modern program," he reported in 1971, "has as destructive an influence on the social fabric of Indochinese life as did the ecocide (destruction of ecology) of the American West upon the American Indian."

NLF sources reported that some 300,000 people were poisoned each year between 1966 and 1969 by exposure to Agent Orange, Agent White, and other chemicals. An epidemic of birth defects was already occurring at that time. Over five million acres had been sprayed with some seventeen million gallons of herbicides, and an area the size of Massachusetts cleared by defoliants. The very soil of Indochina was being destroyed by bombing and defoliation, increasing salinization, flooding, erosion and drought.

Vietnam, once a major exporter of rice, now had to import it from the U.S. due to crop destruction and the disruption of agriculture. Huge tracts of mangrove, evergreen rain forest, and fruit trees were wiped out, leading to the breakdown of associated ecosystems, especially in the Mekong Delta. By December 1970, at least 35 percent of South Vietnam's fourteen million acres of dense forests had been sprayed.

A "food denial" program was also implemented by the Americans to starve the insurgents into submission. This meant massive spraying of croplands and destruction of food stores. Of course, the insurgents, being more mobile, were able to evade some of the circumstances brought about by defoliation, but the villagers left behind starved. Many animal species, particularly birds and aquatic food chains, were destroyed by the chemical warfare.

The hatred for the land and the people knew no limits. A joke circulating at the time was that a proper "final solution" to the "Vietnamese problem" would be to pave the country and make it a parking lot, a joke that was repeated by then California governor Ronald Reagan. Such was the attitude of these American missionaries of a "new civilization." But to the Vietnamese, who blended their Buddhism with strong animist and nature-worship beliefs along with ancestor worship, the land itself was sacred, a constant which centered their universe.

The purpose of American "pacification" of this wilderness was to pave the spiritual and political soil of village identity to make it accessible to American tanks. To "dry up the sea" in which the rebels swam, they had to remove the people from the land itself, forcibly relocating entire villages to so-called "strategic hamlets" (concentration camps), and to the desperation of the cities, turning their ancestral lands into "free-fire zones" where anything that moved was a target. As a result of this campaign and NLF resistance to it, by 1970 a third of the people of South Vietnam had become refugees. In the first six months of that year, another half a million refugees were "generated" by forced removal and wanton destruction. Even this figure is too conservative, since many refugees were never accounted for by official U.S./South Vietnamese government head counts. "The large majority of the refugees, as every objective account agrees, were seeking to escape the free-fire zones and the rain of fire the Americans were showering on them," Kolko reported. "You have to be able to separate the sheep from the goats," said one Pentagon-sponsored analyst. "The way to do it is harsh. You would have to put all military-age males in the army or in a camp as you pacify the country. Anyone not in the army or in a camp is a target. He's either a Viet Cong or is helping them."

Vietnamese culture, as Frances Fitzgerald pointed out, was wrecked by forced relocation and flight to the cities: "As they took life from the earth and from the ancestors, so they would find immortality in their children, who in their turn would take their place upon the earth. To leave the land and the family forever was therefore to lose their place in the universe and to suffer a permanent, collective death."

Of course, many analysts and experts in the pay of the empire found a rosier side to this havoc. For example, Samuel P. Huntington, Chairman of the Department of Government at Harvard University, contributed to *Foreign Affairs* in 1968 a rather cheerful view of history and the American cultural devastation. "In an absent-minded way," wrote the professor from the comfort of his study, "the United States may have stumbled upon the answer to 'wars of national liberation.'"

War, he argued, wasn't in and of itself the answer, but more importantly the "forced-draft urbanization and modernization which rapidly brings the country in question out of the phase in which a rural revolutionary movement can hope to generate sufficient strength to come to power." The solution was to produce "a massive migration from countryside to city." In this way, with bombs and slaughter, did the empire "stir the sleep of a hundred centuries." By 1967 Senator William J. Fulbright remarked that Saigon, representative of all the towns of South Vietnam by being swollen to some four times its previous population, had become "an American brothel."

5. A country shattered

In the end, the U.S. had converted the South, in Fitzgerald's words, into "a country shattered so that no two pieces fit together." Shattering the country — by depopulating the countryside, by defoliation and carpet bombing, by terror and imposed dependence upon the U.S. military — was the method which the crackpot bureaucratic ideologues sanguinely recommended as the solution to the "Vietnamese problem." Destroying that latest incarnation of the "howling wilderness infested by bloodthirsty savages" — the lush Vietnamese rainforests and grasslands where a "VC" was hidden behind every tree — and physically liquidating whoever resisted the salvation America so nobly offered, became the only solution to an unresolvable problem. Only in this way could the "credibility" of the empire be restored and the rising tide of nationalist revolution be halted.

And they went to every length to do so. It became official U.S. policy, in the words of Robert Opton, Jr., a psychologist who was in Vietnam during 1967 and 1968 as a reporter, "to obliterate not just whole villages, but whole districts and virtually whole provinces." At first, residents were moved out, but the vast numbers of refugees created by these operations led military officers to order that no new refugees be "generated." As Jonathan Schell had witnessed, no warnings were issued when air strikes were called in on their villages, and every civilian on the ground was assumed to be the enemy and fired on accordingly. Free fire zones now came to include many inhabited villages.

Opton witnessed U.S. Cobra helicopters firing 20mm cannons into houses, and soldiers shooting the people as they ran out of the houses. "This was termed 'prepping the area' by the American lieutenant colonel who directed the operation. 'We sort of shoot it up to see if anything moves,' he explained, and he added by way of reassurance that this treatment was perfectly routine."

Everyday occurrences of atrocities and brutality against the Vietnamese became so commonplace that they ceased to be reported as news. Pfc. Allen Akers, who served in the 3rd Marine Division, testified at the Winter Soldier Investigation on war crimes in Vietnam (convened by the Vietnam Veterans Against the War in Detroit in early 1971), "We were given orders whenever we moved into a village to reconnoiter by fire. This means to — whenever we step into a village to fire upon houses, bushes, anything to our discretion that looked like there might be somebody hiding behind or under ...we'd carry our rifles about hip high and we'd line up on line parallel to the village and start walking, firing from the hip."

Pfc. Charles Stephens, of the 101st Airborne Division, testified that his battalion had attacked Tui Hoa, reconnoitering by fire, and wounding women and children, who later died due to lack of medical attention. The next day they fired on the village as the people buried their dead, killing another person. "We went down that same day to get some water and there were two little boys playing on a dike and one sergeant just took his M-16 and shot one boy at the dike. The other boy tried to run. He was almost out of sight when the other guy, a Spec 4, shot this other little boy off the dike. The little guy was like lying on the ground kicking, so he shot him again to make sure he was dead." Stephens testified that to prove their body count "we had to cut off the right ear of everybody we killed ... Guys would cut off heads, put them on a stake and stick a guy's penis in his mouth." Kenneth Ruth, a medic in the 1st Air Cavalry Division, reported the torture of prisoners, and test-firing of weapons by firing them indiscriminately at villagers. "Nobody else cared. This is the general attitude. You know, Vietnamese aren't humans, they're targets." He concluded, "I could go on all day. All of us could. And every GI in this room could say the same thing."

Sgt. Scott Camil of the 1st Marine Division reported "burning of villages with civilians in them, the cutting off of ears, cutting off of heads, torturing of prisoners, calling in of artillery on villages for games, corps-men killing wounded prisoners, napalm dropped on villages, women being raped, women and children being massacred, CS gas used on the people, animals slaughtered, passes rejected and the people holding them shot, bodies shoved out of helicopters, teargassing people for fun and running civilians off the road." When asked by the moderator if prisoners being tortured were civilians or North Vietnamese armymen, he replied, "The way we distinguished between civilians and VC, VC had weapons and civilians didn't and anybody that was dead was considered a VC. If you killed someone they said, 'How do you know he's a VC?' and the general reply would be, 'He's dead,' and that was sufficient." He reported that when villagers were searched, "the women would have all their clothes taken off and the men would use their penises to probe them to make sure they didn't have anything hidden anywhere; and this was raping but it was done as searching." All this had taken place in the presence of officers.

The list of brutality is endless, which explains psychologist Robert J. Lifton's observation that of the two hundred or so soldiers that he and his colleagues interviewed, none was surprised by the news of My Lai. "They had not been surprised because they have either been party to, or witness to, or have heard fairly close-hand about hundreds or thousands of similar, if smaller, incidents." Said Camil, "It wasn't like they were humans. We were conditioned to believe that this was for the good of the nation ... And when you shot someone you didn't think you were shooting at a human. They were a gook or a Commie and it was okay. And anything you did to them was okay because like they would tell you they'd do it to you if they had the chance."

Others reported destroying rice and livestock, killing of unarmed persons, running people down on the road with trucks and tanks, desecrating graves, throwing people out of helicopters, throwing cans of C-rations at children by the sides of roads, firing 50-caliber machine guns at villages for sport, nazi-style revenge massacres of whole villages after a GI was killed by a sniper, burning of huts with the people inside, firing at peasants in ox-carts from planes simply to finish off unused ammunition, torturing "VC suspects" by attaching electrical wires to their genitalia (called the "Bell Telephone Hour" by soldiers), rape and murder of women, burning of villages. As Opton wrote in 1970, "'Winning the hearts and minds' of the Vietnamese is now maintained only as a public relations product for consumption on the home market."

And yet among many soldiers there was the grotesque complaint that they were fighting "with one arm tied behind our back," a complaint bellowed today by those who have no shame. What more could they have been allowed in order to carry on their grisly business? Opton noted that among soldiers he interviewed in Vietnam, "many felt that a final solution was the best and perhaps only solution, and many of their officers agreed. Extermination of the Vietnamese people, some officers felt, would be the best way to protect the men under them." So the only way to "save" the Vietnamese would be to annihilate them all, which was probably true in terms of winning the war, since the Vietnamese were willing to fight to the bitter end to throw out the invaders. It was this heroic resistance which impeded the extermination from taking place.

Of course, there was also the fear on the part of war planners that the war could expand beyond their ability to "manage" it effectively. A widening of the war could also draw more massive protest against what was an increasingly unpopular war back home, and resistance in the army itself, which was starting to break down and turn against the war. David Halberstam reports in his book *The Best and the Brightest* that in late 1966, the military was urging Lyndon Johnson to bomb Hanoi and Haiphong and to block the harbor. Johnson replied, "I have one more problem for your computer — will you feed into it how long it will take five hundred thousand angry Americans to climb that White House fence out there and lynch their President if he does something like that?" And Daniel Ellsberg pointed out much later that it was only the resistance to the war by Americans at home that prevented Richard Nixon from committing that ultimate atrocity of dropping nuclear weapons on North Vietnam. Such an escalation could be the only logic of the statement current among those who refuse to face the reality of the hideous crusade, that the U.S. military was "not allowed to win." It is the culmination of the "Indian idea."

6. Bloodbaths

The Americans may not have been able to impose a "final solution" on the Indochinese, but they did enough damage in the course of that war to wreck whole societies and lay the basis for further carnage, as in Cambodia, making Nixon's cynical warning of a "bloodbath" a self-fulfilling prophecy. If some 58,000 American soldiers died in Vietnam and another 300,000 were wounded, and we add to that list the startling number of suicides among veterans since the war, some 50,000, how can these horrifying figures compare to those of three million Vietnamese killed and 4.5 million wounded? What would be the comparable length of a wall like the veterans' memorial in Washington, D.C. if it contained those three million names? And consider some other statistics: ten million refugees, a million orphans, nearly 10,000 hamlets destroyed in South Vietnam alone; 6,600,000 tons of bombs dropped on Indochina, including 400,000 tons of napalm, leaving some 25 million craters; 25 million acres of farmland and twelve million acres of forests destroyed by, among other causes, nineteen million gallons of defoliants sprayed on them. The horror visited upon thousands of American soldiers and their families due to exposure to Agent Orange and other defoliants is only an indication of the far greater numbers and levels of contamination of Indochinese who were and continue to be the victims of the chemical plagues deliberately unleashed by the American masters of war.

The United States went into Vietnam to "save" the south by impeding reunification of the country and stopping the communists from assuming power of the entire country. In so doing it wrecked the possibility of any diversity in Vietnamese society (or Laotian or Cambodian), of anyone but the communists coming to power, by uprooting and destroying the very groups that could have resisted or offset control by the stalinists — the regional political groups and religious sects, the tribespeople of the highlands, the Buddhists, and other political tendencies. The U.S. claimed to wish to prevent domination of the south by northerners. Yet during the Tet Offensive in 1968 and the "Operation Phoenix" program of mass assassinations, jailings and relocations which followed in the early 1970s, it exterminated the mainly southern NLF cadres, making northern domination of the culturally distinct south another self-fulfilling prophecy (indeed, perhaps a necessity for the Vietnamese if they were going to win the war). "The U.S. has changed Vietnam," wrote Fitzgerald, "to the point where it is unrecognizable to Vietnamese ... and flattened the local ethnic, religious, and cultural peculiarities beneath a uniform, national disaster."

Now, ten years later, we could only expect the grotesque spectacle in which history has been rewritten so that Americans can continue to evade individual and collective guilt for the slaughter of the Indochinese and the wrecking of their societies. One particularly repellent example was President Carter's astonishing statement in March 1977, "The destruction was mutual. We went to Vietnam without any desire to capture territory or impose American will on other people. I don't feel we ought to apologize or castigate ourselves or to assume the status of culpability." According to Vietnamese author Ngo Vinh Long, "A professor at Hue University likened [the statement] to a rapist saying that his victims hurt him as much as he hurt them." Yet, incredibly, the refusal by Americans to face the truth of American culpability has brought about exactly such a reversal in many people's minds.

The atrocities and injustices following in the wake of the U.S. war — which could only be seen as the consequences of American devastation, as further proof that a holocaust does not create conditions for reconciliation and freedom but only for more holocaust and tyranny — these crimes are now employed by propagandists as a justification for the original violence that prepared the ground for them. The question never seems to be raised that even if the Indochinese were destined to mutual wars and dictatorship — a frequent occurrence in the troubled Third World — how could that justify the American intervention, the millions dead and wounded, the ruination of traditional forms of life which may have helped to prevent such brutality?

In fact, it is one of the war's tragic ironies that the forced modernization so fondly touted as a solution by U.S. analysts like the Harvard Government professor will now be carried out by the stalinists rather than the fascist puppets of the Americans, and only because the U.S. pulverized that society so thoroughly that the only force left which was capable of creating a new society of any kind was the communists. It is hard to say what would have happened if the Indian fighters had not marched into that valley, but once they did their dirty work, the consequences could only be a foregone conclusion. And the consistent pressure which America now puts on the Indochinese contributes to every act of oppression and brutality which occurs there to this day.

Now that the "lesson" that more American terror and death was necessary in Indochina is widely proclaimed, there are those who would wish to employ it for further holocaust in Central America. Edward N. Luttwak, one of the latest clones of American crackpot military realism, claimed in the *Harper's* symposium that if the "1,000 sorties flown each day in Vietnam" had hit "worthwhile targets," they "would have ended the war in a day," and now prescribes American "victory" for El Salvador, using the same terms and justifications applied by counterinsurgency analysts in the 1960s in Vietnam: "I believe the United States should help the Salvadoran government, which is a democratizing regime, win the war ... The United States can permit the Salvadorans to prevail by using their traditional methods — which simply entail killing as many people as they can until there are no guerrillas left."

And so the graveyards are in flower this spring ten years later, this spring which is witness and prelude to more butchery à la Edward Luttwak. The slaughter is going on at this very moment, in the highlands of Guatemala, in the ravines of El Salvador, along the Honduras-Nicaragua border. We are now told by Richard Nixon (in a book which can only bring to mind the image of Hitler, say in 1955, writing a retrospective on World War II) that the idea of "no more Vietnams" means not that America shouldn't intervene, but that it shouldn't fail. That is *always* the plan. Now the Mayan Indians are being rounded up into strategic hamlets, tortured and massacred, their cultures wrecked and whole language groups decimated. The poor farmers of that earth goddess' necklace of volcanic jewels which is Central America are being exterminated, the "sheep separated from the goats." Even napalm is being used against them in a stunning repetition of history which can only elicit a scream of anguish directly from the heart. Of course these unfortunate people are only "Commies," "subversives" "guerrillas" — targets. They are more jungle to be paved and turned into an American parking lot.

7. America's next Vietnam

Like millions of others, I did what I could to stop that war. I demonstrated, leafletted, sat in, burned my draft card, walked out of school, spoke on streetcorners. In 1967 I was fifteen years old. I would have enlisted in the NLF to fight against the American invasion had I had the opportunity. Because I was young and America was fighting a war so transparently evil, I tended to glorify the resistance, the NLF and the North Vietnamese. The heroism and the dignity of the Vietnamese people blinded me to the authoritarian character of the stalinist politicians who were carried to power. Experience and a deepening understanding of the world made it clear that such illusions are dangerous. Nevertheless, I don't regret waving a "VC" flag, the flag of the empire's enemy, at the gates of a factory in Warren, Michigan, where tanks were produced.

Obviously, everyone always wishes they could have known then what they know now, and I don't confuse my opposition to U.S. intervention in Central America with any illusions about the politicians who run Nicaragua or the political parties involved in the resistance in Guatemala and El Salvador. But the lack of judgment some of us showed in glorifying the Vietnamese resistance cannot be blamed for the misery visited upon those tortured lands. The blame must be laid where it belongs if we are to break the cycle of destruction: on the technocratic fascist war conceived and conducted by the U.S. imperialist war machine, and the daily acts of complicity by Americans with that war machine.

Now the same events are unfolding in Central America (or actually have been unfolding for years, though we are only now becoming increasingly aware of them). The U.S. plays the same dirty tricks, foments its Big Lie, butchers poor farmers and ignites villages in the name of freedom, progress, salvation. Its infernal technology is now being brought to bear on still more victims.

When I look up at the map of Indochina on my wall, I cannot help but wonder: what more could we have done to stop the suffering, to obstruct that smoking, clanking juggernaut cutting its bloody swath through a faraway land? To all the apologists for genocide, paid and unpaid, who promote the imperial lie that the antiwar movement, which eventually became the great majority of Americans, inside and outside the military, "betrayed" the war effort, I can only reply: *We didn't do enough to undermine and betray your war effort.* If there is any lesson to be learned from that war which can aid us in understanding the situation we find ourselves in today, it is this — that now that the soil is being bloodstained by new, hellish wars, now that the engines of holocaust are again filling the air with their terrifying drone, we must find a way to rally our spirits once more, to blockade the beast, to stop its murderous career. Yesterday is today and today is tomorrow. The Vietnam wars are an American creation. It is here — and it is we who must act — where they will be stopped once and for all.

(April-May 1985)

Bibliographic note: Some of the books quoted or consulted in this essay: Richard Drinnon, *Facing West: The Metaphysics of Indian-Hating and Empire-Building* (1980); Frances Fitzgerald, *Fire in the Lake* (1972); *War Crimes and the American Conscience* (testimony from the Congressional Conference on War and National Responsibility, 1970), edited by Erwin Knoll and Judith N. McFadden; John Lewellen, *Ecology and Devastation: Indochina* (1971); Felix Greene, *Vietnam! Vietnam!* (1966); Vietnam Veterans Against the War, *The Winter Soldier Investigation: An Inquiry into American War Crimes* (1972); Noam Chomsky, *American Power and the New Mandarins* (1967) and "After Pinkville," in *Prevent the Crime of Silence: Reports from the Sessions of the International War Crimes Tribunal founded by Bertrand Russell* (1971); Harrison E. Salisbury et al, *Vietnam Reconsidered: Lessons from a War* (1984); and William Appleman Williams et al, *America in Vietnam: A Documentary History* (1985).

WAR IN THE PERSIAN GULF: IMPERIAL DEATH TRIP TO NOWHERE

The Empire, gorged and sclerotic from daily gnawing on the marrow of the world, has now called up its armies and declared its "new world order." Its commander-in-chief, a mediocrity in a civilization of hollow mediocrities, lays aside his golf club and announces a holy war to "defend the American way of life," its basis in the sacred nectar of capital, the "lifeblood of industry and the Western economies," oil. Hundreds of thousands of troops, with more on the way, now await their orders to advance to the conflagration. Or perhaps as you read these lines, the armies have already clashed, littering the sand with corpses and industrial junk.

It would be difficult to devise, in some fiction or film, a war more thoroughly and more classically cynical, hypocritically concocted, and insane. The external Enemy — the bone-grinding djinn Hussein, who gasses soldiers and civilian populations alike, who makes roads of the corpses and drives his tanks over them — has been properly demonized ... now that he has been removed from the payroll.

Studiously forgotten is the role that the United States — and the rest of the industrial capitalist world, for that matter — played in creating this season's Hitler. At the very moment when U.S. centurions were flattening the slums of Panama City to root out last season's Hitler (another former client, even an employee of the empire), the White House announced the lifting of a ban on loans to Iraq.

The U.S. was, in fact, Iraq's largest trading partner up to the invasion. Billions of dollars in loans guaranteed by the U.S. government had been funneled to Iraq during the 1980s, with little doubt that a significant portion went to buy arms and even chemical weapons. When Iraq gassed its Kurdish minority and forced population relocations on half a million Kurds and Syrians, the U.S. looked the other way. When Iraq invaded Iran, gassing thousands of Iranian soldiers, the U.S. provided helicopters, satellite reconnaissance, and other logistical and economic support. When Iraq threatened Kuwait's border because of Kuwaiti sabotage of the Iraqi economy, the U.S. yawned. But when Iraq moved in and took all of Kuwait rather than a slice, the U.S. commander-in-chief denounced "those who would use force to replace the rule of law," called in the marines to protect "our jobs, our way of life, our own freedom," and drew his "line in the sand."

The line Bush drew in the shifting desert sands, as one wit, *Harper's* magazine editor Lewis Lapham, quipped, "was the line between profit and loss." In the first weeks of war hysteria Bush was able to fabricate a consensus for military adventure under the rubric of democracy and freedom. But as the feudal nature of the Saudi and Kuwaiti dynasties, the U.S. ties to Hussein, and the recognition that Americans will die to protect oil companies have all started to dawn on the population, the administration has shifted its rhetoric to the cynical posture of economic necessity. By mid-November, Secretary of State James Baker put it bluntly, declaring the "vital interests" of American capitalism at stake. "To bring it down to the level of the average American citizen," he said, "if you want to sum it up in one word, it's jobs." Workers have in the past been blackmailed with loss of livelihood if they would not allow corporations to slash their wages and safety standards as well as pollute their communities. Now they are being told that to avoid unemployment, they must sell their sons and daughters to the god of war.

Destroy Kuwait to save it

Ironically, Hussein's reasons for war were just as explicitly economic. Hussein invaded Kuwait to defend his national economic interests; what Iraq did to Kuwait, western capital now conspires to do to Iraq. The West masses against the political entity called Iraq, but it should be clear what this means in the real world: the massive bombing of Iraqi and Kuwaiti civilian populations, the phosphorous and anti-personnel bombs, the collapsing apartment houses, the millions of refugees, the burning oil fields and ships, the oil slicks.

When the generals and their sheep talk glibly of "taking out" the Great Satan, they never acknowledge the real victims of their campaign, the mother and child beneath the rubble of their house, the conscripts charred alive in their tanks, the hobbled, the mangled, the mad. In just fifteen years since the end of the Vietnam War, a few Rambo movies and rounds at the space invaders video screen have inured the entire culture to the degree that one can read a passage in *Newsweek* magazine stating with no apparent irony that in an Iraq war, "The damage would be immense. The United States might have to destroy Kuwait — its oil refineries, its port, and much of its capital city — to save it." (August 27, 1990)

The space invaders phenomenon has worked its magic. Americans tend to believe that in war only the faceless other — formerly "gooks," now "A-rabs" (in an environment where anti-Arab racism and violence are pervasive) — are the only ones to die. But Iraq is not Panama. The reality will set in when the shooting actually commences. Military analysts estimate that an attack by U.S. forces "would claim 5,000 U.S. lives and 15,000 wounded in the first ten days of combat alone." (*Boston Globe*) "We are planning for massive casualties," said one officer in charge of a hospital ship. Tens of thousands of body bags (made out of hefty plastic by the petrochemical companies) have arrived in Saudi Arabia. No one on this side of the ocean even bothers to count the Iraqi (or even the allied) dead.[1] (See page 304 for endnotes.) But the most grotesque aspect of the New Order's crusade has yet to be mentioned: the ecological implications. Petrochemical civilization now stands at the threshold of a regional ecological and social catastrophe — massive contamination of the air, soil and waters, massive annihilation by gas, and even perhaps nuclear weapons, of civilian populations, and the rest. And for what? So that global industrialism, led by the capitalist west, can continue its project of heating up and destroying the atmosphere and the basic conditions of life as we know it, through an oil-based, industrial growth-driven economy.

Petrochemical civilization is already suicidal, living as if it were the last human generation on earth. Perhaps the leaders secretly long to join the myriad species their daily business activities send to extinction. But what a glorious excursion down the chute for those riding in the luxury compartments of this slave ship! What giddying power, obscene profits! A war to maintain its privilege of looting and wrecking the ecospheric organism isn't so much like Nero fiddling while his empire burns, as it is a willful torching of the whole world as the final act of an imperial (breadless) circus.

The war in the Middle East is only a continuation of every previous crusade and war against the world in the service of a military-industrial megamachine. Irony of ironies if the ultimate empires find themselves unraveling in the very desert sands that covered the original exhausted civilizations of the ancient Tigris and Euphrates valley. The faces of the cannon fodder are as grim as those of the refugees, the cheap labor from the bottom of the oil dynasty's sordid pyramid scheme, boarding ships and planes to be dispersed back to the wretched colonial provinces from which petrochemical capital had drawn them. There is no stake in it for these expendables, nor has there ever been any.

Ship of fools

Nothing good can come of this crusade, this ship of fools. For the Americans, it is only the same old, age-old story, a journey up a river into the heart of darkness — a river of sand, a river of oil, of blood. The computers malfunction in the desert heat, the sand jams the guns and grounds the helicopters, the mounds of plastic garbage from food rations blow across the horizon. It's the lie of patriotism, played out once again in some distant outpost. Youth dying *for nothing.*[2]

And for the Iraqis, more sacrifice, more bloodshed, more meaningless suffering to sate the blood-drenched god who builds his ziggurat of corpses to erect another billboard of his portrait at the top; who, with Shakespeare's MacBeth, might say,

I am in blood
Stepp'd in so far that, should I wade no more,
Returning were as tedious as go o'er ...

except it's difficult to imagine Hussein seeing ghosts. He builds his stairway to infamy on the bodies of the Iraqi people first.

For the rival empires and jockeying interests, even should the West obtain its objectives quickly, the long-term consequences can only mean mutual ruin. Every conflict, every injustice, every horror will be aggravated and exploded — all the consequences of imperial plunder and industrial distortion brought to bear. It's a death trip to nowhere, and the only near certainty is that such adventures, in the long and grisly run, will unravel the very nation states that embark upon them.

And perhaps this is the only slim silver lining in the whole horrendous nightmare. If things go to pieces, as the death toll mounts and as a draft is implemented in this country (no war of any significant proportions has ever been waged without one), the thin support will evaporate and the possibilities for real opposition, not only to the war but to the system that breeds war, will increase.

As with the ecological crisis that looms over this whole escapade, the resolution will never come from the political and military administrators of the interlocking megamachines; paralyzed by their singular lack of imagination, their cowardice, their greed, by their very conditioning as elites, they are constitutionally incapable of turning their machine back from the devastation it is perpetuating.

Rather, the solutions to the world crisis can only come from the bottom up, from soldiers refusing to fight, fraternizing instead with their "enemies," from people refusing to serve the war machine or the work machine. In other words, it will come from our capacity to mutiny, rapidly and creatively, against all the rival nation states — to make revolution not only against the empires, but against the structure of empire itself, against the oil-fueled industrial machine that is undermining the foundations of complex life on earth.

Calling on troops to mutiny and on captive populations of rival empires to revolt must seem mad to those who cannot envision any turn of events different from the current trajectory toward global war or ecological collapse. But we have no alternative. The more we hesitate, the more general conditions for potential transformation are eroded.

With this in mind, we call on the soldiers to refuse to fight, to sit down on the tarmac, fraternize with enemy troops, create committees of resistance. At home, let us build demonstrations and strikes against the war machine and industrial work machine. Let us not go passively to the graves that the leaders have prepared for us, but rather, turn their crisis into our opportunity. Those who come after us will surely thank us.

(Autumn 1990)

Endnotes

1. As we wrote in the following issue of the *Fifth Estate*, "We were certainly fooled — we thought the Iraqi army would stand up much better to the air war than it did. U.S. intelligence must have known all along they were up against a paper army, and decided to embark on relatively low-risk activities for enormous gain. Others paid the price." ("Detroit Seen," Spring 1991 *Fifth Estate*) Those who paid were mostly the Iraqi people. As I revise and edit this article in the late autumn of 1996, the United Nations has reported that some 4,500 children die in Iraq every month as a result of the war against the Iraqi infrastructure and continuing economic sanctions. In fact, military leaders later acknowledged intentionally exaggerating the dangers, which meant that the excess of troops called up served as hostages to subdue American public opinion. That the opponents of the war for the most part did not recognize that Iraq, after ten years of debilitating war with Iran, would collapse in a desert war, was a terrible mistake. But it did not seem to make much difference in our lack of capacity to stop the war — a sobering lesson.
2. Very few soldiers died in the action, but many now face a vague "Gulf War Syndrome" of illness, probably caused by a combination of released chemical and biological agents, radioactive shell casings and experimental drugs given to soldiers by the army to defend themselves against biological weapons. The "Gulf War Syndrome" is the chemical-biological equivalent of "friendly fire" — an example of new high tech wars and their consequences.

THESE ARE NOT OUR TROOPS;
THIS IS NOT OUR COUNTRY

In George Orwell's novel *1984*, protagonist Winston Smith has acquired a copy of the arch-traitor Emmanuel Goldstein's manual for totalitarian domination, *The Theory and Practice of Oligarchic Collectivism*, in which he reads that the ideal party member "should be a credulous and ignorant fanatic whose prevailing moods are fear, hatred, adulation and orgiastic triumph. In other words it is necessary that he should have the mentality appropriate to a state of war." The novel functions in great part through ironic reversals (the subversive conspiracy is contrived by the police, etc.); it should come as no surprise, then, that the reality the novel now illuminates is not so much the otherness of the state socialist dictatorships that it originally resembled, but rather the oligarchic collectivism of modern corporate capital and its military-industrial garrison states — those states waging their brutal crusade against "Eurasia," now that former enemies appear to be vanquished and incorporated into the empire.

The "credulous and ignorant fanatic" now cheering "Desert Storm" in highly orchestrated hate sessions — be they the nightly news variety on the telescreens, the flag-and-yellow-ribbon affairs organized by local businesses and politicos, or the half-time patriotic stage shows in the sports stadiums — is no longer Orwell's "party member" but the loyal citizen of "democracy," the modern "individual" member of a mob, conditioned to respond appropriately and unquestioningly. The contemporary Thought Police have done an impressive job so far. Probably no other war in history has been more carefully packaged and controlled — not only by the state propaganda machine, but by the manipulation of the structures of meaning itself by the media in mass society. The military "spin-doctors" target the domestic population as meticulously as they chart their bombing missions. As Jean Baudrillard commented in his book *America*, "The Americans fight with two essential weapons: air power and information. That is, with the physical bombardment of the enemy and the electronic bombardment of the rest of the world." (And occasionally one even notes the sanctimonious tone of concern for the enemy soldiers — as they are obliterated — in the military rhetoric of the briefing sessions. The public relations officers have picked up a few tricks from the therapeutic New Age of the 1970s.)

Even the dazzlingly blatant lie that media is undermining the war effort as it allegedly did during Vietnam — when in fact the corporate media, sharing the economic interests and outlook of the rest of the capitalist ruling class, was compliant with the military, and today functions as little more than a government cheering section — is being consciously fabricated by military propagandists and the corporate media ideologues who serve them. This is being done for specific reasons — among them to find a scapegoat for losing the genocidal war against the Indochinese people, to keep the media on a short leash, and to condition the U.S. populace psychologically to respond with indifference when images of the actual suffering and violence inevitably slip through.

In this latter regard they have been enormously successful; witness the indignation expressed by news anchor and good citizen alike over the immorality and cynicism of a "Saddam" to seek propaganda advantages at the expense of the many civilians killed and injured — by allied armed forces. This kind of reversal and psychological projection, a function of denial, has been characteristic of the media manipulation and the response of mass society to this latest military campaign.

A planetary frontier

Certainly, America has always been racist and xenophobic, callous to the suffering of the world's oppressed; long before this war it was already aroused by violence and fascinated with high tech means of destruction. Denial and projection were always central components of U.S. settler-state ideology. The enemies of (or those who were simply obstacles to) U.S. colonial expansion, first on this continent and then elsewhere, had to be painted as "savages" so that every imaginable brutality could be practiced upon them. It started along a frontier misnamed "New England" and continued along a frontier that by the middle of this century, in the words of Richard Drinnon, "had become planetary."

An ideological tradition stretching back through Vietnam to the wars against the Pequots and Narragansetts was leavened with contemporary banality by Marine Brigadier General Richard Neal when he said of a downed pilot rescued inside Kuwait that he "was forty miles into Indian country. That pilot's a happy camper now." The connection was also understood by an Iraqi woman who screamed at a British journalist after cruise missiles had hit a residential area of Baghdad, "You think we are Red Indians, you are used to killing Red Indians."

Today imperial arrogance has more sophisticated technological means for manufacturing public consensus than ever. More importantly, it now manipulates a population that has grown up in the blue light of television, a population in whom the ability to think critically and to reach an understanding based on deep ethical foundations has been deformed and distorted. In his classic study *Propaganda: The Formation of Men's Attitudes*, Jacques Ellul writes of the modern citizen, "Everywhere we find men who pronounce as highly personal truths what they have read in the papers only an hour before, and whose beliefs are merely the result of a powerful propaganda." One week nobody knows of the existence of a Saddam Hussein; in a short time he has become the most dangerous man in the world, a universal bogeyman. The U.S. populace was quickly whipped into a frenzy over Hussein just as they had been over Khomeini, Khadafi and Noriega, while few people can even identify murderous U.S. henchmen like Suharto, Rios-Montt, D'Aubuisson, or Ariel Sharon, and no one gets enraged over a Pinochet. (Readers uncertain of the identities of any of these men prove my point that the state vaporizes any authentic historical understanding in the interests of imperial ideology.)

Television and mass society

But authentic history of the facts of the matter are no longer even relevant. Today's state does not need to control all information, in the manner of a dictatorship; as long as the terms of discourse are controlled, it is more effective for there to be the public illusion of freedom of information. Nor is it necessary for the entire population actively to support imperial military adventures as long as the majority acquiesces to them. And as long as the majority is firmly in the grips of the propaganda machine, fragments of truth that slip through the media barrage are simply ignored because they just don't fit into the overall picture.

Thus the obvious parallel between the U.S. invasion of Panama and the Iraqi invasion of Kuwait can be widely acknowledged, along with the fact that the U.S. was Iraq's major trading partner during the 1980s, supplying it militarily and providing huge loans while it gassed its Kurdish minority and invaded Iran. The information can be widely available, and still have no effect. People are not supporting the war because they have considered the history and the context; they are responding to the most simplified signals. As Nazi propagandist Joseph Goebbels wrote, "By simplifying the thoughts of the masses and reducing them to primitive patterns, propaganda was able to present the complex process of political and economic life in the simplest of terms. . . ." Ellul comments that the massified subject no longer needs to read the newspaper article to the end or hear the entire speech because the content is known in advance. It is not the information itself that matters but the shaping of the discourse, the model itself. The citizen "continues to obey the catchwords of propaganda, though he no longer listens to it ... He no longer needs to see and read the poster; the simple splash of color is enough to awaken the desired reflexes in him."

The hypnotic effects of television have taken this phenomenon to lengths never dreamed of by the Nazis. But the reason television works so well for the institutions of power is because it is a keystone for a whole mass society. When the masses marvel at the technological wonders of intense aerial bombardment, all the conditioned responses are being elicited and manipulated: the thrill of spectacular violence of enormous proportions, psychic numbing in the face of the real suffering that the images flatten and trivialize, the seduction of machines and speed.

As Ellul pointed out in *The Technological System*, one cannot simply talk about the "effects" of television, when this technology of meaning itself "exists only in terms of a technological universe and as an expression of this universe." The entire culture deriving from the industrial capitalist organization of life conspires to brutalize human beings and condition them to become automatons. They accept gargantuan, enormously destructive military campaigns because they have already been prepared by their acceptance of the entire universe of massive planning by technocratic elites in nearly all aspects of their lives. As in construction, so in destruction. The music blares, marching soldiers are shown on the screen, and all context, all history, the reality of the "enemy" as human beings all disappears. This crusade is noble simply because it is; the Nation must stand together.

The state controls discourse

It doesn't matter how many dead Iraqis appear on the screens if the imperial state controls the discourse itself, and people are simply dismissed as "collateral damage," and Iraq can be blamed even for the people burned to death in busses rocketed by American planes (just what did those people think they were doing getting on those busses, after all?) or in civilian neighborhoods and air-raid shelters (they were military targets according to our satellites and our "numerous sources" which are to remain unspecified for security reasons).

As media critic Norman Solomon has argued, "Denial is key to the psychological and political structures that support this war. The very magnitude of its brutality — gratuitous and unmerciful — requires heightened care to turn the meaning of events upside down. Those who massacre are the aggrieved; those being slaughtered with high-tech cruelty are depicted as subhumans, or [in a cynical phrase quoted from *Time* magazine] 'civilians who should have picked a safer neighborhood.'" ("Media Denies, Anesthetizes, Inverts War," *The Guardian*, 2/13/91)

The rage against the butcher of Baghdad is probably the most ingenious manipulation of the propaganda alchemists. Every reflex of hate, fear and rage is gathered into the person of the Great Satan himself, "Saddam." Eighteen million Iraqis magically disappear as the good American citizen endorses the carpet bombing of whole regions (military targets, after all), and even calls for the use of nuclear weapons to "take out" this Saddam. (Imagine using a nuclear bomb against one man. An interesting irony occurs in the latter idea: one lie mobilized to justify attack was that Iraq must be kept from using the nuclear weapons it was allegedly on the verge of building. Now using nuclear weapons against the country, or at least against the positions of its soldiers in Kuwait, is being discussed as a legitimate tactic — another version of the "destroy-it-to-save-it" idea.)

All of the rage and feelings of powerlessness, the miseries and humiliations of living in a society dominated by powerful and mostly anonymous economic and bureaucratic forces are channeled into a partly contrived, partly spontaneous fury against the external enemy. Any action against the Evil Other becomes justifiable. Hussein must not be rewarded for "naked aggression." Yet in fact the U.S. not only commonly aids and abets aggression (for example when it rewarded Hussein for his bloody invasion of Iran), but is itself the world's biggest bully and aggressor, overtly and covertly — in Panama, Grenada, Nicaragua, El Salvador, Mozambique, Angola, and many other countries.

It is asserted that Hussein must be stopped because he is bent on world domination (exactly the objective of the U.S., through its Fourth Reich, the New World Order). Hussein is a dictator (a dictator, that is, who does not serve U.S. interests, in contrast with the stable of tyrants it props up on every continent). Saddam is an environmental terrorist (no mention of massive allied bombing of oil tankers, oil fields, petrochemical facilities, and so on). And Hussein is insane (while the Pentagon bureaucrats charting their bombing raids, of which there have been, on average, *one per minute* since the war started, are quite sane, no, even quite admirable fellows going about their jobs thoughtfully and following orders competently).

Meanwhile, the vicarious sense of power derived from watching the spectral high-tech war on television joins the citizen to the state in a manner most useful to authority: mobilized passivity.

Denial and reversal

Another key element of manipulation has been the slow, incremental intensification of the war, a tightening of a ratchet tooth by tooth. What started out as a deployment to defend Saudi Arabia soon became the basis for attack; the war was going to be short and sweet, perhaps no more than a few bombing raids before the bad guys collapsed. Little by little the trusting citizens were told that no one had ever promised such a thing.

Along the same lines is the ever repeated Big Lie that bombing targets are military targets and military targets only. (This serves a dual purpose of legitimating the massive bombardment of soldiers at the front; civilians are said to be protected so that everything will be permissible in the "theater of operations.") But in this case, as irrefutable evidence started to slip through of massive civilian casualties, the terms were changed all the while civilian deaths were denied. When it became clear to anyone who might be listening closely that Basra was suffering thousands of civilian casualties and massive destruction, military spokesman General Neal replied that the city was "a military town in the true sense of the word." Neal explained to the *New York Times*, "Chemical and oil storage sites, warehouses, port installations, a naval base and other military targets ... are very closely interwoven with the town itself." (February 2, 1991). Thus was an entire city promoted to the status of military target.

And as the U.S. populace becomes hardened to growing civilian casualties, denial and reversal are accelerated. When hundreds of people, mostly women and children, were massacred by U.S. bombs that hit an air raid shelter in Baghdad, U.S. military officials responded that the event probably did not even occur, but if it did, the Iraqi government was to blame for allowing them to take shelter in what U.S. military analysis claimed was a military center. Said one British official. "Nobody's ever claimed we were perfect on these things." A U.S. military spokesman responded laconically, "We're not happy civilians got hurt, as apparently they did." (Note how civilians were apparently only *hurt*; getting burned alive is reduced to twisting an ankle.)

And White House spokesman Marlin Fitzwater, in a stunning utterance of projection: "Saddam Hussein does not share our value in the sanctity of life. Indeed, he, time and again, has shown a willingness to sacrifice civilian lives and property that further his war aims." (*New York Times*, February 14, 1991) One almost forgets who is doing the actual bombing.

Interestingly, Fitzwater's remark repeated almost word for word the comment of General William Westmoreland during the height of the Vietnam War, that the Vietnamese did not share "our value in the sanctity of human life," either, which was why presumably, we had to carpet bomb and napalm them, defoliate their forests and level their villages, bulldoze their cemeteries and herd them into concentration camps to achieve our own war aims. And after Pentagon moralists have destroyed Kuwait in order to save it, levelled Iraqi cities and turned out countless dead, injured, and refugees, they can try the Hitler Saddam Hussein for war crimes, for example Iraqi roughing up and humiliation of Western pilots who, after unleashing multiple Hiroshimas on Iraq, are pictured on the front pages of the empire's newspapers as victims.

The populace succumbs

To a great degree, the populace has succumbed to the signals sent over the telescreens, reflecting what can only be called the profound nazification of U.S. society. A well-dressed woman coming out of church on Ash Wednesday, the symbolic ashes of her peaceful Christ's crucifixion on her brow, tells a reporter that civilian deaths are unfortunate, but after all, that is what happens in wartime. A refinery worker tells a newspaper reporter, "This is a war, and innocent civilians are going to be killed in war." "My opinion stayed the same," says a carriage driver in Philadelphia. "Accidents happen in war. You can't avoid them." A teacher in an affluent Detroit suburb, confronted with the irrefutable evidence of civilians burned to death in the bunker, shrugs her shoulders, saying, "I can't believe a word that man [Saddam Hussein] says." (In his book, *The 12-Year Reich: A Social History of Nazi Germany, 1933-45*, Richard Gruneberger reports that when shown photographs of the death camp at Belsen by a British officer, "a German farmer commented, 'Terrible — the things war makes happen' as if talking of a thunderstorm which had flattened his barley.")

Apart from a courageous, vocal anti-war minority — a legacy of what Noam Chomsky has called "the notable improvement in the moral and intellectual climate" of the country resulting from popular movements opposing imperial power and social regimentation in the 1960s (which is exactly why that decade and those movements have been so defamed by the right wing and trivialized by the media) — the population has remained mostly passive, acquiescent, sheeplike in its obeisance and callously inhumane to the destruction. Discussing this phenomenon as far back as the late 1950s, radical sociologist C. Wright Mills wrote in *The Causes of World War Three*:

In this society, between catastrophic event and everyday interests there is a vast moral gulf. How many in North America experienced, as human beings, World War II? Few rebelled, few knew public grief. It was a curiously unreal business, full of efficiency without purpose … little human complaint was focussed rebelliously upon the political and moral meaning of the universal brutality. Masses sat in the movies between production shifts watching with aloofness and even visible indifference as children were "saturation bombed" in the narrow cellars of European cities. Man had become an object; and insofar as those to whom he was an object felt about the spectacle at all, they felt powerless, in the grip of larger forces, with no part in those affairs that lay beyond their immediate areas of daily demand and gratification. It was a time of moral somnambulence.

In the expanded world of mechanically vivified communication the individual becomes the spectator of everything but the human witness of nothing. . . .

Home is now the state

Mills' description of the social forces leading to nuclear world war fits the present day; in the Pentagon, technocrats calmly map out thousands of bombing raids against the adversary, while the majority of the population, numb to the suffering of the people (and the very land) in the gunsites of their heroes, cheer the battle on from the comfort of their living rooms, pro-war rallies and stadiums.

Such patriotism, though bearing uniquely modern aspects, is very similar to the war fervor nation states have always engendered: loyalty to the political myth of the state, the demonization of the enemy, and a sharing of the triumphalism of military prowess. In reality, however, patriotism is an expression of the defeat of community and the triumph of the state. As authentic community is progressively eroded by anonymous economic and technological forces, the innate desire for community is harnessed by the mass media to reassemble millions of atomized individuals into a pseudo-community of passion for the state and its wars. The state and its spectacle now beckon with outstretched arms to provide the only shelter from a heartless, alienated existence. Home is now the state.

Hitler anticipated this phenomenon in his description of the mass meeting, in which the individual "receives for the first time the pictures of a greater community, something that has a strengthening and encouraging effect on most people. . . ." The individual "succumbs to the magic influence of what we call mass suggestion." One of his co-workers explains to a friend of mine her support for the war: "This is something we can all believe in together." The propagandists have learned their lessons well. In an article on the response of the population to the Gulf War, Peter Applebome writes, "War is one thing with the power to bond the nation into a unified whole," and quotes a UCLA professor's comment that this "moral crusade" functions "as a healing experience in relation to Vietnam." (This man is obviously *not* arguing that a new war can heal this nation from the mass murder and ecocidal destruction it perpetrated in Southeast Asia. He thinks *Americans* were the victims.) An Atlanta woman who makes and sells patriotic pins tells Applebome, "People want something to believe in ... They want some part of their life to have meaning." ("Sense of Pride Outweighs Fears of War," *New York Times*, February 24, 1991)

Its cities in ruins, its economy and infrastructure collapsing, its land massively contaminated, its government sullied in scandal, its foreign adventures sordid and confused, millions of its people crowded into prisons, America today must look to many observers like Weimar Germany did to many Germans. Like the Germans, the loyalties and ideological illusions of Americans have been eroded by all the aspects of imperial decline, but they have not found any real community, values or authentic loyalties with which to replace the nationalist mystique. A crucial element of Reaganism was in fact to provide the spectacle of imperial resurgence while paying off certain privileged sectors economically to ensure their renewed loyalty. So far a large section of the populace has bought it, but for most people it means little more than marching lockstep into deeper economic austerity or even dying in war to defend the very institutions that have bankrupted and scattered what little they had.

Denial and projection are the "answer" — project your rage onto some "subhuman" foreign monster, deny that your own life is in ruins, that your real enemies are here at home signing the marching orders. To arrive at this state of righteous indignation, history — both recent and remote — must be vaporized, or *waxed,* as they are now saying about the people they slaughter. Vaporized, too, is the very context in which world corporate capital functions — a world in which a billion people are starving while resources are stolen from them to pay usurious loans to international banking institutions. None of the violence matters; even when it is acknowledged, the New World Order conscripts are simply tired of hearing about it. America is great again! Free Kuwait! Kick ass! Let's prevent Arabs from killing Arabs by slaughtering Arabs. I am reminded of Thoreau's comment in *Walden*: "They love the soil which makes their graves, but have no sympathy with the spirit which may still animate their clay. Patriotism is a maggot in their heads. . . ." That was a century and a half ago. Now little remains but the maggot.

Baby-killers

Thoreau helps us to respond to one of the most powerful propaganda messages for obedience to the imperial state, the command to "support our troops." This slogan has been an effective manipulation to silence people in the sway of the totalitarian-conformist culture, the line being that whatever one's feeling before the shooting started, "America" must now "close ranks." To refuse to do so is to endanger U.S. military personnel in the Middle East.

Much of the anti-war movement has responded by taking up the flag, insisting that "peace is patriotic" and that supporting the troops means bringing them home. This attitude is held as well by a significant number of the families of soldiers and sailors in the Gulf, for whom the phrase "our troops" brings to mind their relatives, neighbors, friends and lovers.

Most of the troops are nothing but hostages — people recruited by a poverty draft of unemployment and racism that one black observer described as an "affirmative action in reverse." Others joined the reserves assuming that they would be used for cleaning up after tornados and floods or at worst defending U.S. shores from outside attack. They are prisoners of the war machine. Among many of them and their families there is a clear understanding that they are being used as pawns to defend the interests of wealthy elites in the Middle East and the U.S. Said Maria Cotto, the sister of Marine Corporal Ismael Cotto, Jr. from the South Bronx, who was killed in early February, "I saw them on television, saying they were spending billions on this. I saw them on Wall Street and they were cheering. It was sick. They were cheering like it was a game. Don't they know it means that people will die? Not them. Not their families. Not their kids. People like my brother."

There are plenty of troops, nevertheless, along with their families, willing and even happy to do the bidding of the Pentagon. One 23-year-old soldier told the *New York Times,* "Every generation has its war. This is going to be a big one ... I've been waiting for this for 18 years." The pacifist argument that "we want to bring our troops home unharmed" does not address the fact that some of them enjoy their work and that truth and freedom will likely suffer when they are brought home. Nevertheless, they are "our" troops and we are told to support them.

Of course, this command calls up the lie that Americans failed to support the troops in Vietnam, that the anti-war movement mistreated returning soldiers, who were spat on and called "baby-killers." In fact, this is one of the great imperial falsehoods of the century, along with the fascist fantasy that "the Jews betrayed Germany" in the First World War. There is no doubt that soldiers occasionally were called baby-killers by people on their return, if not by anti-war organizers (who saw GIs as victims of the war and potential allies in ending it), then by young people enraged by the images of war that filtered home.

The fact of the matter is that a reasonable number of them had to be baby-killers, or the babies wouldn't have been killed. Abundant evidence exists of the massacre of unarmed civilians and the commission of atrocities by American troops in Vietnam (along with their South Vietnamese and Korean allies). The recognition that the entire population was the enemy had its consequences, many of which were documented by Vietnam veterans themselves at the Winter Soldier Investigation of U.S. war crimes in Indochina held in Detroit in 1971.

The most famous massacre of unarmed civilians took place at My Lai in early 1968. One soldier who participated in another lesser known massacre in a nearby hamlet that same day said, "What we were doing was being done all over." (See Seymour Hersh's *Coverup*, 1972). Robert J. Lifton, a psychologist who along with his colleagues had interviewed some two hundred soldiers, found that none was surprised by the news of My Lai. "They had not been surprised because they have either been party to, or witness to, or have heard fairly close-hand about hundreds of thousands of similar, if smaller, incidents," he wrote. One soldier told him, "I knew we were killing the country and its people. In any other war, what I have seen might be considered war crimes." A wealth of such information exists in America's libraries and in the memory of many of its people, but the latest adventures of the New World Order demand that the truth be suppressed along with common decency and humanity.

Turn the guns around

There is little humanity left in America today, but if any remains at all, we must be honest about these troops. They are not "our troops" but the Empire's. They do its bidding, either enthusiastically or sullenly. As long as they simply follow orders, one cannot support them. One supports human beings, not human beings reduced to mechanisms that acquiesce in killing not only other armed soldiers but unarmed people who die under the bombs they drop from as high as thirty thousand feet. In his essay on civil disobedience, Thoreau commented on such people who go off to fight, even against their wills, that because of their respect for the law, "even the well-disposed are daily made the agents of injustice." Could such automatons be considered men at all, he wondered, or were they instead "small movable forts and magazines in the service of some unscrupulous man in power ... The mass of men serve the state thus, not as men mainly, but as machines, with their bodies."

An enormous machine, made of rigid, interchangeable parts, under the direction of a central authority, acting mindlessly to bring about construction or destruction: if war is the health of the state, said Lewis Mumford in *The Pentagon of Power*, "it is the body and soul of the megamachine ... Hence war is the ideal condition for promoting the assemblage of the megamachine, and to keep the threat of war constantly in existence is the surest way of holding the otherwise autonomous or quasi-autonomous components together as a functioning working unit."

The "support our troops" line has nothing to do with a concern for the well-being of the people at the front who are going to die or be wounded in this horrible, meaningless slaughter. It is a loyalty oath that helps to maintain imperial control over the discourse. The "oppose-the-war-but-honor-the-warriors" variant that has been adopted even by some peace activists is only a variety of the Bitburg syndrome. (Bitburg, for those who have forgotten, was a military cemetery for German Nazi stormtroops where President Reagan honored the warriors of the Hitler regime.) Today the United States may be "taking out" one of the world's most vile dictators, but the U.S. global empire makes and breaks such states all the time. It is the oppressor nation among oppressor nations, which is why it will probably succeed in defeating by utterly destroying its weaker, less organized, less technologically sophisticated and poorer adversary, even if it ultimately fails to impose its will on the region and the world or destroys itself doing so. There is no honor in a colonial war and the saturation bombing of the towns and cities of a poor country.

We must support the troops in only one way — by encouraging them to revolt against the conditions of their slavery. Otherwise, they are only movable forts in a military machine, the U.S. imperial army; the sound defeat of this army, even by the tyrant Hussein, would serve the slim possibility of eventual world peace. For the Iraqis, of course, the situation is the same. The leftist call for "victory to Iraq" is perverse — it means victory to the bloodthirsty satraps who massacre Kurds, Assyrians, Kuwaitis, Iranians, dissidents and rebels. It means victory to the thugs building their own house of horrors, their own local empire — thugs equally vicious in their methods as the Salvadoran death squad regime and the Guatemalan generals. The Iraqi people clearly do not believe in this war — evidenced by their outbursts of joy when any slim hope of peace is held out to them. And they have no stake in it. They would do well, like their counterparts among the allied nations, to turn their guns around. Fighting for Hussein's conquests is suicidal folly. Let both sides be defeated by the troops — let the troops unite against their officers and their respective states!

Support the troops: incite mutiny

One shudders to think what will become of the culture and politics of this country when the troops come home victorious (as they most likely will), relatively unscathed and giddy with triumph. The rulers will have a mandate for more military adventures, and other poor peoples (rarely their leaders) will pay the price in blood. Who will be next? Cuba? A mopping up operation in Central America? All in the name of the New World Order which is, after all, just a buzzword for the renewal of the former World Order of capitalist plunder. And the state will use the opportunity to reinforce the imperial values of a highly militarized, repressive, conformist society at home.

Defeat of the Empire is preferable. If there is any justice left in this world, better that the well-armed and well-fed soldiers of the U.S. die than unarmed civilians (and draftees for that matter) of the Third World. No, these are not our troops, this is not our flag, this is not our country. The Lakota warriors who killed the soldiers and dragged away the U.S. flag from the Little Big Horn, the abolitionists freeing slaves at Harper's Ferry, armed blacks defending themselves from the Ku Klux Klan — these are the warriors we celebrate. But such examples aren't troops so much as human beings fighting for their lives.

And whose country is this, where on cue from the telescreens, citizens scream for the annihilation of their "enemies" thousands of miles away, where they play at the war on board games while their armies smash whole cities, whole regions? This is not our country. Defeat of such a country is preferable (indeed, would better serve its own long-term survival as a viable human culture), to its further descent into blood-drenched elation and conquest. For its own sake as a society, America should lose this war.

Defeat does not guarantee anything, to be sure, but it slows the Empire down, and leaves a small possibility that the automata will be shaken from their somnambulence, humanized, made capable of responding once again to the suffering of the whole world. It is only a possibility, of course; defeat guarantees nothing. But otherwise, one suspects, there will be only a string of these campaigns, of Vietnams, Panamas, Nicaraguas and Iraqs, a necklace of skulls hanging from the belt of the Warrior-Father of All Wars.

Support the troops, all right — incite mutiny. If not against this war, which may end too quickly, then against the next. For there will surely be one.

(1991)

WATCHING THE DOGS SALIVATE: REMARKS ON THE 1992 ELECTIONS

"I know one or two who have this year, for the first time, read a president's message, but they do not see that this implies a fall in themselves rather than a rise in the president. Blessed are the young for they do not read the president's message." — Thoreau to Parker Pillsbury, April 1861

The Empire now has new clothiers, and opportunely for the rulers. As the political management languished and the economy buckled, change became the only way to keep the Empire on its track. The apparatus of organized illusion called the slaves to the Lever: which figurehead could best keep the Empire slouching along? Which party would put them back to work mining the Mystery, with picks and shovels and a small particle of eternity for all, while soothing them with homilies of health and happiness and an economy that would grow and grow forever, amen? Who could provide bread and circuses, feed the unruly to the Coliseum, torch the rebel colonies?

It was Caligula versus Nero, with the option to register (responsible) disaffection by voting for Croesus, the billionaire buffoon. Its atmosphere of sport and scandal, its Big Brother-like electronic "town meetings" and Hollywood hyper-politics drugged the populace like any mass entertainment. Age of complicit cynicism, the spectators could play along even while knowing it was all essentially a hoax. It worked anyway.

It didn't matter if one believed in a party or even voted; what mattered was fascination, as the state and the media, in their double helix of ersatz opposition and legitimation, simultaneously roused and anaesthetized the audience. Just as the Persian Gulf War became popular once initial fears were allayed, this performance involved its audience in organized, active passivity. Hearing the bell ring, the citizens gazed upon the show and told themselves that some momentous event was occurring. The Empire and only the Empire was real, not that receding shadow of what was once the phenomenal world. Watching was enough; publicity did the rest. Meanwhile life continued its downward spiral.

Not that there was no unambiguous difference between the candidates. If essentially they represented only alternative strategies for continuing imperial power, there were also significant differences on the level of mass psychology. Consider the blood-drenched Bush, proud of his massacres and denying the imperial malaise altogether, with bloated thieves at one hand and lead-lined, flint-eyed fascists at the other. One half-step to his right was the puffed-up pretender Buchanan, and one half-step to Buchanan's right was the nazi cretin Duke. Bush appealed to what was most cramped and vengeful in the plebes and to raw avarice in the patricians.

In contrast, the consummate politico Clinton played a traditional game, manipulating a rhetoric (modernized for his television-bred generation) of inclusion, optimism, personal liberty, indignation at injustice and the promise to resolve the built-in miseries of the capitalist system. Clinton promised to make things better — better for the Empire, that is. Thus, he could appeal to plebes and patricians alike.

This good cop/bad cop combination worked well for capital. After a long period of steady economic dislocation and erosion of formal liberties, many people felt beaten-up enough to grasp at straws. Even if Clinton meant more of the same, Bush somehow appeared to signal something even uglier. Or perhaps, to shift analogies, one could say that wanting to avoid Hitler, they pulled the lever for Hindenberg, as Germans fearful of nazism had done during the early 1930s. (Hindenberg soon after brought Hitler into the government.)

If on the level of mass psychology, the abused child has become (along with the abuser, or the serial murderer and his victim) an "indicator persona" in the culture (no matter what the actual conditions of abuse), those desperate souls who voted for the contender evoked the brutalized victim, shakily and hopefully accepting the extended, now seemingly conciliatory hand of the tormentor. As anyone questioning the whole procedure was apt to be told, what choice did they have? One candidate promised to send women to back alleys, to triturate the natural world, to let the poor rot. The other sold the snake-oil of a shapeless optimism.

Of course, this post-modern Hindenberg was the candidate for a more efficient business-as-usual, an Empire "with a human face." The victims were hoping for a breather, but it didn't last even until the inaugural, as it became blatantly clear that many of the same rats were going to join the listing ship of state. And the place still stinks of Weimar (the fascists haven't gone away).

The rule of the caesars has been temporarily streamlined, but the new administrators face the same problems and crises, the same obstacles to rule, and will continue to oversee the decline of their civilization (no matter how protracted the decline may be). Most importantly, they will employ the same means to maintain their rule — austerity and misery for the masses and continued looting of the natural world, all enforced by the armed might of their legions.

*   *   *

"The American people may yet vote themselves dead and buried. I have never voted in my country; but don't let that stop you if it makes you feel better." — Raymond Mungo, Famous Long Ago, *1970*

Despite the palpable fraud, reasoned anarchist arguments against voting never seemed so brittle or flatly rationalistic — something akin to shouting into a vacuum. The declaration that "we" should abstain suggested a coherence in mass society that massification itself had undermined. One could, after all, riot one day and vote the next, but such acts do not in themselves necessarily constitute what radicals have trained ourselves to think they mean, or what dogma might say they mean. Given that one oppressor was going to win, a person might vote the way one might choose to buy (or steal) a specific capitalist product. This, in fact, was one common attitude.

To dispute even this kind of participation was to argue against the totality of humiliations and oppressive relations in mass authoritarian society. But invoking the totality implied just as much the relative meaninglessness of not voting, enmeshed as most people are in the reproduction of daily life under the Empire. Those too oppressed or too self-absorbed to vote don't need to be told not to. Those who take voting seriously can't fathom the idea. In the absence of far-reaching and coherent oppositional movements capable of posing real alternatives, such an argument was like appealing to people to stop being an atomized mass; by definition, they wouldn't be listening.

In fact, those astute enough to see the strings being pulled appeared both to vote or not to vote for the same reasons and for some of the same values. If there was even a slight distinction between the two leaders (and only shrill dogma would assert that there was none), some people decided that all acts being relatively weightless in a world whose major determinants are beyond one's reach, they would settle for the miniscule difference, and carry out that one small act. Thus, in the end, all the arguments against voting added up to a single, quixotic act of refusal.

I was sympathetic to those who voted for the challenger simply because they hated the incumbent's guts. What was one more humiliation if you wouldn't have to hear that nasal rich-boy whine of a monster you had grown to abhor with a bitter puissance, and you could see him repudiated rather than vindicated by his own system of prestige?

Rather, given that conditions seemed to put one within striking distance (if only as a member of the atomized aggregate), why not give old Caligula a major stomach ache? (And those who did so had their way. Stepping out of the voting booth, Bush told reporters, "This has been the worst year of my life." There was a momentary, delicious satisfaction in hearing that story, even though he deserved not so much to lose as to be hanged for his many "years of service.")

* * *

And that 45 percent of eligible voters who abstained, despite the "record turnout" (so much for mass abstention "sending a message" to the rulers) — what were their reasons? One of my co-workers, an amiable enough middle-aged family man, told me that he could not bring himself to vote "this time." In other words, there was something particular to this election that bothered him.

He himself had evaded the draft (while not actively opposing the Vietnam War) in the 1960s, either because he was too smart or too squeamish. One would have thought he would choose Clinton out of a kind of fellowship or for old time's sake. Given his habitual inclination to take part, what exactly did he object to in the candidates?

His was, I suspect, a fairly typical example of not voting. Was he smart or squeamish enough to recognize it was meaningless? But what was meaningless about it to him? Another co-worker, who had actively opposed the Vietnam War and others hence, said he hated "That Motherfucker" Bush so much that since he was apparently vulnerable, he was going to vote against him out of sheer spite. There was time in the day (and he even took off work), so I could hardly argue with him.

I, too, was happy to see That Motherfucker get his stomach ache, to see the lynch mobs with their plastic fetus fetishes sent back, if only temporarily, to their revival tents. Given the multiplicity and enormity of insults in this society, my friend chose which leader to hate for the next quadrennium. It was also his small way of saying to Bush (or so he told me), I couldn't stand your war — not only in the Middle East and Central America but against nature, women and the poor — and I can't stand you.

This was, in so many words, why many people I know voted for the panda in the jogging suit, even as they recognized full well there was no fundamental difference. They held their noses and pulled the lever, voting against the multi-front war, not least against Desert Storm and the myriad lies around it, since it was billed as Bush's chief attraction and proof of his superior character (and is now considered by media pundits and other cheerful robots to be his greatest, indeed his only "achievement").

Yet whatever their personal reasons, those who voted against the incumbent caesar voted for a more efficient, better managed Empire. They voted with the corporate CEOs who wanted a way out of capital's impasse. But perhaps worst of all, they voted alongside that much larger constituency for the most part satisfied with Bush's execution of the Gulf War but unhappy with his management of the imperial economy.

Had Bush been able to turn genocide into high-paying jobs, he might have been re-elected. Thus, the desperate and the outraged had to share the booth with people ("Reagan Democrats," "Clinton Republicans," patriots all) who bring to mind the line that it can't happen here because for all practical purposes it already has.

* * *

Then there was the Croesus vote, the Ross-for-Boss vote — the clown vote. A multibillionaire fascist who made his fortune bilking and milking the state, drew the interest of proles and plebes. He simply bought his way in, and for his megalomania was respectfully dubbed a political "maverick" and an "independent" by the Spin Machine.

Probably even more than his rivals, Perot reflected the total irrationality of the society in general and the elections in particular — their weightlessness, their ghostly irreality. The classic authoritarian character structure contributing to fascism was striking; here was the harsh, punitive father figure central to the complex of abuse and masochism, authority and obedience, rebellion and submisson, in the psychology of modern authoritarian societies.

There was also the slavish fascination with money and its power. Ross would write the checks and flog the profligate. It didn't matter that he himself was a robber baron and swindler even by normal capitalist standards, or that his army of "paid volunteers" and his expensive "info-mercials" probably surpassed the routine venality of elections. In America money talks, and bullshit walks. Ross talked; his brittle cracker voice and corn-pone pablum appealed to the dull-but-cynical and were a direct reflection of their stupefaction and Pavlovian conditioning. An amalgam of "Dallas" tycoon J.R. Ewing and E.T., he was going to lift U.S. capitalism's hood and get that little engine running smoothly again.

A young Latina working mother told a reporter that the billionaire's fire and brimstone sermons on the imperial debt had made her realize she needed to worry about the future, to take responsibility. Worry over the deficit had "politicized" her — in the service of the power system. Not the falling forests, the dying sky, the fetid mountain of petrochemical waste, the ragged poor, the violence, the glazed eyes and withered souls of the young, the high tech televised wars. None of that. A paper debt to usurers: a fantasy.

This Croesus, who could swim in his money like Scrooge McDuck, was called the outsider, the watchdog, the Jeremiah. One of his supporters, a so-called "independent," a chubby, middle-aged, suburban white male known as a "swing voter," thought the corporate clown would "get things done." He explained his own independence in a manner suitable to his hero: "If Ford makes a good pickup truck but a lousy car, I'll buy a Ford pickup and a Chevy car." (Imagine what it would mean to urge *him* not to vote.) Proof that, as a political wit once remarked, America has the best democracy money can buy.

The Croesus vote was in most cases the stupid vote, even more manipulated and enthralled by the fraud than the others. Perot supporters were reminiscent of those unhappy creatures who protested rising meat prices in the 1970s by organizing public dinners to consume dog food. In this case, however, they seemed to be discovering that they rather liked the fare, and were recommending it. They wanted "their country back," and they were willing to eat dog food to get it.

* * *

The elections, like the Persian Gulf War before them, demonstrated how effectively the capitalist system self-stabilizes, balancing itself by using the very erosion of loyalty and confidence it engenders, both to mobilize support for rationalizing its rule and to discard ideologues who are no longer useful. Thus, during the Gulf War, the state successfully manipulated an amorphous anti-war sentiment and fear of casualties to generate support for and compliance with the war by exaggerating the Iraqi threat and then calling up many more reserves and troops (hostages) than needed. This imposed a nervous quiescence in many quarters, followed by sighs of relief when the affair became nothing more than shooting fish in a barrel, as one victor so aptly put it.

The elections continued this imposition of conformist regimentation and imperial loyalty as a kind of mopping-up campaign on the culture; the fear of the proto-fascist right and a desire to return to the good old days of relative misery rather than sliding into absolute misery brought a significant number of dissidents out to endorse an emergent game-plan among the rulers. Consider the alternatives, we will be told, no matter how bad it turns out to be with Nero.

Yet, while it might have been one thing for believers in the democratic state (as well as for believers in nothing) to vote to rid themselves of Caligula, for those claiming a principled opposition to statism in any form it meant a new compliance. If a publication like *The Nation* could counsel its left liberal constituency in October that, given their negligible numbers, they should make their relationship to the elections one of principled self-identity rather than pragmatic realpolitik, how much more such an argument had to mean for the handful of anarchists, anti-authoritarians and antistatist radicals in the country! Yet a significant number opted for the lever.

Of course, none of us knows exactly how to confront the drift and thrust of mass society, its baroque distortion of human intentions and consequences, any more than we knew clearly how to respond to the Gulf War (the first post-modern war?) in order to reach and move people around us. So, even an anarchist who hated That Motherfucker's guts enough to pull the lever must have had his or her reasons. Such a choice had to represent a personal, existential act that suffered no illusion (and held even less hope) about the reduced terrain on which any meaningful, let alone effective, liberatory act might be accomplished. As the taoist sage wrote, "When society is orderly, a fool alone cannot disturb it; when society is chaotic, a sage alone cannot bring order." Social entropy being the order of the day, their shifting under the oppressors' weight was hardly a cause for indignation.

A conscious refusal to participate had and has promise not because of any eternal principles or anti-electoral dogma. Voting might conceivably make sense under certain conditions; it must be clear why it was senseless in 1992, under these. (In fact, even the "None-of-the-Above" slogan was easily recuperated into a "message" of discontent to the leaders like protest voting. A cop in a restaurant laughed and told me he agreed with my "Vote No President" pin but would probably vote anyway — being a cop and therefore being stupid — for Croesus.)

If it can be argued that all acts have the same relative weightlessness in mass society, another response with potentially more exemplary promise might be to articulate opposition to the whole show by focusing on mass society itself, recognizing that for the most part those who voted and those who did not acted under the same operational principles of organized passivity. It was necessary to reveal the emptiness of voting in relation to life's descent continuing behind imperial pseudo-events, and it was inevitably necessary to do so with the most meager of meager means — one's own voice. A pacifist maxim has it that peace begins with oneself. One could say the same of coherence — one's refusal has as much weight as one can expect to muster.

* * *

In Baghdad, people danced in the streets when Bush's defeat was announced. One could hardly blame them; it might have been worth voting just to send them a ray of sunshine and a drop of revenge. Indeed, it was hard to resist the temptation to ruin Bush's day; it was lovely to hear how depressed he became after his defeat, as long as he didn't start firing missiles. (And, lo and behold, he eventually did.)

Ultimately, conscious electoral abstention was a personal act like voting. Being personal, it was automatically political. It was not necessarily rational or reasonable; it might have started from a refusal, despite all distinctions and circumstances, to grasp at the straw, or to salivate when the bell rang. It made sense precisely because so few people were doing it consciously. I earlier called such an act quixotic; but the goal of Don Quixote was to defend an ideal, no matter how archaic and obsolete, against a world steeped in corruption, greed and deception.

In June 1854, Thoreau asked his journal, "Who can be serene in a country where both rulers and ruled are without principle? The remembrance of the baseness of politicians spoils my walks. My thoughts are murder to the State; I endeavor in vain to observe nature; my thoughts involuntarily go plotting against the State. I trust that all just men will conspire."

With the entire planet shrivelling under the weight of this civilization, voting could only be a pathetic, absurd kind of denial or a repetition fetish for absurd, absolutely perilous conditions — a bit of entertainment or busy work for the passengers in steerage on a rudderless, sinking ship. The election and the enthusiasms it provoked permit the continuance of the war that both Caligula and Nero wage, the war against human reason and the gaunt hope for genuine solidarity and community.

An electoral refusal that was more than protest would act not only negatively, but as negation within negation, a "no" in relation to both the "yes" and the "no." It would recognize the sometimes compelling ambiguities and distinctions, and still respond with a "no." Starting from the long view of the Empire and its inevitable decline, such a refusal would seek to illuminate the reality of a mass society that renders all choices meaningless.

But what if the simple act of voting meant saving a single species from extinction, I was asked. This might not be a question of symbols, but something like the Spotted Owl itself. I could only answer — and I am no more satisfied with the answer than my questioner was — how can the owl and the Empire both be saved? I bow humbly to the owl, but still a "no" within the "no." A reply to pragmatism with raw intransigence: a refusal of that bread, and that circus. When Nero proves to be just another version of Caligula, this "no" will remain.

I understand why Iraqis (and others) celebrated Caligula's retirement, and I celebrated with them. But still a "no" within the "no." The baseness of politics and the suffocation of whole worlds, the blare from the screens and the ringing of the bell — only the "no" within the "no" seems to respond adequately.

Some things have changed little since Thoreau's day. Endeavoring in vain to observe nature, my mind goes involuntarily plotting. Plot against the State; plot against the state of affairs. I hope all just women and men will conspire.

(December-January 1992-93)

ON THE ROAD TO NOWHERE:
THE NEW NOMADISM

"After all this long journey ... here it was all come to nothing, everything all busted up and ruined." — Huckleberry Finn

Looking to change my life, at the age of nineteen I decided to pack my belongings into a knapsack and hitch-hike to California. Two miraculous rides carried me through prairies, deserts and mountains into Los Angeles to a friend's place at the edge of Hollywood. In those days, at least, California was considered the ultimate destination for every dream of freedom and opportunity, spiritual and economic.

In one sense, I was following a pattern: it is said that sixty percent of U.S. citizens either arrived here through the immigration center at Ellis Island in New York Harbor, or are descended from them. At least my mother's father seems to have followed that route. As with much of my background, I know little about him — a fairly common situation, evidence of the weightless character of life here.

We Americans are thought to be rootless escapees from every other continent — nomadic, free spirits who get ourselves going when the going gets tough — pulling up stakes and moving on to the next ridge or mountaintop, the next adventure. The country is billed as a Promised Land, a nation of immigrants who made good. (Usually overlooked by this idea are the peoples conquered by the invaders or forcibly dragged here in chains.)

Movement and migration, always a large part of the human experience, have taken on a dramatically different character since early modern times. The rapid pace, enormous dimensions, and universal permanence of movement have become characteristic of what is now a global urban-industrial civilization. The European invasion of America largely financed the emergence of capitalism. In the process, old cultures were entirely uprooted, indigenous peoples slaughtered and displaced, and whole regions pillaged.

It was the unsettling of Europe, Lewis Mumford once remarked, that brought about the settlement of America. Those who came here were themselves uprooted, detribalized people; settlement was itself vastly unsettling, what Frederick W. Turner, in his book *Beyond Geography: The Western Spirit Against the Wilderness,* has called "a spiritual story ... of a civilization that had substituted history for myth as a way of understanding life."

In the opening to his book, Turner recalls finding himself in the Black Hills of South Dakota, the sacred Paha Sapa of the Lakota Sioux (recently slated by the U.S. government as a "national sacrifice area" for mining, energy production and waste dumping). In a sudden flash he recognized how utterly estranged he was from the place, how it could never have the same deep meaning for him it has for the Lakota — not because of the amount of time they have been there but for the way they have lived there.

According to Turner, western civilization's turn from cyclic myth toward an obsession with linear time, and hence with geographic expansion to fulfill its history, underlies the frenzied outward movement of western civilization in general and American civilization in particular. The archaic myth of traditional peoples, which we might visualize as a circle, was transformed into a new mystique of history: a single line, an ever-receding horizon. This turn toward history banished the sacred from nature, Turner argues, making the Europeans "alienated sojourners in a spiritually barren world where the only outlet for the urge to life was the restless drive onward." Such spiritual repression inevitably brought with it colossal levels of violence toward the world they encountered; the westward wanderers' testimonies of "lavish and exhaustless" abundance, Turner writes, were also narratives "of waste, destruction, and frantic despoilation."

Pioneer ideology

Ambivalence toward the land set the tragic conditions of the American experience. The sentimental idea of paradise — a lush, abundant garden — had its corrollary in the image of an immense, threatening wilderness. Incapable of loving the land for what it was, the invaders had to "improve" it, pulverizing and reconstituting everything in their path. Alexis de Tocqueville likened their advance to a march, "turning the course of rivers, peopling solitudes, and subduing nature."

Tocqueville observed the tendency of early nineteenth century Americans to abandon a homestead before even finishing the roof. Typically, the settler was sustained by the idea that the frontier — a middle ground between corrupt civilization and chaotic wilderness — would bring redemption. The utopian urge for movement and change paradoxically reflected a profound desire to set down roots. But the market system at the core of North American ideology and identity, based as it is on abstract economic exchange, is inherently destabilizing and must inevitably undermine roots. Thus each frontier was eventually exhausted and abandoned by the same forces which caused it to be settled in the first place.

Official history says the devastation of the original lands and peoples was a necessary evil to bring about a vital civilization. So deeply ingrained is the mystique of manifest destiny that a 1992 Smithsonian exhibit on the quincentennial of Columbus which merely referred to the incontrovertible fact of genocide and ecological devastation brought about by European conquest, was severely censured by politicians and pundits. The pioneer ideology — a New World version of holocaust denial — remains sacrosanct in many quarters. Every child grows up with it; Davy Crockett and Daniel Boone, and 1950s and '60s television cowboy shows such as *Bonanza* and *Gunsmoke* provided my generation's archetypal heroes, larger-than-life men bringing light to the darkness. We grew up on them, immersed ourselves in the blue light of their ideological shadow play. In this regard we were little different from nineteenth century people who read dime novels and followed frontier reports.

Commonly compared to Columbus and Balboa by the publicists responsible for creating his legend, Daniel Boone was the prototypical folk hero of the national drama. His characteristic misanthropy and urge to escape to the frontier became a familiar theme in American popular culture, from Huck Finn's meander down the Mississippi to Beat novelist Jack Kerouac's pilgrimage west in *On the Road*. Boone's statement that he left "domestic happiness ... to wander through the wilderness of America in quest of the country of Kentucke" reveals the preeminently masculine aspect of the American nomadic mystique. In this story, men abandon "domestic happiness" (a woman's world), with its trivial charms and effete corruptions, for the Great Adventure. Throughout the Boone tale, a sexually charged ambivalence toward the land is visible — his yearning for the "virgin wilderness" and his terror of and loathing for the actual place and the people already living there.

In fact, as historian Richard Drinnon has commented, "under [Boone's] handsome yellow buckskins ... beat the heart of a land company agent." In his indispensable study *Facing West: The Metaphysics of Empire-Building and Indian-Hating*, Drinnon reveals Boone as a land speculator and "professional empire builder" who "went in for body counts" of enemy dead after engaging in numerous punitive expeditions and raids against the locals. "We burnt them all to ashes," Boone writes in a typical account, representative of prior and later wars against America's indigenous tribes, and to future international wars as well. He and his cohorts "entirely destroyed their corn and other fruits, and every where spread a scene of desolation in the country," he reports almost laconically. Such desolation is the public secret underlying the Euroamerican pursuit of happiness.

Everyone must eat hamburgers

If Boone and his ilk were the inventions of real estate promoters, no less was that hero of American heroes, the cowboy. This occupation drew little attention until the cowboy as heroic figure was concocted by Buffalo Bill Cody for his Wild West Show at the end of the last century. By the time Cody was finished, the cowboy was synonymous with America; even the first celebrity cowboy, Cody's protégé Buck Taylor, had become an actor. Since then the actors, from John Wayne to Ronald Reagan, have come to supplant the reality; the myth firmly established, the Wild West has become a gargantuan, lucrative theme of the culture industry.

A cowboy hat and boots now afford masculine potency to their male wearer (and sexual allure to the occasional female), be it in Houston or New York City. Cowboy-inspired clothing is ubiquitous; upscale customers can even buy bluejeans said to have once been worn by "authentic" cowboys. The paraphernalia and symbols are employed not only to sell products like tobacco, alcohol and automobiles, but to sell the macho, individualistic and superficially independent mode of life that, as we are frequently reminded, makes the country great. There is now even a cowboy channel on national cable television for the devoted. Quips western singer Bobby Bare, "Today being a 'cowboy' is more of an attitude than an occupation."

In former days the activities of cowboys represented just another get-rich-quick scheme of the settlers — a horde that first annihilated tens of millions of buffalo to starve out the natives before introducing livestock grazing. "Forage fever" paralleled gold fever, oil fever and other pecuniary thralls, with predictable results: grazing rivals, or surpasses, any other single factor in the ecological destruction of the American West. As Lynn Jacobs reports in his encyclopedic study on livestock grazing, *The Waste of the West*, the real national totem is not the eagle but the cow. One half of all U.S. land outside Alaska is grazed by livestock, mostly cattle, with another fifteen percent used as cropland to feed livestock. Half the water and forty percent of all plant food production go to livestock. The country, Jacobs argues, is a veritable cow factory.

In the American Eden, everyone must eat hamburgers; in the process, grasslands, brushlands, forests and deserts have been "cowburnt" and despoiled. According to U.S. Department of Agriculture estimates (which Jacobs considers very conservative), western rangelands are only about half as productive botanically as they were before the livestock invasion of the 1880s. Western rangeland is losing topsoil, mostly due to ranching, at a rate of five to perhaps twenty times as fast as it is being replaced.

Cattlemen had more than an environmental effect. After slaughtering the natives, they consolidated huge land holdings through theft and coercion. Since then, despite their miniscule numbers, they have dominated state and federal governments, fostering a "frontier justice" based on intimidation and violence — deputizing their cronies and imposing quick trials and quicker punishments, where the sheriff and the judge wear cowboy hats. (In the 1992 Texas gubernatorial race, Democratic and Republican candidates ran on who would execute more criminals more swiftly. The Republican, a son of George Bush, claimed the higher number and won. But cowboy justice seems more popular everywhere in the U.S. today.)

The range war is in fact an apt replica of all aggressive capitalism, its fundamental war-of-all-against-all. The shoot-out and the hostile corporate buy-out are linked spiritually, as Turner might say, certainly symbolically, frequently right down to the western clothing worn by both sets of protagonists. Of course, the cattle barons are now often multinationals or giant eastern insurance companies. Despite the myth's images of neighborliness, community in the West is mostly an aggregate, dominated by the powerful, of atomized individuals, "alienated sojourners" relentlessly whipping and stripping the countryside to scrape off a profit. After being pushed onto reservations and seeing the land suffer under the onslaught of the whites, the Navajos believed their region to be literally bewitched. Anyone who has seen the hysteria on the floor of the commodities exchange, or its result on the landscape, might agree.

The romance of the horizon is a mirage concealing the boom-bust cycle and subsequent dust-bowls of the market. Restless and unsentimental, capital must constantly abandon yesterday's faded paradise to conquer the next or face collapse. The frontier is always somewhere else. Indeed, today's pilgrim may be fleeing yesterday's settlement — perhaps a town like Love Canal, New York, abandoned because of industrial contamination, or some fishing village in Alaska where oil washed up from the Exxon Valdez. Formerly the haven from a heartless world and the site of redemption, the American home, with its toxic leachate seeping through the basement wall, has itself become a kind of horrible condition to escape. In the beginning, the Indians were driven out with the justification that being nomadic, they could lay no claim to the land they occupied. But what came after was fragmentation, not stability, and a contempt for the land still visible in ugly Alaska frontier towns, the denuded industrial landscapes of the Rust Belt, and rural lands everywhere obliterated for "development."

Cowboys and astronauts

Looking honestly at the movements of indigenous nomadic peoples, we would mostly see a peregrination based on a profound awareness of and ability to live with the land rather than against it. Traditional nomads have a spiritual relationship with the land, moving in a kind of sacred circle, or perhaps in an ellipse; in their stories and their migrations they continually return to the source and center of the world.

In contrast, the modern "nomad" moves along a line, following a receding horizon, wrecking and abandoning along the way, never at home, always scheming the next move across shifting, breaking ice. Or maybe the movement is a circle, but it now goes from nowhere to nowhere, around and around like the subway line, or the circulation of money. One thinks of Tocqueville's prescient comment that in America life was "always changing, but it is monotonous, because all these changes are alike." It may be the singular genius of the country of my birth to turn every unique place into the same monotonous Place. The grid plan of early American towns was designed to facilitate land transactions. Now the grid is inescapable, and everywhere one encounters the same sterile housing development, strip mall, power line, "industrial park" or cleared hillside (perhaps stripped to pay off junk bonds, like many of Northern California's redwoods).

The grid and the car go together; if the old household had to be flattened by new expressway construction, the road would lead to "a new beginning," first to the suburbs and the post-war tract home, like the one in which I grew up, and more recently to the semi-rural walled pseudo-villages with country-sounding names harkening to whispering pines or tall oaks long vanished into the shredder. "The long brown path before me leading wherever I choose," wrote Walt Whitman; a plastic bag from a Detroit auto parts store asserts, "It's not your car, it's your freedom."

Early in our history the romance of the landscape shifted to the machine. The railroad and telegraph were destined to "annihilate space and time," according to one observer. As the physical setting was indeed annihilated, wild nature lost its power to dominate the imagination (except increasingly as the site for automobile advertising), and only the machine remains. Today's post-modern nomad channel surfs or wanders in cyberspace, no longer worrying about the world outside or even believing it exists. Consumerism delivers paradise, and the miracles of abundance no longer come from loamy earth but from genetic engineering, space flight and the media. The land is now so displaced that the phantasms of bubble cities and an entirely engineered environment, like the Biosphere II experiment in Arizona, are received with enthusiasm and even hope.

The cowboy is now an astronaut, futures trader or cyberpunk; after porno-, space- and virtual reality-cowboys, it's hard to believe anyone pays him any attention. Yet the frontier idea still elicits loyalty, especially in the high tech mid-sized towns and rural areas of the West and the Sun Belt, where nationalistic, conservative, fundamentalist Christian forces are strongest. There, the old myths have found new vigor in a weird but potent mix of frontier and New Age values. And where the middle class is no longer fascinated by the pioneer, it chases Indian shadows in New Age healing rituals fashioned from purloined fragments of native religion. During the Persian Gulf War millions of Americans were drawn to the hugely successful film *Dances With Wolves*, a white man's romance about living among the Lakota, while the contemporary cavalry incinerated more recently demonized "savages" in the Mideast.

In his 1994 memoir of the Vietnam War, *In Pharaoh's Army*, Tobias Wolff relates how, determined to watch the 1967 *Bonanza* Thanksgiving special in style, he risked getting killed and perpetrated mayhem on Vietnamese civilians along the road in order to drive to a distant U.S. base to find a big screen television. In their refusal to come to terms with the place, he writes, the Americans at the base "had created a profound, intractable bog" smelling of roast turkey and overflowing latrines. In Vietnam, Wolff "saw something that wasn't allowed for in our national myth — our capacity for collective despair." He wonders afterward, "Where were we, really?" (The question has been asked ever since Europeans first stumbled up on a Caribbean beach.) The *Bonanza* special turned out to be, as always, "a story of redemption — man's innate goodness brought to flower by a strong dose of opportunity, hard work, and majestic landscape." Like the American continent, Indochina paid a high price for the acting out of this story. But Wolff's question remains unanswered. We are too busy moving on.

We remain foreigners

As for moving on, I didn't last in California, and after a year or so returned to Detroit. But my family has been scattered to the winds, so it should not be any surprise that I began penning this essay on an airplane headed west to the Hawaiian island of Maui to visit my mother, who moved there twenty-five years ago to work, and then stayed. We're nomads, too.

Just during the last quarter century in which I have visited it, Hawai'i has provided a stunning lesson in the effects of our peculiar nomadism. A small and exquisitely beautiful place stolen from its original inhabitants, it continues to undergo changes both rapid and horrendous. Development of every sort — military, industrial and commercial — is turning it into part Southern California, part Detroit. As I drove from the airport past Kahana Pond this time, I noticed the completion of a new development encroaching on a bird sanctuary there — a huge K-Mart discount store. (K-Mart headquarters in suburban Detroit had just laid off thirteen hundred workers.) There, by the edge of a new asphalt parking lot, stood a beautiful white egret — another immigrant — poking through debris for food, looking like a homeless person at a trash bin.

They "were careless people," Fitzgerald's protagonist Nick Carraway concludes about the people he meets in *The Great Gatsby*. "They smashed up things and creatures and then retreated back into their money or their vast carelessness or whatever it was that kept them together, and let other people clean up the mess they had made." I know the defiled wilderness has also become a common cultural motif. In certain post-modern circles, being "on the road to nowhere," as the Talking Heads song goes, is even counted as a blessing, however precarious. But our wandering comes at a great price — to egrets and to people. Throughout it all, we remain foreigners — in America and everywhere else.

It's true we can't go back to sacred circles long unraveled. We're already torn from our roots, we're made of myriad places. But space and time have not yet been altogether annihilated; it still may be possible to find out where we've been, where we really are, to recognize the integrity of the place and what it has lived. It's time to start cleaning up our mess, to "grasp rock and soil," as the Lakota writer Luther Standing Bear put it. It's time to come home.

(1995)

AUTONOMEDIA NEW AUTONOMY SERIES
Jim Fleming & Peter Lamborn Wilson, Editors

T.A.Z.
The Temporary Autonomous Zone
Hakim Bey

THIS IS YOUR FINAL WARNING!
Thom Metzger

FRIENDLY FIRE
Bob Black

CALIBAN AND THE WITCHES
Silvia Federici

FIRST AND LAST EMPERORS
The Absolute State & the Body of the Despot
Kenneth Dean & Brian Massumi

SHOWER OF STARS
The Initiatic Dream in Sufism & Taoism
Peter Lamborn Wilson

THIS WORLD WE MUST LEAVE
& OTHER ESSAYS
Jacques Camatte

PIRATE UTOPIAS
Moorish Corsairs & European Renegadoes
Peter Lamborn Wilson

40TH CENTURY MAN
Andy Clausen

FLESH MACHINE
Designer Babies & The Politics of New Genetics
Critical Art Ensemble

WIGGLING WISHBONE
Stories of Patasexual Speculation
Bart Plantenga

FUTURE PRIMITIVE AND OTHER ESSAYS
John Zerzan

THE ELECTRONIC DISTURBANCE
Critical Art Ensemble

X TEXTS
Derek Pell

WHORE CARNIVAL
Shannon Bell, ed.

CRIMES OF CULTURE
Richard Kostelanetz

INVISIBLE GOVERNANCE
The Art of African Micropolitics
David Hecht & Maliqalim Simone

THE LIZARD CLUB
Steve Abbott

CRACKING THE MOVEMENT
Squatting Beyond the Media
Foundation for Advancement of Illegal Knowledge

SOCIAL OVERLOAD
Henri-Pierre Jeudy

ELECTRONIC CIVIL DISOBEDIENCE
Critical Art Ensemble

SEMIOTEXT(E), THE JOURNAL
Jim Fleming & Sylvère Lotringer, Editors

POLYSEXUALITY
François Peraldi, ed.

OASIS
Timothy Maliqalim Simone, et al., eds.

SEMIOTEXT(E) USA
Jim Fleming & Peter Lamborn Wilson, eds.

SEMIOTEXT(E) ARCHITECTURE
Hraztan Zeitlian, ed.

SEMIOTEXT(E) SF
Rucker, Wilason & Wilson, eds.

RADIOTEXT(E)
Neil Strauss & Dave Mandl, eds.

SEMIOTEXT(E) CANADAs
Jordan Zinovich, ed.

IMPORTED: A READING SEMINAR
Rainer Ganahl, ed.

AUTONOMEDIA BOOK SERIES
Jim Fleming, Editor

THE DAUGHTER
Roberta Allen

MARX BEYOND MARX
Lessons on the Gründrisse
Antonio Negri

MAGPIE REVERIES
James Koehnline

SCANDAL
Essays in Islamic Heresy
Peter Lamborn Wilson

TROTSKYISM AND MAOISM
Theory & Practice in France & the U.S.
A. Belden Fields

ON ANARCHY & SCHIZOANALYSIS
Rolando Perez

FILE UNDER POPULAR
Theoretical & Critical Writing on Music
Chris Cutler

RETHINKING MARXISM
Steve Resnick & Rick Wolff, eds.

THE DAMNED UNIVERSE OF CHARLES FORT
Louis Kaplan, ed.

THE TOUCH
Michael Brownstein

CLIPPED COINS, ABUSED WORDS,
CIVIL GOVERNMENT
John Locke's Philosophy of Money
Constantine George Caffentzis

HORSEXE
Essay on Transsexuality
Catherine Millot

GULLIVER
Michael Ryan

FILM & POLITICS IN THE THIRD WORLD
John Downing, ed.

THE NEW ENCLOSURES
Midnight Notes Collective

GOD & PLASTIC SURGERY
Marx, Nietzsche, Freud & the Obvious
Jeremy Barris

MODEL CHILDREN
Inside the Republic of Red Scarves
Paul Thorez

COLUMBUS & OTHER CANNIBALS
The Wétiko Disease & The White Man
Jack Forbes

A DAY IN THE LIFE
Tales from the Lower East Side
Alan Moore & Josh Gosniak, eds.

CASSETTE MYTHOS
The New Music Underground
Robin James, ed.

ENRAGÉS & SITUATIONISTS
The Occupation Movement, May '68
René Viénet

XEROX PIRATES
"High" Tech & the New Collage Underground
Autonomedia Collective, eds.

MIDNIGHT OIL
Work, Energy, War, 1973–1992
Midnight Notes Collective

GONE TO CROATAN
Origins of North American Dropout Culture
James Koehnline & Ron Sakolsky, eds.

ABOUT FACE
Race in Postmodern America
Timothy Maliqalim Simone

THE ARCANE OF REPRODUCTION
Housework, Prostitution, Labor & Capital
Leopoldina Fortunati

BY ANY MEANS NECESSARY
Outlaw Manifestos & Ephemera, 1965–70
Peter Stansill & David Zane Mairowitz, eds.

FORMAT AND ANXIETY
Collected Essays on the Media
Paul Goodman

DREAMER OF THE DAY
Francis Parker Yockey & Secret Fascist Underground
Kevin Coogan

THE NARRATIVE BODY
Eldon Garnet7

DEMONO (THE BOXED GAME)
P.M.

WILD CHILDREN
David Mandl & Peter Lamborn Wilson., eds.

¡ZAPATISTAS!
Documents of the New Mexican Revolution
EZLN

THE OFFICIAL KGB HANDBOOK
USSR Committee for State Security

CAPITAL & COMMUNITY
Jacques Camatte

POPULAR REALITY
Irreverend David Crowbar, ed.

CRIMES OF THE BEATS
The Unbearables

WAR IN THE NEIGHBORHOOD
Seth Tobocman

AN EXISTING BETTER WORLD
A Portrait of the Bread and Puppets Theatre
George Dennison

THE MEDIA ARCHIVE
The Foundation for Advancement of Illegal Knowkledge

ESCAPE FROM THE NINETEENTH CENTURY
Essays on Marx, Fourier, Proudhon & Nietzsche
Peter Lamborn Wilson

THE ANARCHISTS
Portrait of Civilization at the End of the 19th Century
John Henry Mackay

BLOOD & VOLTS
Tesla, Edison, & the Birth of the Electric Chair
Th. Metzger

CARNIVAL OF CHAOS
On the Road with the Nomdic Festival
Sascha Altman Dubrul

PIONEER OF INNER SPACE
The Life of Fitz Hugh Ludlow
Donald P. Dulchinos

PSYCHEDELICS REIMAGINED
Introduced by Timothy Leary, Prefaced by Hakim Bey
Tom Lyttle, Editor

ROTTING GODDESS
The Origin of the Witch in Classical Antiquity
Jacob Rabinowitz

SOUNDING OFF!
Fred Ho & Ron Sakolsky, Editors

SEMIOTEXT(E) NATIVE AGENTS SERIES
Chris Kraus, Editor

IF YOU'RE A GIRL
Ann Rower

THE ORIGIN OF THE SPECIES
Barbara Barg

HOW I BECAME ONE OF THE INVISIBLE
David Rattray

NOT ME
Eileen Myles

HANNIBAL LECTER, MY FATHER
Kathy Acker

SICK BURN CUT
Deran Ludd

THE MADAME REALISM COMPLEX
Lynne Tillman

WALKING THROUGH CLEAR WATER
Cookie Mueller

I LOVE DICK
Chris Kraus

THE NEW FUCK YOU
Adventures in Lesbian Reading
Eileen Myles & Liz Kotz, editors

READING BROOKE SHIELDS
The Garden of Failure
Eldon Garnet

AIRLESS SPACES
Shulamith fFirestone

PASSIONATE MISTAKES
Michelle Tea

PLOVER PRESS

THE COURAGE TO STAND ALONE
U. G. Krishnamurti

THE MOTHER OF GOD
Luna Tarlo

AUTONOMEDIA DISTRIBUTION

DRUNKEN BOAT
An Anarchist Review of Literature & the Arts
Max Blechman, ed.

LUSITANIA
A Journal of Reflection & Oceanography
Martim Avillez, ed.

FELIX
The Review of Television & Video Culture
Kathy High, ed.

RACE TRAITOR
A Journal of the New Abolitionism
John Garvey & Noel Ignatiev, eds.

XXX FRUIT
Anne D'Adesky, ed.

BENEATH THE EMPIRE OF THE BIRDS
Carl Watson

LIVING IN VOLKSWAGEN BUSES
Julian Beck

I SHOT MUSSOLINI
Elden Garnet

ANARCHY AFTER LEFTISM
Bob Black

ALL COTTON BRIEFS
M. Kasper

PAGAN OPERETTA
Carl Hancock Rux

SKULL HEAD SAMBA
Eve Packer

BROKEN NOSES & METEMPSYCHOSES
Michael Carter

WATERWORN
Star Black

DIGITAS
New York Digital Review of Arts & Literature

AUTONOMEDIA CALENDARS

AUTONOMEDIA CALENDAR
OF JUBILEE SAINTS
Radical Heroes for the Millennium
James Koehnline & Autonomedia Collective

SHEROES &
WOMYN WARRIORS CALENDAR
Great Revolutionary Womyn of Herstory
*O.R.S.S.A.S.M. (Organisation of
Revolutionary Socialist Sisters and Some Men)*

SEMIOTEXT(E) DOUBLE AGENTS SERIES
Jim Fleming & Sylvère Lotringer, Editors

FATAL STRATEGIES
Jean Baudrillard

FOUCAULT LIVE
Collected Interviews of Michel Foucault
Sylvère Lotringer, ed.

ARCHEOLOGY OF VIOLENCE
Pierre Clastres

LOST DIMENSION
Paul Virilio

AESTHETICS OF DISAPPEARANCE
Paul Virilio

BURROUGHS LIVE
Collected Interviews of William S. Burroughs
Sylvère Lotringer, ed.